'This provocative and timely collection contains rich diversity in both method and content. The average quality of contributions is remarkably high, and the best are gems.'
Henry Shue, *Professor of Ethics and Public Life, Cornell University*

'Booth and Dunne have brought together a star-studded galaxy of authors – intellectuals, academics and thinkers who explore the myriad facets – terror, power, culture – of the attack on the twin towers from the viewpoints of international relations and international political economy. The essays are tightly argued and form a valuable collection for students, teachers, policymakers and policy watchers.'
Lord Desai of St Clement Danes, *Professor of Economics, London School of Economics*

'In a moving and disturbing series of messages, some of the world's smartest and best informed politi... on the causes, meanings and consequences of Septem... ...ging the idea of two well-defined worlds – one good, one bad ... ...gree widely. Taken together, however, their essays issue an eloq... it can for broader, deeper and more humane responses to today's political crises, and lay out many possible elements of those responses.'
Charles Tilly, *Joseph L. Buttenweiser Professor of Social Science, Columbia University*

'As we try to understand September 11, 2001, it would be hard to find a more diverse and interesting set of authors than those assembled here. Agree or disagree, you are bound to learn from them.'
Joseph S. Nye, Jr, *author of* The Paradox of American Power *and former Assistant Secretary of Defense*

'This fascinating and well-written collection of essays provides abundant evidence that scholars sharply disagree not only about the causes of the September 11 terrorist attack on the United States, but also about how best to combat the problem.'
John J. Mearsheimer, *R. Wendell Harrison Distinguished Service Professor, Political Science Department, University of Chicago*

Also by Ken Booth

STRATEGIC CULTURES IN THE ASIA-PACIFIC REGION

Also by Tim Dunne

INVENTING INTERNATIONAL SOCIETY: A History of the English School

Worlds in Collision

Terror and the Future of Global Order

Edited by

Ken Booth

and

Tim Dunne

First published in 2002 by
PALGRAVE MACMILLAN
Houndmills, Basingstoke, Hampshire RG21 6XS and
175 Fifth Avenue, New York, N. Y. 10010
Companies and representatives throughout the world.

PALGRAVE MACMILLAN is the new global academic imprint of
St. Martin's Press LLC Scholarly and Reference Division and
Palgrave Macmillan Ltd (formerly Macmillan Press Ltd).

ISBN 0–333–99804–9   hardback
ISBN 0–333–99805–7   paperback
ISBN 978–0–333–99804–5   hardback
ISBN 978–0–333–99805–2   paperback

This book is printed on paper suitable for recycling and made
from fully managed and sustained forest sources.

A catalogue record for this book is available from the British
Library.

Library of Congress Cataloging-in-Publication Data
Worlds in Collision : terror and the future of global order /
   edited by Ken Booth and Tim Dunne.
      p.cm.
Includes bibliographical references and index.
   ISBN 0–333–99804–9 — ISBN 0–333–99805–7 (pbk.)
   1. Terrorism. 2. World politics—1995–2005. I. Booth, Ken,
   1943– II. Dunne, Timothy, 1965–

HV6431.W635 2002
303.6'25–dc21   2002019596

18   17
11   10   09   08   07
Printed and bound in Great Britain by Antony Rowe Ltd,
Chippenham and Eastbourne

Contents

Part Two: Order

Part Three: Worlds

Preface

Another book about the events and aftermath of September 11 needs no justification. For years to come, if not decades, the 'war on terrorism' will be the defining paradigm in the struggle for global order. There are other and arguably more crucial issues in world historical terms – the growing disparity between the 'haves' and the 'have-nots' and the deterioration of the global environment – but when the victim of terror attacks of spectacular horror happens to be the greatest power on earth, the agenda is set.

In the immediate aftermath of the attacks on the World Trade Center and the Pentagon, every well-known writer joined in the global attempt to try to understand the meaning of that shocking and terrifying morning. Longer pieces then started appearing, and more recently books. What almost all of this analysis and imagining revealed was a sense not only that one historical era had ended, but that something of truly epic significance had occurred which would affect the human international political consciousness with the same impact as the dropping of the atomic bombs, the First World War or the Thirty Years War: the 'events' of that day will become hard-wired into the world historical memory. Six months later, the pictures and sounds of that morning are no less shocking; so shocking, indeed, that one still hopes it is a dream and that in the next re-run the planes will miss their targets.

We have learned over these past months how different states and groups chose to respond to the global crisis. What we do not know, and cannot know, is how it will end. This is one of the most powerful lessons we should all take from the experience: September 11 should have taught us that we cannot assume, for the foreseeable future, that tomorrow will be like today. The global order is being recast, and the twists and turns will surprise us.

To help us think about the importance of these events, both on specific issues and the broadest canvas, we have assembled an outstanding group of academics and public intellectuals from a variety of countries, all expert on questions relating to terror, force, law, ethics and global order. Many of the contributors live and work in the United States, and we make no apology for this, given that the terrorist attacks were aimed at the heart of America. The volume gives voice to a plurality of viewpoints and we believe this diversity of opinions sets it apart from comparable publications. Within these pages, readers will find scholars who are broadly in support of America's war on terror, and others who are more hesitant, conscious that terror is a method that US governments have perpetrated and not just recently experienced. In the spirit of the best American tradition, this book is a home for patriotic and dissident opinions alike.

In bringing this volume to completion, our first acknowledgement must be to our contributors, all of whom are very busy people, but who agreed to write to tight deadlines. This is testimony to the importance they attach to understanding what happened, and their concern that the ways in which people and states respond to September 11 will determine the possibilities for the future global order. As ever, we wish to thank our colleagues in the Department of International Politics at the University of Wales Aberystwyth; their engagement with these issues has been intense, and we have benefited enormously from their conversations and writings. It gives us particular pleasure, finally, to acknowledge Alison Howson, publisher at Palgrave, for her enthusiasm, professionalism and support. This book was her idea.

Ken Booth and Tim Dunne
March 2002

CHAPTER 1

Worlds in Collision

Ken Booth and Tim Dunne

It is curious how a specific date – not a year, but a specific month and a specific day – have almost universally come to define a world historical crisis. The signposts of world affairs in the twentieth century were fixed in particular places: Sarajevo, Munich, Suez, Cuba, Vietnam and the rest. In the case of the attacks on the World Trade Center and the Pentagon it is as if we instantly understood that the meanings of these 'events' were global, beyond locality, an out-of-geography experience. September 11 was a place we all shared.

It was a place we all shared because there was a sense that what we were witnessing, literally, was a collision of worlds. The suffocating smoke and debris from the collapse of the Twin Towers (the image on the cover of this book) not only show the material destruction that follows when worlds collide, but also symbolize the difficulty of understanding colliding thought-worlds. The collisions we pick out in this chapter run through the book: those between different political entities, struggling for power and employing violence and other traditional instruments of policy; and between those thought-worlds characterized by different beliefs about what is reality, what constitutes reliable knowledge and how we should behave. Although what follows are presented as collisions in the context of September 11, we have chosen not to link them by a 'versus', because in our view most of them do not necessarily stand in opposition. We have linked them by 'and'. The one exception – the one unambiguous *versus* – is terrorism itself.

Islam and the United States

In the collision between the United States and Islam two parallel questions have pressed for answers. Why is the United States hated in so many parts of the world? And why is Islam so feared? The answer at one level is easy: the United States is hated because it is feared, while Islam is feared because it is hated. This is a start. In the search for a fuller answer, unfortunately, the chief protagonists shy away. It should be a time for introspection, for the deepening of self-knowledge; instead, self-justification has been the norm.

Introspection in the United States is discouraged by the very circumstances of the attacks. Such was the sense of homeland violation that it was no surprise when President Bush demanded a loyalty test: 'Either you are with us or you are with the terrorists', he told Congress on September 20, 2001.[1]   As a result, to criticize the White House's handling of the crisis, or to seek an explanation for the attacks that is more penetrating than simply asserting the nihilistic mindsets of the perpetrators, is considered to be tantamount to being sympathetic to the terrorists. To try to find reasons is seen as a slippery slope towards concluding that the United States 'deserved it', and hence is treason. Some external friends might have kept quiet out of opportunism. Like the UK, they have stood (more or less) 'shoulder to shoulder' with the United States in its time of crisis, in the hope, one day, that the United States would do the same for them.

So why is the United States hated? 'It' is not: and the very question betrays a powerful stereotyping that feeds global disorder. We do not believe that the 'United States' is hated. There is a large Muslim population in the country not seeking to emigrate; there is a well of respect for American life and people throughout the world. Without doubt, many people have ambivalent feelings towards US society: but so do many of us about our own societies. The 'United States' must be disaggregated. Then it becomes apparent that it is the policies of successive US governments that are so hated: the manner in which the world's sole superpower tends always to get its way; its sometimes brutal foreign policy and profitable project of globalization; its support for tyrants while mouthing the language of democracy and human rights; and the way it uses local proxies to dominate the global order. However benign the US hegemon, it will be feared because it is drawn as no other power into the daily business of running the world, and it will get its way. In any human situation, such structural power tends to provoke the hostility of those who are not listened to, or who do not get their way, ever.

US governments have, without doubt, much to answer for. Set against this, as a society, the US is an idea to which countless victims flock, seeking refuge from tyranny and hunger. Its capacity for economic regenerations is such that it is one of the few countries to treat immigration as an economic resource rather than a burden. One wonders how many of those demonstrating against 'The Great Satan' in places like Iran, Pakistan and Iraq, would pass up the opportunity to join generations of Poles, Italians, Cubans and others who have helped create the land of the free? Many Muslim asylum seekers, migrants and intellectuals have chosen the United States as the site of their hopes for themselves and their families, and not countries at the heart of the Islamic world. The distinction between the US state and US society is vital, and too little heeded by those casually labelling the United States as universally hated, and those critics of this or that policy casually labelling them as 'anti-American'.

Self-knowledge never comes easily. Many Americans are held back from achieving a better understanding of how their government is perceived by knowing so little of their own history, and even less of the history of other peoples. It is not that long since George W. Bush, then on the campaign trail, was unable to name several heads of state, including President Musharraf of Pakistan. After 9/11, Musharraf's agreement to 'full cooperation' in the global war on terror was a decisive part of US coalition building. Lack of knowledge is made worse by the mythological history promoted for profit and entertainment by Hollywood. Intensely law-abiding people who are brought up to believe they belong to the land of the free, the home of the brave, and the shining city on the hill, and who are convinced that their country is a force for good in the world, find it truly shocking when told by one of their own leading intellectuals, Susan Sontag, that 'America is founded on genocide'.[2] The thought is so shocking that it is erased from memory, or she is. Ignorance and myth can breed self-righteousness – a dangerous foundation on which to engage with the world.

The moral high ground is where ethnocentric memories reside. And here, also, is where there are so many similarities between the Bush presidency and the Reagan era. In both cases there is a gap between the self-image of standing firm for liberty, democracy, international law and peace, while conducting policies characterized by inconsistency on free trade, the support of tyrants, economic imperialism, playing fast and loose with international law and, when necessary, being ready, willing and able to use violence. The echoes of the Reagan era are the stronger today because of the return of so many officials of that time to key positions in Washington.

If power is part of the problem with the United States, it is lack of power that besets Islam. In various contexts in recent years, Muslims have been on the receiving end of world politics. They have frequently been victims, although they are invariably represented as perpetrators. As with the US, it is therefore necessary to disaggregate 'Islam'. The stereotype is of suicide bombers, terrorists and fundamentalist clerics. But when one contemplates the 1.2 billion Muslims around the world, the emptiness of the stereotype is evident; most live lives of tolerance, order and decency. It is true that many Muslims regard with distaste some of the excesses of 'Western' life (the breakdown of family life, crime, pornography, and so on) but this is not much different to the feelings of many in the West. If we strip away national structures, militarized security managers and religious fanatics, it is possible to see here a core of shared values. Sections of the Islamic world celebrated the attacks on September 11, but these were drowned out by the expressions of sympathy shown for innocent victims.

However, it cannot be avoided that there were celebrations, and the terrorists did identify with Islam. Introspection is needed, but as with the United States the search for self-knowledge is not a priority. Nor is it encouraged in Islamic states and societies, where tyranny and constraints on freedom of enquiry are widespread. These are circumstances in which it is easier to blame others. So, is 'it' about Islam? For understandable reasons Western political leaders have gone out of their way to say 'No'. Soon after the attacks, Prime Minister Blair, for example, said that 'we do not act against Islam'.[3] He and other leaders attempted to limit intercultural hostility by showing sensitivity to cultural particularities while at the same time underlining common values. Others, without the pressures of office, maintained different views. Salman Rushdie insisted: 'Yes, this is about Islam.'[4] Osama bin Laden, for example, has been part of a radical political movement of Islamists who have had a presence in Egypt, Algeria, Iran and Pakistan. The origins of the Taliban government in 1994 exemplify the rise of Islamism, with its adherence to a particular interpretation of the faith and its desire to fight a holy war against the 'infidel' using a transnational coalition of Islamist warriors.[5] It is partly about Islam, therefore, but there is much more to fathom, from the fantasies of the terrorists of September to the unravelling of the relationships between culture, politics and religion in the Islamic world. The latter is not helped by the fact that many intellectuals in the West treat the subject as 'taboo', the result of physical fear, or guilt for the imperial past, or because of the fashion for not wanting to engage in intercultural critique.[6] The attempt to explain what happened with reference to religion is crude reductionism. Trying to unravel the intricacies of the Muslim world cannot be achieved by 'naive references to the Koran'; this, according to Stephen Chan, would be 'as stupid as trying to understand "the West" by Saddam distributing the Bible and talking about the children of Abraham'.[7] What is more, ideas about defending the faith, by force if necessary, are present in many of the world's religions. It is possible to find passages in Judaism, Christianity and in the Koran 'that legitimate violence, terror and senseless sacrifice'.[8]

We are not suggesting here anything as naive as the simple idea that deeper self-knowledge on the part of Muslims and Americans will stop future collisions of one sort or another, but it would help to change the climate. What we have suggested here, all too briefly, is the critical point that we are not confronted today by a simple 'clash of civilizations'.[9] What we have instead is a confusion of misunderstandings, crude stereotypes, and parallel absences of self-knowledge.[10] The United States and Islam represent major forces in contemporary world politics: one is politically and economically centralized and dominant in terms of both material and soft power, while the other is politically decentralized and weak but ideationally massively influential. An attitudinal shift is needed, and the starting point may have been precisely identified by a Palestinian journalist who, when asked if he could say one thing to Americans in the aftermath of September 11, replied: 'America, we feel your pain. Isn't it time you felt ours?'

The West and the Rest

If we take Osama bin Laden's public statements as our guide, the al-Qaeda network does not believe that it is in a fight with the 'West' so much as with the United States. Yet many commentators and some political leaders have seen the US–Islam collision as a particular manifestation of a much wider one. The collapse of the Twin Towers exposed a gap into which politicians and writers, journalists and academics have poured explanations based on their worries about globalization, fears about anarchy, guilt about Israel, shame about Africa, anxiety about the unknown, and a generalized sense of responsibility for what happened.

The world is not working for countless millions of its inhabitants. There is a growing gap between the 'haves' and the 'have-nots' through profit-led globalization, the buccaneering behaviour of global corporations, the voracious consumption of Western societies, the marginalization of the 'majority world', failed states, human rights abuses, cycles of economic boom and bust, regional crises in the Balkans and central Africa and elsewhere, escalating violence in the

Middle East, Western support for tyranny while ritualistically declaring
its commitment to democracy, increasing numbers of desperate
refugees, societies crippled by debt, the spread of weapons of mass
destruction, environmental decay, the AIDS plague which continues to
terrorize and kill in millions and enervate societies, and so on. These
are seen as the breeding grounds for rage against 'the West' – but does
it explain terror?[11] We know from history that the poor and humiliated
might do anything if roused by voices able to promise them the earth,
or heaven. Does al-Qaeda speak for the global poor? Whatever doubts
may persist about the electoral legitimacy of George W. Bush, nobody
elected Osama bin Laden, and the attacks were not followed by the
discovery of a political testament by the perpetrators.

It does not dishonour those murdered in New York, Washington and
Pennsylvania to point out, as did the leader writers of the *New
Statesman* shortly afterwards, that the dead that day numbered less than
half the total of children who die somewhere in the world each day
from diarrhoea (caused by the lack of clean water). The point is not
about forgetting September 11, but of remembering what the world is
like every day. 'Never forget the other Terror' was the message, and the
great American writer Mark Twain provided the text. Recalling the way
Europe trembled in the 1790s as the terror swept through France, Twain
pointed out that there had been two 'Reigns of Terror'. The first was the
immediate and urgent one, which brought 'the horror of swift death';
the other resulted in 'lifelong death from hunger, cold, insult, cruelty
and heartbreak'. The former 'inflicted death upon a thousand persons,
the other upon a hundred million'. Writing as if for today, Twain said
that the one brief terror 'we have all been … diligently taught to shiver
at and mourn over', whereas the other we had never learnt to see 'in its
vastness or pity as it deserves'.[12] Terrorism is an abomination and must
be countered, but poverty is the world's biggest killer.

Images of terrorism and poverty have fed fears of the 'coming
anarchy' envisioned in the early 1990s by Robert D. Kaplan. He warned
of a world splitting apart – a 'bifurcated world' – with the West inhab-
iting islands of comfort being threatened by a tidal wave of criminal
anarchy on the part of the masses of alien races and cultures. It would
be a violent state of nature in which he thought it doubtful whether the
West could survive in its present form.[13] September 11 has confirmed
this 'new pessimism'. One response has been the call to 'reorder' the
world, by leaders such as Prime Minister Blair. Would any new world
order – echoing the jibe of a decade earlier – simply be another version
of the New World's order?

Some argue that the present crisis reveals how foolish have been the ideals of those who have imagined that the world could ever come together sharing a set of common values. But while the attacks and the reactions to them have revealed incompatibilities, there has been a range of agreement among those of different faiths, and no faiths, on what constitutes proper behaviour. There has been a massive rejection of terrorism as an instrument of politics, for example. Definitional difficulties remain, of course, but here is a case where collectivities have shared values about behaviour, even if they do not share the same prophet. We are not therefore witnessing a comprehensive clash of incompatible values across the world. It is simply not the case empirically. The south and north coexist in New York. The targeting of that city had a logic in terms of it being the highest symbol of modernity, but was inept at the human level, for it is a living example of people of all cultures being able to share the same busy space. The people of many nations and different faiths who were murdered in the World Trade Center are a tragic testimony to that fact. There are no clear-cut 'civilizational' lines. Western leaders in recent months have regularly pointed out their intervention on behalf of Muslim victims in Kosovo in 1999. As the bombs started dropping on Afghanistan in October 2001, the early stages of the trial of former Yugoslav leader Slobodan Milosevic gave some credence to their arguments.

It would be an error of historic proportions to exaggerate the incompatibility between the thought-worlds of the so-called West and the so-called Rest. We in the West may not be able to understand the thinking of the mass murderers of September 11, but few in the rest of the world could comprehend their motives either. In the week after the attacks a leading Muslim writer, Ziauddin Sardar, wrote:

> Islam cannot explain the actions of the suicide hijackers, just as Christianity cannot explain the gas chambers, Catholicism the bombing at Omagh. They are acts beyond belief, by people who long ago abandoned the path of Islam.

The rest of the article is an account of how the actions of the terrorists were outside the faith and reasoning of Islam.[14] Mohammed Atta's mindset was no more comprehensible to the Arab street than that of Timothy McVeigh had been to the American suburb.

All this suggests that the image of the West and the Rest should be challenged. This metanarrative reifies 'the West' and other groupings as if they are the categorical realities of world politics. Again, life is more complex, except for the terrorist. Speaking for the part of the world in which he lives, Umberto Eco writes:

> We are a pluralist civilisation because we allow mosques to be built in our countries, and we are not going to stop simply because Christian missionaries are thrown into prison in Kabul. If we did so, we too would become Taliban.[15]

If the first step is to challenge the notion of a bifurcated world, the second is to accept Mark Twain's warning. There is a relationship between the two terrors, if not a direct one. Even as we in the West seek to deal with the immediate terror resulting from the attacks of September 11, attempting to overcome the terror we have not learned to see will in itself mark the beginning of a victory.

Terror versus Dialogue

Terrorism is a method of political action that uses violence (or deliberately produces fear) against civilians and civilian infrastructure in order to influence behaviour, to inflict punishment or to exact revenge. For the perpetrators, the point is to make the target group afraid of today, afraid of tomorrow, and afraid of each other.[16] Terrorism is an act, not an ideology. Its instruments are assassination, mass murder, hijacking, bombing, kidnapping and intimidation. Such acts can be committed by states as well as private groups.

Western states have consistently sought to deny that states can commit terrorism. The bias of terror has always been 'against people and in favour of governments'.[17] Whether government or group, motivation should play no part in assessing whether terrorism has taken place. Terror is delineated by method, not motives. Even if actors are motivated by noble objectives – such as the liberation of their homeland – these are deformed by terrorist practices. Third World states have consistently sought to deny that liberation movements can commit terrorism. *All* states deny specific accusations of terrorism although *many* routinely use torture, a particular form of terror against individuals. Both terror and torture are justified pragmatically in the context of 'supreme emergency', although neither method is justified morally.[18]

It is worth remembering that the word 'terror' came into prominence during the French Revolution, a moment in history which also witnessed the beginnings of ideas about the inalienable rights and freedoms of individual citizens. In the two centuries that followed,

European states gradually sought to enmesh these values in domestic political constitutions based on dialogue and negotiation. Yet in their external relations, states viewed terror (and terror by proxy) as a legitimate weapon for furthering their interests. One of the tragic paradoxes of the twentieth century is that those states which have most closely self-identified with the path of the Enlightenment have committed acts of barbarism that no modern terrorist group has yet been able to match. As producers of terror, states remain far more significant than non-state groups, although the emerging market in relatively cheap weapons of mass destruction could level this particular killing field in the future.

Acts of terrorism have been seen on every continent. Perpetrators come from diverse religions and ethnic groups, but governments and networks in the Islamic world commit the most extreme forms of terror. This is true of interstate conflict (the Iran–Iraq war) and intrastate conflict (such as the violence perpetrated by Algerian Islamists). According to Walter Laquer, 'Muslim states and Muslim minorities are involved in almost 90 percent of all sub-state terrorist conflicts.'[19] What Laquer fails to make clear is that in many of these cases (such as Bosnia and Palestine), Muslims are not the primary cause of the violence.[20]

If it is not faith, then is it poverty that forces certain states and non-state actors to terrorize? It has been commonplace to read explanations of this kind, as though poverty itself breeds extremism, yet it is just as easy to think of examples where extreme views and wealth march hand in hand (Christian fundamentalism in the United States, for example). Who becomes a terrorist is not simply a consequence of an unjust environment. Osama bin Laden and al-Qaeda do not belong to the poor of the Middle East; they belong to an old tradition in which self-serving elites seize upon and manipulate the grievances of the poor.

Al-Qaeda (literally, 'the base') illustrates the extent to which terrorism has more complex causes than material dispossession. To carry out a war against the West, bin Laden and his associates have built an army of around 5000 trained terrorists. Contrary to the stereotype of al-Qaeda as a band of itinerant cave dwellers, 'they're modern, and they use modern methods'.[21] One of these modern methods is communicating their message using video recordings, broadcast on an Arab satellite channel and reported in the world's media. It is in these messages that bin Laden exploits symbolic references to the fate of the world's Arabs and Muslims. He tells his 'brothers' to 'rise up' and 'die defending Islam' against the 'infidels'. He gives his followers no choice: 'Muslims have to ally themselves to Muslims.'[22] Given the widespread feeling of injustice perpetrated by Western states against

Islamic states, these messages strike a chord among many ordinary Muslims. This anger is not easily dissipated given that many governments in the Middle East lack popular legitimacy, and what is more, the educated middle classes are on the whole unwilling to defend alternative values of negotiation and inclusion. Into this void, extremists get to speak for Islam on virulently anti-American TV networks like al-Jazeera.[23]

Terrorism collides with notions of politics grounded in democratic values. In an ideal polity, political action is based on dialogue, one in which participants rationally seek to persuade others of the universal validity of their moral beliefs.[24] Those holding values and beliefs that are at odds with the majority are listened to, free of the fear of violence; questions of cultural difference are negotiated within a framework of equality.

Even if the war against terrorism succeeds in defeating the al-Qaeda network, it will not bring about a resolution to the political problems that they have exploited. This can only be achieved by nurturing the values that collide with fear, hatred and a willingness to commit any acts in the hope of changing the course of history. Here there is a responsibility on all actors involved in the current conflagration to encourage voices of moderation, human rights and religious toleration. Such an approach would be both moral and prudent in a world where nuclear materials can be acquired with relative ease. Unless dialogue can prevail within and between cultures, nuclear terrorism is a real and horrific possibility.

Force and Law

The worlds of force and law collide in ways that are comparable to terror and dialogue. There is, however, one significant difference. Whereas terrorist acts are always unlawful, there are some circumstances where force is justified. Force may be used to disarm or defeat terrorists. This is the position that the United Nations, and many peoples around the world, have adopted since 9/11. But even if we concede that the worlds of force and law are not always in collision, extreme caution must be exercised on the part of those who take up arms against terrorists to ensure the legality of their actions. The great danger is that fighting terrorism might provoke ruthless behaviours that represent some sort of victory for the terrorists.

To prevent the slide into unlawful violence, a number of conditions must be met. First, leaders of the war 'for freedom and justice' must be certain that all pacific forms of redress have either been exhausted or are ineffective. Second, there should be no doubt about the justice of the cause. And third, those responsible for the conduct of the war must act within the restraints established by the laws of war.

On October 8, 'Operation Enduring Freedom' began as B52s and F14s struck at suspected al-Qaeda bases. Was there an alternative to this strategy of using force against the Taliban? Could the crimes have been met with an international police operation? Many have argued that international law is the appropriate mechanism to establish the guilt or innocence of those suspected of assisting the attacks. True, the US and UK governments published evidence linking bin Laden and al-Qaeda to the atrocities, but this was little more than 'pretty good information', according to Secretary of State Colin Powell.[25] It did not establish guilt beyond reasonable doubt. There is a deeper issue at stake here, and one that is written into the heart of democratic societies: it is not for the victim of a crime (or their political leaders) to establish the guilt of an accused, only an impartial court can do this. Since no court in the US could be expected to be even-handed in this situation, there was a strong case for setting up a court in The Hague, like the trial of ex-president Slobodan Milosevic.

Attempting to capture and prosecute alleged terrorists was only one aspect of a solution that did not involve a global war against terrorists, and those states thought to harbour them. While this approach found some supporters in civil society, they were quickly sidelined. In part this was because of serious practical concerns. A major problem was how to apprehend those suspected of planning the attacks without using military force, especially when they had found protection inside a sovereign state that was believed to be unwilling to give them up. Even if the main suspects could have been captured by careful police and intelligence work, a guilty verdict would not have been acceptable to millions of Muslims if the trial had been conducted in a 'victor's court'. To be effective, the legal process must have a degree of legitimacy in the eyes not only of the prosecution but also of the accused. In the absence of this, the case against bin Laden and his associates would have become little more than a spectacle to be exploited.

Not surprisingly, few in the US supported the idea of an international police action. The White House had to 'do something', and that something was interpreted as military action. This strategy was risky. Even if the military aims had been restricted to the elimination of al-Qaeda's terrorist capacity in Afghanistan, it was unclear what would count as a victory. The problem of fighting a war against terrorism is that one never knows if it has been won. In this 'new kind of war', there will never be a moment when one can be certain that the last piece of the adversary's ground has been occupied, for it might be in Florida. When, then, can the victor's flag be raised? Terrorists can lie in waiting, or they can move to cells in other territories. They may not fight back at once, planning instead a revenge attack that may take place months or years ahead. Out of the clear blue sky, as on September 11, might come another collision to change our world, harming the innocent and spreading further shockwaves of fear.

The pursuit of a military solution faces many obstacles, especially when victory is defined as broadly as 'a series of decisive actions against terrorist organisations and those who harbour and support them'.[26] It may be risky, but is it just? Richard Falk, a longstanding opponent of pervious US military actions, has argued that it was 'the first truly just war since World War II'.[27] It is a just war because the threat posed by Osama bin Laden could not be resolved through dialogue given its genocidal intent against Americans and Jews, and its goal of waging an unlimited civilizational war. Such reasoning combines many kinds of justification, including punishment and deterrence. Yet it was self-defence that representatives of the US government chose to invoke when they needed to make a formal justification for their actions. While there remains an intense legal debate as to what is permitted by self-defence, the crucial point is that the US government's argument was affirmed in two UN Security Council Resolutions (1368 of September 12, and 1373 of September 28) and gained approval in many other international forums. This support, however, should not be interpreted as providing a cover for future military acts against suspected terrorist groups or states that harbour them, not least because of the Taliban's near total ostracism from the international community.

Even if the justice of the cause is thought to be a sufficient reason for using military power, the worlds of law and force will still collide unless every effort is made to minimize harm done to civilians. The official view is that a great deal of care has been taken in identifying targets in Afghanistan, including the involvement of lawyers to assess the likelihood of collateral damage. General Franks, leading the operation, told the Senate Armed Services Committee that 'this is the most accurate war ever fought'.[28] The unofficial view, put forward by human rights groups and researchers, is that there have been thousands of civilian casualties as well as the continuing humanitarian disaster. Who should we believe? It is too soon to tell. When more reliable evidence can be gathered, the question of the extent of civilian casualties will play a prominent role when assessments are made about the rightness of the US strategy.

There may have been no alternative to a military response acceptable to the vast majority of US citizens, but by choosing warfighting rather than crimefighting, critics of US policy argued that it risked reproducing the logic of the terrorists. When we persuade ourselves that war is the only way of prevailing (as the jihadists have), we become self-righteous about our cause (as Islamists are about theirs), and we risk blurring the distinction between warriors and non-combatants (as al-Qaeda has done with its instruction 'to kill the Americans and their allies'[29]). This is not to suggest a moral equivalence between those responsible for the terrorist atrocities of September 11, and those leading the war against terror. Rather, it is a warning that victims all too often become bullies. With this in mind it is crucial to think not only about what our military actions might do to the enemy, but also about what they are doing to us.

States and Networks

September 11 has begun a new chapter in the historic rivalry between states and non-state actors. Since the end of the Middle Ages sovereign states had come to triumph over other kinds of political orders such as city states, empires, religious orders, dynasties and feudal barons. The wave of decolonization in the twentieth century saw the code of the state initially dominant in Europe being copied universally. In Africa and Asia, the boundaries of the political community were framed by a juridical relationship between population, government and a delimited territory. Even when these new states were weak and unable to control their territory, other sovereign states continued to grant them recognition and all the usual prerogatives that come with being a member of the 'international community'.

The reality of the global order has not always conformed to the neat lines on maps. Even strong states have had their sovereignty routinely compromised either by coercion or by consent. The post-Second World War settlement, for example, forced Germany to give up its autonomy in the area of security policy, while the process of European integration led the same country voluntarily to give up a good deal of its economic autonomy. Closer attention to history has shown us that the juridical idea of separate sovereign spaces has always been contested by interventions of a material and ideological kind.[30]

One of the striking aspects of the attacks on the US was the manner in which many of the settled norms of the so-called Westphalian system of states was unhinged. The enemy was not a state, and their immediate aim was not to acquire territory but to alter the ideological balance of power. Such a battle is only one move in what al-Qaeda see as its longer game; namely, a holy war against infidels. The means of fighting this war are also significantly different from the historic pattern of interstate rivalry. Violence is not carried out directly by agents of the state, and the target is not opposing armies but civilians (these are acts that are in breach of existing international legal norms that apply to states and opposition movements).[31]

Terrorist acts in distant lands have become easier with technological advances. Cellphones and the internet allow groups to coordinate their activities (but also to be traced). Documents on the web assisted the 9/11 attackers to access data on the design characteristics of the World Trade Center. What is more, weapons are now available that have greater accuracy, more destructive power and enhanced portability; their availability is also easy, owing to the fact that the world is awash with weapons of all kinds. In addition, there is great potential to divert non-military power (aircraft, industrial explosives, chemicals, and so on) to destructive ends. What the terrorists had to do on 9/11 was to work out how to release such power and redirect it. Two civilian aircraft were able to deliver 'a kiloton of explosive power' into the Twin Towers 'with deadly accuracy'.[32]

Terror networks need more than weapons: they also need bases, and this is why the US used force against the Taliban government which maintained a 'close alliance' with al-Qaeda.[33] Bin Laden's network had provided military and economic support for the Taliban in the civil war that engulfed the country in the late 1990s. In return, the Taliban allowed al-Qaeda to set up a dozen or so training camps in the know-ledge that the warriors and weapons they produced would be used for shared purposes.[34] It was not an alliance destined to prosper. It is commonplace to hear how vulnerable modern societies are to the weapons of the terrorist. This is true. But it does not compare with the vulnerability of weak and failed states to the advanced weaponry of resolute modern societies.

September 11 illustrates the process by which state power is evinced by transnational networks *and* the concomitant attempt by states to reassert the primacy of the interstate realm. Before toppling the Taliban became a stated US war aim three weeks after the bombing began,[35] the US had sought to do business with the new order in Kabul. The prospect of a route to the rich energy resources of central and west Asia propelled US political and corporate elites into an intense round of commercial diplomacy. In 1998, Dick Cheney, now US Vice-President, said: 'I cannot think of a time when we have had a region emerge as suddenly to become as strategically important as the Caspian.' More graphically, a US diplomat saw in this tragic land a vision of a new Saudi Arabia, a country 'with pipelines, an emir, no parliament and lots of Sharia law', to which he added: 'We can live with that.'[36] It would be mistaken, however, to think that the US was motivated solely by geopolitical interests, since it re-evaluated its stance towards the Taliban largely on ethical grounds. Two factors were important in this respect: first, Afghanistan continued to be the largest exporter of opium in the world; second, the government's appalling human rights record jarred with the democratic ideals espoused by the Clinton administration. As a consequence, both in Washington and at the UN, the Taliban became increasingly isolated. In the words of Secretary of State Madeleine Albright: 'We are opposed to the Taliban because of their treatment of women and children' and 'their general lack of respect for human dignity'.[37]

Under the influence of the propaganda of hyperglobalization, many have been dazzled by non-state actors. September 11 underlines the continuing power of states. Al-Qaeda has flourished in places where state structures are either weak or non-existent. Funded by other states and private actors, al-Qaeda was able to establish itself in Afghanistan and the Yemen by brokering deals with the governments to aid them in their own civil wars. The long process of state formation (and decline) in the post-colonial world is connected to transnational networks in complex ways, just as in the era of colonization trading companies and religions aided and abetted the expansion of the states system from its European core to the world beyond its frontiers. In this sense, 9/11 and the global war on terror have not fundamentally altered the dynamic interplay of territoriality and transnationalism.

Communities of Power and the Power of Community

Great practitioners of *raison d'état* like Machiavelli tell us that the first responsibility of leadership is to organize power. This means having strong defences and the capacity to punish others that threaten or use force against your people. In its modern guise, the doctrine places primacy on the state as the protector of the community, the condition for the preservation of its values, institutions and culture. Modern states can therefore be thought of as communities of power.

Like all doctrines, *raison d'état* is open to competing interpretations. It can lend itself to an expansionist understanding, where security leads a state to conquer its neighbours. The fact that *they* are a different community of power, with alternative values and beliefs, is itself thought to constitute a threat to *us*. This is the historic 'security dilemma', the unresolvable uncertainty one state has about the intentions of others.[38] The 'war against terrorism' has already ratcheted up security dilemmas in several regions. Before a satisfactory phrase for the period since the end of the Cold War era had been invented, it looks as though we are on course for a psychological and functional equivalent. The parallels are striking, and we have been here many times: the phrase *guerra fría* originated in the thirteenth century to describe the confrontation between Islam and Christianity in Spain.[39]

The collision between acting as communities of power or promoting the power of community is evident in Western debates about how to respond to 9/11. For the state that was the victim, this represents an old dilemma in the way the United States engages with the outside world, though with a new twist. Can the community be protected by conceiving security as a condition to be achieved *against* others (national security) or can it only be ultimately achieved *with* others (a 'common security')? This distinction is more than semantics. What follows in terms of diplomatic activity and military deployments are poles apart. For the United States in the period ahead the choice is between the search for safety through the exercise of narrowly defined national interests or the cultivation of political community on as wide a scale as possible. It is a choice between thinking about the US as a singular community of fate, as *raison d'état* suggests, or one among many 'overlapping communities of fate'.[40]

Despite emphasizing the right words about 'coalition building' in the period shortly after the attacks on the United States, it seems clear that the Bush administration's impulse to go it alone has won out. Where is NATO now? Or the EU? Or the UN? Some US officials and commentators do not think they need a multilateral approach, nakedly proclaiming, like Charles Krauthammer, that 'the US can do whatever it wants regardless of anyone else'.[41] Even more cautious voices like that of Secretary of State Colin Powell believe that the US does not require authorization for its actions from *any* international institution. A US-led war against Iraq will be a major test of the US-led coalition, particularly in the Arab world. And what if that war happens, and is successful? Will the reaction be a further spreading of US military might around the world? Will the United States then over-reach itself like so many great imperial powers in the past? Is the 'axis of evil' less about the real and present danger they face, but more about rationalizing geopolitical ambitions, together with the tendency of great empires to reach beyond the present frontier?

In the 1980s, the idea of common security coincided with the growing sense that so many problems transcended national boundaries, and that there was a mismatch between narrow national security perspectives and the realization of shared goals concerning peace, the environment and the pursuit of basic rights. The idea of security as a shared value has been dramatically highlighted by the direct attack on the US homeland. September 11 showed that the world's most powerful state is not inviolable. Some parts of the world – notably Western Europe following two world wars – have learned that a shared sense of community is the strongest basis of security. In contrast, it is almost wholly absent in Israel–Palestine relations. Several weeks before the attacks on the United States, Faisal Bodi, a Muslim journalist, wrote an article extolling the virtue of 'Bombing for God'.[42] 'In the Muslim world,' he wrote, 'we celebrate what we call the martyr-bombers'. He referred to polls showing that 75 per cent of people in the Middle East supported the martyr-bombings against Israel. The message of the martyr-bombers was 'brutally clear', he said: 'as long as their people cannot live with dignity and in peace, Israelis should not expect to, either'. This blunt warning is one the now violated United States must heed, while at the same time pursuing the terrorists.

The debate about how the US and its allies should respond to the attacks has focused for the most part on immediate measures rather than long-term strategies. There has been an absence of defining statements of radical alternatives on the lines of common security. A notable exception was Tony Blair's speech to the Labour Party Conference in October 2001. The Prime Minister said:

> Round the world, 11 September is bringing governments and people to reflect, consider and change ... There is a coming together. The power of community is asserting itself. We are realizing how fragile are our frontiers in the face of the world's new challenges.

His tone was evangelical but his themes were Kantian.[43] 'This is a moment to seize. The kaleidoscope has been shaken. The pieces are in flux. Soon they will settle again. Before they do, let us reorder the world around us.' He concluded his speech with the words: 'By strength of our common endeavour, we achieve more together than we can alone.'[44] Blair was both right and wrong. He was mistaken in thinking that a real global community might come from merely re-shaking the existing pieces of the kaleidoscope. A truly reordered world needs new pieces. Where he was right was in thinking that people(s) can achieve more collectively than unilaterally. He was also prescient in guessing that old patterns might soon settle: they have, and the moment has not been seized.

A World of Whose Making?

Who can we trust to guide us through the collisions of thought-worlds and power-plays that shape these stressful times, with some hope of moving beyond the colliding worlds of 9/11? Who is able to see through the smoke and debris of that infamous morning, and understand what really must be done to ensure that nothing like it ever happens again? Who will remake global order? And in whose interests will it be? Timescale is a traditional way of distinguishing mere politicians from great statesmen. For the former, problem solving means attending to today's agenda, and the next election. For great leaders, today's problems are not the real ones. This distinction shades into a difference of approach based on concern for symptoms as opposed to causes. In this respect, the overwhelming priority for the White House has been to attend to the symptoms, by seeking out the terrorists responsible for the attacks and threatening those who harbour them. In the short term this strategy has been more successful than its proponents could have predicted. A low-cost, mostly victorious, almost casualty-free war in 'self-defence' is not only the definition of a model military campaign; it is also the foundation for a successful presidential re-election campaign.

There are many voices around the world for whom today's problems – including 'the war against terrorism' – are not the real problems. September 11 was the deadly symptom of a hot-house global order in which rage germinates, and out of which ruthless leaders are able to pick suicidal accomplices. As it happens, extremism was in season well before the attacks on the United States. At the end of the twentieth century we witnessed a growing disposition of people in many parts of the world to say goodbye to reason. This was evident in the hypernationalism of the Balkans, the genocidal mentality of Rwanda, the fanatical religious beliefs of the Taliban, the fundamentalism of the religious right in the US, the intolerance of parts of the Islamic world, anti-Semitism in Eastern Europe, and the interest in the paranormal, extraterritorial possibilities and 'new age' beliefs in many societies. We not only learned that God is not dead, but also – as G.K. Chesterton put it a century earlier – that many people found it easier to believe in anything rather than believe in nothing.

The terrorists had beliefs that gave their lives meaning, though what those beliefs were remain contested, theoretically, psychologically and politically. What Mohammed Atta left in his delayed luggage, which serves as his only testimony, did not identify with any great political struggles. This is not an option for states and societies, as they construct their frameworks of meaning. At the end of the Cold War the United States lost the Soviet Empire but did not find a role. It did when the 'post-Cold War' collided with the future on 9/11 and became the 'war against terrorism'. Extremism and fear have given the US society a framework of meaning that was never possible from the 24/7 transactions of globalization. Some security measures of course should be taken, for many terrorists are beyond both appeasement and deterrence, but if terrorism is simply matched by escalating violence, then fear will be sovereign in world affairs, and the terrorists will have won some sort of victory. Writing in 1757, in his book *On the Sublime and Beautiful,* Edmund Burke wrote that 'No passion so effectually robs the mind of all its powers of acting and reasoning as fear.' This is an important warning for societies that have already experienced the power of fear in the recent months, and seen the way that it fertilizes suspicion, groupthink and ruthlessness – and sometimes, insidiously, the most primitive of feelings about others. When fear rules, it is not difficult to offer pessimistic scenarios for the months and years ahead.

How much worse can it get? This may seem a strange question, because six months after the attacks, the war in Afghanistan has been declared a victory, the Kashmir crisis did not blow up, the 'friendly' governments of Pakistan and Saudi Arabia are still in power, Osama bin Laden has disappeared from public view and may be dead, and no other major cataclysmic terrorist attacks have occurred. This is all true, but dangers are all around.

In Afghanistan, the situation remains very uncertain, with ground fighting and bombing still continuing, and key members of the Taliban and al-Qaeda having escaped; the country is in turmoil, poverty-stricken and warlord-dominated. It could yet, as so often in history, be a graveyard of hopes. In neighbouring Pakistan, the present 'pro-Western' government is vulnerable, and a coup by fundamentalist forces, incited by events in Kashmir and India, remains a possibility, and with it the nightmare of an 'Islamist bomb'. In India, levels of communal violence between Hindu nationalists and Muslims escalates dangerously, with hundreds already killed. Kashmir is therefore still the most likely site for nuclear use since 1945. If south and west Asia are simmering, the Middle East has already boiled over. The conflict between Israel and Palestine both feeds upon and exacerbates turmoil elsewhere, and threatens to become a bloodbath whose consequences are hard to imagine. If the war against terrorism widens to include Iraq, Saddam Hussein might be expected, as an early gambit, to attack Israel, in order to polarize the region. The 'Arab street' has been ready to erupt, and this would be the spark. As it is, the House of Saud is thought to have shaky foundations (and with it supplies of cheap oil to the West). Could Osama bin Laden yet rise and return to Mecca, like the triumphant Ayatollah to Tehran two decades ago? Further afield, anxieties are frequently expressed about the stability of the Philippines and Indonesia, and indeed any country with large Muslim populations.

Many countries in the West, of course, have extensive Muslim communities. A widening and more violent war on terrorism, with growing numbers of Muslim victims, would strain multiculturalism to breaking point. Already, the erosion of civil liberties in the name of 'security' is a cause for concern in civil society in the US and the UK. Regressive attitudes towards outsiders such as migrants and asylum seekers are widely in evidence. Tougher still, leaders everywhere are using anti-terrorism to legitimize confrontations with their domestic opponents. President Putin is but one leader for whom all this has been an unexpected political bonus.

President Bush always said that it would be a long war, and in this he was certainly correct. How long will it take to suppress al-Qaeda in 40 countries in which it is supposed to have sleepers? Will it ever be possible to have a victory parade in this particular war, given that, as Northern Ireland shows, one is never sure that the last terrorist attack has taken place? In a traditional war, victory is assured by the occupying of ground; in a global war against terrorism not only has territory to be occupied in some sense globally, but also hearts and minds have to be won over. US strategy is gradually spreading its infrastructure of military power across the world in pursuit of the former; its diplomacy is not so far proving as effective in the latter. Although the assertion of US power seems to have been successful in the short run – a degree of business as usual has been re-established – victory is remote. How many suicide bombers were born today? More immediately, a 'spectacular' may be at an advanced state of planning as these words are being written – nuclear, biological, chemical, or simply devastating by traditional means. In the few months between the manuscript of this book being submitted and its publication, the world could yet again be shaken to its international political core.

The choice facing the most powerful Western societies, and especially the United States, is not simply one between short-term and long-term, an age of terror versus the construction of a world of community. The short terms have to be managed if there is to be hope of anything better, beyond. Here it is helpful to recall Albert Camus and his conviction that the means one uses today shape the ends one might perhaps reach tomorrow.[45] This challenges the Machiavellian notion that the ends can justify the means. For Gandhi, 'ends and means amount to the same thing'. A concrete 'end' might be out of reach, but the 'means' are not.[46] This is not a call for human perfection but for a reconceiving of the meaning of victory. Rather than letting terrorism win, by allowing fear to be sovereign, terrorism can be defeated today (if not yet eradicated) by employing the means, however imperfectly, that are the moral equivalent of the ends we seek. The treatment of prisoners in Cuba or of dissidents at home are test cases. In addition to taking necessary security measures, the means approach to victory involves a steady commitment on the part of the world's dominant states to behave as if law is not just an instrument of the powerful, as if the humanizing of globalization is a priority, and as if the creation of a global human rights culture will be the consequence of dialogue not diktat. These means-as-ends would represent a daily victory over terror. If the goal of policy is restricted to one of national security, narrowly defined, then we can say that September 11 was not only our shared yesterday, but risks also being all our tomorrows.

Notes

1. Quoted in Paul Reynolds, 'Washington Readies for War', in Jenny Baxter and Malcolm Downing (eds) *The Day that Shook the World: Understanding September 11th* (London: BBC Books), pp. 84–98, at p. 95.
2. Quoted in Gary Yonge, 'The Guardian Profile. Susan Sontag. The Risk Taker', *Guardian*, January 19, 2002.
3. Tony Blair's speech to the Labour Party Conference. For the full text, see *Guardian Unlimited*,
   <http://politics.guardian.co.uk/labour2001/story/0,1414,562006,00.html>.
4. Salmon Rushdie, 'Yes, This is About Islam', *New York Times*, November 2, 2001.
5. Fred Halliday, *Two Hours that Shook the World: September 11, 2001, Causes and Consequences* (London: Saqi Books, 2002), pp. 44–5.
6. This argument was made by Ibn Warraq, 'Honest Intellectuals Must Shed Their Spiritual Turbans', *Guardian*, November 10, 2001, Review, p. 12.

7. Stephen Chan, 'A Left Too Lazy to Look the "Other" Way', *Times Higher Education Supplement,* December 7, 2001.
8. Halliday, *Two Hours,* p. 46.
9. Samuel P. Huntington, 'The Clash of Civilizations', *Foreign Affairs,* vol. 72, no. 3, pp. 22–49. See also his *The Clash of Civilizations and the Remaking of World Order* (London: Simon and Schuster, 1998).
10. See also Edward W. Said, 'The Clash of Ignorance', *The Nation,* October 22, 2001.
11. See, for example, the op-ed piece by the President of the Philippines: Gloria Macapagal Arroyo, 'Do Both Things: Root Out Terrorists and Overcome Poverty', *International Herald Tribune,* January 31, 2002.
12. Quoted in the *New Statesman,* editorial, November 5, 2001.
13. Robert Kaplan, *The Coming Anarchy: Shattering the Dreams of the Post Cold War* (New York: Random House, 2000).
14. Ziauddin Sardar, 'When the Innocent are Murdered, We All Go into the Dark With Them', *Observer,* September 16, 2001.
15. Umberto Eco 'The Roots of Conflict', *Guardian,* October 13, 2001.
16. Adapted from Bill Clinton, 'The Struggle for the Soul of the 21st Century', The Dimbleby Lecture, 2001 (December 14). Full text: <http://www.bbc.co.uk/arts/news_comment/dimbleby/clinton.shtml>.
17. Eqbal Ahmad, *Terrorism: Theirs and Ours* (New York: Seven Stories Press, 2001), p. 53.
18. The phrase 'supreme emergency' is Michael Walzer's. See his *Just and Unjust Wars: A Moral Argument with Historic Illustrations* (2nd edn) (New York: HarperCollins, 1992).
19. Walter Laqueur, 'Left, Right and Beyond: The Changing Face of Terror', in James F. Hoge and Gideon Rose (eds) *How Did This Happen? Terrorism and the New War* (Oxford: PublicAffairs Ltd/Perseus Books, 2001), p. 75.
20. For an important analysis of 'anti-Muslimism', see Halliday, *Two Hours,* chapter 4.
21. Quoted in Simon Reeve, *The New Jackals: Ramzi Yousef, Osama bin Laden and the Future of Terrorism* (London: Andre Deutsch, 1999), p. 4.
22. These words from bin Laden have been taken from a fax released on al-Jazeera ('Bin Laden's fax', *Guardian,* September 24, 2001), and his taped broadcast of November 3 ('Bin Laden, in a Taped Speech, Says Attacks in Afghanistan are a War Against Islam', *New York Times,* November 4, 2001).
23. Fouad Ajami, 'What the Muslim World is Watching', *New York Times,* November 18, 2001.
24. See Habermas's account of 'discourse ethics' in William Outhwaite (ed.) *The Habermas Reader* (Cambridge: Polity Press, 1996), pp. 180–95.
25. 'NATO Says US has Proof Against Bin Laden Group', *New York Times,* October 3, 2001.
26. 'Get Ready for War, Bush tells America', *Observer,* September 16, 2001.
27. Richard Falk, 'Defining a Just War', *The Nation,* October 29, 2001, p. 1 of 6 (web edition).
28. Barry Bearak, Eric Schmitt and Craig S. Smith, 'Uncertain Toll in the Fog of War: Civilian Deaths in Afghanistan', *New York Times,* February 10, 2002.
29. 'Founding Statement of al-Qa'ida', in Halliday, *Two Hours,* pp. 218–19.

30. See, for example, the chapter by Stephen Krasner in Michael Cox, Tim Dunne and Ken Booth (eds) *Empires, Systems and States: Great Transformations in International Politics* (Cambridge: Cambridge University Press, 2002).
31. David Held, 'Violence, Law and Justice in a Global Age', September 14, 2001, <http://www.opendemocracy.net/document_store/Doc648-5.pdf>.
32. Thomas Homer-Dixon, 'The Rise of Complex Terrorism', *Foreign Policy* (web edition), pp. 3–4. Many of the arguments in the text about changing destructive capacities, and vulnerabilities, have been drawn from this source, <http://www.foreignpolicy.com/issue_janfeb_2002/homer-dixon.html>.
33. Fred Halliday's description, *Two Hours*, p. 42.
34. For a thorough analysis of this relationship see Peter L. Bergen, *Holy War Inc: Inside the Secret World of Osama bin Laden* (London: Weidenfeld and Nicolson, 2001), chapter 8.
35. Jonathan Steele, 'Fighting the Wrong War', *Guardian*, December 11, 2001.
36. Both quotations are from George Monbiot, 'America's Pipe Dream', *Guardian* October 23, 2001, p. 19. The US government under Clinton turned against the Taliban during 1997–98.
37. Quoted in Bergen, *Holy War Inc*, p. 158.
38. Ken Booth and Nicholas J. Wheeler, *The Security Dilemma: Anarchy, Society and Community in World Politics* (Basingstoke: Palgrave, forthcoming).
39. A.B. Bozeman quoted in Philip Allott, 'The Future of the Human Past', in Ken Booth (ed.) *Statecraft and Security* (Cambridge: Cambridge University Press, 1998), p. 335.
40. This phrase is David Held's, 'Violence, Law and Justice'.
41. Charles Krauthammer, 'America Rules OK', *Guardian*, December 17, 2001.
42. Faisal Bodie, 'Bombing for God', *Guardian*, August 28, 2001.
43. Jason Cowley, 'Forward, to the Union of Humanity', *New Statesman*, October 15, 2001.
44. For the text of Prime Minister Blair's speech, see <http://politics.guardian.co.uk/labour2001/story/0,1414,562006,00.html>.
45. See Stanley Hoffmann, *Duties Beyond Borders: On the Limits and Possibilities of Ethical International Politics* (Syracuse, NY: Syracuse University Press, 1981), p. 197.
46. Glyn Richards, *The Philosophy of Gandhi* (Richmond: Curzon Press, 1991), pp. 31–2.

Part I
Terror

CHAPTER 2

History and September 11[1]

Francis Fukuyama

World politics, it would seem, shifted gears abruptly after September 11. During the dot.com era (which today seems like an enchanted, long-ago time), America was on a roll. Communism, the last big competitor to liberal democracy, had collapsed just like fascism and monarchy before it, the US economy was going gangbusters and democratic institutions seemed to be making headway in all parts of the world. Technology, it was said, was bringing the global village closer together in ways that made traditional nation states irrelevant. Today, everything looks different. The United States has gone to war with the Taliban and al-Qaeda in Afghanistan after suffering an unprecedentedly successful attack on its own territory, and after a successful initial stage of the campaign is preparing to take on Iraq. Large numbers of Muslims are now mobilized in opposition to the United States, and countries around the world are being asked to choose sides in the struggle. Security concerns have thrown sand in the gears of the just-in-time economy, which depends on open borders and the free movement of goods and people.

What is going on here? Are we seeing the beginning of a decades-long 'clash of civilizations' pitting the West against Islam, a conflict that expands remorselessly out of the Afghan swamp to engulf ever larger parts of the world? Will the very technologies that seemed to promote freedom, like airplanes and skyscrapers and biology laboratories, be turned against us in ways that we cannot ultimately stop? Or will the present conflict recede and the old world of an ever-integrating global economy come back once Osama bin Laden and the Taliban are swept away and the terror network is rolled up?

More than ten years ago, I argued that we had reached the 'end of history': not that historical events would stop, but that History understood as the evolution of human societies through different forms of government had culminated in modern liberal democracy and market-oriented capitalism.[2] It is my view that this hypothesis remains correct, despite the events since September 11: modernity, as represented by the United States and other developed democracies, will remain the dominant force in world politics, and the institutions embodying the West's underlying principles of freedom and equality will continue to spread around the world. The September 11 attacks represent a desperate backlash against the modern world, which appears to be a speeding freight train to those unwilling to get on board. But we need to look seriously at the challenge we face. For a movement that has the power to wreak immense damage on the modern world, even if it represents only a small number of people, raises real questions about the viability of our civilization. The existence of weapons of mass destruction in the hands of virulently anti-American or anti-Western forces and their possible use has become a real threat. The key questions that Americans face as they proceed forward with this 'war' on terrorism are how deep this fundamental challenge is, which sorts of allies it can recruit and what we must do to counter it.

A Clash of Civilizations?

The distinguished political scientist Samuel Huntington argues that the present conflict could turn into a 'clash of civilizations', one of the cultural conflicts which, he predicted several years ago, would rack the post-Cold War world.[3] While the Bush and Blair administrations have been correctly asserting that the current struggle is against terrorists, not a war between the West and Islam, there are clearly cultural issues at play.

Americans have tended to believe that their institutions and values – democracy, individual rights, the rule of law and prosperity based on economic freedom – represent universal aspirations that will ultimately be shared by people all over the world, if given the opportunity. They are inclined to think that American society appeals to people of all cultures. The millions of immigrants from countries all over the world who vote with their feet to move to America and to other developed societies seem to testify to this fact.

But events since September 11 challenge this view. Mohammed Atta and several of the other hijackers were educated people who lived and studied in the West; not only were they not seduced by it, they were sufficiently repelled by what they saw to be willing to drive planes into buildings and kill thousands of the people among whom they lived. The cultural disconnect here, as for Osama bin Laden and his fellow Islamic fundamentalists, would seem to be absolute. Is it just our cultural myopia that makes us think that Western values are potentially universal ones?

The Logic of History

There are, in fact, reasons for believing that Western values and institutions are immensely appealing to many if not most non-Western people. This is not to deny the historical tie between both democracy and capitalism to Christianity, or the fact that democracy has its cultural roots in Europe: as philosophers from Alexis de Tocqueville and Georg Hegel to Friedrich Nietzsche have pointed out, modern democracy is a secularized version of the Christian doctrine of universal human equality.

But Western institutions are like the scientific method, which, though discovered in the West, has universal applicability. There is an underlying historical mechanism that encourages a long-term convergence across cultural boundaries, first and most powerfully in economics, then in the realm of politics and finally (and most distantly) in culture. What drives this process forward in the first instance is modern science and technology, whose ability to create material wealth and weapons of war is so great that virtually all societies must come to terms with it. The technology of semiconductors or biomedicine is no different for Muslims or Chinese than it is for Westerners, and the need to master it necessitates the adoption of certain economic institutions, like free markets and the rule of law, that promote growth. Modern technology-driven market economies thrive on individual freedom – that is, a system where individuals rather than governments or priests make decisions on prices or rates of interest.

Economic development in turn tends to engender liberal democracy – not inevitably, but often enough that the correlation between development and democracy constitutes one of the few generally accepted 'laws' of political science. Economic growth produces a middle class with property rights, a complex civil society and ever higher levels of education to maintain economic competitiveness. All these factors together create fertile ground in which demands for democratic political participation take shape, which eventually get institutionalized in democratic government.

Culture – religious beliefs, social habits, longstanding traditions – is the last area of convergence, and also the weakest. Societies are loath to give up deeply rooted values, and it would be extremely naive to think that American popular culture, seductive as it is, will soon engulf the entire world. Indeed, the spread of McDonald's and Hollywood around the world has provoked a considerable backlash against the very prospect of globalization.

But while cultural differences remain in modern societies, they tend to be put in a box, separated from politics, and relegated to the realm of private life. The reason for this is simple: if politics is based on something like religion, there will never be any civil peace because people cannot agree on fundamental religious values. Secularism is a relatively recent development in the West: Christian princes and priests in Europe used to mandate their subjects' religious beliefs and persecute those who dissented. The modern secular democratic state emerged out of the bloody religious conflict in Europe during the sixteenth and seventeenth centuries in which different Christian groups slaughtered one another mercilessly. The separation of church and state became a necessary component of modernization precisely because of the need for civil peace – a startling thesis that was argued by philosophers like Hobbes and Locke in a great tradition that culminated in the American Declaration of Independence and Constitution.

This underlying logic of modernization suggests that Western values are not just arbitrary cultural offshoots of Western Christianity, but do embody a more universal process. What we need to ask then is, are there cultures or regions of the world that will resist or even prove impervious to the modernization process?

The West and the Rest

If we look at Asia, it is hard to see insuperable cultural barriers to modernization. Former Singaporean prime minister Lee Kuan Yew used to argue that there were 'Asian values'[4] that supported authoritarianism, not democracy, but in recent years South Korea and Taiwan have democratized as they got richer. India has of course been a successful democracy since independence in 1948 and has recently embarked on a series of economic reforms that could help lift it out of poverty as well.

In Latin America and the former communist states of Europe, the cultural barriers are even less pronounced: for them the problem is more on-the-ground failure to achieve modernization rather than unhappiness with the goal of modernization itself. Sub-Saharan Africa has numerous problems, from AIDS to civil war to wretched government, but it is hard to see how its diverse cultural traditions will prevent societies there from modernizing if they can get their acts together in other respects.

Islam is the one major world culture that arguably does have some very basic problems with modernity. For all the sophistication of Muslim societies, they can boast only one working democracy (Turkey), and have not seen any economic breakthroughs like Korea or Singapore. It is important to be precise, however, in specifying where the basic problem lies.

How Islam is Different

It is doubtful that there is something inherent in Islam as a religion that makes it hostile to modernity. Islam, like Christianity, Hinduism, Confucianism or any of the world's other great religious or cultural traditions, is a system of extraordinary complexity that has evolved in manifold ways over time. In the period noted above, when Christian Europe was torn by wars of religion, different faiths were living peacefully under the Ottoman millet system. In the nineteenth and early twentieth centuries, there were important liberal trends in Islam in Egypt, Iran and Turkey. Kemal Ataturk's Turkish Republic became one of the most thoroughly secular regimes in modern history.

The Islamic world differs from other world cultures today in one important respect. In recent years it alone has repeatedly produced significant radical movements that reject not just Western policies but the most basic principle of modernity itself, that of religious tolerance. These groups celebrated September 11 because it humbled a society that they believed was at its base corrupt. This corruption was not just a matter of sexual permissiveness, homosexuality and women's rights as they exist in the West, but stemmed in their view from secularism itself. What they hate is that the state in Western societies should be dedicated to religious tolerance and pluralism, rather than to serving religious truth. While people in Asia, Latin America, the former socialist bloc or Africa find Western consumerism appealing and would like to emulate it if only they could, fundamentalists like the Saudi Wahhabis, Osama bin Laden or the Taliban see it as evidence of Western decadence.

So this is not simply a 'war' against terrorists, as the American and British governments understandably portray it. Nor, as many Muslims argue, is the real issue American foreign policy in Palestine or toward Iraq. Unfortunately, the basic conflict we face is much broader, and concerns not just a small group of terrorists, but a much larger group of radical Islamists and Muslims for whom religious identity overrides all other political values. It is radical Islamism that forms the backdrop to a broader sense of grievance that is far deeper and more disconnected from reality than elsewhere. It is this type of Islamist who refuses to believe that Muslims were involved in the World Trade Center attacks, attributing them instead to Israel. They may complain about US policy, but they interpret that policy as part of a larger anti-Muslim conspiracy (conveniently forgetting that US foreign policy has in the past supported Muslims in Somalia, Bosnia, Kosovo and Chechnya).

If we recognize that the underlying struggle is not just with actual terrorists but with radical Islamists who see the world as a Manichean struggle of believers and non-believers, then we are not talking about a small and isolated group of fanatics. Osama bin Laden has evoked substantial sympathy throughout the Muslim world since September 11 for standing up to the United States, from slum dwellers in Karachi to professionals in Beirut and Cairo, to Pakistani and Algerian citizens in Britain and France. The Middle East specialist Daniel Pipes estimates this radicalized population to be some 10–15 per cent of the Muslim world.

Islamo-fascism

Why has this kind of radical Islamism suddenly emerged? Sociologically, the reasons may not be that different from those driving European fascism in the early twentieth century. The Islamic world has seen large populations uprooted from traditional village or tribal life in the past generation. Many have been urbanized and exposed to a more abstract literary form of Islam that calls them back to a purer version of the religion, just as extremist German nationalism tried to resurrect a mythical, long-dead racial identity. This new form of radical Islam is immensely appealing because it purports to explain the loss of values and cultural disorientation that the modernization process itself has engendered.

It may therefore clarify things to say that the present conflict is not simply a fight against terrorism, nor against Islam as a religion or civilization, but rather with Islamo-fascism – that is, the radically intolerant and anti-modern doctrine that has recently arisen in many parts of the Muslim world.

A strong finger of blame for the rise of Islamo-fascism must point at Saudi Arabia. The fortunes of the Saudi royal family have been intertwined with those of the puritanical Wahhabi sect for many years. The former have for years sought both legitimacy and protection from the clerics by advancing Wahhabism. But the Saudi rulers made huge new investments in promoting their brand of Islam during the 1980s and 1990s, particularly following the abortive takeover of the Great Mosque in Mecca in 1979. Wahhabi ideology easily qualifies as Islamo-fascist: a textbook mandated for use in Saudi 10th-grade classes explains that 'it is compulsory for the Muslims to be loyal to each other and to consider the infidels their enemies'. The Saudis have promoted this doctrine not just in the Middle East but in the United States as well, where they have reportedly invested hundreds of millions in building schools and mosques to promulgate their brand of Islam. All this money from the Gulf allowed Osama bin Laden and his followers in effect to buy themselves a country, Afghanistan, for use as a base to train a whole generation of Arab fanatics. In this, the United States is blamable as well for having walked away after the Soviet withdrawal and not taking responsibility for the emergence of a stable and moderate political order there.

A final reason Islamo-fascism took off in the 1980s and 1990s has to do with 'root causes' like poverty, economic stagnation and authoritarian politics in the Middle East that are combustible material for political extremism. But we need to be very clear as to what was actually at the root of these root causes, in light of the frequent charge that the United States and other Western countries could have acted to alleviate them in some significant way.

In fact, the outside community, through international agencies like the World Bank, has been assisting Muslim countries all along, as has the United States in its bilateral dealings with nations like Egypt and Jordan. Very little of this aid has done any good, however, because the underlying problem is a political one in the Muslim world itself. The opportunities for economic and political reform were always there, but few Muslim governments, and, in particular, no Arab governments, have undertaken the kinds of policies followed by countries like South Korea, Taiwan, Chile or Mexico to open up their countries to the global economy and lay the foundations for sustained development. No Arab governments have decided on their own to voluntarily step down in favour of democratic rule, like the Spanish monarchy after the dictator Franco or the Nationalists in Taiwan or the various military dictatorships in Argentina, Brazil, Chile and other parts of Latin America. There is not a single instance of an oil-rich state in the Persian Gulf that has used its wealth to create a self-sustaining industrial society, instead of creating a society of corrupt rentiers who over time have become more and more fanatically Islamist. These failures, and not anything that the outside world has done or refrained from doing, is the root cause of the Muslim world's stagnation.

The Future

The challenge faced by the United States and other Western governments today is more than a fight with a tiny band of terrorists. The Islamo-fascist sea within which the terrorists swim constitutes an ideological challenge that is in some ways more basic than the one posed by communism. What will be the broad march of history from this point forward? Will radical Islam pick up ever more adherents and new and more powerful weapons with which to attack the West? We obviously can't know, but certain factors will be key.

The first is the successful outcome of the military operations in Afghanistan against the Taliban and al-Qaeda, and beyond them Saddam Hussein in Iraq. Much as people would like to believe that ideas live or die as a result of their inner moral rectitude, power matters a great deal. German fascism didn't collapse because of its internal moral contradictions; it died because Germany was bombed to rubble and occupied by Allied armies. Osama bin Laden gained an enormous popularity throughout the Muslim world by successfully attacking the Twin Towers. The destruction of his base of operations in Afghanistan and his eventual death or capture at the hands of US forces makes all that he represents much less appealing. A military campaign against Iraq will have great radicalizing potential, unless it is concluded quickly, cleanly, leaving in place a decent and democratic successor regime.

The second and more important development will have to come from inside Islam itself. The Muslim community will have to decide whether to make its peace with modernity, and in particular with the key principle of a secular state and religious tolerance. The Islamic world is at the juncture today where Christian Europe stood during the Thirty Years War in the seventeenth century: religious politics is driving potentially endless conflict, not just between Muslims and non-Muslims but between different sects of Muslims (many of the recent bombings in Pakistan have been the results of Sunni–Shi'ite feuds). In an age of biological and nuclear weapons, this could lead to disaster for everyone.

There is some hope that a more liberal strand of Islam will emerge because of the inner historical logic to political secularism. An Islamic theocracy is something that appeals to people only in the abstract.

Those who have actually had to live under such regimes, for example in Iran or Afghanistan, have experienced stifling dictatorships whose leaders are more clueless than most on how to overcome problems of poverty and stagnation. Even as the September 11 events have unfolded, there have been continuing demonstrations in Tehran and many other Iranian cities on the part of tens of thousands of young people fed up with the Islamic regime and wanting a more liberal political order. For them, earlier chants of 'Death to America!' have been replaced with cries of 'We love you, America', even as American bombs were raining down on the Taliban next door in Afghanistan.

Indeed, it seems that if there is any country that is going to lead the Islamic world out of its present predicament, it will be Iran, which 23 years ago initiated the current fundamentalist upsurge by toppling the shah and bringing Ayatollah Khomeini to power. A generation later, hardly anyone under the age of 30 in that country seems any longer to have sympathy for fundamentalism, and if Iran can create a more modern and tolerant form of Islam, then it will serve as a powerful example to the rest of the Muslim world.

Muslims interested in a more liberal form of Islam must stop blaming the West for painting Islam with too broad a brush, and move themselves to isolate and delegitimate the extremists among them. There is some evidence that this is already happening. American Muslims are waking up to the extent of Wahhabi influence in their own community, and those abroad may come to this realization if the tide turns decisively against the fundamentalists in Afghanistan.

The struggle between Western liberal democracy and Islamo-fascism is not one between two equally viable cultural systems, both of which can master modern science and technology, create wealth and deal with the *de facto* diversity of the contemporary world. In all these respects, Western institutions hold all the cards and for that reason will continue to spread across the globe in the long run. But to get to the long run we must survive the short run. And unfortunately, there is no inevitability to historical progress, and few good outcomes absent leadership, courage and a determination to fight for the values that make modern democratic societies possible.

Notes

1. This first appeared as 'Their Target: The Modern World', December 2001–February 2002, *Newsweek* Special Davos Edition. © 2002 Newsweek Inc. All rights reserved. Reprinted by permission.

2. For a full exposition, see Francis Fukuyama, *The End of History and the Last Man* (London: Penguin, 1993).
3. Samuel P. Huntington, *The Clash of Civilizations and the Remaking of World Order* (London: Simon and Schuster, 1998).
4. Lee Kuan Yew, *From the Third World to First: The Singapore Story* (New York: HarperCollins, 2000).

CHAPTER 3

A New Type of War

Lawrence Freedman

The war that began for the United States on September 11, 2001, has been curious in a number of respects, notably in its combination, on both sides, of modern and primitive forms of warfare. President George W. Bush called for a war against terrorism,[1] but this was not the declaration that began the war. His opponents had declared it many years earlier as they battled against what they claimed to be pernicious American interference in the affairs of Muslim countries. After a series of modest hits against the United States and its assets abroad, they managed a spectacular strike. It had to be assumed that, now emboldened, they would try again. Whether or not to go to war was not an American choice.

Although it became incontestable that the attacks had been perpetrated by al-Qaeda, no claims were ever made nor demands ever issued. Terrorism is normally considered to be a coercive mechanism, part of a guerrilla strategy, in that actions create threats of worse to come if political demands are not met, and these demands (until recently at least) tended to be geared to ending foreign occupation or a secessionist movement. Talk in the 1990s of a new type of terrorism pointed to a readiness to move beyond occasional assassination and localized explosions to weapons of mass effect, including chemical and biological, and objectives that went off the normal political scale, the products of some private torment or zany cult as much as an organized movement for change.[2]

Yet attempts to put al-Qaeda in the same box as the Aum Shinrikyo sect in Japan, notorious for its 1995 Sarin gas attack on the Tokyo underground, or even the unibomber, missed its distinctiveness. It went for spectacular deeds because it wanted to catch attention and was operating at a global rather than a national level, but its aims were neither mystical nor obscure, despite the language in which they were often couched. It shared the presumption that the deed would be eloquent in itself, but it knew that once the link between the actors and the act was established then all would be understood. The attitude to accepting responsibility for the attacks on the World Trade Center and the Pentagon was tactical: a nod and a wink to Islamic brothers but no formal claims that might be used in evidence against al-Qaeda. Pragmatic goals might be discerned – getting the US to lay off Iraq, abandon Israel, cut back on overseas garrisons – but they were never made explicit, and Osama bin Laden's language could be read as urging the striking at infidels and the humbling of the United States as ends in themselves.[3] Perhaps retaliation was welcomed in itself as another likely consciousness-raising exercise, apt to demonstrate American brutality even as doubting elements of international opinion questioned whether those being targeted were culpable for the crimes.

It suited al-Qaeda to give the appearance of being shadowy and ubiquitous, a network of groups spread around the world, harboured unwittingly in Western countries as much as in countries blatantly hostile to the West. The enemy appeared to lack military capabilities, a capital city or even, despite the focus on Osama bin Laden himself, a supreme leader and hierarchical chain of command. Yet this impression was wrong. Evidence gleaned after the fall of the Taliban regime demonstrated that Osama bin Laden was fully *au fait* with the operation. The description of al-Qaeda as being non-state was not accurate in that it had gained its base and sanctuary in Afghanistan by effectively sponsoring and then taking over the Taliban regime, and through the gradual integration of its fighters with those of the Taliban. So long as Afghanistan was left alone this made possible intensive training and a secure headquarters, but it also created a major vulnerability. Unlike traditional armies, guerrilla groups and terrorists do not expect to hold territory. They need time more than space, for it is their ability to endure while mounting regular attacks that enables them to grow while the enemy is drained of patience and credibility. To succeed they must be able to mount a campaign on their own, which requires being able to mount regular attacks to the point where the equilibrium of the target society becomes totally dislocated, and this in turn requires that they survive all attempts to hunt them down. Afghanistan is a large country that offers the perfect terrain for guerrilla warfare, yet al-Qaeda was committed to fighting a war to preserve the Taliban against the depleted and itself rather chaotic Northern Alliance, made up of largely non-Pashtun factions. This meant that it was liable to occupy fixed positions which would be vulnerable to bombing and be drawn into an open battle. By the end of September, as the US began to understand the symbiotic relationship between the two, the focus shifted to take in the Taliban as well as al-Qaeda. The idea that the relationship was one of guest and host had been shattered: the two were clearly intertwined, so that the defeat of one would create a crisis for the other.

Al-Qaeda's global strategy also created difficulties for itself. At issue was how high to raise the stakes for the United States. Traditional terrorist groups, such as the Basque ETA and the Provisional IRA (PIRA), have taken the fight to their opponents' capitals, and in the case of the PIRA this strategy was arguably successful in helping to persuade the British government to seek a settlement (although British strategy was also successful in persuading the PIRA leadership that they had to move to negotiations and not just rely on military pressure). PIRA's strategy, however, became more focused. It went for economic targets, as important to London's economy as the World Trade Center was to New York's, but it never attempted to cause massive loss of life and concentrated on imposing financial burdens and undermining confidence in the ability of London's financial sector to function. By working at the same time to build up a formidable political presence in Northern Ireland, it could demonstrate a coherent strategy.

Beirut in 1983–84 and Somalia a decade later had both demonstrated that long-term changes in American policy might be obtained by targeting American personnel in vulnerable, forward positions. Hezbollah made a similar point in Lebanon, one that was not learned in the second Palestinian Intifada when it moved to suicide bombs in Israeli cities, which had the effect of inflaming Israeli opinion rather than creating a groundswell of sentiment favouring withdrawal from the Occupied Territories. So it was that al-Qaeda's determination to maximize the hurt to the United States, as well as striking against the most celebrated icons of American economic and military power, meant that the issue was never really one of 'Why do these people hate us and what do we need to do to get them to stop?', but rather one of 'How do we punish these people and prevent them from hurting us again?' There was no obvious way to appease al-Qaeda, and for that matter al-Qaeda had no obvious way to appease the United States.

The US objective became one of frustrating, demoralizing and beating back al-Qaeda and its associated groups. Victory would be a matter of degree and unlikely to be decisive. By insisting that it was necessary to get Osama bin Laden 'dead or alive', President Bush set the standard against which his war would be judged, although, as the target lost himself in the wild and lawless Afghan–Pakistani borders, officials made some attempt to downgrade this specific requirement. Nevertheless, just as George Bush Snr's achievement in liberating Kuwait was overshadowed by Saddam Hussein's ability to survive and sustain himself as a nuisance, so any evidence that bin Laden is not only alive and free but also still organizing events will overshadow President Bush.

A counter-terrorist strategy must separate the enemy from those who harbour them, whether in local communities or bases concealed within the borders of another state. The debate over how this might be achieved came to be characterized during the Vietnam War by the competing slogans of 'hearts and minds' versus 'search and destroy'. The instinctive US response to the outrages of September 11 appeared to come into the second category. Somehow those responsible must be found and hit. Countries that provided a haven would have to choose: either abandon their villainous clients or suffer the consequences. Those preferring a 'hearts and minds' approach pointed to the need to remove legitimacy from the enemy by addressing the wellsprings of its support. If this support evaporated then so would sources of new recruits and funds, and eventually, sanctuary. The trouble with 'search and destroy' is that the destruction tends to be more accomplished than the search. If raids failed to differentiate between the guilty, the half-committed and the innocent then the main result would be to generate many new recruits and supporters. Yet a hearts and minds campaign would also be problematic, especially if they implied that nothing could be done without first solving the numerous and intractable problems of the Middle East and Central Asia.

When President Bush's father had gone to war – Desert Storm of January–February 1991 – the conditions were optimum. There were months to get forces into position and excellent bases and ample fuel available in Saudi Arabia. Iraq had no idea of the capabilities of American air power, and had deployed its forces in vulnerable forward positions. The main fighting when it took place was in open desert. Victory came easily and with few casualties.[4] Ten years on, the enemy was far less numerous or well-armed but in every other respect there was reason to suppose that the US and its allies would, to use President Bush's phrase, have to 'smoke out' the enemy. As battle was joined, the human factor would weigh much more heavily than the technical. If it took too long there was a risk that the American people's patience would wear thin or that the fragile international coalition would buckle.

Another comparison would be with the Kosovo War of March–June 1999. During the initial weeks, in addition to cruise missiles, NATO used about 500 aircraft, flying just under 300 sorties per day, about a third of which were attack sorties. The numbers were raised significantly before the attacks made much impression on either Slobodan Milosevic's will or the Serb oppression of Kosovar Albanians.[5] Yet in this case the lack of suitable bases close to Afghanistan meant that air raids would have to be mounted over long distances or from carriers and so the numbers would be limited, which was fine as the air defences of the Taliban were meagre. The infrastructure of Afghanistan was so wretched and primitive that there were few suitable targets to be attacked. What was the point of aiming for power plants in a country where only 6 per cent have electricity? Excessive bombing would risk doing no more than 'rearranging the sand', said to be the main result of the cruise missile attacks against a supposed al-Qaeda conclave in Afghanistan in August 1998 after the attacks on the US Embassies in East Africa. Even worse, the wrong sort of targets might be hit. In Kosovo, ground attacks had been explicitly ruled out at the start of hostilities: in the event, this was recognized as an error. What happened instead was that the role of the Kosovo Liberation Army (KLA) came to be increasingly important – in demonstrating that the Serbs had failed in their basic objective of eliminating this 'terrorist' group, but also in drawing Serb forces into the open and thus rendering them vulnerable to NATO aircraft. In this case, neither Washington nor London claimed that the strategic objectives could be achieved by air attacks alone against a political system that was crude and rugged in its infrastructure. Either a forward operating base would have to be established for US and UK forces or else they would have to get the Northern Alliance to play the role of the KLA.

Backing the Northern Alliance created a risk of the coalition appearing as its air arm, and becoming tied too closely to the Alliance and to its agenda, just as the Kosovo campaign tied the West to the KLA. This would lead to misgivings elsewhere in the region, especially in Pakistan. Furthermore, unless it performed considerably better than it had done when last in power in the mid-1990s, the Northern Alliance was unlikely to attract the loyalties of Afghans and could soon face the old problem of holding only cities and roads while swathes of the country were occupied by stubborn, hostile fighters. This was the argument for getting coalition forces into Afghanistan in substantial numbers. If possible, the best way to accomplish this would be to capture an airstrip in a convenient and defensible location and use it to ferry in troops.

Initially the Americans went for a high-risk military strategy to sustain a low-risk political strategy. That is, they hoped to avoid excessive dependence on any particular Afghan faction or member of the international coalition, by looking for a quick military fix relying on strategic bombing and special force operations to undermine Taliban resistance and encourage defections. As the Taliban collapsed the Americans would install a new, broadly based and UN-sponsored government into Kabul, possibly even including ex-Taliban 'moderates', while their own forces, supported only by the reliable British, would start the search for Osama bin Laden's mountain redoubt. By late October, after a few weeks of bombing, it had become apparent that special force operations required far better logistics and intelligence than available and that the air raids, after the few genuinely important targets had been struck, were doing more harm than good, as civilian losses mounted and Taliban fighters were emboldened. Attempts to forge a new political order for Afghanistan were thwarted by a combination of traditional rivalries and uncertainty over the seriousness of the American intent.

With little to show for their efforts, the US found itself at risk of losing the propaganda war, the battle for 'hearts and minds'. Al-Qaeda had a well-prepared audience for its radical message in countries where the local media has little diversity and regularly denounces Western policies. The spectacle of the strongest nation in the world beating up one of the most wretched was uncomfortable, as was the continuing connection with Israeli policies. The impression gained ground that the bombing continued not because there was much of value to hit but because Washington could think of nothing better to do. Anxious correspondents reported back from the noisy streets constituting the Islamic front line that the US and Britain were hated even more. Every expression of doubt and concern from a supposedly friendly government was soon cited as evidence that although the coalition once seemed so full of solidarity, it was now full of internal tensions and risked falling apart. Even if Bush was determined to mount a substantial land offensive, problems of logistics meant that little could be done before the winter was over.

Yet no matter how many bombs went astray, 'collateral damage' in Afghanistan was never going to cause American public opinion to waver. Nor would other governments change their foreign policies because of mood swings. This would require a recalculation of their national interests. The regimes in the Muslim world where al-Qaeda's message had the greatest appeal fully understood its logic and the dire implications for their rule. In previous wars domestic and international opinion had faltered not because of casualties on either side but rather from a sense that the government had lost the initiative and had become internally divided and uncertain, that sacrifices were being made to no purpose, and that the whole exercise was futile. This is why support for the war in Vietnam collapsed in the US, and why the alliance faced difficulties at a similar moment in the Kosovo campaign, when the bombing had been under way for weeks, causing pain in Serbia but no political movement. It also explains why, despite the difficulties, support held firm during the Falklands War and the Gulf War. The requirement for the propaganda war was the same as that for the real war – a credible strategy that could see the initiative being taken away from the Taliban/al-Qaeda, with some tangible evidence of progress. Yet the main thrust of official statements and unofficial commentary was that it could all take a long time.

In late October the Bush Administration decided on a new approach, involving a lower-risk military strategy although potentially greater political risks.[6] The reduced military risks resulted from focusing the air campaign and gearing it to land operations. The US Army was not, however, to be used. Instead there would be close cooperation with the Northern Alliance, putting to one side misgivings about the Alliance's combat capability as well as the narrowness of its political base. The results were impressive. By November 8, the first major Taliban stronghold in the north, Mazar-e-Sharif, fell, providing control of major highways and two airports. Within days, and to the surprise of many (including this author) the capital city of Kabul fell. There was some serious fighting in Kunduz in the north, where the foreign militants (the 'Afghan Arabs') made their stand and in Kandahar in the south, the heart of the Taliban regime. After those cities had fallen (nothing like as quickly as Kabul), attention moved to the Tora Bora caves where a network of caves and passages had been prepared for sturdy defence. As 2001 closed, operations were still under way, with occasional air raids against suspected gatherings of militants. By this time, as far as Afghanistan was concerned, al-Qaeda and the Taliban were spent forces. This was achieved, as Secretary of State Colin Powell explained, by connecting 'a First World air force' to a 'Fourth World army – B-1 bombers and guys on horses'.[7] Deputy Defense Secretary Paul Wolfowitz explained another basis for the strategy:

One of the lessons of Afghanistan's history, which we've tried to apply in this campaign, is if you're a foreigner, try not to go in. If you do go in, don't stay too long, because they don't tend to like any foreigners who stay too long.[8]

This made sense in that Afghan irritation with foreigners who had outstayed their welcome tended to turn naturally not against the Americans and their allies, but against the Arabs, Chechens, Pakistanis and sundry others inspired by the Taliban's message of pure faith and trained by al-Qaeda.

All this begged the question as to whether the United States had hit upon a new form of warfare or just one that happened to work in the particular conditions of Afghanistan in late 2001. In December, Bush appeared to suggest that a lesson of more general application had been learned. He spoke enthusiastically about the combination of 'real-time intelligence, local allied forces, special forces, and precision air power' that had produced this victory in the first round of the war, adding that this conflict 'has taught us more about the future of our military than a decade of blue ribbon panels and think tank symposiums'.[9] The Pentagon appeared confident that there were few enemies that could not be battered into submission through the application of carefully targeted but also overwhelming air power, even while acknowledging that it worked best when used in conjunction with ground forces – to oblige the enemy to occupy open positions, to identify targets and to follow through after the bombing. A clear preference had been asserted: to use somebody else's troops.

It was probably the case that the combination of the US Air Force and the Northern Alliance, backed by American and British special forces, was less violent for all concerned than alternative means of changing the regime in Afghanistan and expelling al-Qaeda, especially taking into account the reported strength of the belligerents, and the amount of territory that changed hands. Some of the new American equipment, particularly the unmanned aerial vehicles (UAVs) that could be used to find and even attack targets, was impressive. The most important reason for the swift success, however, was that the war was fought as much in a tried and tested Afghan way of warfare as in a new Western way. The Afghan way depends on coercive diplomacy, with protracted sparring to see who has superior power, before the hard bargaining begins on the terms of surrender or, just as likely, defection. Things get really nasty only when the outcome of battle is uncertain. Should victory come through brute force, little mercy is shown to the losing side, with the occasional massacre *pour encourager les autres*. The US special forces may have had impressive new kit to help them operate in unfamiliar terrain, but a critical item in their armoury was large wads of dollars which could provide a formidable inducement to waverers. For those with the sense not to fight to the bitter end, defeat became rather like insolvency, with the faction in question soon trading under another name. Trading is often the operative word, for with territorial control comes the ability to take a share of all economic activity, including trafficking in guns and drugs. Surrender was conditional: remarkably few Taliban fighters appear to have been disarmed and many appeared to have drifted back, still armed, to their villages or into banditry. Many foreigners were able to slip away, and those able to use cash to gain safe passage could escape. The Americans were relieved by the speed of the Taliban surrender but they did not always appreciate its conditional quality. When they objected to attempts to organize conditional deals in the final battle for Tora Bora, in part because they bought time for those attempting to escape, the answer seems to have been that if you want them you go and get them.

Other than the above, there was nothing exceptional in the combination of the postmodern and the premodern. The most effective irregular forces have always proved to be adept at borrowing the more advanced technologies when it suited them – witness the Mujahideen's use of Stinger anti-aircraft missiles to blunt Soviet air power in Afghanistan, or Hezbollah's ability to get videos of their ambushes of Israeli units in Lebanon to the news media, or for that matter al-Qaeda's ability to mount an audacious attack by turning Western technology against itself, with knives acting as the force multiplier at the critical moment as aircraft were hijacked. Al-Qaeda and the White House both thought in global terms, each putting their global coalitions together and mounting attacks into the enemy heartland over long distances, but the principles behind their operations were timeless.

If further rounds of the war on terrorism were to be fought on the same basis, then at each stage it was only going to be as good as the coalition's local allies, with the risks of them floundering and thereby reducing Western options, on the one hand, or allowing an excess of enthusiasm to result in guilt through association with massacres and plunder, on the other. If a strong presence on the ground was eschewed then political influence would be correspondingly diminished. Handing over influence to any group offering itself as an ally, an action probably based on opportunism rather than adherence to Western political norms, could cause problems for otherwise-friendly local neighbours. How serious these problems will turn out to be remains to be seen. The US has enormous political and economic clout which, if it wishes to use it, can make up for its reluctance to get its military forces involved in nation-building exercises.

The lessons of this campaign were as much political as military, and here gained their novelty because of the particular stage of international history at which it was conducted, with the United States and its allies in a position to take on all comers in a conventional war but nervous about unconventional conflicts, enjoying not having to face a radical Great Power challenging it on an ideological and material basis, yet aware that its hegemony was still widely resented. How this war is seen in the future will depend on whether this hegemony is preserved against a crude and vicious attempt to subvert it in the name of an extreme brand of Islam, the future incidence of terrorism directed against the citizens and assets of the US and allies, and the political stability of those allies in the Islamic world most vulnerable to militants. For the moment the most important lesson is the most simple and least surprising: a direct attack on the United States is likely to produce an extremely strong and unremitting response. Given the parallels drawn between the September 11 attacks and Pearl Harbor, it is worth recalling Churchill's recollection in December 1941 of Sir Edward Grey's observation from the First World War, that the United States is 'like a gigantic boiler. Once the fire is lighted under it there is no limit to the power it can generate.'[10]

Notes

1. President George W. Bush, Address to a Joint Session of Congress and the American People, September 20, 2001, United States Capitol, Washington, DC.
2. Bruce Hoffman, *Inside Terrorism* (New York: Columbia University Press, 1998).
3. Magnus Ranstorp, 'Interpreting the Broader Context and Meaning of Bin-Laden's *Fatwa*', *Studies in Conflict and Terrorism*, vol. 21 (1998).
4. Michael R. Gordon, and General Bernard E. Trainor, *The Generals' War* (Boston, MA: Little, Brown and Co., 1995).
5. Benjamin Lambeth, *Nato's Air War for Kosovo* (Santa Monica, CA: RAND Corporation, 2001); 'The Split-screen war: Kosovo and Changing Concepts of the Use of Force', in Albrecht Schnabel and Ramesh Thakur (eds), *Kosovo and the Challenge of Humanitarian Intervention: Selective Indignation, Collective Action, and International Citizenship* (New York: United Nations University Press 2000).
6. Robert Kagan and William Kristol, 'A Winning Strategy: How the Bush Administration Changed Course and Won the War in Afghanistan', *Weekly Standard*, vol. 7, no. 11 (November 26, 2001).
7. *New York Times*, November 13, 2001.
8. Interview, *Face the Nation*, November 18, 2001.

9. Remarks by the President at the Citadel, Charleston, South Carolina, December 11, 2001.
10. Cited in Winston S. Churchill, *The Second World War*, Vol. 3, *The Grand Alliance. 1948–1953* (Boston: Houghton Mifflin; London: Cassell). Churchill was making a similar point about the tendency to underestimate the American will to war, and those who believed that 'They would fool around at a distance. They would never come to grips. They would never stand blood-letting.'

CHAPTER 4

Unanswered Questions

Steve Smith

Despite being overwhelmed with information about the events of September 11, there are still fundamental questions that remain unanswered. This chapter will look at ten of these. The challenge is to provide a summary of what is known without falling into the trap of buying into a historically and culturally specific world view. If some of these questions are, as they will be, questions about what motivated the terrorists or why Osama bin Laden or al-Qaeda ordered the attacks, they run the risk of imposing on to the events a specific, probably Western, notion of rationality and an underlying conception of human psychology. Such an outcome would be exactly what is *not* required if we are to understand these events. What is needed is not some resort to imposing a specific view of rationality on to a model of world politics that features unified state actors acting on the basis of a self-interest dictated by the structure of the international political system.[1] In this sense, what follows is an attempt to pose a set of questions about the events of September 11 in a way that does not reduce the complex to one simple (and ethnocentric) standard of reason.

Although it is tempting to extend the discussion into the events that followed the September 11 attacks, notably the subsequent war against the Taliban, I want to restrict myself to the events of September 11. There are ten 'unanswered' questions that I want to pose.

Who Was Behind the Attacks?

Whilst there now seems little disagreement with the claim that the attacks were orchestrated by Osama bin Laden and al-Qaeda, this has still not been definitively established. Despite the summaries of evidence provided by British Prime Minister Tony Blair and by the US

State Department, a number of key details remain hazy.[2] Even the December 2001 video of bin Laden discussing the attacks is not conclusive in that whilst it shows he was aware of the attacks, he does not state that he ordered them. Then there is the claim that there are significant linkages between Iraq and the attacks. Laurie Mylroie has argued in detail that contrary to the Clinton administration's citing of bin Laden as behind the 1993 attacks on the World Trade Center, in fact the trail leads back to Iraq.[3] David Rose has noted that the three leaders (including Mohammed Atta) of the September 11 attacks met Iraqi intelligence officers on several occasions, and that Iraq runs a training camp in which foreign Islamists are taught to hijack planes using boxcutters.[4] Czech intelligence has revealed that Atta met with a key Iraqi intelligence officer in June 2000.

Despite these conjectures, the evidence linking bin Laden and al-Qaeda to the attacks seems overwhelming. There are two compelling sets of evidence. The first is financial, and focuses on transfers of large sums of money between Mohammed Atta (and other hijackers) and al-Qaeda's chief financial agent (Mustafa Muhammad Ahmed) in the Middle East before the attacks. Over $500,000 was provided to support the hijackers.[5] One of the hijackers, Fayez Ahmed, opened a bank account in Dubai on June 25, and this account was used to fund the final preparations for the hijackings. He gave power of attorney over the account to Mustafa al Hawsawi, an alleged alias for Mustafa Ahmed. On September 6, Fayez Ahmed returned $8055 back to the Dubai account, and three other hijackers wired more than $18,000 to al Hawsawi. On the morning of September 11, al Hawsawi cleared out Ahmed's account and deposited some $25,000 in his own account before flying to Pakistan. Overall, US investigators have accounted for more than $325,000 spent by the hijackers, and have traced most of the transactions whereby that money was transferred from Dubai to accounts in the US.

The second main source of evidence relates to the contacts between the hijackers and al-Qaeda; at least four of the hijackers were trained in al-Qaeda camps in Afghanistan and at least four others have known previous connections with bin Laden's network. Indeed, two of them (Khalid al-Midhar and Nawaq Alhamzi) were wanted by the FBI in the weeks before the attacks. Additionally, intelligence sources have communications evidence linking a senior bin Laden aide, Mohammed Atef, to the attacks. US and British intelligence believe he was 'responsible for the detailed planning of the attacks'.[6] Finally, the attacks seem to have been planned in Malaysia, following which a key bin Laden aide went to two US states to brief the leaders of the mission. This follows the pattern of previous attacks orchestrated by him, whereby a senior leader travels to give the final instructions to each group involved in the attacks.

How Do We Prove Who Did It?

It is one thing to suspect who was behind the attacks, but it is quite another to prove in anything like a conclusive manner that bin Laden planned, organized and ordered the attacks. I am simply not sure that al-Qaeda works like that. It is more of a network of individuals and groups than one organization, and it involves Muslims in up to 60 countries.[7] Bin Laden built up the network but it is not clear that he is in any conventional sense in charge of it. The US and British governments have no doubt that al-Qaeda was behind not just September 11 but also the attacks on US forces in Somalia in 1993, the bombing of the US embassies in Tanzania and Kenya in 1998 and the attack on the USS *Cole* in 2000. The problem is that the evidence in each case has gaps when it moves from a discussion of who carried out the attacks to the linking of these people to al-Qaeda and bin Laden. This does not mean that they were not behind these attacks; only that the task of proving this is a very difficult one. Indeed on the December 2001 video bin Laden comes very close indeed to admitting the planning of the operation; the key moment is when he says: 'They were overjoyed when the first plane hit the building, so I said to them: be patient.'[8] As I note below, bin Laden also spoke in this video of the calculations he had made of the effect of the jet fuel in melting the iron structure of the World Trade Center, causing the collapse of the floors above where the planes hit. But even these statements legally denote nothing more than that he knew about the operation in detail, and this is the reason that I doubt a court or an international tribunal could find him guilty of ordering or planning the attacks. I simply doubt that there is a signed order or a smoking gun.

However, the problem is not really one of whether 'we' know who carried out the attacks; it is that in large parts of the world there is simply no evidence that would convince people of this guilt; hence the scepticism that accompanied the release of the December 2001 video in which bin Laden discussed the attacks in detail, or the reaction to the files found on abandoned al-Qaeda computers in Kabul. In many parts of the world these were simply dismissed as forgeries. Thus it may be impossible to prove guilt to the satisfaction of a large proportion of the world's population. This has significant implications for the legitimacy of the US response and of course threatens to continue to widen and deepen the gap between the West and the Islamic world.

Who Were the Hijackers?

In one sense there is a considerable degree of consensus as to who the 19 hijackers were, but two issues remain unanswered. The first is that it is not clear that the hijackers' identities were authentic, since there is considerable evidence that they may have stolen them. In several cases the real identity of the hijackers may never be known. As a former Justice Department official put it: 'The hijackers themselves may not have known the others' true identities.'[9] According to the FBI, 15 of them came from Saudi Arabia, two from the United Arab Emirates, one from Syria/Lebanon and one from Egypt. None was from Afghanistan or Palestine. Nearly all had lived in the US for months if not years. According to US intelligence sources, there were two distinct groups: the pilots, who came to the US over a year before the attacks; and the 'muscle' who arrived in the months leading up to the attacks.

The second issue relates to exactly what each of the hijackers knew of the plan. There is a major debate over how many of the 19 were aware of the intention to crash the aircraft into buildings. FBI sources argue that perhaps as many as 13 were there only to provide the muscle to prevent passengers overpowering the lead hijackers whose job it was to pilot the planes. Bin Laden has stated that those involved didn't know the details of the hijackings, only that it was a 'martyrdom operation'. As he put it:

> We asked each of them to go to America, but they didn't know anything about the operation, not one letter ... we did not reveal the operation until they were there and just before they boarded the planes ... Those who were trained to fly didn't know the others. One group of people did not know the other group.[10]

Contrary to early reports, there seems to have been only one pilot on each of the four planes, whilst two others had some limited flight training; these six individuals worked closely together in planning the attacks. There was one overall group which was split into the four flights, not four separate cells each planning on its own. Three of the suspected pilots (Atta, Al-Shehhi and Jarrah) had roomed together in Hamburg. The six were helped by 13 Saudi Arabian men, mostly younger and less well-educated. Some FBI investigators now think that

the 13 muscle men may have believed that they were part of a traditional hijacking operation, linked to landing the planes and making
demands. The reasons for this claim are that none of the 13 left farewell
messages, as did five of the six lead hijackers, and that they seemed
jovial in the days before the attacks, again unlike the leaders. On the
other hand, the hijackers engaged in violent behaviour on the flights,
stabbing passengers and crew, which runs counter to the traditional
view that passengers are kept unharmed so that they can be used in
negotiations. Also note that the hijackers told passengers on at least
two of the planes that they were going to die and that they should
make final phone calls to their loved ones.

The degree of coordination was very high. As Amy Goldstein has
written:

> Seven of the hijackers obtained Florida driver's licenses within a 15-
> day span in early summer. Thirteen purchased airline tickets for their
> final flights within five days in late August. And over the course of
> the summer, a dozen ... moved through South Florida apartments.[11]

The 'advance guard' of four arrived in the US between November 1999
and May 2000 and began taking flying lessons: two of them (Khalid al-
Midhar and Nawaq Alhamzi) in California; two (Mohammed Atta and
Marwan Al-Shehhi) in Florida. The California pair were so poor in
flying school that they were told to leave. It seems that they did not
pilot planes in the hijackings. The planes were piloted by Atta (who
piloted American Airlines flight 11, which crashed into the north tower
of the World Trade Center), Al-Shehhi (who piloted United Airlines
flight 175, which hit the south tower of the World Trade Center), Ziad
Samir Jarrah (who had trained as a pilot in Europe, and piloted United
Airlines flight 93 which crashed into rural Pennsylvania) and Hani
Hanjour (who trained to fly in Arizona, had lived in the US for over a
decade, and who piloted American Airlines flight 77 which crashed into
the Pentagon). The second group, the muscle, started arriving in the US
in early 2001, and they trained by undertaking weight training, leaving
a trail of contacts and financial receipts in their wake.

How Many Other Targets Were There on September 11?

This is a fascinating question because there has been a series of leaks
and briefings to suggest that there may have been several other hijacks
planned for the same day. Two other September 11 flights in particular

have aroused suspicion as box-cutters were found on them. Two were stuffed into seat cushions on a flight out of Boston, and one was found in the rubbish bin of a flight from Atlanta to Brussels. In addition, two men, Mohammed Jaweed Azmath and Ayub Ali Khan, were detained on a train in Fort Worth with box-cutters in their luggage. The two men, both of whom had received flight training, had got off a Newark transcontinental flight that was grounded in St Louis after the hijacked planes began to hit their targets. Finally, Zacarias Moussaouri was arrested in Minnesota in August 2001 after he tried to pay, in cash, for training to steer, but not to take off or land, a jumbo jet; he is widely assumed to have been a hijacker for either a further plane or a member of one of the four hijack teams.

We simply do not know how many other hijackings were planned that day, and this remains a genuinely unanswered question, but what is clear is that there is a lot of material that has not been made public, and there remain persistent rumours that at least two more planes were targeted (one strong rumour has it that a flight was not hijacked because a contingent of military – or, in some accounts, basketball players – joined the flight at the last moment). One of these planes was probably intended to hit the White House.

Did They Mean to Cause the Level of Damage They Inflicted?

The issue here is whether the attacks on the World Trade Center were designed to cause the collapse of the towers, or whether the hijackers were 'lucky' in causing the damage they did. In his December video, bin Laden stated that the attacks did far more damage than he had calculated:

> We calculated in advance the number of casualties from the enemy, who would be killed based on the position of the tower ... We calculated that the floors that would be hit would be three or four floors. I was the most optimistic of them all due to my experience in this field, I was thinking that the fire from the gas in the plane would melt the iron structure of the building and collapse the area where the plane hit and all the floors above it only. This is all that we had hoped for.[12]

Some have argued that if the hijackers had wanted to destroy the entire building then they would have flown in at a much lower height, but to answer this would require a very detailed analysis of the flight paths and heights of surrounding buildings. In my view the planes were aimed at a height that would not run the risk of flying too close to buildings in the flight path. These questions cannot really be answered definitively, but it does seem that the collapse of the World Trade Center was a surprise to bin Laden. On the other hand, the level of damage at the Pentagon was probably less than predicted – and of course the plane that crashed in Pennsylvania never reached its target.

Why Was the Attack Ordered?

This is a difficult question to answer because there has been a marked change in the reasons given by al-Qaeda 'spokesmen' since September 11. Within a couple of months of the attacks the reasons were said to be to focus world attention on US support for Israeli policy towards the Palestinians (see in particular his statement released on al-Jazeera TV on December 27, 2001). However, this does not sit easily either with statements made by bin Laden after the attacks or with his previous statements about the underlying causes of the struggle he was engaged in. Put simply, bin Laden has had little to say about the Palestinians in the last decade, with his target instead being the conservative rulers of the Middle East; notably his own home state, Saudi Arabia. His attacks on the US had always been justified because of their support of the Saudi regime, not because of the plight of the Palestinians. This only became an *ex post facto* justification of the attacks, and is unlikely to have been a prominent reason. In my view the reasons for the attacks were twofold: on the one hand, to show the world that the US is vulnerable to attack; on the other, by provoking significant US retaliation, to produce a radicalization of Muslim opinion. But providing any answer to this question leads into deep water because we have to make assumptions about both the values of those who ordered the attacks, and, more problematically, the linkages between events and issues in their world views.

Why Did the Hijackers Do It?

The hijackers did not come from the type of background normally associated with members of terrorist groups. They were virtually all well-educated, mainly middle class, and predominantly Saudi by birth. They were not members of the dispossessed; they were seemingly 'Westernized' Muslims. This makes it very hard to understand why they were willing to die (assuming that all of them knew their fate). As one terrorism expert put it, 'Our profile of the suicide bomber never included pilots, highly educated people.'[13] In comparison to other suspected al-Qaeda operatives in Europe, who were usually of North African origin, who repeatedly failed to pull off their plans and who supported themselves through crime, the leaders of the September 11 hijackings were very different: they were generally older, much better educated, spoke English better and came from Egypt and the Persian Gulf. This meant that they were more likely to get US visas, and would not draw as much attention to themselves during the long planning period. Moreover, it is argued that bin Laden only trusts people from his own region and, having learnt from the considerable failures of earlier attempts to hijack and crash planes, chose those who could most easily live in the US without being discovered. Fifteen of the hijackers obtained their visas in Saudi Arabia, two in Germany and two in the United Arab Emirates. Whilst it is relatively straightforward to explain the actions of many Muslim activists, trying to re-create the intentions and values of the hijackers is very difficult. Many of their families have protested that their sons liked the United States, or expressed disbelief that they would give up their career or education for this cause. US intelligence experts did not really have a category for well-educated professional hijackers, since in their account of terrorism, it is usually undertaken by young, poor, badly educated men, not men who seem to have a stake in Western society (the recent instance of a female Palestinian suicide bomber is the exception that proves the rule). But this characterization fails to understand the deep hatred of the US because of its presence in the sacred lands of the Arabian peninsula and because of its continued support for Israel.

Did They Simply Get Lucky?

In the initial reporting of the attacks, the common view was that the hijackers had been incredibly lucky to have been so successful, but increasingly this view has had to be modified. On the one hand, it is now clear that the attacks were the result of enormous amounts of planning and training: the hijackers spent large sums of money to buy business class seats so that they would be near the front of each plane; the planes chosen were linked to the targets (the two biggest, 767s, with the largest fuel loads, were targeted at the World Trade Center); the routes flown were those that required most fuel; the date, time and routes of the hijacked planes were deliberately chosen because Tuesday early-morning transcontinental flights have very low passenger numbers with the result that there were few to overpower hijackers armed only with box-cutters; the departure airports were close to the targets, thus producing surprise when the planes went off course and also maximizing the amount of fuel on board; and the timing of the flights was chosen to ensure that the attacks were close together.

Yet rumours persist that US intelligence may have intercepted a number of other attacks scheduled for the same day; the point made to me was that in fact the hijackers were relatively unsuccessful overall since so few of their attempts succeeded. I have to say that this seems implausible to me, but we still do not know exactly what else was planned for September 11, and again much remains shrouded in secrecy.

Did Western Intelligence Fail?

This is clearly linked to the previous point, but there is a debate over whether or not the events of September 11 count as a major failure for Western, specifically US, intelligence. There is now incontrovertible evidence that many Western intelligence organizations had been concerned about the activities of several of the hijackers and had passed on their concerns to the FBI, but it proved far more difficult for the FBI to be able to persuade other law enforcement agencies in the US to allow surveillance of the suspects. In the meantime the US focused mainly on threats to US interests overseas. Of particular interest is the case of Zacarias Moussaouri, who was arrested in Minnesota on August 16 after flight instructors became suspicious that, possessing only a licence to fly a single-engine Cessna, he wanted instruction on how to fly a 747-400. They told the FBI that they thought the training could be linked to a planned hijacking. Despite a French intelligence report linking him to a bin Laden group in Chechnya, senior FBI officers felt unable to request a warrant to search his laptop computer. This was because the FBI felt it could not prove that he had committed a crime. The only way they could get round this was to take him (and his laptop) back to his native France and use French laws to search the computer. He was scheduled to go to France on September 17. However, when the computer was examined it revealed no information about hijackings in general or September 11 in particular.

In addition to Moussaouri, and as noted above, at least two of the hijackers were wanted by the FBI in the weeks before the attack. Subsequent investigations by the FBI led to a list of more than 150 individuals living in the US who have 'possible ties' with al-Qaeda, and these individuals are under close surveillance. They are said to be organized into four or five main cells, which suggests that al-Qaeda's presence in the US is far greater than previously thought. Yet this surveillance has led to criticism from civil liberties organizations. In terms of its effectiveness, a former CIA counter-terrorism officer has noted that, 'Insofar as an al Qaeda presence in the United States, they've made very little headway in uncovering it or peeling back the layers and penetrating it ... They don't know what they don't know.'[14] Thus, although it is easy with hindsight to claim that there were intelligence failures, the problem is that there was so much information coming in about possible terrorist attacks against the US that the implications of treating each piece seriously would make the US specifically and the West generally far more of a national surveillance state. But, as before, a lot of the most important information remains classified, so this question cannot really be answered. What is clear is that the model of terrorists and terrorist organizations that the FBI was working with was significantly flawed.

Has the US Understood the Reasons for the Reaction to the Attacks in Many Muslim Parts of the World?

Finally, I want to pose the seemingly simple question of whether or not the US public has understood why some people celebrated and many more quietly thought that the US had got what it deserved.[15] Throughout the 1990s the US asserted its right to lead the world. In 1998, US Secretary of State Madeleine Albright, speaking about US threats to bomb Iraq, put it this way: 'If we have to use force, it is because we are American. We are the indispensable nation. We stand tall. We see further into the future.' In my view the reaction to September 11 has exacerbated this situation, since most US politicians and commentators seem to have resorted to a mixture of unilateralism and isolationism. There has been little interest in trying to understand just why the US is so unpopular in the world, and much more interest in reasserting the superiority of 'the American way'. Thus US television commentators introducing the 2002 Winter Olympics could describe athletes as coming from one of the states said by President Bush to comprise an 'axis of evil'. Similarly, Richard Perle and Newt Gingrich have repeatedly stated that the US will act as it sees fit in its war against terrorism, and that allies can either come in to the coalition on US terms or not come in at all; the US, it was said, does not need allies to win this 'war'. All of this suggests that dominant voices in US foreign and defence policy continue to think that the US can both impose its will on the world, and that the consequences of so doing can be contained. I think this is a fundamentally flawed analysis, and the events of September 11 showed only too clearly that internal US security is linked to US policy overseas. Indeed, if the US sees September 11 as justifying a more unilateralist foreign policy, then the likelihood is more, not less, September 11s.

Conclusion

My specific aim in this chapter has been to indicate that there are still many questions about the events of September 11 that, despite all the analysis and intelligence activity, remain unanswered. For such a major event there are so many things that we still do not know. Perhaps this is in part to do with the way we ask questions about other cultures, notably about how they might see the world in ways very different to the accepted form of life within which we live, think and question. Thus this chapter has suggested a wider and more significant question: to what extent can we fully comprehend the events of September 11 using Western notions of rationality? This of course raises deep philosophical questions about the nature of the mind and whether it operates in the same way regardless of culture. But these philosophical issues actually turn out to have enormously important political consequences, since our assumptions about rationality, about reason and about logic construct our matrix of the key relationships in the social world; from this follow seemingly commonsensical claims about the nature of morality, about responsibility, about legal culpability and ultimately about the linkages between politics and economics, and about the public and private. My overall concern is that understanding September 11 requires careful, informed and detailed analysis of exactly those complexities that have been sidelined, marginalized or ignored by simple resorts to calls for a war against the evil of terrorism.

Notes

1. For an excellent discussion of the weaknesses of rationalist accounts of ethnic conflict see Stuart Kaufman, *Modern Hatreds: The Symbolic Politics of Ethnic War* (Ithaca, NY: Cornell University Press, 2001).
2. For the evidence presented by the British government see United Kingdom, Foreign and Commonwealth Office, *Responsibility for the Terrorist Atrocities in the United States, 11 September 2001,*
   <http://www.fco.gov.uk/news/keythemepages.asp>.
3. Laurie Mylroie, *The War Against America* (London: HarperCollins, 2002).

4. David Rose, 'A Blind Spot Called Iraq', *Observer*, January 13, 2002, p. 16.
5. With some hesitation, I use the term 'hijacker' to denote those who took over the planes that crashed into the World Trade Center, the Pentagon, and on land in Pennsylvania. The term is problematic insofar as it usually refers to people who take control of planes as negotiating devices: however, for the purpose of this chapter, the word 'hijacker' enables a distinction to be drawn between the people who took over the airplanes and those who planned the terror attacks. The use of the term does not mean that I wish to depoliticize the nature of their activity.
6. Dan Eggen and Serge Kovaleski, 'Bin Laden Aide Implicated', *Washington Post*, October 7, 2001, p. A01.
7. For a discussion of Osama bin Laden and al-Qaeda see Simon Reeve, *The New Jackals: Ramzi Yousef, Osama bin Laden and the Future of Terrorism* (London: Andre Deutsch, 1999) and Peter Bergen, *Holy War, Inc. Inside the Secret World of Osama bin Laden* (London: Weidenfeld & Nicolson, 2001). See also Stephen Engelberg, 'One Man and a Global Web of Violence', *New York Times*, January 14, 2001, <http://www.nytimes.com/2001/01/14/world/14JIHA.html>.
8. See 'Text: Bin Laden Discusses Attack on Tape', *Washington Post*, December 13, 2001, <http://www.washintonpost.com/wp-srv/nation/specials/attacked/t.../binladentext_121301.htm>.
9. Quoted in Dan Eggen, George Lardner Jnr and Susan Schmidt, 'Some Hijackers' Identities Unknown', *Washington Post*, September 20, 2001, p. A01.
10. See 'Text: Bin Laden Discusses Attack on Tape'.
11. Amy Goldstein, 'Hijackers Led by Core Group', *Washington Post*, September 30, 2001, p. A01.
12. See 'Text: Bin Laden Discusses Attack on Tape'.
13. Quoted in Karen De Young and Michael Dobbs, 'Bin Laden: Architect of New Global Terrorism', *Washington Post*, September 16, 2001, p. A08.
14. Dan Eggen and Bob Woodward, 'FBI Probe of Al Qaeda Implies Wide Presence', *Washington Post*, December 30, 2001, p. A01.
15. For an excellent essay on this, see Fouad Ajami, 'The Sentry's Solitude', *Foreign Affairs*, vol. 80, no. 6 (November/December 2001), pp. 2–16.

CHAPTER 5

Desperately Seeking Bin Laden: The Intelligence Dimension of the War Against Terrorism

Desmond Ball

The terrorist attacks on the World Trade Center and the Pentagon on September 11 involved the worst intelligence failure by the US intelligence community since Pearl Harbor in 1941. It was a failure at all phases of the intelligence cycle, from the setting of priorities and tasks, through the gamut of collection activities, to the analytical, assessment and dissemination processes which should have provided some warning of the event – and it befell not only the traditional national security and military intelligence agencies but also the myriad law enforcement and specialized agencies involved in counter-terrorist activities. US and allied intelligence agencies had been watching Osama bin Laden closely (albeit fitfully) since 1996, and were well-informed about his intentions towards the US, but were unable to discern his operational plans and preparations.

In retrospect, there is much which could and should have been detected before September 11 (especially concerning the activities of the hijackers in the US in the preceding months). But the warning signs were never explicit, and they were drowned in a mass of confusing and contradictory information, including a series of reports of possible terrorist attacks against US interests in May–July 2001 – which, when proven false, may have contributed to a relaxation of diligence by the relevant agencies. In Roberta Wohlstetter's terms, 'relevant signals, so clearly audible after the event, [were] partially obscured before the event by surrounding noise'.[1] The sophistication of bin Laden's methods of communications, and his capacity for using disinformation and deception, should not have been underestimated.

The magnitude of the intelligence failure raised fundamental questions about the organization of the US intelligence community (still basically structured for roles and missions established during the Cold War), the adequacy of the relevant budgets (currently amounting to about $28 billion, having declined in real terms since the early 1990s), the processes for setting priorities and directing tasks, and the mechanisms for consultation and coordination between the relevant agencies. It also engendered immediate and often ill-considered calls for massive budget increases for the intelligence community, wholesale reorganizations, unprecedented sorts of international cooperation, and a sweeping range of new legal powers for intelligence, internal security and counter-terrorism agencies. Many of the proposals are of problematic utility; some of them would certainly involve deep intrusions into civil liberties.

Intelligence Concerning Bin Laden and Al-Qaeda

By 1996, bin Laden, al-Qaeda and their activities had become high-priority targets for US (and allied) intelligence agencies. In 1995, Western intelligence agencies had learned that he had been involved in planning the bombing of the World Trade Center in 1993. In early 1996, the State Department had identified him as 'the most significant financial sponsor of Islamic terrorist activities in the world today' and 'a serious threat to the national security of the United States'. His network was responsible for the bombing of the US Air Force complex in the Khobar Towers in Dhahran, Saudi Arabia, on June 25, 1996, which killed 19 US military personnel and disrupted US Air Force operations over Iraq. In August 1996, he issued his first *fatwah*, the religious decree which declared war on the US and condoned the killing of innocent civilians in carrying out that war. A covert intelligence war was soon joined.

Conducted mostly in secret, it irrupted into public attention with a sequence of terrorist attacks and subsequent investigations and criminal indictments. On August 7, 1998, bombing attacks on the US Embassies in Nairobi, Kenya (which according to bin Laden was attacked because 'it was considered to be the biggest [US] intelligence-gathering centre in east Africa') and Dar es Salaam, Tanzania, killed 224 people and wounded more than 4000. On November 5, 1998, bin Laden was formally indicted in New York for his role in the Embassy bombings, and on June 7, 1999, he was placed on the FBI's list of 'Ten Most Wanted Fugitives'. The US State Department offered a reward of up to $5 million for information leading to his apprehension or conviction, the largest amount ever offered for a fugitive wanted by the US government.

The US authorities have had some limited success in recruiting useful informants, such as deserters from al-Qaeda or former accomplices of bin Laden who were found and 'turned' during the investigation into the bombing of the US Embassies in Kenya and Tanzania, who provided a wealth of information about the organizational structure of al-Qaeda, its key personalities and its communications networks, and its activities and deliberations up until around 1999–2000. But no Western intelligence agency was able to penetrate al-Qaeda with its own agents (or 'spies').

Most of the intelligence about bin Laden came from extremely sophisticated and highly secret signals intelligence (SIGINT) systems, whereby the National Security Agency (NSA) and its allied counterparts systematically intercepted his various means of radio and telephonic communication. However, already adept at counter-intelligence measures, as he became increasingly aware of the sorts of collection capabilities being used against him, bin Laden responded with increasingly secure techniques.

The nearly simultaneous bombing attacks on the US Embassies in Nairobi and Dar es Salaam on August 7, 1998, evinced not only bin Laden's commitment to major terrorist acts, but also his ability to organize and coordinate major terrorist operations from inside Afghanistan, some 5000 km away, and to do so securely while under extensive surveillance.

By around May 1996, US intelligence had learned that a group of Islamic extremists associated with bin Laden had established a base in Nairobi, Kenya, and by the end of the year US intelligence officials had identified and begun intercepting conversations and faxes on five telephone lines used by the group, including a cellular phone reserved for conversations with bin Laden himself. The interception operations in Nairobi continued right up to the attacks on August 7, but provided no warning of the attacks.

In October 2000, the USS *Cole* was attacked by suicide bombers affiliated with al-Qaeda when it was berthed in Yemen. By the beginning of 2001, several US intelligence agencies were predicting a major terrorist attack, either in the United States or abroad, within the next 12–24 months, with a weapon designed to produce mass casualties.

Bin Laden's Communications Systems

From 1996 to 2000, bin Laden established several alternative headquarters and command centres in fortified locations throughout Afghanistan, including major complexes in the following areas: the caves in the Khorassan Mountains near the border with Iran, a complex constructed in 1996–97; near Kandahar, the spiritual home of the Taliban, in southern Afghanistan, about 100 km from the border with Pakistan; in mountain caves near Jalalabad in eastern Afghanistan, between Kabul and the Kyber Pass; around Khowst, south of Jalalabad and about 30 km from the Pakistan border; in the Pamir Mountains in Kunduz Province, near the border with Tajikistan, which was constructed after the cruise missile attacks on Khowst in August 1998; and in the south-central province of Uruzgan, far from any of Afghanistan's borders. These complexes were equipped with an extensive range of modern communications systems, including HF and VHF radios, telephone and fax connections, and computers for emails and links to websites and electronic bulletin boards as well as maintaining databases.[2]

In November 1996, bin Laden acquired a Compact M satellite telephone set, the size of a laptop computer, from a company in Long Island, New York, which he used extensively for the next couple of years. Allocated the number 873 682505331, and using the INMARSAT international maritime communications satellite parked in geostationary orbit over the Indian Ocean, he used 2200 minutes of satellite time. (A complete record of outgoing and incoming calls between late 1996 and late 1998 was disclosed by prosecutors in the Embassy bombing trial in April 2001.) The most regular recipient of bin Laden's calls (143) was Khaled al-Fawwaz, his London-based operative who had established his Nairobi cell. More than 50 calls were made to Kenya, including four to the home phone number of Wadih el Hage, who was convicted in July 2001 of organizing the Nairobi bombing.

Bin Laden was aware from the outset that satphone communications could easily be monitored, however, and hence limited its use to non-operations purposes. (The NSA even used to play specially-cleared visitors a tape of bin Laden talking to his mother.) But he was evidently unaware, at least until August 1998, of the ability of the US SIGINT satellites to pinpoint the location of satphone transmissions; and he certainly underestimated the extend to which supposedly innocuous calls provided important evidentiary material.

Bin Laden's satphone was sometimes used by his close associates, who might have been less cognizant of the dangers. On August 20, 1998, when Khowst was attacked by cruise missiles, and again the next day, it was used by Ayman al-Zawahiri, his friend and effectively his deputy commander, who talked seemingly unconcerned about the calls being traced and his position pinpointed.[3]

Bin Laden ceased using his satphone in February 1999. Taliban officials have said that they confiscated it in order to constrain his activities, but it is more likely that he stopped for security reasons. On August 21, 1998, National Security Adviser Sandy Berger stated on television that much of the data that prompted the US strikes had been accumulated by monitoring telephone conversations by bin Laden and his associates. Other US officials were reported to have said in subsequent months that spy satellites tapping into bin Laden's phone calls had intercepted details of planned terrorist attacks and enabled them to be prevented.

By the beginning of 1999, bin Laden had constructed a communications network which was versatile and virtually impenetrable to Western intelligence agencies. As a study published by the RAND Corporation later that year noted, it relied on the world wide web, email, and electronic bulletin boards to exchange information without running a major risk of being intercepted by counter-terrorism officials.[4] This advanced technology was complemented with an extensive human courier network, the critical importance of which bin Laden had learned during the Afghan war against the Soviet Union, whereby hand-delivered instructions were passed from the al-Qaeda leadership on to senior military commanders and down to the terrorist cells in the Middle East, Africa and Europe.

The Warning Signs

The US intelligence community was taken completely by surprise on September 11, although there were many indications during the preceding several months that bin Laden was planning a major operation. As US Secretary of State Colin Powell said in October 2001, 'there were a lot of signs [in May–July] that there was something going on', but 'we never got the fidelity and the information that we would have liked to, some warning of what did actually happen'.

On May 29, the US State Department issued an international warning cautioning American citizens that they could become the targets of terrorist groups linked to bin Laden. The US Embassies in Manama, Bahrain and Dakar, Senegal were closed, and US military installations in the Gulf were ordered to the highest state of alert ('Threatcon Delta'). There was a crescendo of reports about possible terrorist attacks immediately before the Fourth of July and then the summit meeting of the industrialized nations in Italy two weeks later. Later in July, the State Department released a warning about possible attacks against US facilities in Japan, South Korea and the Arabian Peninsula.

These warnings were generated by a bin Laden disinformation campaign, designed not only to induce complacency as the alarms proved false, but also to 'spoof' Western intelligence agencies into believing that the threat was against US interests abroad rather than the homeland itself.

The most premonitory report was given to the FBI a month before September 11 when a flight instructor in Minnesota called several times to warn it of the possibility of terrorists using fuel-laden aircraft as flying bombs and the threat posed by one of his trainees – Zacarias Moussaoui, the so-called '20th hijacker'. Moussaoui (who had entered the US in February 2001) was detained by the FBI and Immigration and Naturalization Service (INS) on 16 August on visa violation charges, and has remained in custody ever since, but he provided no information about the September 11 attacks.

The idea of using hijacked fuel-laden aircraft as flying bombs against prominent but undefended buildings should not have been shocking. In December 1994, an Islamic militant group in Algeria hijacked an Air France airliner and threatened to crash it into the Eiffel Tower in Paris. In 1995, Western intelligence services discovered that bin Laden had designed a plan to hijack passenger jets and crash them into various landmark targets in the US, including the World Trade Center in New York, the Sears Tower in Chicago and the CIA headquarters in Langley, Virginia. Details of the plan were widely publicized in 1997 during the trial of Ramsi Youssef, the operational leader in charge of the bombing of the World Trade Center in 1993. The annual reports of the Federal Aviation Administration for 1999 and 2000, published in early 2000 and 2001 respectively, warned that bin Laden and his followers posed 'a significant threat to civil aviation, particularly to US civil aviation', and that an (unnamed) exiled Islamic leader in Britain had said that bin Laden was planning to 'bring down an airliner, or hijack an airliner to humiliate the United States'.[5]

Intelligence and the War on Terrorism

The House Permanent Select Committee on Intelligence reported on September 26 that 'there is a fundamental need for both a cultural revolution within the intelligence community as well as significant structural changes', and said it was imperative that the US increase the number of spies and intelligence analysts, reform the imagery intelligence (IMINT) management and collection processes, and modernize capabilities for processing intercepted voice and data communications. Numerous pieces of new legislation have been proposed, and some already enacted, dealing with terrorism, security intelligence, protection

of critical cyber infrastructure, and additional financial appropria-
tions. There have been vocal calls to remove the 'restrictions' on the
intelligence and counter-terrorist agencies, and to 'unleash' them
against terrorism. Two former directors of the CIA (George Bush Snr
and R. James Woolsey) have called for an end to the classified guide-
lines set in 1995 which prohibit the recruitment of agents who have
committed gross human rights violations. Other former intelligence
officials have said that the US should pursue a vigorous assassination
policy.

Regardless of the outcome of this debate, the future capabilities and
missions of the US intelligence community will be determined far more
by the additional resources allocated to intelligence activities immediately after September 11, and especially the massive investments in new
space-based and airborne collection systems required for the war in
Afghanistan, rather than by any legislative or organizational changes.

Large increases in funding were immediately authorized by both the
White House and Congress. On September 21, the Administration
appropriated $1.15 billion in emergency funds for 'situational aware-
ness and intelligence-gathering'. A few days later, the House of
Representatives approved the Fiscal Year 2003 defence budget ($344
billion), which included an additional $400 million for counter-
terrorism measures. A classified supplemental request from the
Pentagon for Fiscal Year 2002 is reported to include $13 billion for 'situ-
ational awareness, unmanned aerial vehicles and human intelligence'.
President Bush has also committed some $6 billion for (non-defence)
counter-terrorism initiatives.

By the end of September, the US had assembled nearly 50 intelligence, communications, navigation and meteorological satellites to
support military operations in Afghanistan – amounting to some $25
billion. The US intelligence satellites included two DSP missile launch
detection/early warning satellites; two Advanced KH-11 real-time digital
imaging satellites (launched in 1995 and 1996); three Lacrosse imaging
radar satellites; three other specialized, smaller imaging satellites
operated by the National Reconnaissance Office (NRO); two Advanced
Orion geostationary SIGINT satellites; one Mercury/Advanced Vortex
geostationary SIGINT satellite; two Trumpet SIGINT satellites in highly
elliptical orbits; and several smaller low-altitude electronic intelligence
(ELINT) satellites for interception and location of the sources of VHF
and microwave emissions. More were soon to come. On October 5, the
NRO launched a third Advanced KH-11 to enable daily repeat coverage
of Afghanistan – at a cost of $1.3 billion (including the launch vehicle),

or more than the augmentation of emergency intelligence-related funds given to the Pentagon on September 21. On October 10, the NRO launched a data relay satellite (code-named Aquila), costing about $400 million, for relaying SIGINT, imagery and other intelligence data specifically related to military operations in Afghanistan.

Many of the satellite systems used for the war in Afghanistan will require accelerated replacement. Plans to acquire new constellations of geostationary, highly elliptical and low-orbiting SIGINT satellites, the most sophisticated of which will cost $1.5–2 billion each, have been given added impetus. The development of new imaging satellites is also being hastened.

Once military operations began in Afghanistan, the burden of intelligence collection passed from satellites to airborne systems, including unmanned aerial vehicles (UAVs). More than a dozen sorts of intelligence collection aircraft were deployed to the region, including E-3 Airborne Warning and Control System (AWACS) aircraft; upgraded U-2 surveillance aircraft, equipped with radars, electro-optical cameras and SIGINT systems; RC-135 Rivet Joint SIGINT aircraft; E-8C Joint-STARS radar surveillance aircraft; US Navy EP-3 Aries SIGINT aircraft; EC-130H Compass Call communications interception and jamming aircraft; and Navy EA-6B Prowlers also configured for communications interception and jamming. The CIA began using the Predator UAV over Afghanistan in October, and in November the new high-altitude Global Hawk UAV was rushed into service.

Again, the demands of the war in Afghanistan will hasten the replacement and modernization of many of these airborne systems. Plans are being moved forward for the development of new airborne systems, including a US Air Force plan for a multimission reconnaissance and intelligence collection aircraft which would incorporate AWACS, radar surveillance and SIGINT missions; and Navy proposals for a new multimission maritime surveillance aircraft to replace its P-3 Orion, EP-3 Aries and EA-6B Prowler systems. Several new UAVs, equipped with all types of sensors, will enter service over the next few years.

Over the next four years, the Pentagon intends to invest heavily in new and emerging technologies that can significantly enhance the US advantage in intelligence collection and analysis. According to the *Quadrennial Defense Review*, developments in low-observable technologies, nanotechnologies, robotics and biometrics, for example, will enable people to be identified instantaneously by their facial features or the way they walk; reconnaissance systems mounted on platforms the size of mosquitoes will be able to track US adversaries or penetrate their remote facilities; and new forms of electronic combat will be used to disrupt or destroy an adversary's computer and communications infrastructure.

Enhancement of HUMINT

The widespread calls for expanded human intelligence (HUMINT) capabilities have been characterized more by their stridency than their coherence. President Bush, in a speech to military cadets at the Citadel in Charleston, South Carolina, on December 11, 2001, stressed that the US 'must rebuild our network of human intelligence', specifically citing the need for 'people on the ground, ... the people who find the targets, follow our enemies and help us disrupt their evil plans'.

In practice, however, the arguments about enhancing HUMINT concern an array of quite different capabilities and activities, ranging from covert operations (including assassinations) to agent penetrations (that is, 'spies') and analysis and assessment. Some of the calls address peripheral issues; some are probably infeasible; most do not appreciate the extent of the long-term planning or investment in human resources required. The calls for relaxation of operational restrictions on the US military intelligence agencies and the CIA, allowing them to employ criminals in the field or to commit assassinations, are diversions.

The CIA is already moving to expand its human collection capabilities, but penetration of the Islamic terrorist groups is extremely difficult. It will take many years to recruit and train sufficient operatives on the ground, and many cells will remain impenetrable – and some, inevitably, undiscovered. The critical HUMINT requirement is to strengthen the analysis and assessment capabilities. This means not only the recruitment of sufficient trained personnel to adequately analyse all the intelligence collected, but the maintenance of a national educational and research infrastructure able to provide the necessary breadth and depth of expertise in a rapidly broadening range of political, social and technical subjects. Mechanisms for exploiting so-called open-source (or publicly available) intelligence are still gravely deficient. But how these long-term investments and institutional mechanisms should be designed has received little attention.

Organizational Reform

Since the failure of the US intelligence community to foresee the end of the Cold War and the collapse of the Soviet Union, it has been subjected to interminable inquiries and reviews, which have consumed much time and effort but produced little apart from marginal organizational reforms. The most commonly identified weakness, apart from an imbalance in the respective collection and analysis activities, relates to management, tasking and coordination. Many of the inquiries recommended some form of consolidation as well as improved coordination mechanisms. These have become more imperative as an increasing number of agencies accept security-related responsibilities. Some 35–40 agencies are currently involved with some aspect of counter-terrorism, ranging from the national intelligence agencies such as the CIA and NSA to other authorities such as taxation, customs and the INS.

President Bush announced on September 20 in his address to the nation that he had created a new cabinet-level organization, the Office of Homeland Security, to coordinate the efforts of all the federal departments and agencies (including the Department of Defense, the Federal Emergency Management Administration, the Customs Service, the Coast Guard, and so on) and state and local government authorities which have responsibilities affecting homeland defence. However, neither its charter nor its powers have been clarified. It will probably be no more effective than the civil defence organization of the early 1960s or the executive structure organized for the war on drugs in the 1980s. In short, there has been no radical reorganization to date. Indeed, rather than any consolidations, new agencies and offices have been created to deal with the war against terrorism.

While further organizational changes accrete, a range of measures for unprecedented levels and forms of homeland surveillance are also being instituted. This includes provisions for more exhaustive monitoring of private telephone and computer/electronic communications; much more intrusive monitoring of commercial activities (and especially financial transactions); and increased surveillance of internal US airspace.

The US Space Command and the North American Defense Command (NORAD) have been given new domestic responsibilities. For several months after September 11, the USAF maintained a continuous airborne watch by AWACS aircraft over the New York–Washington corridor, looking for errant aircraft that could pose a threat. (The operation could not be sustained by the USAF AWACS fleet, and required the deployment of five aircraft from NATO.) NORAD commanders have now been given the authority to shoot down passenger aircraft being used to threaten US cities.

The central role of emails and the internet in terrorist communications networks, the extensive use of emails by the hijackers in their preparations for the September 11 attacks, and the increasing use by terrorist groups of advanced encryption techniques (including stenography, in which encrypted messages are concealed inside music or picture files on websites) have prompted various initiatives to increase the powers and capabilities of agencies involved in electronic surveillance, and have renewed the arguments concerning the delicate balance between national security and privacy issues.

In the US, numerous intelligence, law enforcement and Treasury Department agencies are involved in electronic surveillance activities, with access to extraordinary databases and files. Within two weeks of the attack, the FBI had located hundreds of emails linked to the hijackers, in English, Arabic and Urdu, sent 30–45 days before the attack, some of which included operational details of the attack.

Some of the proposals to loosen the controls on electronic surveillance are very controversial. The demands for the banning of encryption of email, at least without escrow (whereby the decryption keys are deposited with some government agency), are especially problematic. None of the emails sent or received by the hijackers was encrypted.

In any case, there is no doubt that the techniques currently used for surveillance of facsimile, email and electronic data traffic – such as the Echelon system used by the UK–US SIGINT organizations for monitoring traffic on international circuits, and the FBI's DCS1000 Carnivore system used (under warrant) for intercepting domestic emails – will be dramatically upgraded. Moreover, protocols are quickly being formulated for direct data exchanges between these as well as with similar systems for monitoring electronic financial transactions.

The US government has moved quickly to prepare legislation that will change existing laws on intelligence gathering with respect to the financial infrastructure so as to ease restrictions on covert monitoring of suspicious bank accounts and financial transactions. It also proposes tougher laws against money laundering, which it hopes will enable it to cripple the international financial support networks.

Terrorist operations are relatively inexpensive. The bombing of the World Trade Center in 1993 cost an estimated $20,000. The September 11 atrocity probably had a total cost of about $500,000, used mainly for the living expenses, pilot training and airline tickets of the hijackers. US authorities have traced a 'money trail' involving more than $325,000 via credit card receipts, ATM withdrawals and other transactions connected to the hijackers – but, among 19 people over a period of many months, they were mostly small and not unusual transactions that were unlikely to suggest criminal interest. Another $175,000 was probably spent in cash. Most of the funds were assembled and moved to dozens of bank and credit card accounts in small amounts through the almost paperless (and essentially traceless) hawala process (whereby money is passed 'in trust' through brokers and small merchants belonging to the same clan).

Enhanced Intelligence Collaboration

The war on terrorism will cause a realignment of international relations, with the US having to form new anti-terrorist coalitions and engage in much more extensive intelligence cooperation. The US will require more facilities in the Middle East and central Asia for ground-based listening stations and spy aircraft, overflight permissions, intelligence dissemination networks, and support for special forces operations. Even more importantly, Arab governments are an invaluable source of intelligence about the terrorist networks, personalities, motivations, recruitment and training, and *modus operandi*. They know the Islamic militant groups better than Americans ever can; they are able to penetrate them with agents and informers much more easily than Western intelligence services. There are suggestions of collaborative arrangements in which the US would contribute its prowess in technical intelligence collection (especially SIGINT and overhead imagery capabilities) and the Arab governments their superlative human intelligence.

These new intelligence relationships will be very difficult to forge. The US would have to be much more forthcoming in sharing its intelligence, in order to both persuade Arab authorities of the validity of the US indictments and to assist them in their domestic counter-terrorist activities – and in the process revealing aspects of US capabilities. The US would have to be more frank about its activities in host countries, both to avoid suspicions of espionage and to build confidence that all relevant intelligence acquired by the US is being shared. New approaches to multilateral intelligence cooperation would have to be constructed. Intelligence is a parochial vocation, with the highest-grade material reserved for decision makers and their closest advisers. The most successful cooperative ventures have generally been bilateral, where the highest levels of mutual trust can be maintained and the extent of external dissemination of material minimized. The few multilateral arrangements of the Cold War offer no models.

Prospects

The intelligence community will be burdened by the failures of September 11 for many years to come. There will be many more inquiries and further reorganizations. But the sorts of fundamental changes which might improve intelligence about strategic surprises, from the end of the Cold War through to the war on terrorism, are unlikely to be implemented. Indeed, they are yet to be articulated.

The most palpable consequence of the terrorist attacks, the increase in budgetary resources, will not necessarily improve matters. The primary beneficiaries will be the agencies which have failed against bin Laden since the intelligence war was joined in the mid-1990s. Most of the additional resources will be absorbed by expensive new satellites and other technical systems which will perpetuate current capabilities and modes of operation.

Many required reforms are inhibited by the ingrained philosophies and operational habits which dominate Western intelligence agencies – the surrounding secrecy, the self-defeating compartmentalization, and the sovereignty of the principle of protection of sources and methods. They seem constitutionally unable to address increasingly diverse constituencies, to exploit the growth in open-source intelligence or to harness the technical skills available in the private sector. The long-term investments in education and research capabilities necessary to provide national pools of political, strategic and technical expertise from which the intelligence agencies can draw, remain undefined and unfunded.

The prospective increase in capabilities and legal powers for electronic surveillance will not reduce the fallibility of the intelligence community. Even if all of the email and internet communications of the hijackers now collected had been processed and analysed beforehand by some central authority, it would still probably not have revealed their precise intentions. But a central authority able to assemble and scrutinize electronic communications of all sorts would certainly involve gross infringements of civil liberties.

A decade hence, there will be a larger US intelligence establishment (with its annual budget increased by perhaps $5 billion). It will suffer most of its current weaknesses, including poor tasking, a collection/analysis imbalance, and inadequate intellectual depth and breadth – and be no more able to predict specific events such as the September 11 attacks. Privacy of electronic communications (including commercial transactions) will be more circumscribed. But within another decade there will be another crisis or calamity of strategic proportions which will have caught the new intelligence establishment unawares.

Notes

1. Roberta Wohlstetter, *Pearl Harbor: Warning and Decision* (Stanford, CA: Stanford University Press, 1962), p. 397.
2. Yossef Bodansky, *Bin Laden: The Man Who Declared War on America* (Rocklin, CA: Forum, 1999), pp. 197–8, 308, 312; and Peter L. Bergen, *Holy War, Inc: Inside the Secret World of Osama bin Laden* (London: Weidenfield and Nicolson, 2001), pp. 131, 177, 252.
3. Bodansky, *Bin Laden*, pp. 288–9.
4. Ian O. Lesser et al., *Countering the New Terrorism* (Santa Monica, CA: RAND Corporation, 1999), chapter 3.
5. Matthew L. Wald, 'Warnings: Earlier Hijackings Offered Signals That Were Missed', *New York Times*, October 3, 2001.

CHAPTER 6

Targeting Terrorist Finances: The New Challenges of Financial Market Globalization[1]

Thomas J. Biersteker

Global financial market integration accelerated sharply toward the end of the twentieth century. The flow of foreign exchange across national boundaries exceeded $1.3 trillion per day, a figure that surpassed the foreign exchange holdings of the central banks of all of the OECD countries combined. During the early 1990s, net capital flows to developing countries exceeded $130 billion a year, and even following the Asian financial crisis, direct foreign investment continued to increase in some of the countries hardest hit by the financial market instability in East and Southeast Asia.

Even more important than the dramatic increase in the flow of funds across borders was the conceptual shift that took place within major institutional actors – from individual currency traders and portfolio investors to national regulatory officials. There was a major shift away from a conception of sharply demarcated national financial boundaries toward a conception of an integrated, global financial market, presenting investment opportunities and competitive challenges on a global scale. National attempts to impose effective currency controls, which had prevailed in most countries from the 1930s well into the 1970s, increasingly gave way to financial deregulation, financial liberalization, the gradual elimination of capital controls and the introduction of incentives to encourage cross-border financial transactions. The prevailing imagery was increasingly one of capital 'ricocheting across the globe' instantaneously, on an around-the-clock, 24-hours-a-day basis.

In many ways, the flows of funds, conceptual shift and movement toward financial market liberalization approximated a return to the general patterns and degrees of economic integration prevailing before the First World War. However, there were some important differences at the century's end. Financial market globalization facilitated the emergence of new financial actors – bond traders, currency traders, portfolio investors and money launderers – who developed global investment and hedging strategies to take advantage of the new financial order. More importantly, changes in technology facilitated the emergence of a global financial system that was no longer constituted by exchange regulated and controlled across national financial markets alone. The contemporary global financial system is constituted by 'a network integrated through electronic information systems that entails … more than two hundred thousand electronic monitors in trading rooms all over the world that are linked together'.[2] For good or for ill, this network has become a location of financial power, with the ability to move funds across the globe with relative impunity, to reward those countries that pursue policies it deems prudent and to punish those that pursue policies it deems 'unsustainable'.

Prior to September 11, 2001, most of the discussion about the challenges of financial market globalization concerned its distributional effects and its tendency toward periodic instability (financial fragility). Defenders of financial market globalization lauded its effects on increasing access to finance, potentially reducing inequality between and within states, and its potential for mobilization of capital for development. Critics of financial market globalization emphasized its periodic tendency toward instability, panic and crisis, along with its unequal distributional effects, both within and between states. Because financial market globalization (like globalization itself) is profoundly contradictory, the problematic truth lies somewhere between these two views. Globalization simultaneously increases and decreases inequality at different levels of analysis.

The Challenges of Financial Market Globalization after September 11

After September 11, 2001, much of the discussion about the negative (or 'dark') side of financial market globalization turned away from its distributional effects and tendency toward periodic instability and began to consider how it facilitated the transfer of funds that enabled global terrorism. Money laundering and the operations of transnational criminal organizations had long been identified as side-effects of financial market globalization, but most of the negative consequences associated with these practices seemed to have been more than offset by the general benefits of financial market integration. September 11 changed all of that. Never before had any transnational actor inflicted damage with such a direct – and lethal – effect. The new challenge of financial market globalization was how to track and freeze the financial assets of global terrorist networks.

Like the contradictory distributional effects of globalization, the ease with which transnational actors can move funds across borders in the wake of financial market globalization also has contradictory aspects, for the same technology that enables rapid movements of funds also enables enhanced surveillance and the possibility of tracking those funds.[3] Global terrorism presents a new security threat – that of a networked, transnational actor. However, global terrorism is a networked threat that invites a networked response, and the technology, if not always the political will to employ it, is available.

Different terrorist networks operate with very different structures and sources of financial support. Some are state-supported and financed, some operate as quasi-states (with regional or territorial control and financed by their participation in the drugs trade or by other linkages to global crime), while still others are decentralized, widely dispersed and partially self-funded. We are only beginning to understand the basis of the financing of the al-Qaeda network. However, several recent surveys have suggested useful taxonomies of the forms of financing their operations, which suggest where to try and block, freeze or disrupt the assets of terrorist networks and organizations.

William Wechsler, a former US National Security Council and Treasury Department official, has suggested that beyond the family inheritance of Osama bin Laden, the al-Qaeda network has raised funds from legal businesses and investments, criminal schemes (both large and small), direct solicitation, and also by skimming off contributions to charitable organizations.[4] The movement of funds has been facilitated by legal remittances through routine wire transfers, cash smuggling, direct shipments of gold and the largely unregulated *hawala* system (that enables individuals to provide cash to an agent in one location and ask that it be disbursed at another, circumventing wire transfers and formal bank involvement altogether). Its close ties to the Taliban regime in Afghanistan also enabled the al-Qaeda network to move large amounts of funds and supplies directly through its use of the international airline of Afghanistan. This is one of the reasons the initial focus of United Nations Security Council resolutions targeting the Taliban regime concentrated on the grounding of the official Afghanistan carrier, Ariana Airlines. The *hawala* system has received a great deal of attention since September 11, but it is important to note that much of it exists not as a conduit for disguising the transfers of funds to terrorist networks, but for transfers and remittances from diaspora communities dispersed throughout the world. It is an informal way to remit funds for perfectly legitimate reasons (based largely on trust), and it is often much less costly than using the formal banking system.

Financial deregulation and liberalization policies at the national level in the 1980s and 1990s not only increased the flow of capital across national boundaries, but also decreased the monitoring and regulatory capacity of many states. Once an elaborate system of licensing and controls has been dismantled, it is difficult to replace it with a robust regulatory system at relatively short notice. However, there has been at least one important trend counter to the general pattern of decreased regulation over the past few years. Following widespread criticism of the humanitarian effects of general sanctions (particularly the comprehensive trade and financial sanctions imposed against Iraq), there has been growing international interest in the possibility of targeted sanctions, particularly financial sanctions.

Targeted Financial Sanctions

Targeted financial sanctions entail the use of financial controls to apply coercive pressure on government officials, elites who support them or members of non-governmental entities in an effort to change or restrict their behaviour. Since the sanctions apply only to a subset of the population, they are 'targeted' and therefore hold the potential of minimizing negative impacts on innocent, civilian populations. The use of targeted financial sanctions by the international community has increased substantially during the past decade. The UN Security Council first experimented with them against the Haitian regime of Raoul Cedras in 1994, but the frequency of use of the instrument has grown in the past few years. Targeted financial sanctions have been employed by the UN against the UNITA in Angola (1998), the Taliban regime in Afghanistan (1999, 2000, 2001) and RUF members fighting within Liberia (2001). The European Union imposed targeted financial sanctions on the Milosevic regime in Serbia in 1999.

The successful imposition of targeted financial sanctions entails multilateral coordination, effective national implementation and private sector cooperation. In recent years, there has been increased regulatory cooperation and transgovernmental coordination in this issue area. The Swiss government convened international experts from the worlds of finance, government and international organizations in what became known as the Interlaken Process, to explore ways to refine and enhance the effectiveness of the instrument.[5] At around the same time, the OECD's Financial Action Task Force on Money Laundering (FATF) embarked on a global effort to enhance international cooperation and policy harmonization on money laundering, establishing minimal standards for financial institutions with regard to due diligence and knowing their customers. Voluntary private sector initiatives, such as the Wolfsberg Group of Banks, have also joined the international effort to coordinate policy in this area.

All of this international activity to target individuals and regimes, to coordinate financial policy controls and to engage the private sector in the implementation of new financial restrictions became starkly relevant after September 11. Among the first priorities in the effort to combat global terrorism was the multilateral effort to freeze and suppress both the raising and the movement of funds that support global terrorists. Blocking the financial assets of terrorists and the targeting of financial sanctions are similar in many important respects: both entail the identification of a targeted list of names and corporate (or institutional) entities; both require extensive multilateral coordination to be successful, and both rely on the cooperation and participation of private sector financial institutions for effective implementation.

The international effort to target financial sanctions has had relatively few successes to date. However, serious multilateral efforts to target financial sanctions have only been attempted during the past few years. The biggest challenge for the global enforcement of targeted financial sanctions has been the absence of political will on the part of individual states to devote the resources necessary to establish the institutional mechanisms to make them succeed. In the wake of September 11, the will to do something about terrorist assets has been clearly evident and widely expressed. With the passage of UN Security Council Resolutions 1373 and 1377, and with important changes in national policy throughout the world, from Bahrain to Hong Kong, there have been important expressions of a global willingness to do something about terrorist finances. The absence of political will is not a constraint – at least for the time being.

Degrading the Financial Assets of Terrorist Organizations

There are a number of things that have been learned from efforts to target financial sanctions that are directly relevant to the effort to freeze and suppress the generation and movement of funds that support global terrorism. First, and foremost, given the fact that terrorism is a global problem, responses to it require multilateral cooperation. Clarity and consistency of definition and interpretation across different national legal jurisdictions are vital. Different definitions of what is an 'asset' and efforts to block funds only, rather than transactions involving 'income-bearing assets' have led to inconsistent implementation of targeted financial sanctions between Europe and the US in the past. This created unnecessary loopholes for potential sanctions violators and would provide the same for terrorist organizations. The clarity of the language used in UN Security Council resolutions and in national enabling legislation became a principal focus of the two Interlaken meetings and produced consensual definitions of terms such as 'funds and other financial resources', 'owned and controlled directly or indirectly', to 'freeze', and 'financial services' and 'assets'. These are definitions that can be utilized in contemporary efforts to combat global terrorism.

Second, because private sector financial institutions are on the front lines of implementation of both targeted financial sanctions and efforts to block terrorist finances, they need to be protected from potential claims arising from their compliance with UN Security Council resolutions and other enabling legislation. If they are not provided with this legal protection, the freezing of funds could cause a financial institution to be in violation of its fundamental obligations to its customers. This concern can be readily addressed by the inclusion of a 'non-liability' provision in enabling resolutions or legislation, calling on states to implement the intent of the resolution 'notwithstanding the existence of any rights or obligations conferred or imposed by any other international agreement or contract, license, or permit'. Ironically, most states do not have laws on the books that automatically enable them to apply national measures to give effect to decisions called for in UN Security Council resolutions. Only about 20 states (including the US) have such legislation in place, and this has been a priority of international efforts to coordinate policies on targeted sanctions – both financial sanctions and arms embargoes.

Third, experience with efforts to target financial sanctions suggests that UN Security Council resolutions or national enabling legislation to block or freeze the assets of terrorist organizations should authorize financial institutions to trace funds retroactively. Requiring states to report on the movement of funds within their jurisdiction for a specified period *prior to* efforts to freeze or block the movement of terrorist funds could generate valuable information about the location and movement of financial assets attempting to flee a jurisdiction. Thus, even if the funds cannot be trapped, they can be traced, enabling monitoring of the assets, if and when they attempt to re-enter the global financial system. The identification of funds in this manner also enables the potential 'naming and shaming' of havens for the assets of global terrorist organizations, as the FATF has done with regard to havens for money laundering.

Fourth, efforts to target financial sanctions also suggest that national agencies engaged in international efforts to combat global terrorism need to provide as much identifying information as possible about the targets of the resolutions and enabling legislation. At a minimum, there should be an effort to include the full name, any known or likely aliases, the date of birth and the complete address of any member of a global terrorist organization, as well as details about potential front companies or institutions used by the terrorist organization. The Office of Foreign Asset Control of the US Treasury has long maintained lists of targets of specially designated nationals, narcotics traffickers and terrorists. The recently created lists of specially designated global terrorists and terrorist organizations are more detailed and comprehensive, but they still lack adequate detail about many of the names included on the list. Without this level of information it is difficult for financial institutions to know precisely which transactions should be investigated. Providing more identifying information about potential targets requires multilateral cooperation, including the sharing and coordination of intelligence information. Intelligence coordination is especially important for identifying the potential use of the *hawala* system, since it is not as susceptible to electronic surveillance as the formal banking system.

Fifth, while broad-based multilateral cooperation is necessary for an effective global effort to combat terrorism, the experience with targeting financial sanctions has taught that most countries lack an adequate administrative capacity to implement UN Security Council resolutions effectively. The international effort to pursue sanctions reform has tried to identify 'best practices' at the national level for both targeted financial sanctions and arms embargoes. There are also efforts under way to utilize sanctions assistance missions, technical assistance at the regional level, financial support for those most directly affected by compliance with sanctions resolutions, secondary sanctions, mutual evaluations, 'naming and shaming', transgovernmental cooperation and private sector initiatives to ensure that there is broad multilateral participation in targeted sanctions efforts. Given the urgency of the threat posed by global terrorist organizations, there is a pressing need for dissemination of 'best practices' to offshore financial centres and to the countries most likely to be transit points for terrorist funds.

Sixth, and finally, the computer technology that enables global terrorist networks to exploit financial market globalization and move funds instantaneously across the globe can also be employed against them. Financial institutions throughout the world could be encouraged to utilize one of the many 'name recognition' software programs already widely available on the market. This software could help them determine – electronically and instantaneously – whether they are holding the accounts of any individuals or organizations identified as global terrorists. At present, only the largest, US-based banks make routine use of name recognition software to comply with targeted financial sanctions resolutions. Neither smaller, regional US banks nor major financial institutions in Europe and Japan make use of this technology. Beyond its utility in identifying transactions involving individuals on the list, a new generation of the technology could be deployed to identify patterns of suspicious transactions that deviate from common norms in the frequency, size or destination of transactions. Indeed, it was an individual observation of this kind of deviation from normal patterns of transactions that led a Boston-based bank employee to raise questions about suspicious transactions involving the al-Barakat organization. The use of computerized surveillance technology raises important and legitimate concerns about the potential violation of fundamental civil liberties from this new form of electronic intrusion. However, new norms can be introduced that establish limits on the invasion of privacy and procedures for petition for removal from erroneous inclusion on the list of terrorists. The effort to improve the effectiveness of targeting financial sanctions has produced a recommendation that a right to petition for removal from a list of targets be included in future UN Security Council resolutions for individuals designated erroneously (or sharing a commonly used name).[6]

There are a number of relatively simple and straightforward administrative practices that could be undertaken at the national level in the global effort to combat terrorism. As suggested above, states should ensure that they have legal authority to freeze assets at the national level through national measures. They also need to designate an official agency (or agencies) to administer the assets freeze or blockade. Most states already have regulatory authorities capable of handling these issues, although they may not have special offices devoted to the purposes of freezing the assets of terrorist groups. States need to empower this administering agency with a capacity to develop guidance for banks and other financial institutions as well as to disseminate information to them in an efficient and effective manner. They also need to empower an administering agency to undertake compliance activities, to specify the criteria and process for considering and giving effect to decisions regarding exemptions and exceptions, to determine procedures for the administration of frozen assets, to specify what constitutes a violation of the law and to impose penalties for breaches.

Efforts to target financial sanctions more effectively provide some good institutional precedents for efforts to freeze terrorist finances. However, a comparative assessment of the institutional investment required for the effort – identifying which agencies are able to administer new restrictions – provides some sobering evidence about the magnitude of the challenges that lie ahead. At present, there is *enormous* variation in administrative capacity to implement targeted financial sanctions across different national jurisdictions. Even among major economic powers, there is wide variation in the number of personnel devoted to national implementation. The US Treasury's Office of Foreign Asset Control has more than 100 staff working full time on the implementation of financial sanctions. In contrast, the Bank of England has a staff of about seven. The French Ministry of Finance has two people working part time, the German Bundesbank has one, and the European Commission in Brussels has only one person (and a half-time administrative assistant) working on the sanctions issue.

Although they have national regulatory and supervisory agencies in place, most regional economic powers have no specialized administrative agencies dealing with sanctions issues, arguing that funds are not likely to be placed in their financial institutions and that they have more pressing administrative needs. In response to recent anti-money laundering initiatives from the FATF, some offshore financial centres have created new agencies, or refashioned existing ones, to oversee banking and financial service industries. In some cases, the powers granted to these agencies are similar to those needed for sanctions implementation (record keeping, know your client, and information sharing), but there is only limited evidence that they are being utilized for this purpose. Among smaller countries, administrative capacity to implement sanctions resolutions is directly correlated with the level of development. The more developed the country, the more capable is it likely to be with regard to the implementation of sanctions resolutions. Small, less developed countries tend to comply with UN reporting simply by declaring that they have complied 'to the best of our ability'.

The Emerging Governance of Global Finance

The challenge of multilateral coordination to combat global terrorism
is daunting. It is not impossible, however, and it is striking to note the
virtual 'sea change' that has taken place in the global effort to do something about terrorist finances in the aftermath of September 11. Many
of the operative paragraphs of UN Security Council Resolution 1373
(September 28, 2001) were devoted to terrorist finances, and the resolution created a new committee, the Counter Terrorism Committee
(CTC), to monitor compliance with its provisions. Paragraph 6 of the
resolution called for the submission of formal written reports by UN
member states spelling out the concrete steps they have taken to
comply with the resolution, and 60 reports have been posted on the
CTC's website, most of which spell out specific actions taken against
global terrorism and measures adopted to suppress the financing of
terrorism. States previously better known as offshore havens, and identified in the recent past as 'non-cooperating countries or territories' by
the FATF – the Bahamas, Grenada, Lebanon, Liechtenstein and
Mauritius – have been quick to comply with the reporting requirements
of the resolution. There is substantial evidence of a significant change
of will on this issue. According to the *Financial Times*, more than $104
million in alleged terrorist assets has been blocked since September 11,
and 147 countries have participated in the efforts to block terrorist
funds.[7] The window of opportunity is therefore open, as long as it is
not slammed shut either by American impatience or by its proclivities
toward 'unilateral multilateralism'.

Among the most effective strategies of defence against a global
terrorist network is the development of a networked response.
Transnational networks need to be mobilized, global civil society needs
to be engaged and private sector financial institutions need to be
employed to suppress or freeze the financial assets of terrorist networks.
Given the range of alternative ways to move funds and the relatively
small amounts that appear to be necessary to commit spectacularly
devastating acts of terrorism, the most that can reasonably be accomplished by this effort is the degrading of the assets of global terrorist
organizations. Unlike global criminal organizations that need to move
and launder large amounts of funds, the principal motivation for global
terrorism is not financial gain but a fanatical commitment to a cause.
It did not take a vast amount of resources to mount the terrorist attacks
on the World Trade Center and the Pentagon (as little as $500,000 by
most estimates), but given the human costs of the attacks of September

11, any attempt to degrade the ability of global terrorist organizations appears well worth the effort.

The traditional challenges of financial market globalization – periodic bouts of financial instability and unequal distributional effects – remain in place after September 11, but they have been joined by a new challenge. It is not an insurmountable challenge, but one that will require multilateral cooperation, political will and an innovative use of technology. The global effort to freeze and suppress the funds that support global terrorism provides the international community with an important, multilateral instrument to employ beyond the use of military force. Degrading the value of the financial assets of terrorist organizations increases both the costs and the difficulties of committing future acts of global terrorism.

Notes

1. Much of the analysis in this chapter is based on research conducted over the past three years by the Targeted Financial Sanctions Project of the Watson Institute for International Studies at Brown University. Although I am solely responsible for any deficiencies in this chapter, I have benefited greatly from my interactions with, and would like to acknowledge the many contributions of, my colleagues who constitute the rest of our research team: Sue Eckert, Aaron Halegua and Peter Romaniuk.
2. S.J. Kobrin, 'Beyond Symmetry: State Sovereignty in a Networked Global Economy', in J. Dunning (ed.) *Governments, Globalization and International Business* (Oxford: Oxford University Press, 1997), p. 20.
3. There are important normative aspects of this issue, particularly the protection of privacy, but they will not be explored in this chapter.
4. W. Wechsler, 'Strangling the Hydra: Targeting Al Qaeda's Finances', in James F. Hoge Jnr and Gideon Rose (eds) *How Did this Happen? Terrorism and the New War* (New York: PublicAffairs Publishing, 2001), pp. 130–5.
5. *Targeted Financial Sanctions: A Manual for Design and Implementation* (Contributions from the Interlaken Process), The Swiss Confederation, in cooperation with the United Nations Secretariat and the Watson Institute for International Studies, Brown University, 2001, <http:www//watsoninstitute.org>
6. Ibid., pp. 28–9.
7. 'Complex Finances Defy Global Policing', *Financial Times* (US edition), February 21, 2002, p. 5.

CHAPTER 7

Who May We Bomb?

Barry Buzan

When war breaks out, who is a legitimate target?[1] The near-universal revulsion at the September 11 attacks shows that the civilians in the World Trade Center were not a legitimate target – even for those who oppose American power. The shift of the conflict to Afghanistan made the question of who may be bombed central to the legitimacy of the whole campaign against terrorism. Since the American war on terrorism is open-ended, the possibility of further American attacks on targets in Iraq, the Philippines, Somalia and Sudan, or in principle anywhere, remains on the agenda. The question 'Who may we bomb?' is not going to go away. This question can be fought over on both moral and legal grounds without any decisive answer resulting. But it is also a political and historical question, and it is that angle that I want to explore here. A political approach rests on the questions of how we (and by 'we' I mean the Western democracies) define who our enemies are, and what we are trying to achieve when we resort to war.

The idea that in war, peoples and their governments should be treated separately, has recently become something of a Western fetish, a way of asserting the West's claim to be civilized. In the war against Iraq, great efforts were made to avoid civilian casualties. Similarly, the air war against Serbia targeted the Milosevic regime and its supporting structures. The distinction between combatants and civilians has solid and valuable legal standing in the Geneva Conventions on the laws of war. But that distinction should not lead to the assumption, now becoming a centrepiece of the Western way in war, that all civilians are innocent and that only evil leaderships are the enemy. The Geneva Conventions are aimed at the protection of prisoners, the wounded and civilians, and they impose a range of restrictions on the conduct of war. But they do not outlaw war, nor do they solve the problem of how to distinguish between civilian and military actors.

The exclusion of civilians from definitions of 'enemy' contrasts markedly with the West's behaviour up until quite recently. During the Second World War there was far less concern to draw distinctions between peoples and governments, and both sides freely bombed each other's cities. The home front (production, logistics, conscription) was understood to be as much a part of the military enterprise as the fighting front. No clearer statement of the linkage between government and people could be made than the nuclear incinerations of Hiroshima and Nagasaki. The Cold War was more nuanced in its rhetoric, but much the same in its practice. The West made communism the enemy, rather than the Russian, the Chinese or the Korean people, but the nuclear arsenals would have obliterated their cities just the same. In Vietnam, as in all guerrilla wars, drawing a civilian–military distinction was extremely problematic. As Mao Tse-tung understood, the whole point of guerrilla strategy is to blend the fighters into a supportive population.[2] This blending bears some resemblance to the present dilemma about terrorists, who also hide in, and draw support from, civilian populations. The idea that one has to make war on terrorists, as opposed to dealing with them as criminals, is soberingly captured by the following remark attributed to Egyptian president Hosni Mubarak: 'Those who carry out terrorist acts have no claims to human rights.'[3] To understand wars, whether to fight them or to resolve them, it is vital to appreciate that they are conducted not just between groups of fighters, but between groups of fighters and their networks of support. The distinction between military and civilian has to be understood in that context.

Three factors have contributed to the West's new policy of separating bad governments from their peoples. The first hinges on advances in technology. Since the 1970s, and increasingly over the past decade, it has become possible to deliver warheads with great accuracy to a target. Precision weapons now provide choices about what is and what is not targeted that were not available in earlier wars. This does make a difference, but one side-effect of the 'revolution in military affairs' (RMA)[4] has been to establish unrealistic public expectations of precision in the use of force. Any collateral damage is used by Western critics, and even by target regimes, to cast moral doubt on military action.

The second factor is an evolution in public morality in the West, which at least since the abolition of slavery has been increasingly committed to the idea that all peoples have the right to equal and decent treatment. By combining its technology and its values, the West is able to project its values by injecting an element of law and humanitarianism into the bloody business of war.

Third, Western governments calculate that narrowing the definition of enemy to evil leaderships is in their interests. In the mosaic of historically rooted cultural conflicts that replaced the big ideological divisions of the Cold War, separating peoples from their leaderships during war has many advantages. It moderates charges of cultural imperialism, of one civilization (usually the West) trying to impose its values on others, and it invites the overthrow of tyrants from within, thus keeping open the option of a people remaking itself and gaining quick re-entry into international society. If people can be made to do some or all of the work of removing their bad governments, then the West's casualties are reduced and the legitimacy of both the action and its outcome are increased.

These technological, moral and instrumental explanations for the West's separation of peoples and governments suggest that it is both morally desirable and efficient. But before accepting this view, one needs to return to the questions about how enemies are defined and what wars are fought for. A useful way into the issues is to ask, 'Do people get the governments they deserve?' During the Second World War, the Western answer was broadly 'Yes.' This understanding legitimized mass destruction attacks and the forced remaking of Japan and Germany under occupation regimes.

During the Cold War there was much more ambivalence about the linkage of governments and peoples and a tendency to assume that many of the peoples in the Eastern bloc did not get the governments they deserved. The populations of Eastern Europe definitely, and that of the Soviet Union more arguably, could be seen as victims of a coup, and thus as prisoners of their own governments. It is this position that has now been extended to most post-Cold War conflicts. There are some exceptions – conspicuously in US attitudes towards the Islamic revolution in Iran – but from North Korea through to Burma, Iraq, Libya, Serbia, and most recently to Afghanistan, the West's policy separates bad governments from their peoples and constructs its military strategy accordingly. Doing so supposes that people do not deserve their governments. Is this true?

At one end of the spectrum stand well-rooted democracies with traditions of individual rights, a broad franchise and regular elections. In democracies the demos consequently shares some responsibility for the government's foreign policy, whether people bother to vote or not.

Citizens in democracies do deserve their governments. An extreme version of this link between people and government can be found in the Israel/Palestine confrontation. Arab radicals see no civilian sector in Israel. The Israelis have democracy, a large proportion of the Israeli adult population is in the military reserve and it is common for Israelis to carry, and use, guns. Israeli militants return the compliment by thinking of the Palestinians in much the same terms, as a people united in the pursuit of terrorism. War is cast as an affair between peoples.

Also easy to determine are the cases at the other end of the spectrum, most obviously when countries have their governments imposed by an outside power. In the present international system, this condition is rare, though it might be claimed by Tibetans, Kurds, Kashmiris and other minorities who find themselves prisoners within states not of their own making. Most recently, it was exemplified by Eastern Europe under Soviet occupation. It is true that occupiers are usually assisted by parts of the local population, as the British were in India and the Nazis were in Europe. But as a rule, peoples under occupation are not responsible for their governments.

The middle part of the spectrum is taken up by authoritarian governments of various sorts, which can be differentiated according to their degree of mass support. Just behind democracies come countries where mass revolutionary or nationalist regimes command wide support or acquiescence. These would include communist China, Vietnam, Cuba, Islamic Iran, Nazi Germany and Imperial Japan. Peoples in countries where the government has come to power through popular revolution, or has mass national support, do deserve the governments they get, and this explains the long political hangovers that still affect the Japanese and Germans in international society.

At the centre of the spectrum are countries with authoritarian regimes that command mass acquiescence rather than support. The commonest form of this is found in countries where military rule gains acceptance as a means of restoring stability. One thinks of cases such as Pakistan or, earlier, Nigeria, Brazil, Chile and Argentina. Acquiescence, of course, can be coerced, making the price of individual resistance high and allowing a minority who do support the government to rule over the rest. Such coercion is usually visible, allowing distinctions to be drawn between passive acceptance and terrorized obedience.

Toward the clearly undeserving end of the spectrum one finds blatant tyrannies such as in Burma, Iraq, Syria, Uganda under Amin, Haiti under the Duvaliers, and Zaire under Mobutu. The existence of repression may well be evident in its own right. It may also be shown when substantial sections of the population put up active resistance but fail to unseat the regime or secede from the state. Burma and Sudan are contemporary examples of such failed rebellions, as in some ways is Iraq.

This spectrum suggests a range of fairly clear answers to whether or not people deserve their governments. Yet there are cases where it is impossible to make a judgement. How can one tell whether the North Korean regime has mass support/acquiescence, or is just very efficient at repression and indoctrination? What does one do with split countries where the government is supported by one section of the population and opposed by another, as in Israel, Sudan, Sri Lanka, Turkey and, up to 1994, South Africa? Here one finds a combination of democracy for some of the population and repression for the rest. It would be difficult to argue that the Kurds in Turkey, the Palestinians in Israel or the southerners in Sudan get the governments they deserve.

Equally difficult questions arise about countries with strong structures of tribe and clan, such as Afghanistan, Congo, Libya, Somalia, Iraq, Indonesia and Saudi Arabia. In such places, the choice seems to be between dictatorship and chaotic political disintegration. In the case of Afghanistan, the US declared al-Qaeda and the Taliban to be the enemy. But how much support did the Taliban have amongst the population? They must have had some in order to take over most of the country as swiftly as they did, though they never eliminated armed opposition from the non-Pashtun areas. How much of that support represented real enthusiasm, and how much a simple desire to have any government in place of civil war? Democracy at the level of the state is almost impossible in places where the population is of multiple ethnicities/cultures and where there are no strong social structures shared by the people as a whole. If the state is not held together coercively, it falls apart. It is not clear, for example, that Libya or Iraq would end up with a different type of leadership than the ones they now have, if Gaddafi and Saddam Hussein were removed. In post-Taliban Afghanistan, this question is being put to the test. If it can be claimed that the social structures of a people lead with some certainty to dictatorship or anarchy, are the people who reproduce the cultures collectively responsible?

Culturalist approaches of this sort, or those that focus on ethnic or religious stereotypes, contain the danger of validating racial and xenophobic views, and of promoting 'clash of civilizations' thinking.[5] There is also the problem that any resort to such cultural generalizations has to be preceded by yet another question: what is the historical connection between people and the state they inhabit? In cases where the people have played a role in creating the state over time, the answer is clear. Swedes, Haitians, Egyptians, Iranians, Chinese, Japanese, Americans, French and many other peoples would accept a close identity between themselves and the states they inhabit. But there are many cases where this link is weak or non-existent, most obviously in post-colonial countries.[6] States such as Congo, Iraq, Jordan, Nigeria and Syria have shallow traditions and artificial borders. Since decolonization, they have been held in place by the system of diplomatic recognition that makes them members of international society. Some post-colonial states have taken root and acquired legitimacy, especially those that corresponded in some degree to pre-colonial history, such as India and Vietnam. Many have not. The peoples who live in Sudan, Angola, Indonesia, Chad or Guyana cannot be held responsible for the states they occupy. Where the state itself has failed to take root amongst its people, this often determines the type of government they get.

In sum, the question of whether people get the governments they deserve can often be answered quite simply on the basis of day-to-day observations about the relationship between the demos and the government. This type of observation cannot always give a reliable answer, but is more useful than either sweeping generalizations about culture or simple assumptions that all civilians are innocent.

This brings us back to the question of whether the current Western habit of separating peoples from their leaders makes for better or worse war policy. There can be no doubt that it constrains the sort of military pressure that can be brought to bear. It forces the West into the curious posture, first seen in the war against Iraq, of worrying almost as much about enemy casualties as about its own; and risks undermining support for action when – as is inevitable – civilians are killed by mistake. There is a self-justifying humanitarian argument for keeping casualties to a minimum, as well as the legal constraint of the Geneva Conventions. There is also the instrumental case that such an approach helps to reduce the costs of conflict and makes political rehabilitation easier. Where people do not deserve the government they get, separating the two as far as possible must be imperative in any war policy.

But what of cases where peoples do deserve their governments? Here the questions are trickier. The problem is that if people really do deserve their government, and yet only the government is targeted, the country as a whole remains politically unreconstructed and thus a continuing danger to itself and to the international community. The crushing defeat of both states and peoples in Germany and Japan in the Second World War was instrumental in converting those countries into liberal democracies able to fit comfortably into the international community of the West. The remaking of the two countries is rightly regarded as a huge success and played a big role in the victory of the West in the Cold War.

To take a more recent case, what should the Western response have been during the air war against Serbia when civilians stood on the bridges to prevent them being bombed? If they were there as a result of conspicuous coercion, then the bridges should not have been bombed. But if they were there as a demonstration of support for the Milosevic government then they made themselves legitimate targets. To delink people from their governments, when they are in fact closely linked, is to undermine the political point of resorting to war in the first place. In the end, war is about changing people's minds about what sort of government they want.

Looked at in this way of thinking, Afghanistan was a difficult case. It is not an arbitrary post-colonial construct, but neither is it a coherent self-made historical state. Afghan politics is typically fragmented and fractious, with many local chiefs commanding their own fighters. The Taliban certainly attracted many who actively backed it, but perhaps the bulk of its support was in the form of acquiescence, itself partly a result of effective coercion. During recent decades there was also a great deal of foreign intervention in Afghanistan's domestic politics, which, by changing the internal balance of power, played a major role in determining what sort of government the Afghans got, whether they wanted it or not. Pakistan's role in bringing the Taliban to power was only the latest in a long line of interventions both by Afghanistan's neighbours and by interested great powers. And in a warrior culture like Afghanistan's (or Somalia's), where most men are armed and fighting is a way of life, distinguishing soldiers from civilians is deeply problematic. The picture was thus very mixed. Some Afghans clearly did deserve the government they got, and demonstrated this by supporting its policies and fighting on its behalf. Those who did so made themselves legitimate military targets. Many did not support the Taliban, and demonstrated that by their opposition or by flight. Many were in the middle, acquiescing either out of indifference or fear. Since the Taliban chose to make Afghanistan a danger to international society by allying itself with terrorists, its supporters, and up to a point those who acquiesced, were legitimate military targets. Only by dismantling its concentric circles of support and acquiescence could the Taliban, or any government, be overthrown, and space be created for a government that was more acceptable both to international society and to the Afghan people as a whole. Given the foreign, including US, interventions in its

politics in the past, outsiders had a responsibility both to be quite selective in their violence, and to stay engaged in the process of building a
new Afghanistan.

Unlike in Serbia, and arguably also Iraq, the West got it about right
in Afghanistan. Those elements in the country that were enemies of the
West received the brunt of the war. Those that were not enemies were
spared to the extent feasible, given the limits of the technology and the
uncertainties about who was who. An interesting question that thank-
fully did not have to be answered was what the West should have done
if events had unfolded such that Pakistan had begun to fall apart, and
who might be in control of its nuclear weapons had come into doubt.
Given the unbounded extremism of al-Qaeda, and the close relationship between Pakistan's intelligence service and the Taliban, the West
would have had to make every effort to destroy Pakistan's nuclear
arsenal, including, if necessary the use of nuclear weapons.

Looking ahead, the open-ended character of the war against terrorism
poses several questions about who may be bombed. Given the unusual
character of this 'war', it may well not pose cases where questions about
peoples and governments are a key feature in shaping military action.
The main problem for the 'war against terrorism' will be the longstanding political ambiguity of 'terrorists' versus freedom fighters. If the
enemy is defined as anyone using extreme methods of violence then the
US will be dragged into endless domestic conflicts around the world. It
will find itself in alignment with a variety of unsavoury governments,
and without nearly all of its present coalition allies. If the war is against
al-Qaeda, and any similar outfits (call them international terrorists) that
have declared war on international society, then the campaign becomes
more manageable. The use of violence against the bases of such organizations, and against any political authorities who support or tolerate
them, would be politically legitimate.

Iraq, Somalia and Sudan have all been mooted as possible targets.
How to deal with them depends on how terrorism is defined. On the
narrow answer, these states only become targets if there is evidence that
they are complicit in international terrorism, or that they themselves
pose threats to international peace and security. The problem in
Somalia is not the Afghan one of a government and/or people
constructing itself as an enemy. Rather it is that Somalia has no
coherent government, and this political chaos can allow space for international terrorists to operate autonomously. Military strikes there
would have to be highly selective against the specific targets of international terrorism and their local supporters. Sudan appears to have

been cooperative against al-Qaeda, so the question of military action may well not arise. At the moment there is almost no evidence against Iraq, and since US motives in relation to Iraq are poisoned by other issues, the evidence necessary for the US to attack Iraq under the aegis of the war on terrorism would have to be extremely compelling for the action to acquire political legitimacy. In many places, including within the West, the operations of international terrorists will be hidden within the social framework, and not obviously the knowing responsibility of either governments or citizens. Here the problem is not one of military strategy but one of policing and surveillance, and how these are kept in balance with civil liberties. Between war and police action lie military assistance operations, such as the one in the Philippines, where assistance is given to governments to fight 'terrorists' within their own territory.

Pacifists and the more dedicated type of humanitarians will find these arguments about applied violence unacceptable in principle. A case can be made that the answer to 'Who may we bomb?' should be 'Nobody.' The argument made above is only for those who believe that war still has a role to play in a complex, interdependent and conflictual world, and that that role needs to be both carefully constrained and fully considered. The military strategy and the political logic of war require careful specification of who the enemy is. A blanket assumption that all civilians are innocent will often not be justified. Whether or not people deserve their governments can be a tough question, but answers to it have to be found if ideas about humanitarian intervention are ever to acquire intellectual and political coherence.[7] International society has the right to confront governments and peoples that pose unacceptable threats to peace. If force is going to be used against a country in pursuit of civilizational objectives, the question of citizen responsibility has to be answered before appropriate military strategies can be devised. If the people clearly do not deserve the government they get, then military strategy must be devised as far as possible to target only the state and its army – as has been the case in recent Western interventions. But if people do deserve the government they get, and if that government is in gross breach of standards of civilization, then, as in the Second World War, the war should be against both government and people.

Notes

1. An earlier version of this argument was presented in *Prospect* magazine, December 2001, pp. 38–41 (<www.prospect-magazine.co.uk>).

2. Mao Tse-tung, *On Guerrilla Warfare* (New York: Praeger, 1961).
3. *Economist*, February 2, 2002, p. 52.
4. Lawrence Freedman, 'The Revolution in Strategic Affairs', *Adelphi Paper 318*, London: IISS (1998).
5. Samuel P. Huntington, *The Clash of Civilizations and the Remaking of World Order* (New York: Simon and Schuster, 1996).
6. Bertrand Badie, *The Imported State: The Westernization of Political Order* (Stanford, CA: Stanford University Press, 2000).
7. James Mayall, *World Politics: Progress and Its Limits* (Cambridge: Polity Press, 2000); Nicholas J. Wheeler, *Saving Strangers: Humanitarian Intervention in International Society* (Oxford, Oxford University Press, 2000).

CHAPTER 8

Mr Bush's War on Terrorism: How Certain is the Outcome?

Immanuel Wallerstein

Shortly after the attack of September 11 by al-Qaeda against the Twin Towers in New York and the Pentagon, President Bush addressed the US Congress, declaring a 'war on terrorism' and saying, among other things, that 'its outcome is certain'. Is this true? I am writing this six months after this declaration.[1] What does the picture look like at this point?

The Tactics of the US Government

First, let us look at how the US government has defined its tactics. It seems to have decided that one of the causes of the attack was a wide-spread assumption of US decline and weakness. It followed, by this logic, that the best way to handle such an assumption (not only on the part of Osama bin Laden but on the part of many others, including allies) was to demonstrate that this was manifestly not true. And the way to demonstrate that this was not true was to exhibit the ferocity and effectiveness of US military (but also political) power, as a mode of intimidating any future attempts by forces hostile to the US to engage in such violent attacks on the lives, property and political interests of Americans, individually and collectively.

The US therefore announced as short-term objectives the toppling of the Taliban regime in Afghanistan, the capture of Osama bin Laden (and Mullah Omar) 'dead or alive', and the dismantling worldwide of the al-Qaeda network. As of now, we can see that the US did in fact topple, rather rapidly, the Taliban regime, just as it (via its collaborators, the Pakistani Inter-Services Intelligence) had earlier helped the Taliban topple, rather rapidly, the preceding warring Mujahideen factions. They have not yet captured either bin Laden or Mullah Omar, and it seems unlikely that they will in the near future (although one cannot rule out

95

this possibility). By its own admission, the US has not yet been able to dismantle al-Qaeda; it is not even sure that much of a dent has been inflicted on al-Qaeda's structure, although it is hard to tell since so much on both sides is shrouded in secrecy.

The 'hawks' in the US administration have argued that it is not at all sufficient to oust the Taliban, which they regard as a minor achievement in a secondary zone of the world. Their analysis is that part of the current problem comes from the fact that major opponents of the US had got away with too much too easily in the recent past. There were three notable instances of this, it is argued. In Iraq, the US never finished off the Gulf War. Saddam Hussein is still in power, still defying the UN's efforts to constrain him, and still continuing to augment his store of weapons of mass destruction. In Iran, the heirs of Ayatollah Khomeini, who had so humiliated the US in 1980, are still in power and still pursuing the same anti-US line and action (despite the growth of a strong 'moderate' faction symbolized by the current president of Iran). And the regime in North Korea is unrelenting in its internal Stalinism, its efforts to expand its own military strength and its willingness to aid in the proliferation of nuclear capacity in other countries. This was the origin and the justification of President Bush's 'axis of evil' speech[2] which in effect threatened military action against one or all of these three states. The strong negative reaction in Europe, Russia, South Korea and the Middle East to this speech led the US government to retreat slightly, in effect narrowing down its immediate war threat to Iraq only. This remains an active option as of this point.

The third task the United States assigned itself in the short run was to whip its allies (western Europe and Japan) into line, and to make sure that neither Russia nor China would oppose in any serious way its attempts to restore a US-defined order to the geopolitical arena. The US also apparently decided that it would not use persuasion to do this, but rather use a heavy hand. There were two reasons for this particular decision. First, the US was not at all sure that it could obtain its objectives *vis-à-vis* the allies, Russia and China, merely by persuasion. Second, persuasion seemed to the US government the road of weakness. The US seemed to consider that only by offering these countries an either–or choice ('you are with us, or against us') could they create a situation in which the US could establish a lasting geopolitical order on its own terms. Has this in fact worked?

The reaction to the 'axis of evil' speech and the way the US has handled this reaction makes clear the tactic. First of all, it should be noted that, since 1945, there has never been so strong a negative

European reaction to an announced US policy than after the 'axis of evil' speech. Not only the French, but the Germans, the Spaniards, the Swedes and even major British figures spoke out loudly and strongly in negative terms, describing the project as folly. Publicly, the US reaction to the criticism was disdainful. Secretary of State Colin Powell said that French Foreign Minister Hubert Vedrine was 'having the vapours'; and Vice-President Dick Cheney suggested that, after the huffing and puffing, the Europeans would fall into line. Privately, there has no doubt been a great deal of arm-twisting – and the Europeans have indeed quieted down. In fact, Tony Blair is now leading the softening-up campaign to prepare the world for an American attack on Iraq.

The Difficulties the US Faces

The US government is congratulating itself on the success of its strategy, and many relatively unsympathetic critics are grudgingly admitting that the US seems to be succeeding in getting its way. André Fontaine, France's sage in geopolitical analysis, wrote just such an article in *Le Monde*. Are there not then any negatives in the picture from the US government's point of view? Well, yes, there are two.

First, Israeli Prime Minister Ariel Sharon has taken advantage of the US war on terrorism to pursue an unusually aggressive policy designed to ensure that a Palestinian state will never come into existence. The result has been an escalation of violence that is only a hair's breadth away from all-out war. This threatens not only to be explosive and destructive, but also to hamper the operation that the US is planning in Iraq. Can the US dampen down the conflict? Probably not. The situation seems to be out of control, and the US is overcommitted to supporting Sharon: that is, it will no doubt remonstrate with him, but it is doubtful that it is ready to do what it takes to make him back down seriously and consider, for example, the Saudi initiative.

Second, there is the potential cost of implementing the war on Iraq. In 1991, the US did not march on Baghdad for a very simple reason: the US anticipated a very serious struggle, with a high cost in US lives as well as finances. The first President Bush (as well as large portions of the US military) did not relish the idea of a second Vietnam War, with its internal US consequences. And, if that were not reason enough, there was the fact that none of the surrounding countries (with the exception of Kuwait) wanted the US to march on Baghdad. They all feared that, if the US won, the resulting political situation in Iraq would be one that would be worse for them than having Saddam Hussein in power.

Have either of these two factors changed? There are some who argue
that the intervening decade has seen such an increase in US military
capacity that it would be easier to win a war without paying such a
devastating price. If this argument were so telling, there would not still
be so much internal debate within the US government, including
inside the Pentagon. As for the surrounding countries, none has
changed the views it held in 1991 about the potential negative consequences for them of such a war. And the far greater tensions in
Israel/Palestine over 1991 reinforce this sentiment.

On the other hand, President Bush is a politician in a country with
a closely divided electorate. The war on terrorism has certainly aided
him politically, and probably the Republican Party as a whole. His political advisers do not wish him to lose this advantage. They certainly
don't want to see anything that would, by showing failure or weakness,
push centrist voters back into the Democratic camp and alienate a part
of his right-wing supporters. This is a strong argument for following
through on his Iraq rhetoric.

Let us suppose that the fears about the fallout from a war on Iraq are
justified objectively, and that the fears of his political advisers are
equally justified. In this case, President Bush is up against an impossible
choice, for he would lose politically within the US whatever he did. Of
course, he could finesse this, by starting a war on Iraq circa October
2002. This would be too early for the negative reaction and just in time
for the positive feedback, and this might help the Republicans to win
the Congressional elections. But 2004, when Bush comes up for re-
election, would loom ahead – and he is haunted by the fate of his
father.

There is also the question of how long the Europeans will be so timid
(or perhaps the right word is 'intimidated'). Why are they so flabby?
First of all, a third to a half of their electorate is cheering on the US.
They share the Bush view that this is a war of the civilized against the
barbarians, and that only the US can man the barricades effectively. But
what about the others? They are increasingly uncomfortable with what
they see as the insufferable arrogance of the present US government.
And they have serious economic differences of interest with the US.
Above all, if they are to construct Europe – and most of these persons
wish to construct Europe – it must stand for something, politically and
culturally, and this inevitably means distinguishing it from the US.

Suppose they don't protest too much when the US goes into Iraq.
What will they be saying six months later, if there is a long, drawn-out
war? And if there begins to be an anti-war movement in the US, can the

European establishment afford to be far behind? It seems very dubious. And, if Europe begins to object, can Russia and China afford to be quiescent? The present US casual political dominance in the world system might disintegrate quite rapidly; as rapidly, perhaps, as the Taliban regime.

In addition, there is the question of the state of the world economy. The gurus make predictions in every direction. If, in fact, all goes up again, as Mr Bush is hoping and predicting, the economy disappears as an issue. For Bush, this would be a plus. But the economy needs only to stay uncertain, not to speak of a further world deflation, and the disorder is unleashed. One, two, many Argentinas might be the slogan. And protectionism will rear its ugly head. Indeed, it already has. The US tariffs on steel may be seen, in historical retrospect, as marking the end of the World Trade Organization era and the return to a trimodal system of protected spheres. Notice that Bush exempted Canada and Mexico from the tariffs. He targeted Europe in effect, and the Europeans are aware of this. This has economic motives but it also has political motives. It is not only that Bush thinks this will win some votes in crucial states within the US, but that it will hurt Europe and thereby teach Europe the lesson that it had better toe the line. The Europeans may be ready to swallow, at least for the moment, an attack on Iraq, but are they ready to swallow a decline in their own standards of living to improve the US situation? Again, this seems doubtful.

The basic problem with the Bush strategy is the audacious and very hard to believe assumption that the US can control all the crucial variables in a chaotic world situation. It is playing *va banque*. And the US is probably overplaying its hand. Neither Machiavelli nor Sun Tzu would have counselled this.

And, oh yes, the terrorists, against whom a war is being waged. Of course, one cannot conduct a war against terrorists. One can try to wipe them out, if one is strong enough. Given the loose and inclusive definition the US government is now giving the term 'terrorism', it seems highly improbable that this would be achieved. The British government never wiped out the IRA. The Spanish government has not wiped out ETA. The Israelis have not wiped out Hamas or Hezbollah. The Russians have not wiped out the Chechen rebels. The Colombians have not wiped out FARC. The Philippine government cannot even wipe out the small band of Abu Sayyaf. The apartheid government of South Africa could never dent the militarily feeble ANC. And of course, the Viet Minh defeated the US armed forces in all their might. The reason in each case is the degree of political support these groups have had locally, because they were seen locally as standing both for something and against something. If they lose that support, as did Sendero Luminoso, they can be wiped out. Otherwise, in the end, after endless bloodshed and horrors, there lies the road of negotiations and some form of compromise. Intolerable for Ariel Sharon and perhaps for George W. Bush, but it seems a lesson that might be drawn from history.

The outcome is, to say the least, quite uncertain.

Notes

1. This chapter was written in March 2002.
2. State of the Union Address, January 29, 2002.

CHAPTER 9

In Terrorem: Before and After 9/11[1]

James Der Derian

Before 9/11 and after 9/11: it is as if the history and future of international relations were disappeared by this temporal rift. Old rules of statecraft, diplomacy and warfare have been thrown out by terrorist and anti-terrorist alike, and in this interregnum – best described by Chris Patten, the last governor of Hong Kong and current European Union Commissioner for External Affairs, as one of 'unilateralist overdrive' – critical enquiry is threatened by a global *in terrorem*.[2]

Obviously, the sheer scale, scope and shock of the events themselves are partially to blame for the paucity as well as the poverty of the response by the field of International Relations. Perhaps we witness once again what happened at academic conferences after the fall of the Berlin Wall, when social scientists were reluctant to posit cause and effect from a single data point. Or perhaps something more is at work, a great deal more. After terrorist hijackers transformed three commercial jetliners into highly explosive kinetic weapons, toppled the Twin Towers of the World Trade Center, substantially damaged the Pentagon, killed over 3000 people and triggered a state of emergency – and before the dead are fully grieved, Osama bin Laden's head brought on a platter, justice perceived as done, and information no longer considered a subsidiary of war – there is very little about 9/11 that is *safe* to say. Unless one was firmly situated in a patriotic, ideological, or religious position (which at home and abroad drew uncomfortably close), it is intellectually difficult and even politically dangerous to assess the meaning of a conflict that phase-shifted with every news cycle, from 'Terror Attack' to 'America Fights Back'; from a 'crusade' to a 'counter-terror campaign'; from 'the first war of the twenty-first century' to a now familiar combination of humanitarian intervention and remote killing; from kinetic terror to bioterror; from the spectacle of war to a war of spectacles.

Under such conditions, I believe the task is to uncover what is *dangerous* to think and say. Or as Walter Benjamin put it best in an earlier interim of violence and uncertainty, 'in times of terror, when everyone is something of a conspirator, everybody will be in a situation where he has to play detective'.[3]

Detective work and some courage are needed because questions about the root causes or political intentions of the terrorist acts have been either silenced by charges of 'moral equivalency' or rendered moot by claims that the exceptional nature of the act placed it outside political discourse: explanation is identified as exoneration.[4] Reflecting the nature of the attacks, as well as the chaos and confusion which followed, the conventional boundaries of the infosphere expanded during the first week to include political, historical and ethical analysis by some voices not usually heard on primetime. However, as the flow of information became practically entropic, there was a willingness (as judged by the unholy trinity of polls, pols and programming) to accept as wisdom President Bush's early declaration that evil – which expanded from a person to a network to the now notorious 'axis of evil' – was to blame. From that moment, policy debate and political action downshifted to a simple declarative with an impossible performative: to eradicate evil. Binary narratives displaced any complex or critical analysis of what happened and why. Retribution required certainty, and certainty was produced as salve for the actually as well as symbolically injured.

More sophisticated analysts like Michael Ignatieff also downplayed the significance of social or political enquiry by declaiming the exceptionality of the act:

> What we are up against is apocalyptic nihilism. The nihilism of their means – the indifference to human costs – takes their actions not only out of the realm of politics, but even out of the realm of war itself. The apocalyptic nature of their goals makes it absurd to believe they are making political demands at all. They are seeking the violent transformation of an irremediably sinful and unjust world. Terror does not express a politics, but a metaphysics, a desire to give ultimate meaning to time and history through ever-escalating acts of violence which culminate in a final battle between good and evil.[5]

By funnelling the experience through the image of American exceptionalism, 9/11 quickly took on an *exceptional ahistoricity*. For the most part, history was only invoked – mainly in the sepia tones of the

Second World War – to prepare the US for the sacrifice and suffering that lay ahead. The influential conservative George Will wrote that there were now only two time zones left for the United States:

> America, whose birth was mid-wived by a war and whose history has been punctuated by many more, is the bearer of great responsibilities and the focus of myriad resentments. Which is why for America, there are only two kinds of years, the war years and the interwar years.[6]

Under such forced circumstances, of being beyond experience, outside of history and between wars, 9/11 does not easily yield to philosophical, political or social enquiry. The best one can do is to thickly describe, robustly interrogate and directly challenge the authorized truths and official actions of all parties who posit a world view of absolute differences in need of final solutions. I do so here by first challenging the now common assumption that 9/11 is an exceptional event beyond history and theory, especially those theories tainted, as Edward Rothstein claimed in the *New York Times*, by 'postmodernism' and 'post-colonialism'.[7] Second, I examine the representations, technologies and strategies of network wars that have eluded mainstream journalism and traditional social science. I conclude by uncovering what I consider to be the main dangers that emerged from the counter/terror of 9/11.

An Exceptional Act?

On the question of exceptionalism, consider a few testimonials; the first from an editorial in the *New York Times*:

> If the attack against the World Trade Center proves anything it is that our offices, factories, transportation and communication networks and infrastructures are relatively vulnerable to skilled terrorists ... Among the rewards for our attempts to provide the leadership needed in a fragmented, crisis-prone world will be as yet unimagined terrorists and other socio-paths determined to settle scores with us.[8]

Another from a cover story of *Newsweek*:

> The explosion shook more than the building: it rattled the smug illusion that Americans were immune, somehow, to the plague of terrorism that torments so many countries.[9]

And finally, one from the *Sunday Times*:

> He began the day as a clerk working for the Dean Witter brokerage
> on the 74th floor of the World Trade Center in New York and ended
> it as an extra in a real-life sequel to *Towering Inferno* ...[10]

It might surprise some to learn that these are all quotes taken from 1993, the first and much less deadly terrorist attack on the World Trade Center. They are presented here as a caution, against reading terrorism only in the light – the often-blinding light – of the events of September 11. Obviously the two WTC events differ in the scale of the devastation as well as the nature of the attack. 9/11 defied the public imagination of the real – not to mention, as just about every public official and media authority is loath to admit, the official imagination and pre-emptive capacity of the intelligence community, federal law enforcement, airport security, military and other governmental agencies. Shock and surprise produced an immediate and nearly uniform reading of the event that was limited in official discourse to condemnation, retribution and counter-terror. But there is a professional as well as a public responsibility to place 9/11 in a historical context and interpretive field that reaches beyond the immediacy of personal tragedy and official injury. Otherwise 9/11 will be remembered not for the attack itself but for the increasing cycles of violence that follow.

If 9/11 is not wholly new, what is it? As we have seen too well, the official response was a struggle of evil against good – of which, given the rhetorical excess deemed necessary by our leaders to mobilize the public to action, there have been more than a few cases in American history. As an actual practice of warfare we again received a better picture of what 9/11 is not than what it is: from the President and Secretary of Defense and on down the food chain of the national security hierarchy, we heard that this would not be the Gulf War or Kosovo, and it most definitely would not be Vietnam or Mogadishu. And they were partially right – certainly more so than commentators from the kneejerk factions of both the right and left, who flooded the airwaves with sloppy historical analogies from the Second World War (Pearl Harbor and the Reichstag fire being most prominent) and convergent conspiracy theories (the Israeli Mossad and Big Oil pulling all the strings).

From my perspective, new and old forms of representation and violence synergized on 9/11. The neo-medieval rhetoric of holy war reverberated from the minaret to the television and, at an unprecedented level, to the internet. A hypermodern war of simulation and surveillance was played out at flight schools, airports and in practically every nook, cranny and cave of Afghanistan. A remote aerial war was directed from Central Command in Tampa, Florida, 7750 miles away from targets that were surveyed by drone aircraft like the Predator and Global Hawk, and destroyed by smart GPS-guided JDAMs (Joint Direct Attack Munitions with a circular error probability of about 10 feet), CBU-87 and CBU-103 'cluster bombs' (Combined Effects Munitions containing over 200 bomblets that have anti-tank, anti-personnel as well as an incendiary capability), and dumb bombs, topped by the 15,000 pound 'Daisy-cutter' (BLU-82) that explodes 3 feet above the ground and incinerates anything within 600 yards. And in a dirty war of blood and bluff, special operations forces led an anti-Taliban coalition in a limited and, by early reports, highly successful land campaign.

This strange new hybrid of conflict fully qualifies, perverse as it might sound, as a *virtuous war*. Post-Vietnam, post-Cold War, post-modern, virtuous war emerged prior to 9/11, from the battlespace of the Gulf War and the aerial campaigns of Bosnia and Kosovo in which the killing was kept, as much as it was technologically and ethically possible, virtual and virtuous. Virtuous war relies on computer simulation, media manipulation, global surveillance and networked warfare to deter, discipline and, if need be, destroy potential enemies. It draws on just war doctrine (when possible) and holy war (when necessary). Post-9/11, virtuous war now looks to be the ultimate means by which the US intends to re-secure its borders, maintain its hegemony and bring a modicum of order if not justice back to international politics. The difference from pre-9/11 is that the virtual enemy – at least at home – now comes with a face (indeed, 22 faces; all of them displayed on the FBI's new website of most-wanted terrorists[11]).

In the name of the holy trinity of international order – global free markets, democratic sovereign states and limited humanitarian interventions – the US has led the way in a revolution in military affairs (RMA) which underlies virtuous war. At the heart as well as the muscle of this transformation is the technical capability and ethical imperative to threaten and, if necessary, actualize violence from a distance – but again, with minimal casualties when possible.

This is not to claim that people do not die in virtuous wars, but rather that new technologies of killing skew the casualty rates, both off and on the battlefield. In the 9/11 attack, 19 terrorist hijackers killed over 3000 people in the United States. By the end of January, 20 American military personnel were killed overseas in the line of duty, the majority of whom died in accidents or by friendly fire: only one soldier, Sergeant First Class Nathan Chapman, was actually killed by hostile fire.[12] As was the case in the Kosovo campaign, more journalists *covering* the war were killed by hostile fire (ten by the end of January) than American military fighting the war. The high incidence of friendly-fire deaths (as well as ratio to hostile fire deaths) reflects the increased lethality of precision munitions when they are mistargeted: three members of the US Army 5th Special Forces Group team were killed and 19 soldiers wounded after they mistakenly gave their own geocoordinates for satellite-guided JDAMs. It also reflects a 'low risk, low yield' military strategy that some see as a lingering legacy of the 'Vietnam Syndrome' (the erosion of public support if body bags come home in high numbers) which resurfaced at the beginning and then was declared 'kicked' at the end of the Gulf War by the first President Bush in 1991.[13] On the other side of virtuous war, enemy casualties are increasingly hard to come by. As the war was winding down in December, estimates of enemy combatant deaths ranged wildly, from 3000 to 10,000. And when a lone economics professor, Marc Herold at the University of New Hampshire, researched the number of Afghan non-combatant casualties at 3767, a maelstrom of controversy erupted.[14]

Network Wars

From the start, it was apparent that 9/11 was and would continue to be a war of networks. Whether terrorist, internet or primetime, most of the networks were linked by a push/pull propagation of violence, fear and dis/mis/information. For a prolonged moment, in the first week of confusion and chaos where there was no detached point of observation, these networks seemed almost neurally attached, immersing viewers in a 24/7 cycle of tragic images of destruction and loss. A national state of emergency and trauma reached into all levels of society. It was as if the American political culture experienced a collective Freudian trauma, which could be re-enacted (endlessly on cable and the internet) but not understood at the moment of shock. And in a state of emergency, as in war, the first images stick. There was an initial attempt by the media to transform these images of horror into responsible discourses of reflection and action, but the blame game kicked in with a fury. Moving at the speed of the news cycle and in the rush to judgement, there was little time for deliberation, for understanding the motivations of the attackers, or for assessing the potential consequences, intended as well as unintended, of a military response.

It quickly became apparent that the war networks were not merely nodes connected by wiring of one sort of another. They conveyed, mimicked and in some cases generated human attributes and intentions, as suggested by *Wired* founding editor Kevin Kelly, who defined a network as 'organic behavior in a technological matrix'. But 9/11 knocked akilter this always problematical relationship between meat and wire. Technologically driven events outpaced organic modes of comprehension, and human actions, whether out of trauma or information overload, seemed increasingly to resemble machinic reflexes. Indeed, the first reaction by most onlookers and television reporters was to deem the event an accident. The attack on the second tower destroyed the accidental thesis, and also, it seemed, our ability to map cognitively the devastating aftermath. Instead, into the void left by the collapse of the WTC towers and the absence of detached analysis, there rushed a host of metaphors, analogies and metonyms, dominated by denial ('It's a movie'), history ('It's Pearl Harbor') and non-specific horror ('It's the end of the world as we have known it').

In our public culture, the media networks rather than the family, the community or the government provide the first and, by its very speed and pervasiveness, most powerful response to a crisis. Questions of utility, responsibility and accountability inevitably arose, and as one would expect, the media's pull-down menu was not mapped for the twin-towered collapse of American invulnerability. Primetime networks did their best (Peter Jennings of ABC better than the rest) to keep up with the real-time crises. But fear, white noise and technical glitches kept intruding, creating a cognitive lag so profound between event and interpretation that I wondered if superstring theory had not been proven right, that one of the ten other dimensions that make up the universe had suddenly intruded upon our own, formerly ordered, one, exposing the chaos beneath.

Indeed, after the looped footage of the collapse of the towers began to take on the feeling of *déjà vu*, I seriously wondered if the reality principle, as in nothing so much as *The Matrix,* had not taken a fatal blow. Like Ignatieff, I discerned a nihilism at work, but of a different kind, of the sort vividly on display in the movie. It first appears when some punky-looking customers in search of bootleg virtual reality software come to see Neo, the protagonist played by Keanu Reeves. He pulls from a shelf a green leather-bound book, the title of which is briefly identifiable as Jean Baudrillard's *Simulacra and Simulation*. When he opens the hollowed-out book to retrieve the software, the first page of the last chapter appears: 'On Nihilism'. Clearly a homage by the two directors, the Wachowski brothers, it all happens very quickly; too quickly to read the original words of Baudrillard, but here they are:

> Nihilism no longer wears the dark, Wagnerian, Spenglerian, fuliginous colors of the end of the century. It no longer comes from a Weltanschauung of decadence nor from a metaphysical radicality born of the death of God and of all the consequences that must be taken from this death. Today's nihilism is one of transparency, this irresolution is indissolubly that of the system, and that of all the theory that still pretends to analyze it.[15]

With the toppling of the WTC a core belief was destroyed: it could not happen here. Into this void the networks rushed, to provide transparency without depth, a simulacrum of horror, a much purer form of nihilism than imagined by moralist commentators like Ignatieff or Rothstein. In official circles, there was a concerted effort to fence off the void: the critical use of language, imagination, even humour, was tightly delimited by moral sanctions and government warnings. This first strike against critical thought took the peculiar form of a semantic debate over the meaning of 'coward'. In the *New Yorker* and on *Politically Incorrect,* the question was raised of whether it is more cowardly to commandeer a commercial airliner and pilot it into the World Trade Center, to bomb Serbians from 15,000 feet, or to direct a cruise missile attack against bin Laden from several thousand miles away. The official response was swift, with advertisements yanked, talk show condemnations, and Ari Fleischer, White House Press Secretary, saying that people like Bill Mahar of *Politically Incorrect* 'should watch what they say, watch what they do'.

Other protected zones of language began to take shape. When Reuters news agency questioned the abuse-into-meaningless of the term 'terrorism', George Will, on a Sunday morning news programme, retaliated by advocating a boycott of Reuters.[16] Irony and laughter were permitted in some places, not in others. At a Defense Department press conference Secretary of Defense Rumsfeld could ridicule, and effectively disarm, a reporter who dared to ask if anyone in the Department of Defense would be authorized to lie to the news media.[17] President Bush was given room to joke in a morale-boosting visit to the CIA, saying that he had been 'spending a lot of quality time lately' with George Tenet, the director of the CIA.[18] And then there was *New York Times* reporter Edward Rothstein, taking his opportunistic shot at postmodernists and post-colonialists, claiming that their irony and relativism was 'ethically perverse' and produced a 'guilty passivity'.[19]

Some of us were left wondering where that view would place fervent truth-seekers and serious enemies of relativism and irony like Osama bin Laden: terrorist foe but epistemological ally?

The Mimetic War of Images

The air war started on October 7, 2001, with a split-screen war of images: in one box, a desolate Kabul seen through a nightscope camera lens, in grainy-green pixels except for the occasional white arc of anti-aircraft fire followed by the flash of an explosion; in the other, a rotating cast of characters, beginning with President Bush, followed over the course of that day and the next by Secretary of Defense Rumsfeld, Chairman of the Joint Chiefs General Meyers and Attorney-General John Ashcroft, then progressively down the media food chain of war reporters, beltway pundits and recently retired generals. On the one side we witnessed images of embodied resolve in high resolution; on the other, nighttime shadows with nobody in sight.

Strategic and narrative binaries cropped up in President Bush's war statement, incongruously delivered from the Treaty Room of the White House: 'as we strike military targets, we will also drop food'; the United States is 'a friend to the Afghan people' and 'an enemy of those who aid terrorists'; 'the only way to pursue peace is to pursue those who threaten it'. And once more, the ultimate either/or was issued: 'Every nation has a choice to make. In this conflict there is no neutral ground.'[20]

However, the war programming was interrupted by the media-savvy bin Laden. Shortly after the air strikes began, he appeared on Qatar's al-Jazeera television network ('the Arab world's CNN') in a pre-taped statement that was cannily delivered as a counter air-strike to the US. Kitted out in turban and battle fatigues, bin Laden presented his own bipolar view of the world: 'These events have divided the world into two camps, the camp of the faithful and the camp of infidels.' But if opposition constituted his world view, it was a historical mimic battle that sanctioned the counter-violence: 'America has been filled with horror from north to south and east to west, and thanks be to God what America is tasting now is only a copy of what we have tasted.'[21]

Without falling into the trap of 'moral equivalency', one can discern striking similarities. Secretary of Defense Rumsfeld and others have made much of the 'asymmetrical' war being waged by the terrorists. And it is indeed a canny and even diabolical use of asymmetrical tactics as well as strategies when terrorists commandeer commercial aircraft and transform them into kinetic weapons of indiscriminate violence –

and then deploy commercial media to counter the military strikes that follow. Yet a fearful symmetry is also at work at an unconscious, possibly pathological level; a war of escalating and competing and imitative oppositions, a *mimetic war of images*.

A mimetic war is a battle of imitation and representation, in which the relationship of who we are and who they are is played out along a wide spectrum of familiarity and friendliness, indifference and tolerance, estrangement and hostility. It can result in appreciation or denigration, accommodation or separation, assimilation or extermination. It draws physical boundaries between peoples, as well as metaphysical boundaries between life and the most radical other of life, death. It separates human from god. It builds the fence that makes good neighbours; it builds the wall that confines a whole people. And it sanctions just about every kind of violence. President Bush announces that Iran is now part of the 'axis of evil'; Iran complies by staging the first large-scale anti-American demonstration since the moderate Khatami regime came to power.

More than a rational calculation of interests takes us to war. People go to war because of how they see, perceive, picture, imagine and speak of others; that is, how they construct the difference of others as well as the sameness of themselves through representations. From Greek tragedy and Roman gladiatorial spectacles to futurist art and fascist rallies, the mimetic mix of image and violence has proven to be more powerful than the most rational discourse. Indeed, the medical definition of mimesis is 'the appearance, often caused by hysteria, of symptoms of a disease not actually present'. Before one can find a cure, one must study the symptoms – or, as it was once known in medical science, practise *semiology*.

MIME-NET

It was not long before morbid symptoms began to surface from an array of terror and counter-terror networks. Al-Qaeda members reportedly used encrypted email to communicate; steganography to hide encoded messages in web images (including pornography); Kinko's and public library computers to send messages; underground banking networks called *hawala* to transfer untraceable funds; 24/7 cable networks like al-Jazeera and CNN to get the word out; and, in their preparations for 9/11, a host of other information technologies like rented cell phones, online travel agencies, and flight simulators.

In general, networks – from television primetime to internet real-time – delivered events with an alacrity and celerity that left not only viewers but also decision makers racing to keep up. With information as the life-blood and speed as the killer variable of networks, getting inside the decision making as well the image making loop of the opponent became the central strategy of network warfare. This was not lost on the American national security team as it struggled after the initial attack to get ahead of the network curve. Sluggish reactions were followed by quicker pre-emptive actions on multiple networks. Congress passed the 'Uniting and Strengthening America by Providing Appropriate Tools Required to Intercept and Obstruct Terrorism (USA PATRIOT) Act', which allowed for 'roving wiretaps' of multiple telephones, easier surveillance of email and internet traffic, more sharing between foreign and domestic intelligence, and the divulgence of grand jury and wiretap transcripts to intelligence agencies.[22] National Security adviser Condoleeza Rice made personal calls to heads of the television networks, asking them to pre-screen and to consider editing al-Qaeda videos for possible coded messages.[23] Information about the air campaign as well as the unfolding ground interventions was heavily filtered by the Pentagon, which set up an 'Office of Strategic Influence' to correct unfavourable news reports and, supposedly, to plant favourable ones in the foreign press. Open information flows slowed to a trickle from the White House and the Defense Department after tough restrictions were imposed against leaks. Psychological operations were piggy-backed on to humanitarian inter-ventions by the dropping of propaganda leaflets and food packs. The Voice of America began broadcasting anti-Taliban messages in Pashto. After the 22 'Most Wanted Terrorists' were featured on the FBI's website, the popular TV programme *America's Most Wanted* ran an extended programme on their individual cases. The infowar was on.

Some of the most powerful networks are often the least visible, but it was hard to keep a secret when Hollywood was added to the mix. The entertainment industry journal *Variety* first broke the news about a meeting between White House officials and Hollywood executives. The stated intention was ominous enough, to 'enlist Hollywood in the war effort':

> The White House is asking Hollywood to rally round the flag in a style reminiscent of the early days of World War II. Network heads and studio chiefs heard that message Wednesday in a closed-door meeting with emissaries from the Bush administration in Beverly Hills, and committed themselves to new initiatives in support of the war on terrorism. These initiatives would stress efforts to enhance the perception of America around the world, to 'get out the message'

on the fight against terrorism and to mobilize existing resources, such as satellites and cable, to foster better global understanding.[24]

Although some big media picked up this aspect of the story, none except for *Newsweek* took note of an earlier meeting organized by the military and the University of Southern California's Institute for Creative Technology.[25] I knew about the ICT because I had covered its opening for *Wired* and *The Nation* back in1999, when the army ponied up $43 million to bring together the simulation talents of Hollywood, Silicon Valley and the US military.[26] Now it seemed that they were gathering top talent to help coordinate a new virtual war effort:

> In a reversal of roles, government intelligence specialists have been secretly soliciting terrorist scenarios from top Hollywood filmmakers and writers. A unique ad hoc working group convened at USC just last week at the behest of the US Army. The goal was to brainstorm about possible terrorist targets and schemes in America and to offer solutions to those threats, in light of the twin assaults on the Pentagon and the World Trade Center. Among those in the working group based at USC's Institute for Creative Technology are those with obvious connections to the terrorist pic milieu, like 'Die Hard' screenwriter Steven E. De Souza, TV writer David Engelbach ('MacGyver') and Joseph Zito, who directed the features 'Delta Force One,' 'Missing in Action' and 'The Abduction.' But the list also includes more mainstream suspense helmers like David Fincher ('Fight Club'), Spike Jonze ('Being John Malkovich'), Randal Kleiser ('Grease') and Mary Lambert ('The In Crowd') as well as feature screenwriters Paul De Meo and Danny Bilson ('The Rocketeer').[27]

It would appear that 9/11 christened a new network: the military-industrial-media-entertainment network (MIME-NET). If Vietnam was a war waged in the living rooms of the United States, the first and most likely the last battles of the counter/terror war are going to be waged on global networks that reach much more widely and deeply into our everyday lives.

Counter/Terror Dangers

Terror came to America on 9/11 not by rogue state or ballistic missile or high-tech biological, chemical and nuclear weapons of mass destruction – as presaged by the intelligence and national security experts – but by an unholy network, hijacked airliners and the terrorist's favourite 'force-multiplier', primetime, cable and internet weapons of mass distraction and disruption. Have we learned the right lessons since then? Or will the 'evil' regimes, missiles and high-tech create more blindspots from which new threats will emerge with devastating effects? What lies ahead?

My greatest concern is not so much the future as how past futures become reproduced; that is, how we seem unable to escape the feedback loops of bad intelligence, bureaucratic thinking and failed imagination. From my own experience, when confronted by the complexity and speed of networked conflicts, the fields of political science and international relations are too slow to respond when it matters most. This leaves another intellectual void into which policy makers, military planners and media pundits are always ready to rush. Currently the RMA-mantra among the techno-optimists in the Pentagon is to swiftly implement 'network-centric warfare'. As first formulated by Vice Admiral Arthur Cebrowski (formerly President of the Naval War College and hand-picked by Defense Secretary Rumsfeld to head the Pentagon's new Office of Force Transformation), network-centric war is fought by getting inside the decision making loop of the adversary's network and disrupting or destroying it before it can do the same to yours. The basic idea is that people make war as they make wealth, and, in the information age, networked technology has become the enabler of both (probably not a view currently shared by Enron stockholders). Information and speed are now the key variables in warfare: whoever has the fastest network wins.

I interviewed Cebrowski about network war while he was still President of the Naval War College. He came across as very smart, highly articulate, deeply religious and quirky.[28] His comments were laced with quotes from an unusual cast of characters, such as former head of Disney's Imagineering, Bran Ferren ('The advent of interconnectivity is comparable to the advent of fire'), and Executive Editor of *Wired*, Kevin Kelly ('The first thing you need for innovation is a well-nurtured network'). In light of 9/11, one answer stood out from the rest. I asked him about the implications of network wars, where the goal is always to be faster than the opponent: Would this not squeeze out deliberation time? Did he really want machine-time to replace human-time? He replied, 'As soon as you can.' The goal was 'to relieve humanity of a lower level decision making process'.

The shift from state-centric to network-centric modes of deterring and defeating new threats makes sense within a rational framework.

However, diminishing the role of human decisions, *especially* ones in which emotion plays such a significant part, might not be the best way to confront future threats of terrorism. Furthermore, after the Pentagon released the bin Laden home video in December, where dreams and theology mix with strategies of destruction and slaughter, there was little evidence of any kind of rational purchase for a network-centric deterrence to work.[29] And after witnessing that same day the revival of missile defence as the *deus ex machina* cure for American vulnerability, the consignment of 'lower levels of decision making' to networked technology seems practically (rather than as it had been in the past, mutually) suicidal.

It is clear that the allure of technological solutions reaches across cultures and often beyond rationality. Bandwidth as well as bombs might offer short-term fixes for the immediate threats posed by terrorism. But no matter how weak the flesh, neural networks, human spirit and political will are still needed to make the future safe again. In the rush to harden and to accelerate networks, all kinds of checks and balances are being left behind. There seems to be little concern for what organizational theorists see as the negative synergy operating in tightly coupled systems, in which unintended consequences produce cascading effects and normal accidents, in which the very complexity and supposed redundancy of the network produce unforeseen but built-in disasters. Think Three Mile Island in a pre-1914 diplomatic-military milieu. Think Pentagon *and* Enron when Paul Virilio writes of the 'integral accident':

> The proliferation of atomic weapons, freshly boosted by India, Pakistan and probably other destabilized countries on the Asian continent, is prompting the United States – the last great world power – to accelerate the famous 'revolution in military affairs' by developing that emergent strategy known as 'information war', which consists in using electronics as a hegemonic technology: a role it now takes over from nuclear physics ... It is in this context of financial instability and military uncertainty, in which it is impossible to differentiate between information and disinformation, that the question of the *integral accident* arises once again ...[30]

My second concern is as much political as it is theoretical: are the social sciences intrinsically unsuited for the kind of investigation demanded by the emergence of a military-industrial-media-entertainment network? President Eisenhower in his 1961 farewell address famously warned the US of the emergence of a 'military-industrial complex', and of what might happen should 'public policy be captured by a scientific and technological elite'. Now that Silicon Valley and Hollywood have been added to the mix, the dangers have morphed and multiplied. Think *Wag the Dog* meets *The Matrix*. Think of C. Wright Mills' power elite with much better gear to reproduce reality:

> The media provide much information and news about what is happening in the world, but they do not often enable the listener or the viewer truly to connect his daily life with these larger realities. On the contrary, they distract him and obscure his chance to understand himself or his world, by fastening his attention upon artificial frenzies that are resolved within the program framework, usually by violent action or by what is called humor ... There is almost always the general tone of animated distraction, of suspended agitation, but it is going nowhere and it has nowhere to go.[31]

So, for the near future, virtuous war as played out by the military-industrial-media-entertainment network will be our daily bread and nightly circus. Some would see us staying there, suspended perpetually, in between wars of terror and counter-terror. How do we break out of the distractive, often self-prophesying circles? Are there theoretical approaches that can respond critically without falling into the trap of the interwar? One that can escape the nullity of thought which equates the desire to comprehend with a willingness to condone terrorism? The use of sloppy analogies of resistance as well as petty infighting among critics does not give one much hope. We need to acknowledge that the majority of Americans, whether out of patriotism, trauma, apathy or sheer reasonableness, think it best to leave matters in the hands of the experts. That will not change, the cycle will not be broken, until a public rather than expert assessment is made of what distinguishes new from old dangers, real from virtual effects, terror from counter-terror – and whether we are then ready to live with new levels of uncertainty about those very distinctions.

Otherwise, the last word might well come from the first words I heard of the last war the US fought. Circling ten years ago over Chicago O'Hare airport, the captain came on the PA to inform us that the bombing of Iraq had just begun. In the taxi on the way to my hotel, I heard the first radio reports of stealth aircraft, smart bombs and incredibly low casualty rates. But what stuck from that evening were the last and only words of my cab driver. In the thickest Russian accent, in a terribly war-weary voice, without the benefit of any context but the overexcitement of the radio reports, he said: 'They told us we would be in Afghanistan for ten weeks. We were there for ten years.'

Notes

1. This chapter draws from earlier postings at <www.infopeace.org>, <http://www.ssrc.org/sept11/essays/der_derian.htm> and <http://muse.jhu.edu/journals/theory_&_event/>.
2. '*in terrorem*, as a warning, in order to terrify or deter others' (*Oxford English Dictionary*).
3. Walter Benjamin, *A Lyric Poet in the Era of High Capitalism* (London: Verso, 1997).
4. For an earlier discussion of the ideological, epistemological and ontological obstacles facing any enquiry into terrorism, see my 'The Terrorist Discourse: Signs, States, and Systems of Global Political Violence', *Antidiplomacy: Spies, Terror, Speed, and War* (Cambridge, MA, and Oxford: Blackwell, 1992), pp. 92–126.
5. Michael Ignatieff, 'It's War – But it Doesn't Have to be Dirty', *Guardian*, October 1, 2001.
6. George Will, 'On the Health of the State', *Newsweek*, October 1, 2001, p. 70.
7. Edward Rothstein, 'Attacks on US Challenge the Perspectives of Postmodern True Believers', *New York Times*, September 22, 2001, p. A17.
8. Mark Edington, *New York Times*, March 2, 1993.
9. *Newsweek*, March 8, 1993, p. 22.
10. *Sunday Times*, February 28, 1993, p. 10.
11. See <http://www.fbi.gov/mostwant/terrorists/fugitives.htm>.
12. See <http://abcnews.go.com/sections/us/DailyNews/STRIKE_Casualties.html>, and *New York Times*, February 9, 2002, p. A7.
13. By comparison, 35 of 148 US troops killed in action in the Gulf War were hit by US fire, with 11 killed by accidental US air strikes; and of 467 US military personnel wounded, 72 were hit by friendly fire.
14. See <http://www.media-alliance.org/mediafile/20-5/dossier/herold12-6.html>. On the difficulty of assessing civilian casualties in Afghanistan, see http://www.washingtonpost.com/ac2/wp-dyn?pagename=article&node= &contentId=A59457-2002Jan3 and <http://www.arizonarepublic.com/news/articles/0125attacks-civilian25.html>. More recently, the Project on Defense Alternatives, using mainly media sources, has put the number of Afghanistan civilian casualties at between 1000 and 1300. See 'Uncertain Toll in the Fog of War: Civilian Deaths in Afghanistan', *New York Times*, February 10, 2002, p. A1.
15. Jean Baudrillard, *Simulacra and Simulation*, trans. Sheila Glaser (Ann Arbor, MI: University of Michigan Press, 1994), p. 159.
16. *ABC Sunday News*, September 30, 2001.
17. See <http://www.defenselink.mil/news/Sep2001/t09252001_t0925sd.html>.

18. See <http://www.washingtonpost.com/wp-srv/nation/specials/attacked/transcripts/bushtext_092601.html>.

19. See *New York Times*, September 22, 2001 (<http://query.nytimes.com/search/abstract?res=FA091FF6355F0C718EDDA00894D9404482>).

20. See <http://www.whitehouse.gov/news/releases/2001/10/20011007-8.html>.

21. See <http://www.cnn.com/2002/US/01/31/gen.binladen.interview/index.html>.

22. See <http://www.eff.org/Privacy/Surveillance/Terrorism_militias/20011025_hr3162_usa_patriot_bill.html>.

23. In a videotape interview with the Arabic cable network, al-Jazeera (which they never aired but was partially seen on January 31 on CNN), bin Laden displayed his affinity for information technology while scoffing at the White House 'request' that American television networks not broadcast his statements: 'They made hilarious claims. They said that Osama's messages have codes in them to the terrorists. It's as if we were living in the time of mail by carrier pigeon, when there are no phones, no travelers, no Internet, no regular mail, no express mail and no electronic mail.' See <http://www.washingtonpost.com/wp-dyn/articles/A5371-2002Jan31.html>.

24. See *Washington Post*, September 26, 2001 (<http://www.variety.com/index.asp?layout=story&articleid=VR1117854476&categoryid=10&query=H%27wood+enlists+in+war>).

25. Disclaimer: I provided the information to them. See <http://www.msnbc.com/news/642434.asp>.

26. See my 'Virtuous War Goes to Hollywood', *Virtuous War: Mapping the Military-Industrial-Media-Entertainment Network* (Boulder, CO, and Oxford: Westview Press/Perseus, 2001), pp. 153–78.

27. See <http://www.variety.com/index.asp?layout=story&articleid=VR1117853841&categoryid=10&query=Institute+for+Creative+Technology>.

28. See my *Virtuous War*, pp. 123–51.

29. See <http://www.defenselink.mil/news/Dec2001/b12132001_bt630-01.html>.

30. Paul Virilio, *The Information Bomb*, trans. Chris Turner (London and New York: Verso, 2000), p. 132.

31. C. Wright Mills, *The Power Elite* (New York: Oxford University Press, 1957), pp. 314–15.

CHAPTER 10

Terror and the Future of International Law

Michael Byers

The United States government wields more power than any regime since the Roman Empire. With 12 aircraft carriers, the only significant heavy air-lift capacity and the only major stocks of precision-guided missiles and bombs, it can defeat almost any opponent while suffering only minimal loses. And thanks to its massive defence budget, the US is the only country that regularly makes major advances in military technology. The determination to build a national missile defence (NMD) system is but one example of a continued willingness on the part of the world's richest country to invest heavily in high-tech weapons so as to increase an already unassailable lead.

Decisions made on Wall Street and in Washington reverberate around the world. Corporate America, the regulatory infrastructure that supports it and the pension funds that propel it are the dominant influences on economic policy in Europe, Asia, South America and elsewhere, not to mention on the World Bank, the IMF and the WTO. The collapse of Enron may have demonstrated the fragility of corporate structures, but it also exposed the incestuous relationship between business and political elites. Until its demise, Enron was more influential than all but a handful of nation states. Last spring, I asked an Argentine diplomat what he thought about his country becoming part of the Free Trade Area of the Americas, currently being negotiated at the initiative of a number of US-based corporations. He said, with evident regret: 'We have no choice.'

US Unilateralism

A country as powerful as the US has many choices. Prior to the terrorist attacks of September 11, the new Bush administration had set itself firmly on a unilateralist path. During the first eight months in office, it publicly rejected the Anti-Ballistic Missile Treaty, the Kyoto Protocol, the Rome Statute of the International Criminal Court (ICC), a convention on the sale and transfer of small arms and a protocol to the Biological Weapons Convention.[1]

Many thought that the initially measured response to the atrocities of September 11 heralded the beginning of a dramatically different, multilateral approach to foreign affairs. A 'coalition' was constructed to facilitate the freezing of terrorist assets and the gathering of intelligence overseas. The support of numerous countries was sought and received for military action against the al-Qaeda terrorist network and the Taliban government of Afghanistan.

However, the United States' allies delude themselves if they think that the attacks on New York and Washington have persuaded the Bush administration of the more general value of multilateral approaches. Since September 11, Bush and his advisers have rejected offers of a UN Security Council resolution authorizing the war on terrorism, preferring instead to rely on an extended claim of self-defence. New alliances have been forged with illiberal regimes in Pakistan, Kyrgyzstan, Tajikistan and Uzbekistan, reversing years of carefully coordinated efforts to promote human rights. Hundreds of Afghan civilians have been killed or maimed as a result of careless targeting, and unexploded cluster bomblets will harm thousands more. The destruction of the al-Jazeera TV bureau in Kabul, plans for special military commissions with low evidentiary standards and the refusal to accord detainees captured in Afghanistan presumptive prisoner of war status – as required by the 1949 Geneva Convention – all indicate a casual disregard for international opinion and the laws of war.

Most disturbing, however, are some of the threats uttered by President Bush. The assertion that 'you're either with us or against us' obviates a central aspect of state sovereignty – the right not to be involved – and recasts the US as the ultimate arbiter of right and wrong. The identification of an 'axis of evil' comprising Iran, Iraq and North Korea challenges one of the twentieth century's greatest accomplishments: the prohibition of the threat or aggressive use of force in international affairs. In an age of ever-increasing interdependence, cooperation and shared values, Bush and his advisers are deliberately out of step with most of the Western world.

In many respects, Bush's team is a reincarnation of the second Reagan administration, which was also stridently unilateralist: it, too, drew explicit distinctions between good and evil, claimed extended rights, promoted missile defence and relied on the threat of terrorism to justify it all. Following the terrorist bombing in 1986 of a Berlin discotheque frequented by American servicemen, the then Secretary of State George Shultz said that it was 'absurd to argue that international law prohibits us from capturing terrorists in international waters or airspace; from attacking them on the soil of other nations, even for the purpose of rescuing hostages; or from using force against states that support, train and harbour terrorists or guerrillas'.[2]

George W. Bush's speechwriter couldn't have put it better, though there are important differences between the situation then and now. First, the end of the Cold War transformed the US into an unrivalled superpower, making it more likely that such claims would meet with acquiescence on the part of other countries. More important, the events of September 11 have transformed a traditionally isolationist population into one that wants the president to act decisively on the world stage. And Bush's advisers have taken steps to ensure that Americans continue to feel this way, by connecting the 'war on terrorism' to deeply held conceptions of nationhood. The US is the shining 'city on a hill', representing the best of the entrepreneurial, individualist spirit, and once again under assault from believers in a different God.

Powerful countries have always shaped the international system to their advantage. In the sixteeenth century, Spain redefined basic concepts of justice and universality so as to justify the conquest of indigenous Americans. In the eighteenth century, France developed the modern concept of borders, and that of the balance of power, to suit its continental strengths. In the nineteenth century, Britain introduced new rules on piracy, neutrality and colonialism – again, to suit its particular interests as the predominant power of the time.[3]

The present-day US is no different, apart from the fact that, following September 11, hardly anyone has been prepared to challenge its lead. The president's advisers are taking full advantage of the situation, applying pressure in pursuit of a wide range of goals that, in normal circumstances, might not be achieved. In January 2002, Bosnia handed over five Algerians to the US, despite the fact that the Bosnian Supreme Court had ordered them to be released due to lack of evidence: they are now in Guantanamo Bay. Around the same time, Canada was told to rescind its pledge to ratify the Kyoto Protocol, and to bring its immigration system into line with American procedures as part of the new emphasis on 'homeland defence'. It has already put hundreds of its soldiers under direct US command, and is considering doing the same with all of the rest. The UK is leading the stabilization operation in Kabul and providing key support on both NMD and the issue of detainees.

Russia, for its part, has acquiesced in the establishment of American military bases in the former Soviet republics of Kyrgyzstan, Tajikistan and Uzbekistan. China, having already witnessed the aggressive character of the Bush administration on two occasions – first in April 2001, after the crash-landing of a US surveillance plane, and then on its western border in Afghanistan – is keeping quiet, hoping that the US will go after Iran instead. The discovery of 27 listening devices in a Boeing 767 purchased for President Jiang Zemin has passed without complaint.

Expanding the Right of Self-Defence

Of the changes being pushed by the Bush administration, some of the most dramatic concern the international rules governing the use of force. Widespread sympathy in the aftermath of September 11 and heightened concern about terrorism have made possible the securing of a long-sought-after goal: an extension of the right of self-defence to include military responses against states that support or harbour terrorist groups.[4]

Article 51 of the UN Charter stipulates that acts of self-defence must be reported to the Security Council, but it does not define the content of that right. Self-defence is part of customary international law – an informal, unwritten body of rules derived from the practice and opinions of states. Necessity and proportionality are the key requirements. During the 1837 rebellion in Upper Canada, British forces captured an American ship that was being used to supply the rebels on the Canadian side of the Niagara River, set it on fire and sent it over Niagara Falls. The US asserted that the UK had to show that this was a necessary and proportionate act of self-defence. The UK agreed with the American assessment of the legal requirements, and the modern law of self-defence was born.

The UK was also involved in a more recent precedent: the response to the Falklands/Malvinas invasion was a legitimate act of self-defence. But most claims of self-defence arise in circumstances that are less clear cut, with their contribution to the ongoing development of customary international law turning on whether they are widely accepted by other states. In 1976, Israeli commandos stormed a hijacked plane in Entebbe, Uganda, killing the pro-Palestinian hijackers and rescuing most of the passengers and crew. Although many of the passengers were Israeli, Israel itself had not been attacked. Nor had it sought Uganda's permission for the raid. But most states tacitly approved of what Israel had done and, as a result, the requirements of necessity and proportionality were loosened somewhat with regard to the rescue of nationals abroad. In contrast, when Israel destroyed an Iraqi nuclear reactor in 1981, its claim of self-defence was firmly rejected by other states. A nuclear strike was not even imminent, and the requirements of necessity and proportionality were not fulfilled.

For decades, the US, Israel and apartheid South Africa argued that the right of self-defence extends to military responses to terrorist acts. But while the argument was accepted in a few specific instances, the pattern of response was never clear enough to establish new customary international law. Israel claimed to be acting in self-defence when it attacked the headquarters of the Palestine Liberation Organization in Tunisia in 1985. The UN Security Council strongly condemned the action. In 1998, after the bombing of its embassies in Kenya and Tanzania, the US fired cruise missiles at targets in Sudan and Afghanistan and claimed self-defence. A number of governments expressed concern about the fact that the territorial integrity of sovereign states was violated in an attempt to target not the states themselves but terrorists believed to be present there.

Even when the country concerned is directly implicated in terrorism, acts of self-defence directed against it have – in most instances – received at best a mixed response. The US responded to the 1986 terrorist attack on the Berlin discotheque by bombing Tripoli, and claimed self-defence. The claim was widely rejected, with many states expressing doubt as to whether the attack on Libya was necessary and proportionate. In 1993, in Kuwait, an assassination attempt was made on George Bush Snr. The US responded by bombing the headquarters of the Iraqi Secret Service. It claimed self-defence on the basis that the attack on the ex-president was tantamount to an attack on the US itself. Again, the claim received little support from other states.

In late September 2001, the US found itself in something of a legal dilemma, though not an entirely unhelpful one. In order to maintain the coalition against terrorism, its military response had to be necessary and proportionate. This meant that the strikes had to be carefully targeted against those believed responsible for the atrocities in New York and Washington. But if the US singled out Osama bin Laden and al-Qaeda as its targets, it would have run up against the widely held view that terrorist attacks, in and of themselves, did not justify military responses against sovereign states. Even today, most countries would not support a rule that opened them up to attack whenever terrorists were thought to operate within their territory.

In response to this dilemma, the US adopted a two-pronged legal strategy. It began by expanding its focus to include the Taliban. By giving refuge to bin Laden and al-Qaeda and refusing to hand him over, the Taliban were alleged to have directly facilitated and endorsed his acts. The US in this way broadened the claim of self-defence to include the state of Afghanistan. Although it would normally still be contentious, this was much less of a stretch from pre-existing international law than a claimed right to attack terrorists who simply happened to be there. As a result, the claim to be acting in self-defence – and the modification of customary international law inherent within that claim – had a much better chance of securing widespread expressed or tacit support.

The US then worked hard to secure that support in advance of military action. The formation of the coalition, including the invocation of Article 5 of the 1949 North Atlantic Treaty even though NATO was never called upon to engage in military action, helped smooth the path for the self-defence claim. UN Security Council resolutions adopted on September 12 and 28, 2001, did not authorize the use of force under the UN Charter, but instead were carefully worded to affirm, within the context of a broader response to terrorism, the right of self-defence in customary international law.[5]

The strategic effort to secure advance support built upon an approach previously used in 1998. A few short hours before he ordered the cruise missile strikes against terrorist targets in Sudan and Afghanistan, Bill Clinton telephoned Tony Blair, Helmut Kohl and Jacques Chirac and requested their support. Without having time to consult their lawyers, all three leaders agreed – and followed this with public statements immediately after the strikes. Criticism of the military action by other states was, consequently, more restrained than it might have been. And this relatively restrained response facilitated the eventual modification of customary international law that has now occurred: states now have the right to engage in self-defence against states which actively support or willingly harbour terrorist groups who have already attacked the responding state.

This change to international law will be of considerable significance in future. Having seized the opportunity to establish self-defence as an accepted basis for military action against some terrorist attacks, the US will now be able to invoke it again – even when the circumstances are less grave.

The US may now be employing similar strategies to develop a right of anticipatory self-defence. Until September 11, claims of a right to pre-emptive action were invariably contested. In fact, Article 51 of the UN Charter states that the right of self-defence arises when 'an armed attack occurs' and most countries have, since 1945, been very reluctant to claim a right of anticipatory self-defence. Israel justified the strikes that initiated the 1967 Six Day War on the basis that Egypt's blocking of the Straits of Tiran was a prior act of aggression. The US justified its 1962 blockade of Cuba on the basis of Chapter VIII of the UN Charter, as regional peacekeeping, and the 1988 downing of an Iranian civilian Airbus as a response to an ongoing armed attack. There is almost no support for a right of anticipatory self-defence as such in present-day customary international law.[6]

This does not mean that this aspect of the law will remain unchanged. In a letter to the president of the Security Council on October 7, 2001, US Ambassador John Negroponte wrote: 'We may find that our self-defense requires further actions with respect to other organizations and other states.'[7] When this sentence is read together with subsequent statements indicating a willingness to act against countries such as Iran, Iraq and North Korea, on the basis that they are developing weapons of mass destruction threatening to the US, it becomes clear that the Bush administration is contemplating wide-spread military action that it would justify as anticipatory self-defence. Whether this action, and the attempt at its legal justification, extend the right of self-defence yet further will depend on how other countries respond. If they do not protest against the US action, if and when it comes, their behaviour could well constitute acquiescence in yet another change to customary international law.

The Making of Exceptional International Law

The Bush administration also seems to be engaged in a parallel effort to remake – in favour of the US – the rules according to which international law is made, interpreted and changed. It increasingly adopts an approach to treaty interpretation that focuses on the supposed purposes of the treaty rather than what the words actually say. It accords considerably more weight to physical acts than to statements when weighing state behaviour with regard to customary international law, and discounts entirely the resolutions and declarations of the UN General Assembly. It pays little if any attention to decisions of the International Court of Justice – even though most other countries regard them as authoritative pronouncements on the existence and content of specific rules of international law. As a result, international

law as applied by the US increasingly bears little relationship to international law as understood elsewhere. It remains to be seen whether,
and to what degree, this divergence will influence the approach taken
by other countries.

It is possible, however, that instead of seeking change in the existing
rules, the US is in fact attempting to create new, exceptional rules for
itself alone. Similar exceptional rules have been created by other countries in the past, albeit on a more limited basis. In 1984, West Germany
abandoned its universally accepted claim to a three-mile territorial sea
in the waters off Hamburg and claimed a new, unprecedented limit on
the basis of a 16-mile box defined by geographical coordinates. The
new claim, which was explicitly designed for the limited purpose of
preventing oil spills in those busy waters, met with no public protests
from other states. This was perhaps because the balance of interests in
that situation was different from that which existed more generally –
different enough that other countries were prepared to allow for the
development of an exception to the general rule.

The same might be said of the position and interests of the single
superpower in the post-Cold War period, in which case the development of exceptional rules would depend on the responses of other
countries to the exceptional claims. And given the potentially substantial political, military and economic costs of opposing the US in any
particular law-making situation, acquiescence might well occur – at
least with regard to those claims that are not substantially contrary to
the most important interests of others. In short, although international
law is what countries choose it to be, the power dynamic behind the
law might in fact leave the less powerful believing that they have little
choice but to allow the creation of precisely such an exceptional legal
regime.

What would such a regime look like? The Bush administration
would clearly wish it to have an imperial tinge, with the US serving as
global law-maker and sheriff, setting the rules and acting alone or at the
head of a posse of compliant allies to impose discipline and stamp out
foreign threats. The security regime established by the UN Charter in
1945, whereby the five permanent members of the Security Council –
China, France, Russia, the UK and the US – were collectively given executive powers to maintain international peace and security, imposes
potentially inconvenient limits on the discretionary powers of a newly
confident hegemon and must, therefore, be firmly pushed aside.

Efforts at the creation of an exceptional regime are also being made
elsewhere. The Anti-Ballistic Missile Treaty and the Geneva Convention

have both been described as 'outdated', implying that the US is not bound by treaties entered into before the end of the Cold War. International human rights are similarly regarded as no longer binding on the US: in addition to the new links with illiberal regimes, the Bush administration has dismissed reports of abusive treatment of detainees in Afghanistan and Guantanamo Bay on the basis that the treatment is consistent with US standards. However, we can expect international human rights to remain part of the diplomatic arsenal of the State Department when it comes to the behaviour of other countries, such as China, Iran, Iraq and North Korea.

The greatest threat to the long-term survival of the human species may well be climate change rather than terrorism. But the Bush administration, heavily funded by the oil industry and inherently suspicious of 'entangling alliances', has rejected the developing international regulatory system on the emission of greenhouse gases. It has taken a similar stance towards the ICC.[8] When the ICC comes into being next year, it will face the active opposition of a single superpower angry that the actions of its soldiers – and thus its military policy – might be held up to scrutiny by foreign judges. Others may wish to promote an illusionary common good through the Kyoto Protocol and the ICC, but the US acts alone.

Terrorism can cause great destruction and upheaval, but efforts to stamp it out can also be a smokescreen for the pursuit of other, less worthy goals. Friends and allies of the US, while providing strong overall support, should offer their cooperation on specific issues only after thinking carefully about what is best for themselves. Recent statements by European Union Commissioner Chris Patten, French Prime Minister Lionel Jospin and German Foreign Minister Joschka Fischer show that some prominent Europeans are at last voicing concern about American unilateralism in the post-September 11 world. These voices should not be dismissed as anti-American. Respect for diversity of opinion is, after all, a central aspect of American society, and differing points of view are never far away. Most Americans currently support the president, but less than half of them voted for him. The Democratic Party has been revitalized by the Enron scandal and Bush's advisers are acting as if they have something to hide. Even within the administration there are public differences over such issues as the treatment of detainees.

The views expressed by Patten, Jospin and Fischer reflect deep-seated concerns on the part of the United States' best friends that the Bush administration is taking the country away from some of its most valuable and deep-seated traditions. One regularly hears talk of a 'democratic deficit' with regard to supranational institutions such as the UN and the EU, but perhaps it is time to start speaking of a similar deficit with regard to the US. The importance of decisions made in Washington today eclipses that of decisions made in the UN – and not just for Americans. Citizens of other countries find themselves in a position of considerable historical irony: the victims of a twenty-first-century form of 'taxation without representation', subject to the governance of a foreign power but deprived of any voice.

Maintaining the integrity and equal application of the international legal system is the most effective way in which we can begin to address this problem. Although imperfect, the international rules and institutions rejected by Bush and his advisers are more consistent with the founding principles of the US than the imperialist principles to which they subscribe. Even the Declaration of Independence recognized that the representatives of the US were required to have a 'due regard for the opinions of other nations'. It is high time that more of the United States' friends made themselves heard, and insisted that the immense power of the US be challenged through existing international rules and institutions, and thus used to improve the world – for everyone.

Notes

1. The following internet sites contain the texts of most international treaties: <http://untreaty.un.org/>; <http://fletcher.tufts.edu/multilaterals.html>.
2. George Shultz, 'Low-Intensity Warfare: The Challenge of Ambiguity', Address to the National Defense University, Washington, DC, January 15, 1986, reproduced in (1986) 25 *International Legal Materials* 204 at 206.
3. On the geopolitical history of international law see Wilhelm Grewe, *The Epochs of International Law* (Berlin: Walter de Gruyter, 2000).
4. For a more detailed analysis see Michael Byers, 'Terrorism, the Use of Force and International Law after 11 September', *International & Comparative Law Quarterly*, vol. 51 (2002).
5. For the text of Security Council Resolutions see <http://www.un.org/documents/>.
6. For a more detailed analysis see Christine Gray, *International Law and the Use of Force* (Oxford: Oxford University Press, 2000), pp. 111–15.
7. See <http://www.un.int/usa/s-2001-946.htm>.
8. See generally William Schabas, *An Introduction to the International Criminal Court* (Cambridge: Cambridge University Press, 2001).

CHAPTER 11

Who Are the Global Terrorists?

Noam Chomsky

After the atrocities of September 11, the victim declared a 'war on terrorism', targeting not just the suspected perpetrators, but the country in which they were located, and others charged with terrorism worldwide. President Bush pledged to 'rid the world of evildoers' and 'not let evil stand', echoing Ronald Reagan's denunciation of the 'evil scourge of terrorism' in 1985 – specifically, state-supported international terrorism, which had been declared to be the core issue of US foreign policy as his administration came to office.[1] The focal points of the first war on terror were the Middle East and Central America, where Honduras was the major base for US operations. The military component of the re-declared war is led by Donald Rumsfeld, who served as Reagan's special representative to the Middle East; the diplomatic efforts at the UN by John Negroponte, Reagan's Ambassador to Honduras. Planning is largely in the hands of other leading figures of the Reagan–Bush (Snr) administrations.

The condemnations of terrorism are sound, but leave some questions unanswered. The first is 'What do we mean by "terrorism"?' Second, 'What is the proper response to the crime?' Whatever the answer, it must at least satisfy a moral truism: if we propose some principle that is to be applied to antagonists, then we must agree – in fact, strenuously insist – that the principle apply to us as well. Those who do not rise even to this minimal level of integrity plainly cannot be taken seriously when they speak of right and wrong, good and evil.

The problem of definition is held to be vexing and complex. There are, however, proposals that seem straightforward, for example, in US Army manuals, which define terrorism as 'the calculated use of violence or threat of violence to attain goals that are political, religious, or ideological in nature ... through intimidation, coercion, or instilling fear'.[2]

That definition carries additional authority because of the
was offered as the Reagan administration was intensifying
terrorism. The world has changed little enough so that the ......ent
precedents should be instructive, even apart from the continuity of
leadership from the first war on terrorism to its recent reincarnation.

The first US war on terror received strong endorsement. The UN
General Assembly condemned international terrorism two months
after Reagan's denunciation, again in much stronger and more explicit
terms, in 1987.[3] Support was not unanimous, however. The 1987 resolution passed 153 to 2, Honduras abstaining.

Explaining their negative vote, the US and Israel identified the fatal
flaw: the statement that 'nothing in the present resolution could in any
way prejudice the right to self-determination, freedom, and independence, as derived from the Charter of the United Nations, of people
forcibly deprived of that right ..., particularly peoples under colonial
and racist regimes and foreign occupation'. That was understood to
apply to the struggle of the African National Congress against the
apartheid regime of South Africa (a US ally, while the ANC was officially
labelled a 'terrorist organization'); and to the Israeli military occupation, then in its 20th year, sustained by US military and diplomatic
support in virtual international isolation. Presumably because of US
opposition, the UN resolution was scarcely reported (if at all) and has
been effectively erased from the historical record; that is fairly standard
practice.[4]

Reagan's 1985 condemnation referred specifically to terrorism in the
Middle East, selected as the lead story of 1985 in an Associated Press
poll. But for Secretary of State George Shultz, the administration
moderate, the most 'alarming' manifestation of 'state-sponsored
terrorism', a plague spread by 'depraved opponents of civilization itself'
in 'a return to barbarism in the modern age', was frighteningly close to
home. There is 'a cancer, right here in our land mass', Shultz informed
Congress, threatening to conquer the hemisphere in a 'revolution
without borders' – an interesting fabrication exposed at once but regularly reiterated with appropriate shudders.[5]

So severe was the threat that on Law Day (May 1) 1985, the president
announced an embargo 'in response to the emergency situation created
by the Nicaraguan Government's aggressive activities in Central
America'. He also declared a national emergency, renewed annually,
because 'the policies and actions of the Government of Nicaragua
constitute an unusual and extraordinary threat to the national security
and foreign policy of the United States'.

'The terrorists – and the other states that aid and abet them – serve as grim reminders that democracy is fragile and needs to be guarded with vigilance', Shultz warned. We must 'cut [the Nicaraguan cancer] out', and not by gentle means: 'Negotiations are a euphemism for capitulation if the shadow of power is not cast across the bargaining table', Shultz declared, condemning those who advocate 'utopian, legalistic means like outside mediation, the United Nations, and the World Court, while ignoring the power element of the equation'. The US was exercising 'the power element of the equation' with mercenary forces based in Honduras, under Negroponte's supervision, and successfully blocking the 'utopian, legalistic means' pursued by the World Court and the Latin American Contadora nations – as Washington continued to do until its terrorist wars were won.[6]

Reagan's condemnation of the 'evil scourge' was issued at a meeting in Washington with Israeli Prime Minister Shimon Peres, who arrived to join in the call to extirpate the evil shortly after he had sent his bombers to attack Tunis, killing 75 people with smart bombs that tore them to shreds, among other atrocities recorded by the prominent Israeli journalist Amnon Kapeliouk on the scene. Washington cooperated by failing to warn its ally Tunisia that the bombers were on their way. Shultz informed Israeli Foreign Minister Yitzhak Shamir that Washington 'had considerable sympathy for the Israeli action', but drew back when the UN Security Council unanimously denounced the bombing as an 'act of armed aggression'. The United States abstained in the vote.[7]

A second candidate for most extreme act of Mideast international terrorism in the peak year of 1985 is a car-bombing in Beirut on March 8 that killed 80 people and wounded 256. The bomb was placed outside a mosque, timed to explode when worshippers left. 'About 250 girls and women in flowing black chadors, pouring out of Friday prayers at the Imam Rida Mosque, took the brunt of the blast', Nora Boustany reported. The bomb also 'burned babies in their beds', killed children 'as they walked home from the mosque' and 'devastated the main street of the densely populated' West Beirut suburb. The target was a Shi'ite leader accused of complicity in terrorism, but he escaped. The crime was organized by the CIA and its Saudi clients with the assistance of British intelligence.[8]

The only other competitor for the prize for the most extreme terrorist atrocity in the Mideast in the peak year of 1985 is the 'Iron Fist' operations that Peres directed in March in occupied Lebanon. They reached new depths of 'calculated brutality and arbitrary murder', a

Western diplomat familiar with the area observed, as the Israeli Defence Forces (IDF) shelled villages, carted off the male population, killed dozens of villagers in addition to many massacred by the IDF's paramilitary associates, shelled hospitals and took patients away for 'interrogation', along with numerous other atrocities.[9] The IDF High Command described the targets as 'terrorist villagers'. The operations against them must continue, the military correspondent of the *Jerusalem Post*, Hirsh Goodman, added, because the IDF must 'maintain order and security' in occupied Lebanon despite 'the price the inhabitants will have to pay'.

Like Israel's invasion of Lebanon three years earlier that left some 18,000 dead, these actions and others in Lebanon were not undertaken in self-defence but rather for political ends, as recognized at once in Israel. The same was true, almost entirely, of those attacks that followed, up to Peres' murderous invasion of 1996. But all relied crucially on US military and diplomatic support. Accordingly, they too do not enter the annals of international terrorism.

In brief, there was nothing odd about the proclamations of the leading co-conspirators in Mideast international terrorism, which therefore passed without comment at the peak moment of horror at the 'return to barbarism'.

The well-remembered prize-winner for 1985 is the hijacking of the *Achille Lauro* and the brutal murder of a passenger, Leon Klinghoffer. It was doubtless a vile terrorist act, and surely not justified by the claim that it was in retaliation for the far worse Tunis atrocities and a pre-emptive effort to deter others. Adopting moral truisms, the same holds of our own acts of retaliation or pre-emption.

Evidently, we have to qualify the definition of 'terrorism' given in official sources: the term applies only to terrorism against *us*, not the terrorism we carry out against *them*. The practice is conventional, even among the most extreme mass murderers: the Nazis were protecting the population from terrorist partisans directed from abroad, while the Japanese were labouring selflessly to create an 'earthly paradise' as they fought off the 'Chinese bandits' terrorizing the peaceful people of Manchuria and their legitimate government. Exceptions would be hard to find.

The same convention applies to the war to exterminate the 'Nicaraguan cancer'. On Law Day 1984, President Reagan proclaimed that without law there can be only 'chaos and disorder'. The day before, he had announced that the US would disregard the proceedings of the International Court of Justice (ICJ), which went on to condemn his administration for its 'unlawful use of force', ordering it to terminate these international terrorist crimes and pay substantial reparations to Nicaragua (June 1986). The ICJ decision was dismissed with contempt, as was a subsequent Security Council resolution calling on all states to observe international law (vetoed by the US) and repeated General Assembly resolutions (US and Israel opposed, in one case joined by El Salvador).

As the ICJ decision was announced, Congress substantially increased funding for the mercenary forces engaged in 'the unlawful use of force'. Shortly after, the US command directed them to attack 'soft targets' – undefended civilian targets – and to avoid combat with the Nicaraguan army, as they could do thanks to US control of the skies and the sophisticated communication equipment provided to the terrorist forces. The tactic was considered reasonable by prominent commentators as long as it satisfied 'the test of cost-benefit analysis', an analysis of 'the amount of blood and misery that will be poured in, and the likelihood that democracy will emerge at the other end' – 'democracy' as Western elites understand the term, an interpretation illustrated graphically in the region.[10]

State Department legal adviser Abraham Sofaer explained why the US was entitled to reject ICJ jurisdiction. In earlier years, most members of the UN 'were aligned with the United States and shared its views regarding world order', but since decolonization a 'majority often opposes the United States on important international questions'. Accordingly, the US must 'reserve to ourselves the power to determine' how it will act and which matters fall 'essentially within the domestic jurisdiction of the United States, as determined by the United States' – in this case, the terrorist acts against Nicaragua condemned by the ICJ and the UN Security Council. For similar reasons, since the 1960s the US has been far in the lead in vetoing Security Council resolutions on a wide range of issues, with Britain second and France a distant third.[11]

Washington waged its 'war on terrorism' by creating an international terror network of unprecedented scale, and employing it worldwide with lethal and long-lasting effects. In Central America, terror guided and supported by the US reached its most extreme levels in countries where the state security forces themselves were the immediate agents of international terrorism. The effects were reviewed in a 1994 conference organized by Salvadoran Jesuits, whose experiences had been particularly gruesome.[12] The conference report takes particular note of the effects of the residual 'culture of terror ... in domesticating the expectations of the majority vis-a-vis alternatives different to those of the powerful', an important observation on the efficacy of state terror that generalizes broadly. In Latin America, the September 11 atrocities were harshly condemned, but commonly with the observation that they are nothing new. They may be described as 'Armageddon', the research journal of the Jesuit University in Managua observed, but Nicaragua has 'lived its own Armageddon in excruciating slow motion' under US assault 'and is now submerged in its dismal aftermath', and others fared far worse under the vast plague of state terror that swept through the continent from the early 1960s, much of it traceable to Washington.[13]

It is hardly surprising that Washington's call for support in its war of revenge for September 11 had little resonance in Latin America. An international Gallup poll found that support for military force rather than extradition ranged from 2 per cent (Mexico) to 11 per cent (Venezuela and Colombia). Condemnations of the September 11 attacks were regularly accompanied by recollections of their own suffering – for example, the death of perhaps thousands of poor people (Western crimes, therefore unexamined) when George Bush Snr bombed the barrio Chorillo in Panama in December 1989 in Operation Just Cause, undertaken to kidnap a disobedient thug who was sentenced to life imprisonment in Florida for crimes mostly committed while he was on the CIA payroll.[14]

The record continues to the present without essential change, apart from the modification of pretexts and tactics. The list of leading recipients of US arms yields ample evidence, familiar to those acquainted with international human rights reports.

It therefore comes as no surprise that President Bush informed Afghans that bombing will continue until they hand over people the US suspects of terrorism (rebuffing requests for evidence and tentative offers of negotiation). Or, when new war aims were added after three weeks of bombing, that Admiral Sir Michael Boyce, chief of the British Defence Staff, warned Afghans that US–UK attacks will continue 'until the people of the country themselves recognize that this is going to go on until they get the leadership changed'.[15] In other words, the US and UK will persist in 'the calculated use of violence to attain goals that are political ... in nature': this is international terrorism in the technical sense, but is excluded from the canon by the standard convention. The rationale is essentially that of the US–Israel international terrorist operations in Lebanon. Admiral Boyce was virtually repeating the words of the eminent Israeli statesman Abba Eban as Reagan declared the first war on terrorism. Replying to Prime Minister Menachem Begin's

account of atrocities in Lebanon committed under the Labour government in the style 'of regimes which neither Mr Begin nor I would dare
to mention by name', Eban acknowledged the accuracy of the account
but added the standard justification that 'there was a rational prospect,
ultimately fulfilled, that affected populations would exert pressure for
the cessation of hostilities'.[16]

These concepts articulated by Eban and Boyce are conventional, as
is the resort to terrorism when deemed appropriate. Furthermore, its
success is openly celebrated. The devastation caused by US terror operations in Nicaragua was described quite frankly, leaving Americans
'United in Joy' at their successful outcome, the press proclaimed. The
massacre of hundreds of thousands of Indonesians in 1965, mostly
landless peasants, was greeted with unconstrained euphoria, along with
praise for Washington for concealing its own critical role, which might
have embarrassed the 'Indonesian moderates' who had cleansed their
society in a 'staggering mass slaughter' that the CIA compared to the
crimes of Stalin, Hitler and Mao.[17] There are many other examples. One
might wonder why Osama bin Laden's disgraceful exultation over the
atrocities of September 11 occasioned indignant surprise. But that
would be an error, based on failure to distinguish their terror, which is
evil, from ours, which is noble, the operative principle throughout
history.

If we keep to official definitions, it is a serious error to describe
terrorism as the weapon of the weak. Like most weapons, it is wielded to
far greater effect by the strong. But then it is not terror; rather, 'counter-
terror', or 'low-intensity warfare' or 'self-defence' and, if successful,
'rational' and 'pragmatic', and an occasion to be 'united in joy'.

Let us turn to the question of proper response to the crime, bearing
in mind the governing moral truism. If, for example, Admiral Boyce's
dictum is legitimate, then victims of Western state terrorism are
entitled to act accordingly. That conclusion is properly regarded as
outrageous. Therefore the principle is outrageous when applied to
official enemies; even more so when we recognize that the actions were
undertaken with the expectation that they would place huge numbers
of people at grave risk. No knowledgeable authority seriously questioned the UN estimate that '7.5 million Afghans will need food over
the winter – 2.5 million more than on Sept. 11':[18] a 50 per cent increase
as a result of the threat of bombing, then the actuality, with a toll that
will never be investigated if history is any guide.

A different proposal, put forth by the Vatican among others, was
spelled out by military historian Michael Howard: 'a police operation

conducted under the auspices of the United Nations ... against a criminal conspiracy whose members should be hunted down and brought before an international court, where they would receive a fair trial and, if found guilty, be awarded an appropriate sentence'.[19] Though never contemplated, the proposal seems reasonable. If so, then it would be reasonable if applied to Western state terrorism; something that could also never be contemplated, though for opposite reasons.

The war in Afghanistan has commonly been described as a 'just war'; indeed, evidently so. There have been some attempts to frame a concept of 'just war' that might support the judgement. We may therefore ask how these proposals fare when evaluated in terms of the same moral truism. I have yet to see one that does not instantly collapse: application of the proposed concept to Western state terrorism would be considered unthinkable, if not despicable. For example, we might ask how the proposals would apply to the one case that is uncontroversial in the light of the judgements of the highest international authorities, Washington's war against Nicaragua; uncontroversial, that is, among those who have some commitment to international law and treaty obligations. It is an instructive experiment.

Similar questions arise in connection with other aspects of the wars on terrorism. There has been debate over whether the US–UK war in Afghanistan was authorized by ambiguous Security Council resolutions, but that is beside the point. The US surely could have obtained clear and unambiguous authorization (not always for attractive reasons – Russia and China eagerly joined the coalition in the hope of gaining US support for their own terrorist atrocities, and the UK and France would not have exercised the veto), but that course was rejected, presumably because it would suggest that there is some higher authority to which the US should defer, a condition that a state with overwhelming power is not likely to accept. There is even a name for that stance in the literature of diplomacy and international relations: establishing 'credibility', a standard official justification for the resort to violence – the bombing of Serbia, to mention a recent example. The refusal to consider the negotiated transfer of the suspected perpetrators presumably had the same grounds.

The moral truism applies to such matters as well. The US refuses to extradite terrorists even when their guilt is well-established. One current case involves Emmanuel Constant, the leader of the Haitian paramilitary forces that were responsible for thousands of brutal killings in the early 1990s under the military junta, which Washington officially opposed but tacitly supported, publicly undermining the

Organization of American States' embargo and secretly authorizing oil shipments. Constant was sentenced *in absentia* by a Haitian court. The elected government has repeatedly called on the US to extradite him, again on September 30, 2001, while Taliban initiatives to negotiate the transfer of bin Laden were being dismissed with contempt. Haiti's request was again ignored, probably because of concerns about what Constant might reveal about ties to the US government during the period of the terror. Do we therefore conclude that Haiti has the right to use force to compel his extradition, following as best it can Washington's model in Afghanistan? The very idea is outrageous, yielding another *prima facie* violation of the moral truism.

It is all too easy to add illustrations.[20] Consider Cuba, probably the main target of international terrorism since 1959, remarkable in scale and character, some of it exposed in declassified documents on Kennedy's Operation Mongoose and continuing to the late 1990s. Cold War pretexts were ritually offered as long as that was possible, but internally the story was the one commonly unearthed on inquiry. It was recounted in secret by Arthur Schlesinger, reporting the conclusions of JFK's Latin American mission to the incoming president: the Cuban threat is 'the spread of the Castro idea of taking matters into one's own hands', which might stimulate the 'poor and underprivileged' in other countries, who 'are now demanding opportunities for a decent living' – the 'virus' or 'rotten apple' effect, as it is called in high places. The Cold War connection was that 'the Soviet Union hovers in the wings, flourishing large development loans and presenting itself as the model for achieving modernization in a single generation'.[21]

True, these exploits of international terrorism – which were quite serious – are excluded by the standard convention. But suppose we keep to the official definition. In accord with the theories of 'just war' and proper response, how has Cuba been entitled to react?

It is fair enough to denounce international terrorism as a plague spread by 'depraved opponents of civilization itself'. The commitment to 'drive the evil from the world' can even be taken seriously, if it satisfies moral truisms – not, it would seem, an entirely unreasonable thought.

Notes

1. *New York Times*, October 18, 1985.
2. *US Army Operational Concept for Terrorism Counteraction* (TRADOC Pamphlet No. 525–37, 1984).

3. General Assembly Resolution 40/61, December 9, 1985; Resolution 42/159, December 7, 1987.
4. See my *Necessary Illusions* (Boston, MA: South End Press, 1989), chapter 4; and my essay 'International Terrorism: Image and Reality' in Alex George (ed.) *Western State Terrorism* (Cambridge: Polity Press/Blackwell, 1991).
5. George Shultz, 'Terrorism: The Challenge to the Democracies' (State Department, Current Policy No. 589, June 24, 1984); 'Terrorism and the Modern World' (State Department, Current Policy No. 629, October 25, 1984). For Shultz's congressional testimony 1986, 1983, the former part of a major campaign to gain more funding for the contras, see Jack Spence 'The US Media: Covering (Over) Nicaragua' and Eldon Kenworthy 'Selling the Policy' in Thomas Walker (ed.) *Reagan versus the Sandinistas* (Boulder, CO, and London: Westview Press, 1987).
6. George Shultz, 'Moral Principles and Strategic Interests' (State Department, Current Policy No. 820, April 14, 1986).
7. *New York Times*, October 17, 18, 1985; Amnon Kapeliouk, *Yediot Ahronot*, November 15, 1985; *Los Angeles Times*, October 3, 1985; Geoffrey Jansen, *Middle East International*, October 11, 1985; Bernard Gwertzman, *New York Times*, October 2, 7, 1985.
8. Nora Boustany, *Washington Post Weekly*, March 14, 1988; Bob Woodward, *Veil* (New York: Simon & Schuster, 1987), p. 396f.
9. *Guardian*, March 6, 1985. For details and sources, see my 'Middle East Terrorism and the American Ideological System', in *Pirates and Emperors* (New York: Claremont, 1986; Montreal: Black Rose, 1988), reprinted in Edward Said and Christopher Hitchens (eds) *Blaming the Victims* (London: Verso, 1988).
10. For details, see my *Culture of Terrorism* (Boston, MA: South End Press, 1988), p. 77f.
11. Abraham Sofaer, *The United States and the World Court* (State Department, Current Policy No. 769, December 1985).
12. Juan Hernandez Pico, *Envio* (Managua: Universidad Centroamericana, March 1994).
13. *Envio*, October 2001. For a judicious review of the aftermath, see Thomas Walker and Ariel Armony (eds) *Repression, Resistance, and Democratic Transition in Central America* (Wilmington, NC: Scholarly Resources, 2000).
14. *Envio*, October 2001; Panamanian journalist Ricardo Stevens, NACLA *Report on the Americas*, November/December 2001.
15. Patrick Tyler and Elisabeth Bumiller, *New York Times*, October 12, 2001, p. 1; Michael Gordon, *New York Times*, October 28, 2001, p. 1.
16. *Jerusalem Post*, August 16, 1981.
17. For an extensive review, see my *Necessary Illusions*; *Deterring Democracy* (London: Verso, 1991) (Nicaragua); *Year 501* (Boston, MA: South End Press, 1993) (Indonesia).
18. Elisabeth Bumiller and Elizabeth Becker, *New York Times*, October 17, 2001.
19. *Foreign Affairs*, January/February 2002; Tania Branigan, *Guardian*, October 31, 2001.
20. For a sample, see George, *Western State Terrorism*.
21. *Foreign Relations of the United States*, 1961–63, vol. XII, American Republics, pp.13f., 33.

Part II
Order

CHAPTER 12

The Public Delegitimation of Terrorism and Coalitional Politics

Robert O. Keohane

The terrorist attacks of September 11, 2001, were widely condemned.[1] The enormity of these attacks made them impossible to defend in international fora. Terrorism has long been legally outlawed: 12 Conventions related to terrorism have been deposited at the United Nations or other international organizations.[2] However, many states have long been willing to make exceptions for the 'freedom fighters' in causes they espoused, and other states did not give their opposition to terrorism priority over other foreign policy objectives. Since September 11 it has been more difficult for public officials around the world passively to tolerate terrorism or even quietly to support it. The frightening prospect of terrorists using means of mass destruction makes attempts to prevent terrorism even more urgent and toleration of lower-level terrorism even more problematic. One result of the September 11 attacks has been the *public delegitimation of terrorism.*

By 'public delegitimation' I do not mean that people everywhere have suddenly renounced their support of terrorism to achieve political objectives. What I do mean is that apparent support of terrorism can now be more effectively criticized and its supporters embarrassed. The great powers of the world – the United States, the European Union, China and Russia – all have good reasons to fear terrorism. None of them believes that it can achieve its own anti-terrorist objectives without supporting a global effort against terrorism. Hence, there is suddenly a broad coalition against terrorism based not only on American power, but on the perceived self-interest of other powerful states.

The thesis of this short chapter is twofold. In the short run, the public delegitimation of terrorism has changed the interests and positions of a variety of states in a way that affects both coalition formation

141

and outcomes of political disputes. New coalitions and alignments are now emerging as state interests change in the wake of the actions of September 11. Adjustments are occurring in the relative power of various states and non-state movements, stemming from the public delegitimation of terrorism as a means of political action.

In the longer term, terrorism recalls other forms of non-state violence – notably piracy – that thrived under certain conditions but were eventually eliminated by a combination of state action and changes in structures of opportunity. If the piracy analogy has any merit, there may be hope of sharply reducing the dangers from those forms of terrorism that operate transnationally with the support or tolerance of states. Such an accomplishment will depend, however, on the public delegitimation of terrorism becoming much more universal, as a result of increasing opportunities for otherwise frustrated people as well as effective state action.

Changes in Interests and Coalitions

The key distinctive attribute of *terrorism* as a form of organized informal violence – as contrasted with criminal action, guerrilla warfare or assassination – is that terrorism seeks to intimidate an audience rather than to eliminate an enemy. In terrorist activity, 'the direct targets of violence are not the main targets'.[3]

Not all terrorism operates transnationally, with either sponsorship by states or their acquiescence. Timothy McVeigh, who carried out the bombing in Oklahoma City, and the Aum Shinrikyo cult, which launched a gas attack in the Tokyo subways, were home-grown. As Joseph Nye has recently pointed out, technology is putting destructive power not only into the hands of states and non-state actors closely or loosely tied to states, but also into the hands of individuals and groups within democratic societies.[4] In this chapter, however, I focus only on transnational terrorism – 'terrorism with a global reach', in the language of President Bush.[5] When I use the word 'terrorism' here, I mean transnational terrorism, sponsored by or at least tolerated by governments.

Despite the wide consensus against terrorism, it is wise to remind ourselves that world politics is a competitive activity in which conflicts of interest are rife; hence the construction of a norm against terrorism is only the beginning of a political process, not the end. Given such a norm, much activity in world politics becomes a *competition for specifying what the norm means*. Who qualifies as a terrorist? Of what does 'harbouring terrorists' consist? Both militant non-state groups and states will seek to frame the issue in such a way that informal violence in which they engage, or that they support, is not defined as terrorism, while violence that they seek to combat is so defined. Israel, for instance, would like to exempt from 'terrorism' any action by states such as itself, focusing attention on non-state actors. It wishes also to define as terrorism violence against Israeli police and soldiers. Palestinian groups, by contrast, seek to exempt attacks on police and soldiers, but regard Israeli assassinations of Palestinian civilians and destruction of Palestinian homes as terrorist acts designed to intimidate others.

Since much is at stake politically, the word 'terrorism' has not yet been defined in a coherent way by governments. Indeed, the United Nations resolutions of September, 2001, condemning terrorism and support of terrorists, did not attempt to define the term. In the immediate future, terrorism is likely to be defined inductively and operationally – as those acts of informal violence that an overwhelming coalition of states regards as illegitimate. Long-run delegitimation of terrorism, however, will require a clearer consensus on what the word means.

Two ways to analyse prospective shifts in coalitional politics are to explore how the events of September 11 have changed the interests of major actors in world politics, and how they have changed the political situations of states whose fundamental interests may not have shifted so much. Interests have changed for states that previously did not see themselves as targets of terrorism. Political situations have changed markedly for states that were involved, on one side or another, in struggles involving terrorism.

Changes in Interests

Consider first the United States. The attacks have made the United States more dependent on other states for assistance in its 'war against terrorism'. Normally, when a state asks others for assistance, some form of reciprocity is required. Not surprisingly, therefore, the US is being more solicitous of Pakistan's requests for economic aid than it was before September 11. The appeals for aid from Turkey – a secular Islamic country with a repressed fundamentalist Islamic resistance movement – are also likely to find more receptive ears in Washington than they did before the attacks on the World Trade Center and the Pentagon. Yet at the same time, the increased salience of terrorism issues to the US means that its threats toward states that defy its wishes are more credible than they seemed earlier. Countries such as Sudan and Syria have reportedly

Worlds in Collision

begun to cooperate with US anti-terrorist measures as the price of non-cooperation has gone up. The US has a new interest both in aiding its anti-terrorist allies and in punishing states that defy it.

The shifts in American interests toward international organizations such as the United Nations are equally complex. Despite its previous dismissive attitudes toward international agreements and institutions, the Bush administration turned in September 2001 to the United Nations for resolutions on terrorism. Clearly, the UN was not to be the director of the anti-terror coalition, but was expected to become a source of *collective legitimation* for American actions. Only the UN can provide the breadth of support for an action that can elevate it from the policy of one country or a limited set of countries, to a policy endorsed on a global basis.[6] Yet the United States has also shown, in its conduct of the war in Afghanistan, that it seeks to remain unfettered in its military strategy. Indeed, its interests in remaining independent of serious multilateral constraints have, if anything, been reinforced as a result of September 11. As a result, the UN is serving as the legitimating institution for an essentially unilateral effort by the US. Military objectives defined by the US take precedence over the much more problematic task of long-term reconstruction of Afghanistan, which is being left in the hands of the UN.

Other countries also seem to have adjusted their interests in response to the terrorist attacks. Some have discovered that they are more vulnerable than they may have realized both to terrorism and to charges by the United States that they are doing too little to combat it. Increased police surveillance and intelligence gathering, coupled with attempts to break up terrorist rings based in their countries – whether in Europe or in Singapore – have resulted from these shifts in perceptions of interest. The government of the Philippines has even invited American military advisers to help it defeat an Islamic guerrilla movement allegedly linked to al-Qaeda.

Finally, it seems clear that China has become more concerned about Islamic fundamentalism in its vast western territories, inhabited largely by non-Chinese Muslims. Two quite significant shifts in Chinese policy seem to reflect this shift in interests. First, China voted for the September 28 UN Resolution, which gave, in effect, *carte blanche* to the US to take whatever actions it thought justified to attack sanctuaries for terrorism, even if those sanctuaries were provided by sovereign states. The contrast with China's opposition to NATO's action in Kosovo in 1999, largely on grounds of concern for sovereignty, is striking. The big difference, of course, is that in the case of terrorism, the Chinese government fears for its own control over its own territory and population. Actions that limit the sovereignty of other states, such as Afghanistan, become justified when they may protect the sovereignty of China. The other notable shift in Chinese policy is its rapprochement with India. Chinese Prime Minister Zhu Rongji made the first visit by a Chinese prime minister to India in over a decade in mid-January 2002, as Indian troops were on a war footing with China's long-term ally, Pakistan. China's concern over terrorism in its northwest provinces gives it common interests with India, fighting terrorism in Kashmir, despite concern about growing Indian power.[7]

Changes in Political Situation

Equally dramatic as these changes in interests are the changes in the political situations of countries that have been involved, on one side or another, in terrorist struggles. Some countries are beneficiaries of the delegitimation of terrorism; others have been losers from this normative change.

Among the major beneficiaries is India. For over 50 years, India and Pakistan have struggled over Indian rule in parts of Kashmir whose population is principally Muslim. India seized the territory in the 1947 war that ensued after the British relinquished political control of the subcontinent, and has subsequently refused to enable a plebiscite to determine the will of the area's people. Pakistan has for a long time supported terrorist actions designed to dislodge India from control of Kashmir. Even after September 11, such support of terrorism by Pakistan did not generate serious condemnation by the West. In December 2001, however, an attack took place on India's parliament, which according to India was carried out by Pakistani-based militants. India responded by threatening war. Threats of war and mobilization often produce pressure on the country making the threats; but in this case, India's actions led to pressure by the US and Britain on Pakistan's government to disavow terrorism, close down terrorist organizations and arrest terrorist suspects. As one expert commented, 'Since the September 11 terrorist attacks, India has sat back and watched the United States pressure Pakistan into doing everything that India has been seeking for years.'[8]

Why should the US, despite its dependence on Pakistan for help against the Taliban, take India's side in this dispute? Surely there are multiple reasons. India credibly threatened to use its overwhelming military force against Pakistan, which meant that the only feasible way to avoid war was for Pakistan to back down. But another part of the answer may lie in the normative consensus against terrorism that the US is trying to construct. A key element in any normative argument is *universality*. General normative arguments cannot differentiate on parochial grounds. If an issue is not salient, inconsistency can be quietly maintained. But when India's parliament was attacked and India mobilized in response, Pakistani state-sponsored terrorism became front-page news. Under those conditions, the US could hardly build a coalition against Islamic terrorism directed against itself if it regarded fundamentalist Islamic terrorism against democratic India as less worthy of response. In other words, US interests in this respect are not defined entirely by its material interests, or even by its interest in defeating the Taliban and capturing al-Qaeda leaders. On the contrary, its interests now encompass *constructing a credible normative order* that delegitimizes terrorism. It must therefore support India even when doing so runs some risk of destabilizing a government of Pakistan, run by General Musharraf, that has been loyally supporting US policy since September 11 at considerable risk to itself.

Another beneficiary of the delegitimation of terrorism is Israel. Terrorism has been a principal weapon of Palestinian militants, whether aligned with the Palestinian Authority of Yasser Arafat or not. Arafat was under enormous pressure in the months after September 11 not only to disavow terrorism but to stop it, as a condition for the United States being willing to re-enter discussions with the Palestinian Authority. Israel's attacks on Palestinian militants are less often identified as terrorism. One reason for such a judgement may be that Israel claims to target activists who have planned terrorist acts: in this view, it is seeking to eliminate an enemy rather than to intimidate an audience.[9] But a less solid basis for exempting Israel from charges of terrorism is the assumption that only non-state actors can engage in terrorism. Such an assumption is questionable: 'state terrorism' is not an oxymoron. Yet the identification of terrorism with non-state actors gives all states – including Israel – an advantage over their non-state opponents. Since states control the discourses of international organizations, such organizations may be inclined to adopt, or implicitly to accept, definitions that privilege the behaviour of states.

The delegitimation of terrorism helps not only governments whose territory has been attacked by organizers of informal violence based across international borders, it also benefits governments that fight armed internal rebellions. How the issue is framed becomes crucial in the struggle to justify action. Is violent repression of armed militants inside one's own country violation of human rights by the government, or is it struggling against terrorism? Russia's fight against Islamic militants in Chechnya now can be framed as a struggle against terrorism – akin to American efforts in Afghanistan – whereas previously it was viewed as repression of a minority group, on the analogy of Serbian behaviour in Bosnia or Kosovo. Different analogies have different implications. The current emphasis on terrorism makes that analogy available to observers, helping the Russian government persuade them that it is behaving properly. The emphasis of the 1990s on human rights had the opposite effect, creating a natural analogy between unjustifiable repression of human rights in the Balkans and Russian actions in Chechnya. Algeria has also sought to justify its repression of Islamic militants on anti-terrorist grounds, and even Syria (which has long been on the American list of pro-terrorist states) now intimates that its repression of the Muslim Brotherhood was an early example of the fight against terrorism![10]

It follows from this discussion of beneficiaries of the delegitimation of terrorism that there are losers as well. Pakistan's fight to regain Kashmir and Palestinian attempts to regain control of the West Bank have both suffered setbacks, partly as a result of the events of September 11. So have fundamentalist Islamic movements in a variety of countries. Saudi Arabia's reputation as a 'moderate' state has been badly damaged by revelations of the support for Islamic fundamentalism by Saudi elites and the Saudi state, and by the substantial numbers of Saudi citizens involved in al-Qaeda. As terrorism becomes a central focus of coalitional politics, coalition leaders will have strong incentives to join with repressive regimes to fight terrorists, on the principle 'the enemy of my enemy is my friend'. Human rights in various regions of the world are likely to suffer as a result, and strategically placed tyrants will benefit.

The Delegitimation of Non-State Violence in the Eighteenth and Nineteenth Centuries

What we have observed so far is only the public delegitimation of terrorism in the wake of a devastating attack against the United States. It is very difficult to draw conclusions about long-term developments from such current events. Yet there would be a historical precedent for a more thoroughgoing delegitimation of terrorism, or even for its virtual elimination, in what happened to slavery and the practice of non-state violence in the eighteenth and nineteenth centuries.

The delegitimation of slavery is a familiar story. Less than a century elapsed between the first public campaign against slavery, in Great Britain in 1787, and its abolition in Brazil, the last state in which it was legal, in the 1880s.[11] Slavery was virtually universally accepted as a practice in 1785; universally condemned by 1885.

The suppression of non-state violence, including piracy, is more directly analogous to the issue of terrorism. In 1700, non-state violence was an accepted part of world politics. Mercantile companies such as the Dutch and British East India Companies wielded enormous power, which flowed from the barrels of their cannon. In addition, mercenary armies were often used in warfare; private citizens were authorized by states to act as 'privateers', attacking and capturing merchant ships belonging to subjects of adversary states; and piracy was widespread from the Indian Ocean to the Caribbean. Yet by 1900, the mercantile companies had been liquidated, many states punished their subjects for serving in a foreign army, and piracy had virtually been driven from the seas. This task was largely accomplished by the navies of major states, led by Great Britain, but it was also the result of political change – including imperialism, which expanded the scope of European control.[12] A landmark in this process – although occurring after most piracy had already been eliminated – was the Declaration of Paris (1856), which was signed by all European Great Powers but not by the US. It legally abolished privateering, which had been a major source of piracy.

The key to these restrictions on non-state violence lies in the actions of states. In 1700, states used measures such as privateering to further their own goals; indeed, powerful elites in Great Britain and its American colonies even financed pirates such as Captain Kidd.[13] Only when states devised a clear definition of piracy and outlawed privateering could they eliminate it. 'Piracy could not be expunged until it was defined, and it could not be defined until it was distinguished from state-sponsored or -sanctioned individual violence.'[14] Legal and political actions were at least as important as military measures in eliminating piracy. State sovereignty was strengthened. On the whole, powerful, well-organized states, their elites and the societies they governed, benefited most from this process. Marginalized actors such as pirates and weak states that sought to use privateers against more powerful naval powers were losers.

This precedent may be relevant today. Terrorism is a weapon of the weak, most useful to groups that are not powerful enough to confront their adversary in direct battle, or even to wage effective guerrilla warfare. It is also a weapon of the highly organized, the fanatical and those without moral scruples. The delegitimation of terrorism and effective war against it will strengthen powerful states, which are (apart from terrorism) able to police their borders and deter attacks by other states. It will also benefit democracies, which are both most vulnerable to terrorism due to their openness and least able to engage in it due to the secrecy involved and the dangers that supporting terrorist organizations will undercut democracy itself.

The delegitimation of terrorism, like the delegitimation of piracy and privateering, suggests an interesting dialectic in world politics. Technological advances such as ocean-going commerce in the sixteenth century and global patterns of interdependence and alliance in the twenty-first, have created targets for wielders of non-state violence such as pirates and contemporary terrorist movements. Corresponding technological advances have also created the means for non-state actors to wield violence, whether as a result of sailing vessel technology or jet aircraft and mobile phones. One of the most disturbing aspects of contemporary terrorism is the potential availability to terrorists of the means of mass destruction, which could magnify by a thousandfold the damage that they could inflict. But the organizational capacities of states have not stood still; so when the threat from non-state violence has been sufficiently large, states have been able to counter-attack effectively, using law and policing as well as military force. This is the story of suppression of non-state violence in the eighteenth and nineteenth centuries. Whether it will also be the twenty-first-century story of the suppression of terrorism, with its vastly greater potential for destruction, remains to be seen.

State action and the delegitimation of terrorism may not be sufficient. One source of piracy in the seventeenth century was the repression of the lower classes prevalent in England. For adventurous spirits, a short life as a pirate might be preferable to submissiveness in misery at home.[15] Analogously, in the twenty-first century the lack of opportunity facing many young men in Muslim countries makes engaging in 'holy war' more attractive than continuing to feel frustrated and humiliated in refugee camps or urban slums. As opportunities for energetic people increased in the eighteenth and nineteenth centuries – albeit partly as a result of imperialism – the comparative attractions of piracy must have declined. By analogy, countries threatened by terrorism today have a long-term interest in helping to transform the conditions of life, as well as the dominant patterns of education and indoctrination, in the regions from which terrorists now derive or from which they could come in the future.

Conclusion

The coalition against terrorism, organized by the United States after the horrible events of September 11, has exerted effects on conflicts around the world. The anti-terrorist coalition has made it harder for countries such as Pakistan and entities such as the Palestinian Authority to support terrorist activity. Their opponents have capitalized on the opportunity, altering the political map to their advantage.

My broader argument about the public delegitimation of terrorism is more speculative. Yet the analogy with the delegitimation of non-state violence in the eighteenth and nineteenth centuries is particularly suggestive. As with contemporary transnational terrorism, piracy depended on support from states and state elites. The history of its suppression shows that when such non-state violence becomes a serious inconvenience states can act effectively against it. Public delegitimation at a symbolic level has to be accompanied by efforts to define the illegitimate activity in an operational way so that it can be identified and rooted out. At a deeper level, eliminating transnational terrorism, like eliminating piracy, will require a multitrack strategy. Military and police action will be essential. So will sustained efforts to prevent the revival of state support for terrorism. Finally, long-term measures that expand opportunities for people to live productive lives will be necessary if the sources of transnational terrorism are genuinely to be eliminated. Even then, democratic societies will have to maintain safeguards against the use of highly destructive violence by individuals and small groups of individuals, whether with transnational ties or purely domestic in origin.

The violent actions of September 11 had major effects on the lives of thousands and the livelihoods of millions. They threatened the security of societies whose states had seemed sufficiently powerful to protect that security. In response, the US has projected awesome military force halfway around the globe. Yet the long-term political success of the 'war against terrorism' depends on the legitimacy or illegitimacy of practices as well as on military power, intelligence gathering and police work. To win the battle against transnational terrorism, transnational terrorism must become widely regarded as illegitimate, as are slavery and piracy today. Slavery and piracy have not been eliminated in the world, but they have been marginalized. The deepening delegitimation of transnational terrorism is a necessary condition for its disappearance as a major force in world politics.

Notes

1. The author is indebted to Tim Dunne, Peter J. Katzenstein, Nannerl O. Keohane and Joseph S. Nye for comments on an earlier version of this chapter.
2. Eight other United Nations Conventions related to terrorism have been deposited with other international organizations. One of these involves marking plastic explosives; seven deal with violence in or against aircraft and ships, or against oil platforms. The UN also lists seven regional conventions on terrorism. See the UN website: <http://untreaty/un.org/English/Terrorism.asp> (visited January 17, 2002).
3. Alex P. Schmid, 'The Response Problem as a Definition Problem', in Alex P. Schmid and Ronald D. Crelinsten (eds) *Western Responses to Terrorism* (London: Frank Cass, 1993), p. 8.
4. Joseph S. Nye Jnr, *The Paradox of American Power: Why the World's Only Superpower Can't Go It Alone* (New York: Oxford University Press, 2002).
5. President George W. Bush, Address before Congress, September 20, 2001. *New York Times*, September 21, 2001, p. B4.
6. Inis L. Claude, *The Changing United Nations* (New York: Random House, 1967).
7. See *Financial Times*, January 15, 2002, p. 5.
8. Stephen Cohen of the Brookings Institution, quoted in *Financial Times*, January 14, 2002, p. 3.
9. It could be argued that terrorism has been intrinsic to the strategy of militant Palestinian groups, including both Fatah and Hamas, but not to that of Israel: that even if Israel has occasionally resorted to terrorism, it has not relied on it. The actions of the current prime minister, Ariel Sharon, to some degree undercut such a defence of Israeli policy, at least for periods during which he has been in office. A commission of responsibility assigned him 'indirect responsibility' for massacres by Israeli allies of hundreds of Palestinians in refugee camps in Lebanon in 1982, when he was defence minister. Since Sharon came to power in 2001, Israel has assassinated a number of Palestinian civilians on the grounds that they planned or executed terrorist acts. Recently, Prime Minister Sharon stated his regret that Israel did not 'liquidate' Yasser Arafat in 1982 (*New York Times*, February 1, 2002, p. A1).
10. *New York Times*, January 14, 2002, p. A8.
11. For a concise review, with citations see Margaret E. Keck and Kathryn Sikkink, *Activists Beyond Borders: Advocacy Networks in International Politics* (Ithaca, NY: Cornell University Press, 1998).
12. The analogy between the 'white man's burden' of imperialism and current efforts at 'nation building', accompanied by assumptions of Western cultural superiority, has recently been noted. See 'Kipling Knew what the US may now Learn', *New York Times*, January 26, 2002, p. A17.
13. Robert C. Ritchie, *Captain Kidd and the War Against the Pirates* (Cambridge, MA: Harvard University Press, 1986), chapter 2.
14. Janice E. Thomson, *Mercenaries, Pirates and Sovereigns* (Princeton, NJ: Princeton University Press, 1994), pp. 117–18. This is a valuable study on which the discussion in this section draws heavily.
15. See Ritchie, *Captain Kidd*, p. 123.

CHAPTER 13

Meanings of Victory: American Power after the Towers

Michael Cox

If 'the post-Cold War security bubble finally burst' on September 11,[1] what also shattered along with it was a series of cosy assumptions about the world within which we happened to live – one of the most influential of which was that under conditions of globalization the propensity for international conflict would more likely diminish than increase.[2] As the terrorist attacks on New York and Washington revealed only too graphically, globalization not only appeared to have as many determined enemies as well-meaning friends, but enemies of a quite novel (and undeterrable) character. What it also revealed – again to the discomfort of those who assumed the world was becoming a better, safer place – was that the worst sometimes happens. But even the most imaginative of right-wing conspiracy theorists could not have predicted that a group of fanatics, many of them originally organized and trained by the CIA (but now financed by the multi-millionaire son of one of the richest Saudi families) could have carried out an attack which devastated two apparently indestructible buildings in the heart of New York, and then make a series of ghoulish videos boasting of the fact to loyal followers around the world. It was all too fantastic for words, yet its consequences upon political discourse in the US should not be underestimated. Before the act, liberals at least had a voice: after it happened, they went quiet. Perhaps it was not just the lives of 4000 innocent people that al-Qaeda destroyed on September 11, but the narrow ground upon which liberal America had previously been perched. As one conservative astutely pointed out (more in triumph than in sorrow), the tragedy visited upon the United States was the nation's wake-up call, reminding all those who seemed to have forgotten that we still live in a dangerous international system where only tough words, and even tougher measures, suffice.[3]

If the big political winner of September 11 has been the political right in general and George W. Bush in particular, the most embarrassed group has been all those (and there were more than a few) who were once sceptical about the United States' capacity to respond in a time of crisis. Indeed, even if we accept that the world has not been turned completely upside down by what happened on that most photographed of autumn mornings[4] we could hardly ignore the impact which events after September 11 have already had upon perceptions of American power. Before the war, the fashionable view was that the US was a confused and crippled giant led by an inexperienced and possibly illegitimate president. After victory, words alone did not seem to be enough to describe just how formidable the last remaining superpower had suddenly become. It was a most extraordinary reversal. Thus according to one rather typical report, written not long after the defeat of the Taliban, the US was not so much a 'superpower' but a 'behemoth' strutting its stuff 'on the planetary stage'.[5] The *Financial Times* came to much the same conclusion: in fact, it made the point several times over in a series of five articles devoted to the phenomenon of American power.[6] Even that old guru of US decline, Paul Kennedy, had to recant on past intellectual misdemeanours. The US, he sadly confessed, was now the 'only player' left on the field of world politics. The eagle, whose wings he thought had once been clipped, was now flying higher than ever.[7] But it was Mrs Thatcher, not Professor Kennedy, who made the point with the greatest force, and in a moment of rare poetic inspiration even quoted Milton to describe the United States in its new muscular form. 'Methinks I see in my mind a noble and puissant nation rousing herself like a strong man after sleep, and shaking her invincible locks.' Go ahead America, she continued in a slightly less literary vein, make the world a safer place.[8]

Of course, much of what has passed for serious comment since September 11 has been hyperbole. Moreover, most of it seems to have ignored the rather important fact that the 'new' American hegemony of which many now speak in tones of almost awed reverence, is not really new at all, but rather the by-product of a number of significant (and largely ignored) trends that had been transforming the shape of world politics throughout the 1990s.[9] That said, we still have to come to terms with what has happened since the fall of the Twin Towers: for in a relatively short space of time, the US did not just recover its breath but willed an unlikely coalition into being, defeated an enemy, impelled others to change course, and emerged at the other end in an even more favourable international position than the one it was in before. Critics may attack what was done and how it was done. Nonetheless, it was done, and done in such a way as to leave enemies and admirers alike dazed and impressed. Even left-wing opponents were stunned into a rare silence as the Taliban retreated and Kabul celebrated the defeat of its medieval oppressors.

Yet as Walter Lippmann once remarked to Woodrow Wilson, it is a lot easier to win wars than construct peace. And in spite of a quite dazzling performance by the US since September 11, the world is not yet a secure place – and one of the reasons for this is the US itself. What the war has done, basically, is to confirm the Bush administration's view that because stability in an uncertain world derives from power, then the best way of maintaining and sustaining a stable order is not through multilateral agreement, international treaties or international law, but through the threat or the use of force – American force. From this perspective the problem is not that the US has too little power – an argument frequently used in the past to explain why the international system might be under stress – but that it now has too much. The process may have begun before September 11, but it took September 11 to make things clear and reveal the truth. Our story begins, therefore, with the act itself on that beautiful Tuesday morning.

September 11 and After

There are many reasons why September 11 was so shocking to American sensibilities, not the least of which was the scale of the attack itself and the fact that it happened when Americans – according to their own opinion polls – had never been feeling more secure. In fact, not since the British burned the White House in 1812 had the US homeland been subject to a direct attack with the threat, in late 2001 at least (though not 1812), of more appalling acts of carnage to follow. As disturbing, perhaps, was what the atrocity said about the world beyond US borders: that in spite of all the glitz about Americanization and the spread of a Hollywood culture, there are people 'out there' who not only do not share the American world view, but actually hate what the US represents. Perhaps few people were prepared openly to applaud what happened. Indeed, if one recent survey is to be believed, then the most sensitive group of all – Muslims in Islamic countries – actually felt a great deal of sympathy for the US immediately after the attack itself.[10] Nonetheless, there were more than a few who appeared to take quiet satisfaction in seeing the hegemon hit where it hurt most in those quintessential symbols of American power: the Twin Towers and the

Pentagon.[11] Osama bin Laden and his associates had chosen their targets well.

The immediate costs of September 11 were without doubt huge. Yet every crisis, as the president was to remind the American people on several occasions thereafter, represents an opportunity as well as a challenge. Thus how the United States responded to this particular challenge was going to be crucial. Few doubted that the US would take military action, but hardly anybody could have anticipated the speed with which the back of the regime in Afghanistan was broken, and the extent to which the United States then inserted itself into the region as a whole only a few weeks after having launched a war that many originally predicted would end in disaster. The war also seemed to provide the US with a larger rationale. Thus whereas before September 11 the United States appeared to be floundering without purpose, within a blink of an eye it was playing a most active leadership role directing a loose but surprisingly obedient alliance of states of various repute in an ill-defined but very real 'war' against something called international terrorism. And the results were not unimpressive: at least one source of global disturbance in the shape of the Taliban regime was destroyed; the US acquired new bases in countries within the former Soviet Union where before it had had hardly any influence at all;[12] it secured at least one important source of oil;[13] for a while it even seemed to get close to Iran; it sucked in the Russians; and it literally ordered a number of countries like Pakistan, Indonesia and the Philippines to deal with their own fundamentalists. Imperialism might be an inadequate and conspiratorial term by which to describe the process through which the United States increased its global influence post-September 11; but increase it, it undoubtedly did. Indeed, in much the same way that the international struggle against communism led to an expansion of American influence after 1947, the war against the new global enemy known as terrorism helped to extend American power after September 11. Little wonder that certain analysts saw important parallels between the two.[14]

The war also revealed a great deal about the character of alliances in general and the United States' growing indifference to its own allies in particular. Drawing what it felt was the central lesson from its previous engagement in Kosovo – that friends (to quote the 17th Lord Derby) were 'politically useful but militarily a damned nuisance' – the United States decided from the outset to fight the war in Afghanistan without too much interference from its associates. Hence NATO did little more than declare its solidarity by invoking Article 5; meanwhile, other members of the coalition were primarily important either as bases or as cheerleaders. As Kennedy observed rather cryptically, in Afghanistan the US did 98 per cent of the fighting; the British, 2 per cent, while the Japanese 'steamed around Mauritius'.[15] The result was one of the more one-sided wars in recent history – the more obvious one between the United States and its enemies on the ground in Afghanistan, and perhaps also the more important one between the US and its friends in Europe. Tony Blair's hyperdiplomacy may have obscured the fact, but few failed to see what was going on: the Europeans had been sidelined almost completely in an American war fought for largely American ends by American military personnel.

Of course, some wars lead to peace. This one, however, led to renewed American demands for forging ever more effective means of destruction. In reality, the Bush military build-up which followed only confirmed what many already knew to be true: that the gap in military capabilities between the US and the rest of the world was so vast as to be politically embarrassing. However, like the astute politician he was fast becoming, Bush was keen to take advantage of a quiescent Congress and a traumatized nation, and so announced the biggest military increase in US defence expenditure in over 20 years. So huge was the new programme that some, including the president himself, hoped it would kick-start an ailing American economy.[16] Rarely in recent American history has a peacetime leader been quite so explicit in making the connection – but he did, and in the process added another $36 billion to an already planned military budget of $328 billion for 2002, and $48 billion for 2003: a 15 per cent boost in all, and the largest in two decades. This alone would make the United States' spending on defence double that of all the European Union countries put together; and over five years would add another $120 billion to a total defence outlay of nearly $1700 billion. President Bush also requested $38 billion for homeland security programmes for 2003 – double the level of spending for 2002 in a category of expenditure which did not even exist in 2001. As even Paul Kennedy was forced to admit, the 'world's policeman' was not only likely to remain very well-armed, but 'in military terms' it was now the only combatant left in the ring.

Finally, in terms of measuring the United States' response to September 11 we have to take account of its impact upon the US itself. Of one thing we can be sure: the country will never be the same again. Aside from the creation of a new cabinet post whose purpose is to deal with the problem of homeland defence, the Bush administration acted speedily in an attempt to reassure the American people that no such attacks would take place again. This was not easy. Too little would achieve nothing; too much might threaten civil liberties. Bush was in no doubt where his priorities lay. Nor was he alone, and on October 12, Congress passed the aptly named 'USA Patriotic Act' which gave the government significant new powers in dealing with the terrorist threat. This was then followed a month later by the even more incredible executive order signed by President Bush himself (without consulting Congress) which made it legal to try alien terrorists in military tribunal courts with no criminal law or evidential rules of protection.[17] Such measures proved remarkably popular in a country which, having recovered from the initial shock of September 11, was now engaged in a spasm of nationalism whose most visible expressions were the mass flying of the American flag and the almost perpetual singing of the American national anthem – understandable acts of catharsis perhaps, but not without their political consequences. Indeed, this almost unending wave of patriotism not only did much to bolster the Bush presidency, and Bush himself, but also served to unite the country and generate a sense of shared identity. In a hostile world where further action might be required to deal with the terrorist threat, this new sense of ideological cohesion was not to be underestimated. After all, if the US was to take action against Iraq, Iran or even North Korea – the three countries specifically described by Bush as constituting an 'axis of evil' in his State of the Union Address in January 2002 – then it would need the backing of the American people. The so-called Vietnam Syndrome might not have been overcome completely as a result of what happened; nonetheless, September 11 has done much to make Americans a good deal less reluctant to support US military action abroad.

The Future

The argument advanced here is a simple and hopefully controversial one: that, whatever short-term costs the US has had to bear because of what took place – and these should not be underestimated – the longer-term result has been to enhance US credibility and make it much easier to project force around the world,[18] and to cement the country together in ways that have not been seen since the early days of the Cold War. September 11 and the war which ensued have also helped to justify a massive military build-up which will leave the US in an even more dominant position than before. Moreover, all this has occurred in an atmosphere in which legitimate dissent has become synonymous with treachery, where defence of the Geneva Convention now looks decidedly suspect,[19] and in which most American liberals – who were especially vocal in their criticism of Bush before September 11 – can see no alternative (for the moment) but to go along with what is happening.[20] One should not exaggerate. The US is not about to launch a pre-emptive strike against all known enemies. Nor is Joseph McCarthy waiting in the senatorial wings ready to brandish lists of presumed subversives. However, these are troubling times.

This brings us, then, to the problem of the future. As has no doubt been repeated *ad nauseum* since the Taliban fell, it is critically important that the US now draws the right set of lessons from what has happened, and at least two seem obvious to any objective observer: that the enemy state from which the aggression was originally planned was not especially secure or strong, and that the very nature of the attack legitimized some sort of response in the eyes of most people in that entity which has come to be known as the 'civilized world'. Furthermore, in spite of bin Laden's best efforts, his group failed to attract any serious international support, leaving him and his organization highly vulnerable to attack. Indeed, while many Muslims and Arabs might have had little liking for the United States (and even less for the war it then waged) they had even less perhaps for the Taliban who harboured a network of international terrorists whose activities gave Islam a bad name, and whose political rage was just as likely to be directed against other regimes in the Muslim world as it was against the West.

This litany of well-known facts draws us to our first, fairly self-evident conclusion: that attacking and destroying the regime in Afghanistan was a relatively easy task. Attempting to take the war against international terrorism forward against other countries which have no intention of attacking the United States and have far greater capabilities, would not only be far more difficult, but also extraordinarily dangerous. Yet, if presidential rhetoric and recent revelations are to be believed, that is precisely what is now being contemplated, at least in the highest circles around Washington. As one recent report pointed out, it is becoming increasingly clear (though how clear remains open to speculation) 'that the US is not now engaged in a war against terrorism at all. Instead this is a war against regimes the US dislikes', and Iraq is clearly the regime which the US dislikes the most.[21] How and when the 'war' against Saddam will be launched is not known. Whether it will be launched and what form it will take is unclear. Nonetheless, regime change now seems to be the order of the day. Even the more 'moderate' Colin Powell has been reported as saying that such a move 'would be in the best interests of the region, the best interests of the Iraqi people ... we are looking at a variety of options that would bring that about'.[22]

Success in the war against Afghanistan is thus encouraging the United States to think 'creatively' about how to deal with other states and organizations it does not like. But it is also generating a series of perhaps equally important tensions between itself and its European allies. These were simmering beneath the surface long before 9/11, but were to be momentarily checked by the horror of the terrorist attacks on the World Trade Center and the Pentagon. However, these unresolved differences (on the Kyoto Protocol and the Anti-Ballistic Missile Treaty, to name but two) have not gone away. Moreover, the war has only made matters worse – partly because of the way in which it was conducted, and increasingly because of the American urge to carry it forward against other countries. But these are only short-term issues. The longer-term problem arises because of the sheer disparity of power between the US and its different NATO allies. NATO has always been an unequal partnership, but the chasm between one of its constituent parts and the rest has grown exponentially, with potentially major implications for the future cohesion and even meaning of the alliance. The war in Afghanistan did not cause this to happen; what it did do was reveal how great the gap has become, and how much greater it is likely to become in the future. This will not undermine NATO. It is simply too important. Nonetheless, it could easily change its basic character. As the US ambassador to NATO, Nicholas Burns, warned, 'without dramatic action to close the capabilities gap, we face the real prospect of a future two-tiered alliance'; one part composed of what Lord Robertson has called the 'military pygmy' known as Europe and the other being the United States.

Finally, any assessment of the future has to come to terms with another simple fact of international political life: the extent to which the United States itself is moving in an increasingly unilateralist direction.[23] This is not something new. In many ways, there has never been a time when the US – because of its identity, geography and Constitution – has not always reserved the right to act when it likes, how it likes and basically where it likes. This in some ways is the rare privilege enjoyed by all very powerful states. Even the Clinton administration was not immune to the lure of unilateralism. As Madeleine Albright once put it, 'we will behave multilaterally when we can and unilaterally when we must'. However, the Bush administration has taken this whole approach on to a different, almost philosophical plain. This seems to be especially true of those around Donald Rumsfeld, whose world view, it seems, is that to achieve results the United States should not be too sensitive about the political feelings of others. As one member of the Rumsfeld group recently admitted, the Secretary of Defense and his team are very firm 'believers in unilateral American military power'.[24] Nor is this outlook likely to have been dented by what happened in Afghanistan. If this is the case, then the future direction of US foreign policy is likely to be very different from what we have come to expect. When the war began there were those who hoped this would curb the unilateralist inclinations of the Bush administration and that it would emerge on the other side converted to the cause of coalitions and multilateralism. In reality, the war has had almost the opposite effect. This might not please important European leaders;[25] it may upset the United States' allies; and it could in part be checked by those in the foreign policy bureaucracy who recognize that effective action on most issues requires cooperation. But the United States in its current mood appears little inclined to listen to such voices. If anything, the loudest sound coming from Washington is being made by those who think that in a world where the US is all-powerful and the threats against it are all too real, then the country must act alone – if it has to – and with others, if they keep quiet. We live in interesting times.

Notes

1. Ashton B. Carter, 'The Architecture of Government in the Face of Terrorism', in *International Security*, vol. 26, no. 3 (Winter 2001/02), p. 5.
2. For a wide-ranging assessment of the impact of 9/11 on international politics see *inter alia* 'September 11 – and After', *International Relations*, vol. 16, no. 2 (Summer 2002). The two quickest books off the publisher's block were Fred Halliday, *Two Hours that Shook the World* (London: Saqi Books, 2001), and Strobe Talbott and Nayan Chanda (eds) *The Age of Terror and the World After September 11th* (Oxford: Perseus Books, 2002).
3. Adam Garfinkle, 'September 11: Before and After', *Foreign Policy Research Institute*, vol. 9, no. 8.
4. For a sceptical view on the historical importance of September 11 see Chris Brown, 'The "Fall of The Towers" and International Order', *International Relations*, vol. 16, no. 2 (Summer 2002).
5. Peter Beaumont and Ed Vulliamy, 'Focus – American Power: Armed to the Teeth', *Observer*, February 10, 2002.
6. See *Financial Times* series, February 18–22, 2002.
7. Paul Kennedy, 'The Eagle has Landed', *Financial Times*, February 2–3, 2002.
8. Margaret Thatcher, 'Go Ahead and Make the World a Safer Place', *International Herald Tribune*, February 12, 2002.
9. I discuss this in my 'Whatever Happened to American Decline? International Relations and the New United States Hegemony', *New Political Economy*, vol. 6, no. 3 (2001), pp. 311–40, and 'September 11th – Or Will the Twenty First Century be American Too?', *International Studies Perspective*, no. 3 (2002), pp. 53–70.

10. 'Muslims are Strongly at Odds with the US, Survey Shows', *Financial Times*, February 27, 2002.
11 See *Financial Times*, September 12, 2001.
12. 'Three Central Asian Nations Seem Open to US Military', *Wall Street Journal Europe*, September 21–22, 2001.
13. Richard Butler, 'Russia and the US Can Both Win the New Oil Game', *International Herald Tribune*, January 19–20, 2002.
14. See Anatol Lieven, 'Fighting Terrorism: Lessons from the Cold War', *Policy Brief*, no. 7 (October 2001), Carnegie Endowment for International Peace, and Walter A. McDougall, 'Cold War II', *Orbis*, December 2001.
15. Kennedy, 'The Eagle has Landed'.
16. As Dan Plesch of the Royal United Services Institute put it: 'The current rise in US military spending ought to be compared to the decision in the First World War to order up more cavalry when the first wave had been mown down by machine-guns' (quoted in *Observer*, February 10, 2002).
17. See Irene Khan, 'Curtailing Freedom', *The World Today*, vol. 58, no. 2 (February 2002), pp. 7–8.
18. Quoted in *Observer*, February 10, 2002.
19. See Aryeh Neier, 'The Military Tribunals on Trial', *New York Review of Books*, February 14, 2002, pp. 11–15.
20. See Brian Knowlton, 'On US Campuses, Intolerance Grows', *International Herald Tribune*, February 12, 2002.
21. See Hans von Sponeck and Dennis Halliday, 'The Hostage Nation', *Guardian*, November 29, 2001; Evan Thomas, 'Chemistry in the War Cabinet', *Newsweek*, January 28, 2002.
22. Julian Borger and Ewen MacAskill, 'US Targets Saddam', *Guardian*, February 14, 2002.
23. See Paul Rogers, 'Right for America, Right for the World', *The World Today*, vol. 58, no. 2 (February 2), pp. 13–15.
24. Quoted in *Observer*, February 10, 2002.
25. See in particular Chris Patten's attacks on what he called the US 'instinct' to go it alone, in the *Financial Times*, February 15, 2002.

CHAPTER 14

Upholding International Legality Against Islamic and American *Jihad*[1]

Abdullahi Ahmed An-Na'im

While condemning the terrorist attacks of September 11 on the United States in the most categorical and unqualified terms, I also hold that the failure of the international community in any way to check or to regulate the massive and indefinite unilateral response by the United States is a fundamental challenge to international legality. In retaliation since October 7, the United States has acted militarily on a global scale exclusively on its own perceptions of the immediate or anticipated danger to itself, without any assessment of those perceptions through accepted institutional arrangements and processes of international law. To simplify and illustrate the seriousness of this situation in domestic law terms, it is as though someone's house had been attacked and the aggressor had been killed in the attack, but the victim had then taken his gun and gone into the town killing those he believed to be responsible for or associated with the attack. This failure of international legality promotes the cause of militant Islamic fundamentalism and undermines possibilities of support for international peace and protection of universal human rights in Islamic societies.

Space would not permit discussion and assessment of the legality of all the actions of the United States since October 7, and it is probably too early to do so. But my main point in this respect is the *institutional and procedural failure* of international legality, even if the actions of the United States were found to be legal and appropriate if properly scrutinized and evaluated. The essence of the principle of legality, whether at the domestic or the international level, is essentially about the *standards and process* of independent and impartial investigation and adjudication of disputes, rather than subjective determinations of 'entitlement' to act in certain ways. Legality fails whenever actors resort to

self-help and vigilante justice, which is even more serious when perpetrated by the world's sole superpower and permanent member of the
Security Council, which is supposed to be the guardian of international
peace and security.

The serious implications of this failure can better be appreciated
when it is viewed against a background of Western colonial and post-
colonial hegemony and aggression in many parts of the world.
Afghanistan itself was the target of repeated attempts at conquest by
Britain and Russia in the past, and the site of Cold War confrontation
between the Soviet Union and the United States in the 1980s and of
regional conflicts up to the present. This context also includes the use
or sponsorship of terrorism by the United States on the territory of
other countries, especially in South and Central America, and its long-
term support of the same forces it is now seeking to destroy in
Afghanistan. As far as international legality is concerned, one should
recall that the United States simply ignored the judgments of the
International Court of Justice regarding its illegal activities in Nicaragua
in the early 1980s, and invaded Panama in order to kidnap its president
and bring him to trial in the United States, where he is still serving a
prison sentence.

I am unable to appreciate any moral, political or legal difference
between this *jihad* by the United States against those it deems to be its
enemies and the *jihad* by Islamic groups against those they deem to be
their enemies. The Arabic term *jihad* simply means 'self-exertion' or
'special effort', and is used in Islamic discourse to refer to a variety of
activities undertaken in furtherance of the will of God. In fact, the
primary religious meaning of *jihad* for Muslims is 'self-control',
including checking any temptation to harm others.[2] However, the term
can also refer to religiously sanctioned aggressive war to propagate or
'defend' the faith. What is problematic about this latter sense of *jihad* is
that it involves direct and unregulated violent action in pursuit of political objectives, or self-help in redressing perceived injustice, at the risk
of harm to innocent bystanders. It is in this very limited and specific
sense of the term that I am comparing the actions of the United States
since October 7 to claims of *jihad* by Islamic terrorists. The fact that one
approach is rationalized as 'American exceptionalism' and the other as
a religious duty is immaterial for my purposes here, as it relates only to
the motivation of the actors and not to their deliberate intention to act
in this way, nor to the consequences of their action. Moreover, these
recent events have clearly shown that religious motivations have no
'advantage' over mundane calculations of material advantage.

In my view, the aftermath of the attacks of September 11 proves the fallacy of Samuel Huntington's 'clash of civilizations' thesis,[3] in addition to the grave risks it creates for peaceful international relations. The fallacy of this thesis is clear in that the attacks were motivated by specific political, security and human rights grievances against the foreign policy of the United States, rather than by an irrational, generalized Islamic hostility to so-called 'Western civilization' as such. More importantly, there was no indication of a clash of civilizations in the actual positions of any Islamic country, as they all either supported the massive and sustained military retaliation by the United States or acquiesced to it. Instead of standing in solidarity with the Muslims who are alleged to have attacked the United States, or the states accused of harbouring or supporting them, as Huntington's thesis would lead one to expect, all the governments of predominantly Islamic countries have clearly and consistently acted based on calculations of their own economic, political or security interests. What is happening everywhere is simply the politics of power, as usual, and not the manifestation of a clash of civilizations. Yet Huntington's thesis can be a dangerous self-fulfilling prophecy because its underlying premise may be 'vindicated' if either or both sides to this or other conflicts take it seriously and act upon it.

In this light, it becomes clear that the aftermath of September 11 and October 7 is more about the *difference in power* between the two sides of the conflict and their allies, regardless of cultural/religious affiliation, than the *power of difference* between so-called Islamic and Western civilizations. As would be the case everywhere in the world, culture and religion are important dimensions of the conflict only in relation to how events are perceived, interpreted, and reacted to by all sides; they are not independent and static variables. Recent global events do raise the risk of a deepening cultural/religious divide that will undermine the universality of human rights, but this alarming prospect is the product of moral and political choices constantly being made by all sides to this or other similar conflicts, and is not inherent in the nature of cultural/religious difference as such.

It is also important to emphasize that a failure of legality cannot be justified by its outcome. In this instance, the removal of the oppressive and violent Taliban regime from power in Afghanistan may be claimed as 'vindication' of the American military campaign, which has achieved immediate improvement of the protection of human rights for the vast majority of the population, as well as creating favourable conditions for peace, political stability and economic development for the country as a whole. Even if this is a true and sustainable outcome in this case, which is far from clear anyway, such retroactive rationalization violates the essence of the principle of legality which requires legitimate results to be achieved in accordance with generally established principles and processes. Otherwise, other actors will use this dangerous precedent as justification for a wide variety of speculative adventures, some of which are bound to have disastrous consequences.

Underlying the whole analysis is my belief in the critical importance of the rule of law as a framework for responding to this challenge. It should be emphasized, however, that the rule of law in this sense means 'law' that is consistent with international human rights law, and not simply in any formal sense of the term. In my view, this is the only effective and sustainable response to the reality of *our shared vulnerability* as human beings everywhere – even the most privileged and apparently secure persons and groups, as painfully and dramatically illustrated by the attacks of September 11.

The Challenge of Terrorism for Islamic Societies

A major issue facing Islamic societies today is the role of Islam in their national politics and international relations; especially regarding whether, and to what extent, traditional formulations of Sharia should apply today. Different positions on this basic issue have been reflected in the extensive public debate among Muslims since September 11, ranging from a categorical disassociation between Islam and the attacks, at one end, to strong support for them as justified, if not dictated, by Sharia, at the other. In fact, the relationship between Sharia and terrorism has always been an extremely contested subject among Muslims, ever since the first civil war (*al-fitnah al-Kubra*) following the rebellion against Uthman, the third Caliph, and his murder in the year 35 of *Hijrah* (656 CE).[4] Since *textual* sources (the Qur'an and Sunna, or traditions of the Prophet) as well as precedents in early Islamic history can be cited in support of either side in this controversy, I suggest that resolution should be sought in *contextual* mediation between these views; that is, competing textual sources can only be understood and reconciled with reference to a contextual framework for their meaning and practical application today.

The main premise of this contextual mediation is that Islamic sources are supposed to provide moral and political guidance for drastically different Muslim communities living under radically different conditions – from the small city state of Medina in seventh-century

Arabia, to today's nation-state societies, and into the future.[5] The historical context within which Sharia was elaborated during the first three centuries of Islam was an extremely harsh and violent environment, where the use of force in intercommunal relations was the unquestioned norm. It was simply conceptually incoherent and practically impossible for Sharia regulation of intercommunal (international) relations to have been based on principles of peaceful coexistence and rule of law in the modern sense of these terms. The dominant traditional view is that Sharia restricted the causes of the legitimate use of aggressive force in *jihad* to propagating Islam. Sharia also regulated the conduct of hostilities, including the strict prohibition on killing children, old men, women and non-combatants.[6] But it is also clear that there is much ambiguity and diversity of opinion in the theory of Sharia on this subject, and that practice has been far from consistent with that theory throughout Islamic history.

Despite my deep concerns about the current serious threat to the credibility of international legality, I maintain that the traditional understandings of *jihad* are totally untenable today.[7] In my view, the serious threat to international legality posed by the recent conduct of the United States and the complicity of major world powers in this regard does not justify a re-enactment of that sense of *jihad*, and the realities of global power relations would not permit its practice today. The challenge facing Islamic societies today is how to authoritatively and effectively repudiate those notions of *jihad* in the hearts and minds of Muslims, and not only in the official policy and practice of their states. Since Islam addresses the individual Muslim directly, there is a strong sense of obligation to comply with what is believed to be Sharia, regardless of the official policy or action of the state as such. When there is no redress to grave injustice under the rule of law, individual Muslims are likely to invoke religious justification for direct violent action against corrupt regimes at home and perceived enemies abroad.[8]

There are internal and external dimensions to the proposed transformation of the nature and role of Sharia in the lives of modern Islamic societies. The internal dimension includes theological and theoretical debates about the rationale or justification of change, and ways of coping with its traumatic impact on personal and communal lives. This internal dimension also includes the political and sociological 'space' for such debates and experimentation with new ideas and lifestyles. The strong acceptance and effective implementation of universal human rights are critical for all of these facets of social change and cultural transformation.

Regarding the external dimension, if a society feels threatened or under attack, a siege mentality will take hold, whereby people and groups tend to become more conservative and entrenched in their traditional ways of seeing and interpreting things. From this perspective, US foreign policy contributes to the erosion of the internal prerequisites for social change and transformation, as well as reinforcing a sense of external threat that encourages conservative entrenchment. It also encourages strong scepticism about the validity of universal human rights, whether by supporting oppressive regimes like Saudi Arabia or by enabling that of Iraq to consolidate its control by citing the external pressure of sanctions and the constant threat of air strikes as justification for its behaviour. These long-term negative consequences are now drastically compounded by the military campaign in Afghanistan.

This recent failure of international legality severely undermines the conceptual and political premise of arguments against the traditional understanding and practice of *jihad* in Islamic society. This sequence of events is a betrayal of Muslim advocates of international legality because it undermines the conceptual as well as the political basis of their internal Islamic argument against *jihad* and in favour of the universality of human rights. The proponents of *jihad* as an aggressive war are more likely to be supported by the majority of Muslims in a world where military force and self-help prevail over the rule of law in international relations.

The Challenge of American *Jihad* to International Legality

I am not suggesting that the United States should passively submit to repeated atrocious attacks against its citizens and interests at home and abroad, nor am I drawing any conclusions about the possible legal justification(s) for its military campaign in Afghanistan. Rather, my position is simply that the actions of the United States since October 7 cannot be accepted as being in conformity with international legality unless they are scrutinized and approved by the *institutional and procedural* requirements of that system. Whatever legal justification(s) may be claimed for the actions of the United States, they can never authorize it to act as prosecutor, judge, jury and executioner in its own cause and still claim the legitimacy of international legality.

While a detailed assessment of the legality of these actions is beyond the scope of this chapter, it is important to note that the limited activities of the UN Security Council in this regard only confirm the failure of international legality. The Security Council adopted two resolutions prior to October 7: Resolution 1368 of September 12, 2001, and Resolution 1373 of September 28, 2001. The first simply condemned the attacks and decided 'to remain seized of the matter' without making any other decision. The second affirmed the right of self-defence in its preamble, but did not sanction any use of force under Chapter VII of the UN Charter. In my view, the failure of international legality lies in the fact that the American military campaign began four weeks *after* the attacks of September 11, and continued for more than three months (at the time of writing), and yet the Security Council neither authorized, endorsed nor condemned any of these actions, let alone acted itself to preserve international peace and security, as required by the Charter.

Terrorism is a serious threat to human rights precisely because there is a powerful temptation to sacrifice principled commitment to the due process of law in the name of defending national security and public safety. The ultimate objective of terrorism, in all its forms and from whatever source it may come, is to diminish the humanity of its victims and to reduce them to its own level of barbarity. To respond to this challenge, each society needs to reflect on its own enlightened and humane best interests in the face of such grotesque behaviour. In particular, since direct retaliation will only feed into a downward spiral of mutual destruction, each society has to strive to understand and address the possible causes of what appears to be utterly senseless carnage, however alien and incomprehensible that may be to that society's own sense of rationality.

Failure to acknowledge and address the rationality of the terrorists is to deny their humanity, and thereby to forfeit any possibility of universality of human rights. This is why it is critically important to take into serious consideration the grievances articulated by terrorists, like the various pronouncements and international media interviews given by bin Laden before and after the attacks of September 11, without implying that such views justify or legitimize terrorism as a means of redress. Understanding the motivation of any terrorist is essential for a reasoned and sustainable response, and should not be seen as condoning the crime or blaming the victim. It is from this perspective that I insist that it is relevant, indeed necessary, to consider the relationship between the attacks of September 11 and US foreign policy. This perspective applies to US policy in relation to particular regions of the world – the Middle East, in this case – and to its subversive impact on international legality.

Upholding International Legality for Human Rights

One of the consequences of the recent failure of international legality is that it precludes any meaningful discussion of the legal characterization of both the terrorist attacks of September 11 and the military retaliation by the United States and its allies since October 7. Instead of engaging in a hypothetical or speculative discussion of these issues, I prefer to focus here on clarifying what I mean by this failure of international legality, and its drastic implications for the universality of human rights. My point here can easily be appreciated from the old maxim, 'Justice must not only be done, but must also *be seen* to be done.' In this case, the apparently arbitrary, unfettered and unilateral power of the US to do what it pleases across the world is as damaging to the legitimacy and credibility of international law (and human rights) as an affirmation that it actually has the legal authority to do so.

However, it is also pertinent to ask, 'What is the alternative? How can the United States protect its own citizens and safeguard its sovereignty and territorial integrity, even its national dignity and pride as the world's sole superpower?' The answer is simply that the attacks were international crimes of the utmost seriousness that must be vigorously investigated in order to hold those responsible accountable under the law. From this perspective, and according to the available and verifiable facts, the legal issue between the US government and the Taliban government of Afghanistan immediately after the attacks should be characterized as an extradition matter, and pursued as such. This approach may have been unrealistic regarding the attacks of September 11, but it was never given a serious chance by the US, whose actions since October 7 make such an approach even less viable in similar cases in the future.

If there is the political will to treat the attacks as a matter for law enforcement, not military retaliation, I believe that there are enough normative and institutional resources to begin the process of criminal accountability under international law. Available models include *ad hoc* international tribunals established by the UN Security Council and tribunals established as a result of negotiations between concerned states, as happened in the case of the bombing of the Pan Am flight over Lockerbie in Scotland. In fact, during the first week of October, a few days prior to the commencement of the American military campaign, Iran made an offer via the British Foreign Secretary to use the mediation of the Organization of the International Islamic Conference (which was to meet the following week in Bahrain) to agree on a forum whereby suspects in the September 11 attacks could be brought to trial based on the evidence. The Taliban regime made a similar offer for mediation by the International Islamic Conference and the UN. The United States rejected both offers and demanded the immediate and unconditional surrender of Osama bin Laden and al-Qaeda leaders, exclusively on the grounds of its own assertion of their responsibility for the attacks, without allowing for any independent and impartial verification of the evidence. According to some press reports at the time, the United States showed the evidence it had against Osama bin Laden and his associates to its NATO allies, some of whom felt that it would not stand in a court of law – but even if they all found the evidence sufficient for a conviction, that would still not be good enough from the viewpoint of due process of law.

It may be true that the institutional capacity and practical efficacy of the international legal order are insufficient for these purposes, but this claim is not available to the United States simply because it never gave international legality a chance to work in this case. Moreover, the only way to remedy the weakness or inadequacies of international legal processes is to invest in the development of the system over time. The point is clearly illustrated in the legal history of the United States itself. When organized crime unleashed a streak of violence, intimidation and corruption in the 1920s that seriously threatened public safety and undermined the administration of justice in many parts of the country, the US government persisted in its commitment to the rule of law and gradually built a credible domestic judicial system without compromising on due process. Without similar determination and perseverance, the time will never come when the rule of law replaces self-help and vigilante justice in international relations.

The problem here is that the United States is committed only to the protection of the civil liberties of its own citizens, with little regard for the human rights of other people elsewhere in the world. This can be seen in the treatment of non-citizens within the US since September 11, including the military directive of President Bush authorizing the trial of foreign nationals, and including lawful permanent residents of the US itself, suspected of terrorism before military tribunals, with no due process protection.[9] In this light, and given its strong opposition to efforts to establish the International Criminal Court, one may wonder whether the United States' rush to military action was not part of a deliberate policy to subvert any possibility of international criminal accountability for the terrorists attacks of September 11.

In the final analysis, however, since it was so clear that the United States was unwilling to give due process of international law a chance, why did the Security Council fail to intervene to uphold the mandate of the Charter of the United Nations itself for the peaceful settlement of disputes? Why did the Security Council fail, in the two resolutions it passed on the matter prior to October 7, either to expressly authorize the use of force by the United States and clearly define the scope and objectives of its military operations, or to call for the establishment of a UN force for the purpose? The apparent answer to these and related questions is that the members of the Council itself, especially the five permanent members, have conspired to paralyse and marginalize the UN system for their own political interests. It is relevant to recall here, I believe, that none of the major actors in that subversion of international legality come to this with clean hands. While a host of countries, including the United States and Russia, have used terrorist methods or sponsored terrorists for decades, others have either done so in the recent past or have their own peculiar political reasons for failing to challenge those who do.

Notes

1. This chapter is based on a paper I presented at an International Meeting on Global Trends and Human Rights – Before and After September 11, organized by the International Council on Human Rights Policy, Geneva, January 10–12, 2002.
2. Al-Kaya al-Harasiy, *Ahkam al-Qur'an* (The Precepts of the Qur'an) (Beirut: al-Muktabah al-ilmiya, 1983), vol. 1, pp. 78–89.
3. Samuel P. Huntington, *The Clash of Civilizations and the Remaking of World Order* (New York: Simon and Schuster, 1996).
4. Wilfred Madelung, *The Succession of Muhammad: A Study of the Early Caliphate* (Cambridge: Cambridge University Press, 1997), chapter 4.
5. Abdullahi Ahmed An-Na'im, 'Islamic Ambivalence to Political Violence: Islamic Law and International Terrorism', *German Yearbook of International Law*, vol. 31 (1988), pp. 307–44.
6. Muhammad Hamidullah, *The Muslim Conduct of State* (Lahore: Sh. M. Ashraf, 1966), pp. 305–9.
7. Abdullahi Ahmed An-Na'im, *Toward an Islamic Reformation* (Syracuse, NY: Syracuse University Press, 1990).
8. Khaled Abou El Fadl, *Rebellion and Violence in Islamic Law* (Cambridge: Cambridge University Press, 2001), pp. 337–42.
9. Aryeh Neier, 'The Military Tribunals on Trial', *New York Review of Books*, vol. XLIX, no. 2 (February 14, 2001), pp. 11–15.

CHAPTER 15

The United States and the Israeli–Palestinian Conflict[1]

Avi Shlaim

Major wars have a habit of generating a peace agenda which goes beyond the immediate security objectives of the campaign to outline a vision of a better world, of international order based on universal values such as justice and morality. This is particularly true of wars that are fought not by one country but by a coalition of countries. The broader peace agenda is needed to keep the coalition together and to justify the sacrifices that have to be made in the course of fighting the war against the adversary.

Thus, the First World War was the war to end all wars. The Second World War was fought to free the world from the scourge of fascism and to make it safe for democracy. On January 16, 1991, George Bush Snr stated that military action against Iraq would make possible a 'New World Order, a world where the rule of law, not the law of the jungle, governs the conduct of nations'. Similarly, George Bush Jnr embarked on the war against the al-Qaeda organization and the Taliban regime in Afghanistan with the broader agenda of freeing the world from the scourge of international terrorism.

Linkage Politics

There are other striking parallels between the Gulf War and the war in Afghanistan. In the first place, on the American side, some of the key positions today are held by veterans of the Gulf War, including Dick Cheney, Paul Wolfowitz and Colin Powell. Second, in both conflicts the incumbent US president sought to build a broad international coalition to confront the aggressor. Third, in both wars Israel was kept at arm's length in order to preserve the coalition. Fourth, in both cases a link was quickly established between the conflict at hand and the Palestine problem.

In 1990 Saddam Hussein pioneered the concept of 'linkage' by making Iraq's withdrawal from Kuwait conditional on Israel's withdrawal from all the Arab lands that it occupied in 1967.[2] Thus, before threatening the 'mother of all battles' if Iraq was attacked, Saddam Hussein unleashed the mother of all linkages. President Bush rejected the proposed linkage so as not to appear to reward Saddam's aggression, and in order to deflate his claim to be the champion of the Palestinians. But Bush could not, without exposing himself to the charge of double standards, insist that Iraq should comply immediately and unconditionally with UN orders to withdraw from Kuwait without accepting that Israel should be made to comply with strikingly similar UN resolutions that had been on the table since 1967. Bush's way round this problem was to intimate that the US would address the Arab–Israeli conflict as soon as Iraq pulled out of or was booted out of Kuwait. In other words, while rejecting simultaneous linkage, Bush implicitly accepted deferred linkage.

After the guns fell silent in the Gulf, the Bush administration came up with a five-point plan for the future of the Middle East. The elements of this plan, the 'five pillars of wisdom' as one observer dubbed them, were democracy, economic development, arms control, Gulf security, and a settlement of the Arab–Israeli conflict. It was a sound and well-thought-out plan, but it simply fell by the wayside. The much-vaunted New World Order turned out to be the old world order minus the Soviet Union. In the aftermath of victory, the US, the sole surviving superpower, and its Arab allies reverted to their bad old ways. No serious attempt was made to introduce democracy to the Arab world, to promote greater economic equality, to curb arms sales to the region, or to lay the foundations for an independent system of Gulf security.

The one element of the programme for postwar reconstruction that did receive sustained attention was the Arab–Israeli conflict. The American-sponsored peace process was launched with the conference in Madrid towards the end of October 1991. The basis of the conference was UN Resolutions 242 and 338 and the principle of land for peace that they incorporated. All the parties to the conflict were there, including the Palestinians who presented their own case for the first time at a major international gathering. In his opening speech, President Bush was faultlessly even-handed: he gave a pledge to work for a settlement based on security for Israel and justice for the Palestinians.[3]

Two tracks for bilateral negotiations were established at Madrid: an Israeli–Arab track and an Israeli–Palestinian track. But as long as Yitzhak Shamir, the leader of the right-wing Likud Party, remained in power, no real progress could be achieved on either track. Shamir, in line with the ideological position of the party that he headed, was adamant that the West Bank was an integral part of the Land of Israel. Bush was equally insistent that the project of Greater Israel had to be abandoned and that the building of new Jewish settlements on the West Bank had to stop. A battle of wills ensued. By forcing Israelis to choose between US aid and continuing colonization of the West Bank, Bush contributed to Shamir's electoral defeat in June 1992 and to his replacement by a Labour government headed by Yitzhak Rabin. But the bruising battle was also a factor in George Bush's own defeat in the presidential elections later that year. Deferred linkage did not materialize due to Israeli intransigence. Two years after the liberation of Kuwait, the Palestinian problem remained unresolved. George Bush Snr failed to deliver on his pledge 'to push the Israelis into a solution'.

Bill Clinton's 'Israel First' Approach

On becoming president, Bill Clinton gave free rein to his pro-Israeli sympathies. He abruptly reversed the even-handed policy of his predecessor and replaced it with an 'Israel-first' policy reminiscent of the Reagan years. The new approach was laid out by Martin Indyk, a senior official on the National Security Council, in a speech he gave to the Washington Institute for Near East Policy on May 18, 1993. Two elements were listed by Indyk as central: Israel had to be kept strong while the peace process continued, and Iraq and Iran had to be kept weak. The second element was called 'dual containment' and one of its aims was to protect Israel on the Eastern front.

Regarding the Middle East peace process, said Indyk, 'our approach to the negotiations will involve working with Israel, not against it. We are committed to deepening our strategic partnership with Israel in the pursuit of peace and security.' Withdrawing from territory, Indyk argued, involved risks to Israel's security, and Israel would only take these risks if it knew that the United States stood behind it. Real progress in the talks could only come with this kind of special relationship between the US and Israel. No similar pledge was made to work with the Arabs or the Palestinians. As a result, the US in effect abdicated its independent role as the manager of the peace process and took the side of one of the protagonists. After ten rounds, the bilateral negotiations in Washington reached a dead end.[4]

The breakthrough announced in September 1993 on the Palestinian track was made in Oslo, not in Washington. The Declaration of

Principles on Palestinian self-government in Gaza and Jericho was negotiated directly between Israel and the Palestine Liberation Organization (PLO) in the Norwegian capital without American help or even knowledge. Israel recognized that the Palestinians have national rights while the PLO renounced terrorism. Bill Clinton served essentially as the master of ceremonies when the Oslo Accord was signed on the White House lawn and clinched with the hesitant handshake between Yitzhak Rabin and Yasser Arafat. Clinton did recognize, however, the need for an active American role in supporting the experiment in Palestinian self-government. But while Israel continued to receive $3 billion a year, as well as extra funds to finance its withdrawal from Gaza and Jericho, only modest 'seed money' was advanced to the Palestinian Authority.

The rise to power in May 1996 of a Likud government headed by Benjamin Netanyahu dealt a heavy blow to the Oslo peace process. Netanyahu was a bitter opponent of the Oslo Accord, viewing it as incompatible both with Israel's security and with its historic right to the biblical homeland.[5] He spent his three years as prime minister in an attempt to arrest the exchange of land for peace that lay at the heart of the Oslo Accord. This Israeli retreat from the historic compromise struck at Oslo called for a reassessment of the American role, but no real reassessment took place. President Clinton maintained an active personal involvement in the Israeli–Palestinian peace talks, but he achieved only very modest results in the shape of the Hebron Protocol of January 15, 1997, and the Wye River Memorandum of October 23, 1998. Israeli feet-dragging was the primary cause of the loss of momentum on the road to peace. But the redefinition of the American role, following Clinton's entry into the White House, inadvertently facilitated this feet-dragging. It left the Palestinians largely to the tender mercies of a right-wing government which remained committed to the old vision of Greater Israel.

The electoral victory of Ehud Barak in May 1999 promised a fresh start in the struggle towards comprehensive peace in the Middle East. It also provided an opening for Bill Clinton to resume the role he had always wanted to play, that of helping Israel to assume the risks involved in exchanging territory for peace. Like his mentor Yitzhak Rabin, Barak was a soldier who turned to peacemaking late in life. Israel's most decorated soldier, however, turned out to be a hopelessly incompetent domestic politician and maladroit diplomat. He approached diplomacy as the extension of war by other means. He was much more interested in an agreement with Syria than with the

Palestinians because Syria is a military power to be reckoned with whereas the Palestinians are not. Accordingly, Barak concentrated almost exclusively on the Syrian track during the first eight months of his premiership, but his efforts ended in failure. It was only after his policy of 'Syria-first' failed that Barak reluctantly turned to the Palestinian track. Throughout this period, Clinton remained solidly behind Barak and made no attempt to play an independent role in the management of the Middle East peace process.

The critical point in the Israeli–Palestinian final status negotiations was reached at the Camp David summit in July 2000. On the causes of failure there are two radically different versions. The Israeli version is that Barak presented a most generous package at Camp David but Arafat rejected this out of hand and chose to revert to violence. The Palestinian version is that Barak laid a trap for Arafat and sought to impose on him, with the help of the American 'peace processors', a fundamentally unfair and unsound final status agreement.

A most revealing first-hand account of Camp David was published by Robert Malley, Special Assistant on Arab–Israeli Affairs, and Hussein Agha, a Palestinian expert. Three main points emerge from their account. First, the idea of setting aside Israel's interim obligations and tackling all the issues together at a summit meeting was proposed by Barak to Clinton. Second, Arafat pleaded for additional time to prepare the ground and warned Clinton of the danger that the summit would explode in his face unless progress was made in narrowing the gap between the two sides. Indeed, both the concept and the timing of the proposed summit reinforced in Arafat's mind the sense of an Israeli–American conspiracy. Third, Clinton assured Arafat that he would not be blamed if the summit did not succeed. 'There will be no finger-pointing', he promised. What is not clear is why Clinton put all the blame on Arafat after the failure of the summit. The answer suggested by Malley and Agha is that Camp David exemplified for Clinton the contrast between Barak's political courage and Arafat's political passivity, between risk-taking on one side and risk-aversion on the other side. But they also point to the complex and often contradictory roles that the United States played at the summit: as principal broker of the putative peace deal; as guardian of the peace process; as Israel's strategic ally; and as its cultural and political partner.[6] It is difficult to avoid the conclusion that Clinton's strong commitment to Israel undermined his credibility as an honest broker and was therefore one of the factors that contributed to the collapse of the Camp David summit.

Clinton himself seems to have drawn the right lessons from the failure at Camp David. On December 23, 2000, five months after the meeting in Maryland and two months after the outbreak of the second Palestinian Intifada, he presented a detailed plan for the resolution of the Israeli–Palestinian dispute. The plan reflected the long distance that Clinton had travelled towards meeting Palestinian expectations since the American 'bridging proposals' tabled at Camp David. His plan envisaged an independent Palestinian state over the whole of Gaza and 94–96 per cent of the West Bank; Palestinian sovereignty over all the Arab parts of Jerusalem except for the Jewish Quarter in the Old City and the Western Wall; and the right of the Palestinian refugees to return to their homeland in historic Palestine, subject to Israel's sovereign decision to absorb them in its own territory.[7] Considerable progress towards a final status agreement was made by Israeli and Palestinian negotiators at Taba, Egypt, in January 2001, on the basis of these proposals or 'parameters'. They basically accepted the parameters, although each side had many outstanding doubts and reservations.[8] But time ran out on two of the main actors. On January 20, Clinton was succeeded as president by George W. Bush, and, on February 6, Ehud Barak was defeated by Ariel Sharon in the direct election of the prime minister.

The new Republican president departed from the approach of his Democratic predecessor in two respects. First, whereas Clinton was prepared to devote as much of his presidency as it took to resolve the Israeli–Palestinian dispute, Bush Jnr adopted a 'hands-off' attitude of leaving it to the two sides to sort out their own differences. Second, whereas Clinton had a special bond with the leaders of the Labour Party in Israel as well as with Yasser Arafat, Bush cold-shouldered the Palestinian leader and established surprisingly warm relations with the right-wing Israeli leader. After their first meeting at the White House, Bush commented on Sharon's 'marvellous sense of history'. More importantly, the Bush administration seemed receptive to the Sharon line that Yasser Arafat is a terrorist, that the Palestinian Authority is a terrorist entity, and that they should be treated as such. Sharon's refusal to resume the political dialogue with the Palestinian Authority until there is a complete cessation of violence, struck a sympathetic chord in Washington. Vice-President Dick Cheney went as far as to justify in public Israel's policy of assassinating Palestinian activists suspected of orchestrating the violence.

September 11 and the War against Terrorism

The terrorist attacks on the World Trade Center and the Pentagon on September 11 violently shook the kaleidoscope of world politics. It had far-reaching consequences for almost all aspects of US foreign policy, including relations with Israel and the Palestinians. Many Israelis hoped that the events of September 11 would engender greater sympathy and support in the US for their own war against Palestinian militants. Ariel Sharon reportedly said to Colin Powell, 'Everyone has his own bin Laden and Arafat is ours.' Sharon also hoped to make common cause with the US in the war against international terrorism. All these hopes, however, were quickly dashed. Colin Powell made it clear that 'Israel will not be part of any anti-terror military action.' The attempt to demonize Yasser Arafat backfired. While Israel was firmly excluded from the emergent anti-terror coalition, some of its enemies, such as Syria and Iran, were being considered for membership. Hizbullah, Hamas, and Islamic Jihad were conspicuous in their absence from the list of 27 terrorist organisations that had their assets frozen by Congress. They were treated on this occasion as local movements fighting against occupation, not as global terrorist networks like the one headed by Osama bin Laden. Far from gaining respectability, Israel felt that it was being treated almost as a pariah and as an impediment to the American effort to build an anti-terror coalition.

Worse was to come. Two weeks after the attacks President Bush issued the strongest statement yet endorsing an independent Palestinian state with East Jerusalem as its capital. The Bush administration's plan, which was said to have been in preparation prior to September 11, envisages the handing back of nearly all the West Bank to Palestinian control. Departing from its standard operating procedures, the State Department prepared its own plan rather than forwarding Israeli proposals with minor modifications. The plan itself was anathema to Mr Sharon, who was committed to keeping the whole of Jerusalem under Israeli control. He seemed reluctant to yield to the Palestinian Authority more than the 42 per cent of the West Bank that it currently controls; and he envisaged a weak Palestinian entity made up of isolated enclaves with no territorial contiguity.

Sharon reacted to the United States' peace plan with an astonishing outburst of anger which reflected his deep fear that the US might abandon the strategic alliance with Israel in favour of an alliance of convenience with the Arab states and the Palestinians. He warned President Bush not to repeat the mistake of Neville Chamberlain in

1938 of trying to appease Nazi Germany by offering Hitler part of Czechoslovakia. 'Do not try to appease the Arabs at our expense', said Mr Sharon. 'Israel will not be Czechoslovakia. Israel will fight terrorism.' The analogy with Munich is preposterous: Israel is not Czechoslovakia but an occupying power; the Palestinian Authority is not Nazi Germany; and Yasser Arafat is no Adolf Hitler. After being compared to Neville Chamberlain of all people, Bush must have regretted his remark about Sharon's marvellous sense of history. In any case, the official American response reflected extreme displeasure. 'The prime minister's comments are unacceptable', said Ari Fleischer, the White House spokesman:

> Israel has no stronger friend and ally in the world than the United States. President Bush has been an especially close friend of Israel. The Unites States has been working for months to press the parties to end the violence and return to political dialogue. The United States will continue to press both Israel and the Palestinians to move forward.

Although Mr Sharon expressed regret for provoking this public row, his allegation of appeasement and of treachery continued to rankle.

Israel's reaction to the assassination of tourism minister Rehavam Ze'evi by the Popular Front for the Liberation of Palestine (PFLP), in Jerusalem on October 17, deepened the crisis in the relations with the US. The radical right and racist former general, who advocated the 'transfer' of Palestinians from Palestine, was a personal friend of Ariel Sharon. The assassination was a straightforward retaliation for Israel's 'targeted killing' of the PFLP leader, Abu Ali Mustapha, in August. Sharon warned Arafat of 'all-out war' unless he handed over the assassins. Without waiting for a reply, he ordered the Israeli Defence Forces to reoccupy six cities in Area A on the West Bank in the most drastic assault on Yasser Arafat's Authority since limited self-rule began seven years ago. The scale and ferocity of the incursion shocked many Israelis, including Shimon Peres, the foreign minister and leading advocate of the policy of negotiation as opposed to the policy of retaliation. It appeared to serve the not-so-secret agenda of the hardliners in the government and in the army of destroying the peace process by banishing Arafat and bringing about the collapse of the Palestinian Authority.

The aggressive move against the Palestinian Authority placed Israel on a collision course with the US. The US denounced the move in uncharacteristically blunt terms and called on Israel to quit the West Bank cities immediately and unconditionally. It also warned Sharon that the war against the Palestinians threatened the fragile coalition against the Taliban regime and Osama bin Laden. Sharon flatly rejected the American demand in a remarkable display of defiance towards an ally that gives his country $3 billion in aid every year. But he was forced to recognize his error in thinking that the terrorist attack on the US provided Israel with an opportunity to redefine the rules of the game in the local conflict with the Palestinians. Having declared that Israel would act unilaterally in defence of its own interests, he was compelled to take American interests into account. A gradual withdrawal from the West Bank cities was set in motion.

The pro-American Arab regimes, led by Egypt, Jordan and Saudi Arabia, viewed the escalation of violence in Palestine with mounting anguish and anxiety. They had been shamed and discredited in the eyes of their own people by their inability to help the Palestinians or to modify the United States' blatant partiality towards Israel. Osama bin Laden was quick to seize the plight of the Palestinians as an additional stick with which to beat these Arab regimes following the Anglo-American assault on Afghanistan: 'Israeli tanks are wreaking havoc in Palestine – in Jenin, Ramallah, Rafah and Beit Jala and other parts of the land of Islam, but no one raises his voice or bats an eyelid.' Like the Iraqi dictator, bin Laden exploited the plight of the Palestinians for his own ends. But his motives did not detract from the centrality of the Palestine question. His plea struck a sympathetic chord in much of the Arab and Islamic world. And by swearing that the US would have no peace until Palestine was free, the besieged bin Laden succeeded in setting the agenda for Arab demands on Palestine.

Yasser Arafat was the first Arab leader to denounce the horrific terrorist attacks of September 11. He had paid a heavy price for his support of Saddam Hussein following the invasion of Kuwait, and he was not about to make the same mistake again. Arafat and his colleagues, and all thoughtful Palestinians, sought to distance themselves from bin Laden, the Lucifer of international terrorism. Bin Laden's war against the West is a religious war, whereas the Palestinians' struggle against Israel is essentially a political and national struggle, although there is an undeniable religious dimension to it. Palestinians also draw a firm distinction between the kind of unbridled terrorism practised by bin Laden and their own resort to violence in self-defence. A further distinction they make concerns Israeli violence, which they regard as illegitimate because its purpose is to perpetuate the occupation of their land and their own resistance to Israeli occupation. The US stands accused of double standards, of subscribing to a definition of terrorism that, until very recently, suited only Israel. Arab and Muslim groups have been pressing for some time for a new definition of terrorism that excludes movements resisting occupation. The lack of one helps to explain their lukewarm response to the American led coalition against it.

Clearly, a link existed between the war in Afghanistan and the conflict in Palestine. For the majority of Arabs and Muslims, Palestine is a central issue. Their attitude towards the United States' war in Afghanistan was determined to a large extent by its stand on the Palestine question. And the dominant perception was one of American double standards, of one standard applied to Israel and another to the Palestinians. Consequently, the US did not receive unambiguous Arab support in its war against international terrorism because it did not satisfy the moderate Arab demands on Palestine, meaning the Clinton parameters: a deal that would establish the borders for an independent and sovereign Palestinian state, that would allow for the return of some refugees, and that would divide Jerusalem between Israel and the Palestinians. President Bush took a critical step forward in invoking international justice to justify the war in Afghanistan. To be consistent, he had to uphold the same standard of justice for the Palestinians. Verbal commitments no longer carry much credibility. His father promised justice for the Palestinians after the Gulf War and failed to deliver. He himself will be judged not by words but by actions.

Conclusion

From this brief review of US policy towards the Israeli–Palestinian conflict during the last decade, a number of conclusions emerge. First, on their own the two sides are incapable of reaching a resolution of their 100-year-old conflict. They came tantalizingly close at Taba in January 2001, but they did not get there. Second, the policy of using American moral, material and military support to give Israel the confidence to go forward in the peace process has not achieved the desired results. The best proof is Bill Clinton. He was, in the words of one Israeli newspaper, the last Zionist. Yet even he could not sweet-talk Israel into a final settlement. If Clinton could not do it, nobody can. That leaves only one possible path to progress: an externally imposed solution.

An externally imposed solution sounds rather coercive and brutal towards Israel but it need not be. Indeed, if it is brutal, it will backfire.

The key to progress is to bring about a change in Israeli public opinion in favour of ending the occupation and conceding to the Palestinians the right to genuine national self-determination. Improbable as it may look today, such a change is not inconceivable. The Israeli public has never been as resistant to the idea of Palestinian statehood as the politicians of the right. At the last elections, Ariel Sharon promised peace with security and has decidedly failed to deliver either. Today, Sharon does not have a plan with the remotest chance of being acceptable to the other side, and he knows it. Hence his stubborn opposition to the resumption of the final status negotiations. At the same time, he is being subjected to the most intense pressure by his coalition partners. The left is pressing him to quit the West Bank; the right is pressing him to reoccupy it. His main aim is survival and that precludes the option of voluntary withdrawal from the West Bank. So once again, as so often in the past, the peace process is held hostage to domestic Israeli politics.

Only the US can break the deadlock in Israeli politics. If it does not, no one else will. The credentials of the US as a friend are impeccable. Since 1967, it has given Israel more than $92 billion in aid and this aid continues to the tune of $3 billion a year. The US should involve the United Nations, the European Union, Russia, and its Arab allies in a concerted effort to generate internal pressure on Sharon to move forward on the political front, but its own leadership role is crucial. The key point to drive home in this educational campaign is that the US remains committed to Israel's security and welfare, and that the country's security will be enhanced rather than put at risk by ending the occupation of the West Bank and Gaza. Arguably, the US would be doing Sharon a favour by walking him into a peace deal against which, given his ideological provenance, he is bound to protest loudly in public. Moreover, a fair number of sensible, level-headed Israelis would be grateful to the US for liberating them from the 35-year-old colonial venture which has so disastrously distorted the Zionist political project. In the end, it might be a question, as George Ball once put it in an article in *Foreign Affairs*, of how to save Israel against itself.

Notes

1. Avi Schlaim would like to thank the United States Institute of Peace for their support.
2. Lawrence Freedman and Efraim Karsh, *The Gulf Conflict, 1990–1991: Diplomacy and War in the New World Order* (London: Faber and Faber, 1993), pp. 101–2.

3. Avi Shlaim, *The Iron Wall: Israel and the Arab World* (New York: W.W. Norton, 2000).
4. Avi Shlaim, *War and Peace in the Middle East: A Concise History* (New York: Penguin Books, 1995), pp. 120–2.
5. Benjamin Netanyahu, *Fighting Terrorism* (New York: Farrar Strauss Giroux, 1995), pp. 102–5.
6. Robert Malley and Hussein Agha, 'Camp David: The Tragedy of Errors', *New York Review of Books*, August 9, 2001.
7. Bernard Wasserstein, *Divided Jerusalem: The Struggle for the Holy City* (London: Profile Books, 2001), pp. 347–9.
8. Akiva Eldar, 'The Peace that Nearly Was at Taba', *Ha'aretz*, February 15, 2002.

CHAPTER 16

The Reconstruction of Afghanistan

William Maley

The crushing of the Taliban movement represents only the first stage in the return of Afghanistan to membership of the international community. Afghanistan's problems are awesome, and reconstruction is not a straightforward task. To put the country back on its feet, it is necessary to accomplish the interconnected tasks of reconstituting the state, rebuilding trust at elite and mass levels, overcoming the threat of predatory warlordism, redeveloping a shattered infrastructure and meeting the urgent needs of the most vulnerable Afghans without disrupting market mechanisms and norms of reciprocity which have sustained a large proportion of the population through decades of turmoil. All these objectives must be pursued in a climate of uncertainty as to the exact amount of aid that will be made available in the long run, and in the face of rising expectations on the part of ordinary Afghan men and women, a very large number of whom are deeply traumatized as a result of their experiences of war. Such difficulties would be challenging for any rulers, but for rulers coming to power after years of being neglected by the wider world, they are especially daunting.

A range of factors allowed Osama bin Laden's al-Qaeda to put down roots in Afghanistan. During the 1980s, bin Laden had spent time in Peshawar and supported Arab volunteers in Afghanistan, although there is no evidence that he did so with American backing, or that the Arabs he backed played a significant role in the anti-Soviet resistance. Nevertheless, he had a sense of engagement with Afghanistan, which made it a natural destination after his Sudanese experience began to turn sour. He was also able to offer services to the Taliban movement, which had taken shape in late 1994 through Pakistani patronage: bin Laden provided the substantial sums of money that the Taliban used to 'buy' local commanders as part of their final push to Kabul in September 1996. The Taliban – whose pathogenic, anti-modernist, neo-fundamentalist core was augmented by a motley collection of former communists and opportunists who supported it out of Pashtun ethnic solidarity[1] – then accorded bin Laden the hospitality which the tribal code of the Pashtuns embodies and which lies at the heart of Pashtun identity. He also benefited from ties with other extremist groups which had gravitated to Taliban areas, notably Pakistan-backed Kashmiri militants that Islamabad was happier to see trained in Afghanistan, in a 'plausibly deniable' fashion, than on its own territory. But the key factor in the rise of both the Taliban and the entrenchment in Afghanistan of al-Qaeda was the disintegration of the Afghan state. State collapse facilitates such developments in two ways. First, it permits self-interested neighbours to interfere in the affairs of a country in which the instrumentalities of the state have broken down. Had moderate Islamist forces inherited a functioning state, the Taliban's prospects of ever securing a political foothold with Pakistani support would have been negligible. Second, state collapse distorts communications between domestic political actors and the wider world. The Taliban had little knowledge of the world, and limited opportunity to lighten the burden of their ignorance. Bin Laden exploited them shamelessly, and they paid a heavy price.

Reconstructing a Polity

One of the greatest challenges in Afghanistan is therefore the rebuilding of appropriate state instrumentalities. The task is a much larger one than simply assembling a 'government', for the state in Afghanistan effectively ceased to exist years ago. Throughout the 1980s, successive regimes depended for their survival on a flow of resources from the USSR, which had invaded Afghanistan in December 1979, and from the end of 1991 this lifeline was severed, creating a crisis which resulted in the collapse of communist rule in April 1992.[2] Since then, Afghanistan has had a range of power centres, but not a cohesive state. On December 5, 2001, following the collapse of the Taliban movement, an agreement signed in Bonn between anti-Taliban Afghan groups put Afghanistan on a new path of political development, directed not at dividing the spoils of 'victory' but at rebuilding institutions. An 'Interim Administration', chaired by Hamed Karzai, was charged with commencing the process, and the Bonn Agreement specified the steps which would then follow, culminating in the holding of a free and fair election by June 2004. The aim of the process is to reconstitute basic state functions and win them sufficient legitimacy to sustain them in the long run.

Is 'democracy' feasible in the new Afghanistan? Some have criticized the very notion as a fantasy,[3] and it is certainly the case that there is much more to a functioning democracy than simply the holding of one election. Furthermore, a trip to the polls before a basic consensus exists on the rules of the political game can have incendiary effects. Nonetheless, it is also the case that the basic democratic principle that ordinary people should have access to mechanisms for changing their rulers without bloodshed is a very important one, and one which matters a great deal to Afghans, who have been denied this basic right for far too long. In addition, since electoral choice is built into the heart of the Bonn Agreement, any attempt to discard it could lead to a breakdown of the transition process. For better or for worse, Afghanistan is set on this path.[4] Yet within this framework, there are important choices to be made, choices which raise important questions of political theory. Should the functions of the state be extensive or limited? Should the institutions of the state be centralized or diversified? Should the constitutional structure be monarchical, presidential or parliamentary? Should voting systems be chosen to foster majoritarianism or proportionality? Should political institutions be designed to bring together ethnic groups in a grand coalition, or should they rather be designed to foster cross-ethnic alliance formation? How should the institutions of state and civil society relate to each other? These choices are for Afghans to make, but the wisdom with which they choose will significantly shape their country's future.

Ensuring an adequate degree of elite stability is a major problem. The importance of the political choices to be made during a transition almost guarantees that there will be differences of opinion over how to proceed, and where levels of trust are low there is always a danger that the process will unravel. Avoiding concentrations of power is a wise long-term strategy,[5] but it is important that the wider world provide incentives for the different elements within the elite to hold firmly to the commitments which they accepted in Bonn, and for those groups which were not present in Bonn to accept the Bonn process as the only viable path forward. One way to assist this is through the flow of externally supplied resources. Another is through the deployment of neutral security forces. Such forces can help to overcome intrastate security dilemmas, where distrust tempts an insecure party to strike preemptively against its 'enemies' before they can strike pre-emptively against it. This is a key (if unstated) purpose of the British-led International Security Assistance Force (ISAF).

Assisting the reconstitution of an Afghan national army is an important task for ISAF. However, equally important is the redevelopment of a capacity for effective civilian *policing*. Whereas military force is classically used to destroy or deter an external enemy, policing is concerned with the enforcement of law, and preferably with minimal use of coercive instruments. It is designed to foster confidence in the rule of law, and while police powers can be massively abused, they can also provide an important foundation for the flourishing of civil life. Hamed Karzai has signalled a commitment to struggle against the widespread corruption which contributed to the delegitimation of the Afghan state before the communist coup of April 1978. Corruption and nepotism, enormously alluring as sources of income for officials in a system struggling to overcome the burdens of decades of war, are almost entirely corrosive in their wider effects, not least because they undermine the notions of impartial service and impartial justice. Here, it is notable that the Bonn Agreement provides for three important institutions which have not been much discussed: a Civil Service Commission, a Judicial Commission and a Human Rights Commission. Tempting as it may be for donors to fund the construction of tangible assets that can then be reproduced in glossy photographs, there is a powerful case for ensuring that the day-to-day operations of these three commissions are properly resourced. They supply mechanisms for a constructive separation of powers, for 'guarding the guardians'. It would be a tragedy if they were to wither.

Economic and Social Reconstruction

Afghanistan's reconstruction needs are enormous. A joint study by the Asian Development Bank, the UNDP and the World Bank, prepared for a Ministerial Meeting in Tokyo on January 21–22, 2002, produced estimates of the costs of reconstruction which, over a ten-year period, ranged from a base figure of $14.6 billion to a high of $18.1 billion.[6] Infrastructural damage in Afghanistan has been severe, and roads, water supply, aviation, energy and communications facilities are all in a parlous state.[7] Of particular concern is the decay of the health care system, in terms of both primary health care and facilities for treating more complex complaints. While credible baseline data are in short supply, it is estimated that 1 million Afghans are disabled in some way, with consequent burdens on a large number of families. Life expectancy in Afghanistan is a mere 44 years, a consequence of infant and child mortality rates among the worst in the world. The other area that Afghans themselves routinely recognize as a priority is education, especially at the primary level to which only 38 per cent of boys and 3 per cent of girls presently have access. Education is widely seen as a means of escaping from the rut into which the Afghan people have been plunged by decades of war.

The emergence of the Taliban in late 1994 largely reflected the desire of the government of Pakistan to find new means by which to promote its interests in Afghanistan, but it was strongly backed by a range of commercial actors. In particular, smugglers and narcotics producers backed the Taliban as a force which could secure the roads in Afghanistan along which they wished to move their wares. This led to a significant 'criminalization' of the Afghan economy,[8] not so much in terms of the proportion of the workforce engaged in 'illicit' activities, but rather in terms of the value of the illicit output as a proportion of overall national income. As a result of a ban on opium cultivation imposed by the Taliban on the relatively small number of producers, the production of opium fell from a massive 4600 tonnes in 1999 to just 185 tonnes in 2001. There is thus a window of opportunity to detach Afghanistan from the global drugs market, although the pressures on individual farmers are so great that without plausible alternatives they will surely seek to re-plant and harvest on a large scale. Oddly enough, before drought struck in 1999, there had been some notable achievement in the area of agriculture, with the cereal output in 1998 totalling 3.85 million tonnes. However, the drought led to a 40 per cent fall in cereal output, and the international community must now step in to ensure that supplies reach the most vulnerable Afghans, while at the same time avoiding the mistake of inadvertently destroying the incentives for farmers to produce cereals for sale.

As has been the case for most of the last two decades, markets will continue to be the principal source of sustenance for the bulk of the Afghan population. Claims that the Afghan economy has 'collapsed' are misleading: private production and trade are the mainstay of the daily lives of millions of people. However, there are opportunities to improve the ways in which markets operate. First, improvements in transport and communications infrastructure expand the scope for contractual exchange. Second, the reconstitution of the state can offer mechanisms for adjudication in contractual disputes, and for the enforcement of tortious liability. Third, the development of a reliable banking sector permits the mobilization of savings, which in some hands in Afghanistan are substantial but currently are not accessible to fund investment. There are also good reasons to ponder whether some of the services historically delivered by the state might not better be delivered by private suppliers. For example, non-governmental organizations (NGOs) such as the Swedish Committee for Afghanistan have an excellent record of running schools in rural Afghanistan, and there may be local educational entrepreneurs willing to follow their lead.

It is very important that social capital not be degraded in the course of reconstruction. Norms of reciprocity are extremely powerful in Afghan society, and especially within family structures. The strength of Afghan society, in particular the capacity of its units to unite in the face of an external threat, in large measure accounted for the disaster which befell the Soviet Union as a result of its Afghanistan adventure; the United States intervened more successfully in 2001 because a substantial number of Afghans were ready to welcome an external force committed to overthrowing the Taliban and rescuing them from the consequences of Pakistan's 'creeping invasion' of their country. High levels of social capital can lubricate the reconstruction process, and it is useful to design individual programmes and projects with an eye to their ability to nurture the development of social capital. One sphere of activity which has been particularly effective in this respect is mine action, where a creative partnership between the United Nations and Afghan NGOs has provided a venue for cooperation in pursuit of a superordinate national goal.

As agents of reconstruction, women have a particularly important role to play.[9] Educated women from urban areas suffered enormously under the Taliban, but the gender policies of the Taliban did have the effect of highlighting to the wider world the losses to Afghanistan of excluding women from active roles as educators and health workers.[10] While women have received symbolically important positions in the Interim Administration, it will be quite some time before the more enlightened attitudes at the upper echelons of the new system spread to all the reaches of Afghan society. Given experiences in other developing countries, there may be a case for promoting the supply of microcredit to women with an interest in establishing small enterprises.

Threats to the Reconstruction Process

One of the greatest threats to reconstruction comes from the resurgence of warlordism in Afghanistan, in part because of the blithe way in which the United States funded groups which marketed themselves as potential opponents of the Taliban in southern and eastern Afghanistan. Warlords pursue a strategy of predatory extraction, securing prudential support by distributing to clients some of the resources which they extract. The warlord's personal interest in following this course often exceeds the personal interest of any one of its victims in seeing predation eliminated. Thus, it may be necessary either to deploy state power to crush the warlord, or to pay the warlord a premium (possibly in the form of some national office) for acting cooperatively, a premium which in value exceeds the possible gain from predation. Each of these courses has its dangers. The latter runs into the difficulty of 'moral hazard': paying people to behave properly may encourage other people to misbehave as a way of securing a similar payment. The former runs the risk of prompting a warlord to act more directly as a spoiler, targeting his forces against the institutions of the embryonic state. It rarely pays to announce that one's intention is to eliminate or marginalize a warlord – this simply invites a pre-emptive attack – but as the central state gradually builds up its power, the cost to the warlord of non-cooperation may also mount. Here, sequencing is important: initially it is important to build up some national structures as a way of overcoming warlordism,[11] but in the longer run, it is important to diffuse power to legitimate communities and governance structures. Both of these processes will take time, and in Afghanistan as elsewhere, time is a scarce commodity.

A second threat comes from the sheer scale of deskilling which Afghanistan has experienced in recent years. There is no doubt that large numbers of Afghans are highly entrepreneurial, and will seize with gusto the opportunities presented by the unexpected obliteration of the Taliban. Millions, however, have been stuck in neighbouring countries as refugees, or have been internally displaced in their homeland. Refugee camps are not appropriate venues for acquiring the practical skills which turn an Afghan youth into a competent farmer or herdsman. The process of reconstituting human capital is likely to be laborious, and the temptation for the unskilled to offer their services to predators may be considerable. The return of refugees is also likely to be a turbulent process, setting the scene for disputes over property rights, over access to commonly owned resources and over participation in the work of new political institutions.

A further threat, virtually unaddressed in the literature on Afghanistan, relates to the burden of war-related trauma. In Afghanistan, one encounters a vast number of people who either have developed, or are at risk of developing, post-traumatic stress disorder.

There are almost no services available for the diagnosis or management of such complaints, and the result is a large number of walking wounded, prone to surges of emotion which they can neither understand nor control. For cultural reasons, this is not an issue about which Afghan men can readily speak, or about which they can expect much real understanding from their peers. Yet in a very real sense, it represents a psychosocial time-bomb. Measures to address the problems of grief, disempowerment and diminished self-esteem are easy to recommend in the abstract, but to give them concrete form is much more difficult. There is certainly a case for thoroughly briefing international agency staff on these issues, so that when they encounter symptoms of these problems, they can respond in ways which are sensitive to the underlying suffering to which the symptoms point.

There is also a danger that sharply rising popular expectations in Afghanistan will confront the new authorities with demands they are simply incapable of meeting, and that the loss of legitimacy which results from inadequate performance will be too great to be overcome by 'legal-rational' legitimation through the procedures set out in the Bonn Agreement. It is therefore important that the international community and the Afghan authorities work together to ensure that expectations are realistic, by sharing factual information with the Afghan people through radio and other media. A transparent process will be easier to defend than a secretive one. But it is equally important that some of the weaknesses exposed in the course of past exercises in complex peacebuilding be avoided: it would be a tragedy if preventable mistakes of an organizational or logistical character were to undermine so important a transition process.

In the international sphere, it is important above all to maintain international commitment. The Afghan people have had the bitter experience of being abandoned in the past, most notably in the 1990s when the US walked away from Afghanistan and left it fatally exposed to Pakistan's clumsy meddling and to the fantasies of American oil and gas companies. Americans came to appreciate the scale of the Clinton administration's follies only with the terrorist attacks of September 11, 2001: the Afghans, unfortunately, had been exposed to them much earlier. The euphoria surrounding the establishment of the Interim Administration will pass, and other problems will surely appear on the horizon. It is at this point that it is vital that the wider world not lose sight of Afghanistan. If it abandoned Afghanistan once more, the consequences could be incalculable. It is particularly important that Pakistan comes to grasp that the days in which it could claim a right to determine

who should rule in Afghanistan are over. Apart from Moscow, no capital
has brought more misery to Afghanistan than Islamabad, and
Islamabad's own gains from its years of manipulation have proved negligible. It is widely distrusted in Afghanistan, and its leaders are now faced
with the problem of managing indigenous extremists whose sectarian
extremism has cost the lives of many innocent people.[12]

In particular, it is vital that states interested in seeing Afghanistan and
its neighbours stabilized stand ready to commit to an expanded international force in Afghanistan. It is not surprising that in his briefing to
the UN Security Council on February 6, 2002, Ambassador Lakhdar
Brahimi, the Special Representative of the Secretary-General for
Afghanistan, stated that proposals for the expansion of ISAF beyond
Kabul to the rest of Afghanistan should 'receive favourable and urgent
consideration by the Security Council'. Amongst ordinary Afghans,
there is overwhelming support for increasing the size of ISAF and
expanding its geographical mandate, and key figures in the Interim
Administration have also backed such a proposal. The fragile authority
of new institutions can easily be compromised if they prove unable to
deliver basic security, and it is here that ISAF has a profoundly important role to play – not necessarily in combating 'spoilers' directly, but
rather in *disinclining* Afghan actors to support anti-state actors rather
than the new authorities. However, if those states which can readily
support such a force wait for others to volunteer first, the positive
momentum generated by the Bonn meeting and the commencement of
the transition process could be lost. Are there grounds for optimism in
Afghanistan? In the long run, certainly. Afghanistan has turned a very
important corner. But as Ambassador Brahimi remarked to the Security
Council on February 6, 2002, 'the road is still very long and fraught with
danger'. The Afghan people should not be left to tread that road alone.

Notes

1. See William Maley, 'Introduction: Interpreting the Taliban', in William
   Maley (ed.) *Fundamentalism Reborn? Afghanistan and the Taliban* (New York:
   New York University Press, 1998), pp. 1–28; Ahmed Rashid, *Taliban: Militant
   Islam, Oil and Fundamentalism in Central Asia* (New Haven: Yale University
   Press, 2000).
2. See William Maley, *The Afghanistan Wars* (London and New York: Palgrave,
   2002), chapter 8.
3. Marina Ottaway and Anatol Lieven, *Rebuilding Afghanistan: Fantasy versus
   Reality* (Washington, DC: Policy Brief, Carnegie Endowment for
   International Peace, January 2002).

4. See Jeff Fischer, *Post-Conflict Peace Operations and Governance in Afghanistan: A Strategy for Peace and Political Intervention* (Washington, DC: International Foundation for Election Systems, 2001).
5. See Caroline A. Hartzell, 'Explaining the Stability of Negotiated Settlements to Intrastate Wars', *Journal of Conflict Resolution*, vol. 43, no. 1 (1999), pp. 3–22.
6. *Afghanistan: Preliminary Needs Assessment for Recovery and Reconstruction* (Manila, New York and Washington, DC: Asian Development Bank, UNDP and World Bank, January 2002), p. 47.
7. William Maley, 'Reconstructing Afghanistan: Opportunities and Challenges', in Geoff Harris (ed.) *Recovery from Armed Conflict in Developing Countries: An Economic and Political Analysis* (London and New York: Routledge, 1999), pp. 225–7, at pp. 234–6.
8. See Barnett R. Rubin, 'The Political Economy of War and Peace in Afghanistan', *World Development*, vol. 28, no. 10 (2000), pp. 1789–803.
9. Amartya Sen, *Development as Freedom* (New York: Anchor Books, 1999), pp. 189–203.
10. See William Maley, *The Foreign Policy of the Taliban* (New York: Council on Foreign Relations, 2000), pp. 18–21; Rosemarie Skaine, *The Women of Afghanistan under the Taliban* (London: McFarland & Co., 2002).
11. Astri Suhrke, Arne Strand and Kristian Berg Harpviken, *Peace-building Strategies for Afghanistan. Part I: Lessons from Past Experiences in Afghanistan* (Bergen: Chr. Michelson Institute, 14 January 2002), p. 22.
12. William Maley, 'Talibanisation and Pakistan', in Denise Groves (ed.) *Talibanisation: Extremism and Regional Instability in South and Central Asia* (Berlin: Conflict Prevention Network, Stiftung Wissenschaft und Politik, 2001), pp. 53–74.

CHAPTER 17

State–Society Relations: Asian and World Order after September 11

Amitav Acharya

Politics, not geopolitics or culture, may ultimately determine how September 11 and the American response reshape world order in the early twenty-first century. Many see these events as ushering in a clash of civilizations, or at least a renewed power rivalry among nations. But September 11 may exert its most profound impact on the relationship between states and societies, where a new struggle for authority and legitimacy looms, whether in Muslim or non-Muslim worlds.

Asia, the world's most multicivilizational continent, the only part of the world where Great Power war remains a possibility, and the last major frontier of authoritarianism, offers an important window for assessing the implications of September 11 for world order. The response of states in Asia to September 11 and the US strike on the Taliban was not necessarily along civilizational lines. What is more important, reactions to September 11 show a greater convergence among government positions than between them and their peoples. Thus, the most important legacy of September 11 in Asia may be the reshaping of state–society relations. Its reshaping of world order will depend on how the international community reconciles the multifront war against terrorism with the demands and aspirations for freedom and normal living.

Why This Was Not a Clash of Civilizations

Writing in *Newsweek* magazine, Samuel Huntington argues that '[R]eactions to September 11 and the American response were strictly along civilization lines.' But the evidence coming from Asia suggests otherwise, at least where government responses were concerned. While, as Huntington observes, the governments and peoples of Western countries were 'overwhelmingly supportive' of the US and made commitments to join its 'war on terrorism',[1] it was the governments of India and Pakistan which were among the first to offer military facilities to the US. Pakistan, a Muslim nation, proved to be the most critical link in the logistics chain that ensured victory for the US against the Taliban.

Governments, including those presiding over Islamic nations, not only condemned the terrorist attacks on the US, many also recognized its right to retaliate against the Taliban. Governments in Muslim Central Asia braved a popular backlash by offering material and logistical assistance to the US. From Saudi Arabia to Pakistan, from Iran to Indonesia, Islamic nations distanced themselves from the theology of Osama bin Laden. Pakistani President Musharraf denounced his homegrown extremists for giving Islam a bad name and for threatening the modernist vision of Pakistan's founder, Ali Jinah. Iran, having for decades spearheaded the Islamic revolutionaries' *jihad* against the 'great Satan', made no secret of its disdain for the Taliban's Islamic credentials.

In responding to September 11, states acted more as states than as civilizations.[2] From Hindu India to Muslim Indonesia, from Buddhist Thailand to the Catholic Philippines, the response of governments was the same. Asked to choose between the US and the terrorists, they overwhelmingly sided with Washington, and they did so despite reservations about the US support for Israel, concerns about civilian casualties in the Afghanistan war, and misgivings about US military and economic dominance of the world. And they chose this course despite the Bush administration's decision to give short shrift to multilateralism and coalition-building.

Why governments acted this way speaks more to pragmatism and principle than to their cultural predisposition and civilizational affinity. National interest, regime security and modern principles of international conduct were placed ahead of primordial sentiment and religious identity. Pakistan, for example, obtained badly needed American aid and *de facto* recognition of its military regime. Indonesia, whose support as the world's most populous Islamic nation was crucial to the legitimacy of the US anti-terrorist campaign, received both economic and political support for its fledgling democracy. The Saudi regime, which along with Pakistan had created the Taliban, simply followed the dictates of its security dependence on the US. Iran saw an opportunity to rid itself of an unfriendly regime in its neighbourhood and extend its influence beyond its eastern frontiers.

For some governments, concerns for domestic stability and regime security proved decisive. In Malaysia and Pakistan, the war against terrorism presented a fresh opportunity for governments to rein in domestic Islamic extremists which had challenged their authority and created public disorder. Malaysian Prime Minister Mahathir Mohammed made it difficult for Malaysian *jihad* supporters to travel to Afghanistan to fight alongside the Taliban.

In rejecting the open call to *jihad* issued by the Taliban and its supporters, some Islamic nations acted out of interest, others out of principle, but most out of a combination of both. Many nations recognized the US counter-strike as an exercise in a nation's right of self-defence under Article 51 of the UN Charter. They would not grant the same right to the Taliban, whose apologists had portrayed terrorism as a legitimate weapon of the weak against an unjust, anti-Islamic and overwhelmingly powerful imperialist. A combination of national interest and common interest remains the basis of international relations. Religion and civilization do not replace pragmatism, interest and principle as the guiding motives of international relations.

The clash of civilizations thesis assumes a degree of homogeneity among Islamic rebellions, which they evidently do not possess. Many extremist groups now being branded as Islamic or terrorist (or both), are fighting their own governments, whether or not these governments are allied with the US. Thus Islamic militants in Malaysia seek to create an Islamic state by supplanting a regime known for its anti-Western foreign policy rhetoric. It is therefore very much a case of a clash within a civilization rather than between civilizations. The Abu Sayaaf in the Philippines is motivated primarily by mercenary instinct, not religious sentiment. The armed rebellion in Aceh pursues a political rather than a religious goal.

Great Power Geopolitics since September 11

Instead of Huntington's civilizational thesis, it may be useful to see the repercussions of September 11 in terms of the traditional Great Power rivalries, especially great power geopolitics. Its impact on Sino–US relations, the major strategic contest in East Asia, is noteworthy. In this contest, China, geopolitical pundits have observed, comes out a 'loser' on several fronts.[3] Pakistan has become less dependent on China than before, and India's influence in Afghanistan has grown while its strategic position *vis-à-vis* China has been strengthened by American sympathy and support for India's own war on terrorism. Chinese insecurity is furthered heightened by the dramatically enhanced US military presence in Southeast Asia and Central Asia; especially the latter, where China had painstakingly built up its own anti-terror alliance and was in the process of securing its own long-term access to the Caspian Sea oil. These developments, along with China's renewed insecurities about the awesome display of US power projection in Afghanistan, complicate and worsen the Sino–US strategic rivalry. The strategic tension between China and Japan has also intensified. Using the pretext of conducting operations in support of the US strike on the Taliban, the Japanese navy entered the waters of the Indian Ocean. This, and Japan's growing defence ties with India, increases China's anxiety and anger.

These are important changes which could undermine regional stability in Asia, but their impact would be offset by a number of developments. American hegemony has been strengthened so much that it now acts as a significant check on regional conflicts. By consolidating its influence over both India and Pakistan, the US has acquired an unprecedented ability to restrain their rivalry, one of the most dangerous flashpoints in Asia and the world. A new US–Russian understanding over transnational terror has narrowed the strategic gulf between them over missile defence and minority rights. Sino–US relations may be heading in a similar direction. Throughout Asia, transnational terrorist networks are filling in as *the* common threat against which states can build new networks of security cooperation. Already, this has led to renewed American strategic engagement in Southeast Asia; something regional governments, if not their peoples generally, regard as a positive force for regional stability. The terrorist threat in Malaysia, Singapore, Indonesia and the Philippines has already produced the first multilateral gathering of their defence intelligence chiefs.

State–Society Relations Post-September 11

While September 11 produced changes in interstate and intercivilizational relations, they pale in comparison with its roots in, and effects (and potential effects) on, state–society relations. Several signposts of this have emerged.

The first is the divergent perception of, and reactions to, September 11 on the part of governments and peoples. Throughout the Islamic world, including Saudi Arabia, Malaysia, Pakistan and Indonesia, societies showed less sympathy and support for the US than did their own governments, and a lot of this popular anger is directed against their own governments – especially those which had sided with the US or had not been sufficiently forthcoming in condemning the US military action in Afghanistan. Popular resentment of American support for Israel made it difficult, though not impossible, for their governments to show understanding and support for the US. President Megawati of Indonesia made a much publicized visit to the White House to show solidarity with the US, but domestic disapproval of this stance soon forced her to criticize the US attack on Afghanistan. Domestic pressures also explain why Prime Minister Mahathir of Malaysia, after making it difficult for his own citizens to travel to Afghanistan to fight with the Taliban, also attacked the US military campaign in Afghanistan. The war against terror is thus more divisive when it comes to the relationship between governments and their subjects than that between governments.

The perpetrators of September 11 were inspired as much by a hatred of their own governments as hatred of American hegemony. Osama bin Laden's turn to full-blown mass terrorism was sparked by his well-known dislike of the US, but also of the autocratic ways of the Saudi royal family. Mohammed Atta, the apparent ringleader of the September 11 terrorists, has been described by his German friends as having spoken with 'increasing bitterness about what he saw as the autocratic government of President Hosni Mubarak and the small coterie of former army officers and rich Egyptians gathered around Mr Mubarak'.[4] Anti-Americanism of the kind that breeds the bin Ladens of the world goes hand in hand with authoritarianism in the Middle East, where governments routinely permit their media to fuel anti-American sentiments so as to deflect attention from their own repressive rule. In this sense, the US war on terrorism, as Ellen Amster reminds us, is in reality one in which Washington is interposing in a fight between Islamic radicals and Arab governments.[5]

The nexus between terrorism and authoritarianism has been a matter of some debate in Asia, and is an important aspect of the changing state–society relationship in the post-September 11 era. In the past, the debate about democracy was centred on questions of whether democracy is good for development, and whether democratic transitions (as in Indonesia) are a catalyst for regional disorder. The debate on democracy in Asia after September 11 is about two questions: whether lack of democracy is a 'root cause' of terrorism, and whether democracy limits the ability of states to respond effectively to it.

On the first question, Anwar Ibrahim, the deposed and jailed Deputy Prime Minister of Malaysia, has observed: 'Osama bin-Laden and his protégés are the children of desperation; they come from countries where political struggle through peaceful means is futile. In many Muslim countries, political dissent is simply illegal.'[6] Anwar sees himself as a victim of authoritarian rule in Malaysia, and his comments reflect unresolved domestic struggles there. The issues of terrorism and democracy come together in Malaysia; its government faces ongoing demands for political liberalization while responding to a serious challenge from homegrown and Afghanistan-trained terrorists. Farish Noor, a Malaysian scholar of Islam, makes a direct link between terrorism and authoritarian politics in Malaysia:

> It is the absence of ... democratic culture and practices in the Muslim world in general that leads to the rise of self-proclaimed leaders like the Mullahs of [the] Taliban, Osama bin Laden and our own Mullahs and Osama-wannabes here in Malaysia. And as long as a sense of political awareness and understanding of democracy is not instilled in the hearts and minds of ordinary Muslims the world over ... we will all remain hostage to a bunch of bigoted fanatics who claim to speak, act and think on our behalf without us knowing so.[7]

If the absence of democracy breeds terrorism, does democracy pre-empt and defeat the terrorist challenge? Some advocates of democracy in the Muslim world hope that 'With more democracy ... and a stronger voice for advocates of democracy, popular frustrations are less likely to be misdirected, and the resort to violence and terror reduced, particularly among an increasingly disaffected and vulnerable young population.'[8] In Southeast Asia, Surin Pitswuan, a former Foreign Minister of Thailand who is a Muslim and who has been a leading voice for democracy in Southeast Asia, argues that democracy reduces the danger of terrorism by enhancing the conditions for interethnic harmony in pluralist societies. 'As we pursue our aspirations of democracy', he contends, 'we know that we shall be free to practise our faith fully and on an equal basis with others who also have their own religious faith and rituals sacred to them'.[9]

However, critics of democracy are unlikely to be convinced by the logic of such arguments. As the cases of the US, Israel and India demonstrate, democratic governance does not make a country immune to transnational terrorism. Thomas Homer-Dixon argues that the advanced industrial nations of the West are uniquely vulnerable to terrorism because of their growing complexity and interconnectedness, and their tendency to concentrate vital infrastructure in small geographic clusters.[10] The fact that these nations also tend to be democracies is not inconsequential, since democracies are also theoretically restricted in their ability to conduct the kind of arbitrary detention and coercive investigation needed to prevent acts of terrorism.

In supposedly 'mature' democracies, however, such restrictions may be withering as governments wake up to the dangers caused by traditional pitfalls of civil liberties in combating terror. This was demonstrated, for example, by the case of Zacarias Moussaoui, a French national whose laptop computer (presumably with information about the impending September 11 attacks) could not be seized legally by the US authorities in time to save the World Trade Center. Ironically, it is the immature new democracies, such as Indonesia and the Philippines, which may now be more vulnerable to terrorism because of their inability to imitate Attorney-General John Ashcroft's America.

Democratization has not made these states less prone to terrorist conspiracies and attacks, whether from within or without (both being interlinked in most cases), but they also offer the least defence against terror in a region where the main weapon against the terrorists has been the Internal Security Act (ISA), a holdover from colonial days which has been used to silence political opponents as effectively as religious fanatics. Indonesia's inability to replicate the efforts of its neighbours, Malaysia and Singapore, in suppressing suspected terrorists has been blamed on democratization (apart from the rise of Islam as a political force since the late Suharto period, and the various other kinds of ongoing domestic violence that make Indonesians relatively impervious to terrorism of the bin Laden kind). After repealing the notorious Anti-Subversion Law of the Suharto era, Indonesia under its new democratic constitution does not provide for an Internal Security Act similar to those of its two neighbours. In the Philippines, President Arroyo has walked a political minefield and risked substantial domestic discontent in soliciting American help in her own war against terrorism, even though the public is generally unsympathetic to the militants' cause.

The response of Southeast Asian governments to terrorism provides ammunition to those who see democratization as part of the problem, rather than the solution, in confronting the terrorist challenge. The case for democratization is undermined when one compares the responses of Malaysia and Singapore (with swift detention under the ISA) with that of Indonesia and the Philippines. As Indonesian scholar Irman Lanti notes:

> While it may be true that democracy might provide a long-lasting solution, certainly democratization (as a process) might not, especially

if it is conducted without clear agenda and planning ... What best can be done ... is [the] opening up of political space for the society to engage in discussion with the state on various issues *within* the framework of the existing system. An ambitious project of democratizing these nations might further complicate the already complex problems there.[11]

With democracy on the defensive (perhaps temporarily – only time will tell) in the debates about the causes of and responses to terrorism, who is to prevent governments from using national security as a camouflage for regime survival? By creating a sense of national unity and purpose, however brief and superficial, the war against terrorism, like any war, presents governments with an opportunity to outmanoeuvre their political opponents. This might be happening in Malaysia today. The war against terrorism thus easily translates into a war against freedom.

In the post-September 11 world, terrorism is rapidly emerging as a convenient and overarching label under which governments and academic analysts can lump any and all kinds of challenges to state authority and regime security. Self-determination, the much vaunted norm of the post-Cold War global political order, becomes a major casualty in this altered political and intellectual climate. Witness the haste with which Chinese official commentators, while showing some empathy for the US after September 11, demanded American understanding of China's own brush with 'terrorism and separatism' in Xinjiang, Tibet and Taiwan, even though the Tibetans and Taiwanese have no record of terrorism. Already, months before September 11, the Shanghai Forum, a regional grouping of China, Russia, Kazakhstan, Kyrgyzstan, Tajikistan and Uzbekistan, had issued a joint declaration by its defence ministers pledging 'real interaction of the armed forces and other power structures of their countries in the fight against terrorism, separatism, and extremism'.[12] To be sure, terrorism and self-determination are not always separable. But in the absence of a common understanding of what terrorism means, governments can be expected to conflate terrorism and separatism to crush legitimate demands for self-determination, even the terror-free variety. Where terrorist acts are carried out in the name of self-determination, governments now have less reason to separate the tactics from the cause. Who tells the nations belonging to the global anti-terror alliance that their fight against a tactic (terrorism) must not come at the expense of a willingness to address the cause (demands for self-determination)?

The post-September 11 world order has suddenly become less hospitable for human rights around the world. A US which detains and secretly holds legal and illegal aliens suspected of terrorism and imposes a blanket denial of Geneva Convention rights on its Afghan prisoners in Cuba, loses its moral high ground as an advocate for human rights and democracy in the world.[13] This message is unlikely to be lost on Asian governments, especially those who have accused the US of double standards when it comes to promoting human rights and democracy; they would feel even less constrained (if they ever were) in challenging the universality of human rights norms, especially when their domestic stability is at stake. This compounds another possible consequence of September 11, the decreased space for civil society, as discoveries are made of how some terrorist organizations thrived by claiming NGO status and adopting their *modus operandi*.

Finally, state–society relations post-September 11 will be challenged by the inevitable redefinition of 'security'. Before September 11, the security agenda of nations was steadily reorientating towards 'non-conventional' issues: for example, the environment, refugees, migration, abuse of human rights, and so on. The paradigm of human security, or security for the people, had emerged as an alternative to national security, or security for states (and in real terms, regimes). Transnational terrorism may well be classified as a non-conventional threat, but the response to this menace is very much spearheaded by conventional configurations of states. And with a vengeance, states everywhere are striking back and re-empowering themselves against societal forces. They are doing so in a variety of ways: by regulating financial flows with a view to curbing the economic lifeline of terrorist networks, by tightening immigration controls, and by remilitarizing borders. The US–Canadian border is no longer the longest undefended border in the world. The power balance between globalization and government has shifted in favour of government.

Security is changing in another, more fundamentally ironic, manner. The 'traditional division of security threats into external and internal threats', declared Defence Minister Tony Tan of Singapore in the aftermath of September 11, 'no longer held'.[14] The American model of 'homeland security' is finding roots in Singapore and in other parts of Asia and the world. Though ostensibly geared to defeating the terrorist menace, homeland security is also a highly elastic notion that could be made to cover all aspects of fighting 'low-intensity' threats and controlling day-to-day lives. Going by the thinking of America's leading experts on future wars, the real heroes in the coming war on terrorism will not be the 'Daisy-cutters' and 'Predators' of Afghanistan, but the 'pervasive sensors' found in America and its fellow-travelling nations, sensors which could be 'attached to every appliance in your house, and to every vending machine on every street corner', and which would then register 'your presence in every restaurant and department store'.[15]

In projecting the growing sense of insecurity within the US, homeland security blurs the once fashionable distinction between Western and Third World security approaches, in which the latter focused on their domestic fronts while the former pursued defence against foreign military aggression. With Americans on American soil made to feel and act more insecure than their counterparts in India and Malaysia, the home front against terrorism has brought the United States' security predicament closer to that of the Third World. As both situations converge, it is well to remember the words of David Ignatius: 'But security is different. Like life itself, it is something for which people will pay almost any price.'[16]

Notes

1. Samuel P. Huntington, 'The Age of Muslim Wars', *Newsweek*, Special Davos Edition, December 2001–February 2002, p. 13.
2. Amitav Acharya, 'Clash of Civilizations? No, of National Interests and Principles', *International Herald Tribune*, January 10, 2002, p. 6.
3. Robyn Lim, 'Calmer Seas in Asia', *Wall Street Journal*, December 19, 2001.
4. Neil MacFarquhar, 'In Cairo, Father Defends Son as Too "Decent" to be Hijacker', *International Herald Tribune*, September 20, 2001, p. 3.
5. Ellen Amster, 'The Attacks Were a Bid for Power in the Arab World', *International Herald Tribune*, September 18, 2001, p.10.
6. Anwar Ibrahim, 'Growth of Democracy is the Answer to Terrorism', *International Herald Tribune*, October 11, 2001.
7. Farish Noor, 'Who Elected You, Mr Osama?', *Malaysiakini.com*, October 10, 2001, <http://www.worldpress.org/asia/1201malaysiakini.com>, p. 4.
8. Shaha Aliriza and Laila Hamad, 'A Time to Help Mideast Democrats', *International Herald Tribune*, October 20–21, 2001, p. 6.
9. Surin Pitswuan, 'Islam in Southeast Asia: A Personal Viewpoint', *The Nation*, September 22, 2001.
10. Thomas Homer-Dixon, 'The Rise of Complex Terrorism', *Foreign Policy*, January 2002.
11. Irman Lanti, personal communication, January 31, 2002.
12. 'Shanghai Forum Ready to Fight Terrorism, Separatism and Extremism', *Pravda* (online English edition), May 15, 2001, <http://english.pravda.ru/world/2001/06/15/7789.html>.
13. 'The Home Front: Security and Liberty', Editorial, *New York Times*, September 23, 2001, p. 16.

14. *The Straits Times*, November 5, 2001.
15. David Ignatius, 'Pervasive Sensors Can Net Bin Laden', *International Herald Tribune*, November 12, 2001, p. 8.
16. Ibid.

CHAPTER 18

Catharsis and Catalysis: Transforming the South Asian Subcontinent

C. Raja Mohan

Although international terrorism has long been associated with the Middle East, the locus of extremism and violence had begun to shift to the subcontinent in recent years. The peace process in the Middle East during the early 1990s and the American successes in limiting the activities of state sponsors of terrorism appeared to ease the danger in the Middle East. But the same period saw the centre of gravity of international terrorism moving towards South Asia.[1] Among the factors responsible for the shift were the growth of extremism and violence among all religious groups and many ethnic communities across the subcontinent, the rise of the Taliban in Afghanistan which provided state support and an infrastructure for nurturing international terrorism, Pakistan's tolerance of extremist activities from its soil, and the increasing regional instability. Together they had provided a fertile ground for the growth of religious extremism, the effects of which were so dramatically demonstrated in New York and Washington on September 11.

The subcontinent was thrust on to the centre stage of world politics in the wake of September 11, and the American war against terrorism saw the first ever direct American military intervention in the region. All indications are that the political engagement and military presence of the US in South Asia are likely to be enduring. The subcontinent is likely to be the arena in which many of the great issues that have come up for debate since September 11 will be played out. These include the challenges of reconciling the tension between Islam and the West, coping with the anti-Western and anti-American resentment brewing in the world, rescuing failed states, and universalizing Enlightenment values amidst renewed resistance from obscurantist and orthodox forces.[2]

While there is considerable criticism in Europe, the Middle East and elsewhere in the world of both the concept and the mechanisms the United States has adopted in fighting the war against international terrorism after September 11, the subcontinent has greeted the demise of the Taliban with great relief. The Taliban movement had epitomized the new threat to the region from religious totalitarianism. What is more, contrary to the old political instincts in the region, the protest against the likely long-term American military presence has been limited. There is a strong view in both Pakistan and India that the new American involvement in the region has the potential to change both the internal dynamics and the external orientation of the subcontinent in a positive way.

If the subcontinent was helplessly trapped in a permanent crisis of inter- and intrastate conflict during the 1990s, September 11 and the American war against terrorism have imparted powerful external stimuli to change course. For the elite in Pakistan, increasingly frightened by the growing dominance of religious radicals over society, the American ousting of the Taliban offered a badly needed way out of the looming danger of the 'Talibanization' of their nation. The Indian leadership, increasingly frustrated at its inability to get Pakistan to stop support of cross-border violence and accept a *modus vivendi*, welcomed the American war on terrorism for creating a new international framework to engage Pakistan.

The terrorist attacks on New York and Washington on September 11 had their roots in the policies the United States had initiated in Afghanistan in the late 1970s.[3] Osama bin Laden was the prized child of the American proxy war against the Soviet Union in Afghanistan. To cope with the blowback effect that has ended the longstanding invulnerability of the American homeland, the US has had to return to the subcontinent with a radically different agenda than that of the late 1970s. If the first American intervention in Afghanistan turned out to be disastrous for the region, the second is likely to prove to be both transformational and positive.

Catharsis

More than two decades ago, the Soviet intervention in Afghanistan pushed the Western parts of the subcontinent into the frontlines of the Cold War. In the American strategy to trap the Soviet bear in Afghanistan and bleed it to death, Pakistan was the indispensable base. The army in Pakistan became the principal vehicle for the training, arming and nurturing of the Afghan Mujahideen to fight against the Soviet occupation of Afghanistan. As the Central Intelligence Agency unveiled the Reagan Doctrine in the early 1980s aimed at choking Moscow's clients in the Third World, the army in Pakistan became the executor of the Doctrine in Afghanistan and the principal beneficiary of American largesse. The Reagan Doctrine turned out to be a powerful one that put the Soviet-backed Third World regimes on the defensive and turned the West into an aggressive sponsor of insurgency and low-intensity conflict. Any group, however reprehensible its character, was welcome to join the new Crusade. Whether it was the genocidal Pol Pot fighting the Soviet- and Vietnamese-backed regime in Cambodia or the Contras in Central America or the primitive Mujahideen confronting the Afghan communists, the US kept a company that was despicable by any standard. Whatever its moral dimension, the Reagan Doctrine worked far beyond the expectations of even its most ardent supporters in Washington. After forcing Russian troops out of Afghanistan by the end of the 1980s, the US declared victory and turned its back on the subcontinent. But in the end there was a price to pay – on September 11.

The Jihadis,[4] whom the Americans trained in the schools of terror organized in Pakistan, successfully defeated the 'Godless communists' in Afghanistan and their backers in Moscow. While the Americans walked away in triumph, the Jihadis had their own larger agenda. They were not just 'anti-communist'; but were more fundamentally 'anti-Western' and 'anti-modern'. There was even greater triumphalism among the Jihadis for having routed a great European power, and they were looking for more. The conscious American mobilization of Islamic volunteers from across the Middle East, the so-called Arab Afghans, as well as funds from the conservative kingdom of Saudi Arabia, fused one of the great reservoirs of anti-Western resentment with the modern technology of low-intensity conflict. It also created an infrastructure for terrorism and violence in Afghanistan and Pakistan. Extremists from Tanzania to Tajikistan, from Mindanao to Manhattan, could find shelter and solace, weapons and theology from Taliban-controlled Afghanistan and the lawless frontier that seamlessly connected Pakistan and Afghanistan. No nation, it seemed, would be immune from the powerful new force with its seething resentment of modernity, that was being nurtured in Afghanistan and Pakistan.

While there is a belated recognition in the West of the consequences of the United States' Afghan policy in the 1980s, there is much less understanding of its impact on the subcontinent. The bitter conse-quences of the United States' Afghan strategy were visible in four different areas: the internal degeneration of Pakistan, the worsening of Indo-Pakistan relations, the nuclearization of the subcontinent, and the rise of anti-Western ideologies in the region.

The strategic necessity for access to Pakistan's geographic space led to the strong American support for an institution, the army in Pakistan, that had been widely discredited in the 1971 defeat at the hands of India. General Zia ul Haque was a pariah when he ousted the regime of Zulfiqar Ali Bhutto in 1977. But the Afghan end-game in the Cold War resulted in the strong American endorsement of the military rule with disastrous long-term effects on the prospects for democracy in Pakistan. Although democracy returned to Pakistan in the late 1980s, the civilian leaders could never shake off the army's dominance – both in shaping national policies and in deciding the distribution of national resources.

More importantly, the CIA and the Inter-Services Intelligence (ISI) of the Pakistan army forged by the conflict in Afghanistan created a powerful monster in Pakistan that would run wars abroad and manipulate the political processes at home. The linkage that developed between the ISI and the Jihadis turned out to be an enduring one as Pakistan became the principal arbiter of political developments in Afghanistan after the US turned its back on the scene. In looking for the elusive 'strategic depth' in Afghanistan, Pakistan extended support for the Taliban and its religious totalitarianism. Meanwhile, the Jihadi groups, and the extreme ideological formations backing the Taliban in Afghanistan, wanted a similar future for Pakistan. They gained a free run incrementally at home in shaping the ideological discourse, in fomenting sectarian violence, and in putting the moderate and secular forces in the Pakistani polity on the defensive. Neither the elected politicians in the 1990s nor the army chiefs appeared capable of resisting the advances of the Jihadi groups in Pakistan despite the dangers that were increasingly apparent. It was only the US president's blunt warning to Pakistan after September 11 – 'either you are with us or against us' – that forced Pakistan to agree to throttle the Taliban and scrap two decades-worth of material and emotional resources it had invested in Afghanistan.

The pressure to appease the Jihadis at home had also become imperative in the context of their increasing role in the pursuit of the popular Pakistani cause to 'liberate' areas of Jammu and Kashmir subject to Indian 'occupation'. Kashmir as an issue had remained largely dormant in Indo-Pakistan relations during 1971–88. But as the Pakistan army sensed triumph in Afghanistan, it applied the same model to Kashmir – combining traditional insurgency with religious motivation and modern weaponry. India's own disastrous handling of the political grievances in Kashmir gave Pakistan a successful handle in fomenting unprecedented trouble in the disputed state. As Pakistan discovered that it had created a low-cost but highly effective instrument of low-intensity conflict, its support for terrorism in India went way beyond Kashmir. The expansion of the strategy culminated in the attack on the Indian parliament on December 13, 2001. This was the last straw for India. After absorbing the impact of Pakistan's support of violence for nearly a decade, India said enough is enough and threatened go to war unless Islamabad put an end to the strategy of 'death by a thousand cuts'.

Another legacy of the American–Afghan war was the intense miniaturization of Indo-Pakistan relations and the eventual nuclearization of the subcontinent. The American arms sales and assistance to Pakistan in the 1980s, amounting to nearly $6 billion, induced a competitive military build-up in India. While the acquisition of conventional arms by India and Pakistan slowed in the 1990s thanks to the economic crunch in both the countries, the two nations crossed the nuclear threshold and began to introduce missiles into their arsenals. Dependent on Pakistani support to pursue Cold War objectives in Afghanistan, the US winked at the nuclear and missile programmes in Pakistan during the 1980s. India responded with its own programmes, and both countries became overtly nuclear by the 1990s. The new nuclear dimension to the Indo-Pakistan conflict saw a series of military crises – in 1987, 1990, 1999, and finally the most explosive one at the end of 2001, when India and Pakistan massed their military forces on the border after the December 13 terrorist attack on Parliament House in New Delhi. Given the real danger of the military tensions escalating to a nuclear level, the international community deepened its engagement of India and Pakistan and demanded an end to Pakistan's support of cross-border terrorism and substantive negotiations between New Delhi and Islamabad to resolve the Kashmir dispute.

The greatest damage from the United States' Afghan war in the 1980s was the legitimization of anti-modern, extremist and intolerant forces in the region. American and Pakistani state support of militant and fundamentalist Islamic groups in defeating the Soviet Union reinforced the rise of religious radicalism in a region that until the 1980s had kept religion largely at bay in the conduct of state affairs. Even Pakistan, an avowedly Islamic state, had been moderate in its religious orientation. But as General Zia ul Haque coopted the religious forces to lend legitimacy to his military dictatorship and promoted religious radicals across the border to defeat the Soviet army, Pakistan saw the rise of extremism and sectarianism. Pakistan's shift inevitably had an impact on Muslims in the rest of the subcontinent and elsewhere in the world. The rise of Islamic radicalism added grist to the mill of growing Hindu fundamentalism in India in the late 1980s and 1990s. Together, they added to the intensification of Hindu–Muslim tensions across the subcontinent, and more fundamentally gave a boost to anti-Enlightenment ideas in the region. Majoritarianism, sectarianism, obscurantism, opposition to the traditional regional notions of tolerance, and rejection of the Western idea of separating religion and state became increasingly powerful. The US–Taliban confrontation, resulting in the defeat of those who wanted to take the region backwards, was a blessing for the region.

Catalysis

The cathartic events of September 11 and the American engagement in the region have helped to arrest some of the negative tendencies in the region and have the potential to catalyse a redirection of the region towards political moderation, social modernization and regional harmony. Legitimate criticism of the American strategy and tactics in Afghanistan since September 11 and the fact that the US was guilty of promoting the Taliban in the first place do not take away the historic significance for the subcontinent of the Western confrontation and defeat of the forces of religious extremism. American engagement in the region also offers the opportunity to transform Pakistan into a moderate Islamic state, to promote a historic reconciliation between New Delhi and Islamabad and to facilitate a more rapid economic advancement of the subcontinent as a whole.

While the potential for a new, positive phase on the subcontinent is real, so too are the political obstacles; but the conjunction of international circumstances has never been so favourable for a new beginning in the region. Nowhere is the tension between the likely positive gains from September 11 and the difficulties of realizing them more visible than in Pakistan, which holds the key to a different future for the subcontinent. Under pressure from the United States to choose either a long-term relationship with the US or continued support of the Taliban, the leader of Pakistan, General Pervez Musharraf, chose to abandon the Taliban. Later facing the threat of war by India and the United States' diplomatic urging of the abandonment of all support for terrorist groups, not just those in Afghanistan, General Musharraf declared on January 12, 2002, a commitment to launch Pakistan on a new course that involved a crackdown on extremist groups and the modernization of the education system in the Madrassas that had become the fountainhead of extremist ideas in the nation.[5]

By any measure, General Musharraf's speech was a historic moment in the evolution of Pakistan. In returning to the original ideal of Pakistan's founder, Mohammad Ali Jinnah, to build a modern secular state, General Musharraf was discarding the previous two and a half decades of political accommodation and manipulation of religious forces. In rejecting a theocratic vision for Pakistan, in challenging the claims of the Jihadi groups to speak for Muslims, General Musharraf was asserting what few leaders in the Islamic world were willing even to state in public. No wonder that General Musharraf has been hailed in the West as 'Ataturk II' and his plans for modernization of Pakistan have been pronounced as a veritable model for the rest of the Islamic world. While there is anger and resentment in the Middle East at the policies of the US towards the Muslim world, here was a leader and a nation ready to bridge the divide between Islam and the West.

General Musharraf's bold vision raises hopes for a positive future for the subcontinent; but can the West and India depend on just one man, an unelected military leader, for the deliverance of Pakistan towards political moderation and economic modernization? The history of Pakistan, with its string of failed civilian and military rulers, does not necessarily fuel much confidence in the eventual success of General Musharraf. Getting Pakistan to move in the direction of moderation will be necessary to preserve the gains of the war against terrorism in the region, but it will also be the biggest political challenge for the US and India, who will have to develop imaginative policy instruments. The desired outcome of a stable and moderate Pakistan is not beyond the reach of the international community.

General Musharraf's ability to launch Pakistan on a new course is intimately tied into the future of Indo-Pakistan relations. A Pakistan that is at peace with India will be in a better position to grow and prosper than one that is in perpetual hostility with its neighbour. Here, again, September 11 might have generated at once a huge military crisis and a historic opportunity for reconciliation between the two. The attack on the Indian Parliament House on December 13 intensified the decade-long military tensions between India and Pakistan into full-blown confrontation. India initiated its biggest military mobilization ever with an implicit threat to go to war unless Pakistan put an end to cross-border terrorism once and for all. Under simultaneous pressure from India and the US, General Musharraf, in his speech on January 12, has promised to end it. If he can overcome internal resistance in

Pakistan to his plans, the Indo-Pakistan military crisis at the turn of 2002 could lead to substantive negotiations to resolve all outstanding disputes, including those regarding Jammu and Kashmir, and a full normalization of bilateral relations.

However, there is considerable reluctance in Pakistan to give up the one instrument – cross-border terrorism – that many in Islamabad believe has been effective in putting political pressure on New Delhi to rethink its policy on the Kashmir dispute. There is apprehension that if Pakistan gives up the instrument of cross-border violence, India will have little incentive to negotiate. India, on the other hand, believes it had made a big leap in recent years towards the idea of seeking a final settlement with Pakistan on the Kashmir issue instead of avoiding a negotiation. The Indian prime minister, Atal Behari Vajpayee, has repeatedly emphasized the importance of ending the bitter legacy of partition by resolving the Kashmir dispute,[6] but given the intense mutual distrust, India is not in a position to assure Pakistan of its good intentions; and that is precisely where the American role on the subcontinent after September 11 has come into play.

Since the covert nuclearization of the subcontinent in the late 1980s, the United States has had to interject repeatedly to defuse the Indo-Pakistan military crises. The fear of a conflict between India and Pakistan escalating to the nuclear level had ensured American involvement in the region. However, since September 11, the United States has had the opportunity to look beyond crisis management towards a final conflict resolution between India and Pakistan. The unprecedented simultaneous improvement of American relations with both India and Pakistan since September 11 has made a peace process in the subcontinent, encouraged and sustained by the United States, a real possibility. Throughout the Cold War, American relations with India and Pakistan remained a zero sum game, but as India began to shed the anti-Western orientation of its foreign policy and drew closer to the United States in the 1990s, New Delhi began to find that Washington could become a credible interlocutor in normalizing the crisis-ridden relationship with Islamabad.

The Bush administration's unambiguous commitment to fight terrorism everywhere and its pressure on General Musharraf to end cross-border terrorism after September 11 have allowed India to countenance discreet third-party facilitation of tension reduction and conflict resolution with Pakistan. India has for decades rejected with great vehemence any external intervention in its disputes with Pakistan. The Cold War estrangement between India and the West meant that there was no way that India would accept the US as an objective inter-locutor on Kashmir. Since September 11, for India, the US and Britain have emerged as the only channels of political communication with Pakistan. Anglo-Americans, long distrusted in India for their alleged tilt towards Pakistan on Kashmir during the Cold War, are now seen in New Delhi as potential partners in the transformation of the subcontinent.

A normalization of Indo-Pakistan relations, including a resolution of the Kashmir dispute, will liberate the subcontinent from the politics of hate, religious extremism and violence that have so consumed it since partition. The unending spiral of conflict between India and Pakistan has maintained the region as one of the most backward in the world. Kashmir, as the residual item of partition, begs an answer to the original question of how Hindus and Muslims should structure their relations within the subcontinent. The United States, having established good relations with both India and Pakistan after September 11, may now be in a position to nudge the subcontinent towards reasonable resolution of the Kashmir dispute, regional economic cooperation and internal democratization. The normalization of Indo-Pakistan relations will hold the key to a transformation of the subcontinent.

Such a transformation will have an impact way beyond the region. The subcontinent is home to more than a third of the world's Muslim population, and a triumph of the Enlightenment values in the region will tilt the global struggle against the anti-modern political passions that drove the attackers of September 11. The subcontinent is home to some of the oldest Islamic revivalist movements, and debates on the tension between Islam and modernity in the region have had a profound effect on Muslim thinkers from Maghreb to Malaysia. A decisive shift of the Muslim world view in the subcontinent towards a reconciliation with the ideas of Enlightenment will send positive ripples towards both the Middle East and Southeast Asia.

Speaking in the wake of the unexpectedly swift victory in Afghanistan, President Bush proclaimed in his controversial State of the Union Address of January 29, 2002, that the US 'will lead by defending liberty and justice because they are right and true and unchanging for all people everywhere'.[7] While insisting that the US has no desire to impose its values on other nations, President Bush suggested that the promotion of democracy in the Islamic world would have to be among the key political objectives of the continuing American war against international terrorism. 'America will take the side of brave men and women who advocate these values around the world, including the Islamic world, because we have a greater objective than eliminating threats and containing resentment. We seek a just and peaceful world beyond the war on terror', Bush added.

The idea that the focus must now shift to the promotion of democratization in the volatile Asian region fits in with India's own sense that political pluralism is a universal value and not culturally relative. India has never subscribed to the view that democracy is a Western virtue and is incompatible with either Islamic or Asian values. Warts and all, India's own democratic experiment is a testimony to that. India now recognizes that without an expansion of the democratic values in its neighbourhood, its own future as a multiethnic and multicultural nation may be at risk from rising religious extremism of all hues. While India might quibble with the United States on some of the methods Americans might have in mind for the next phase of the war against terrorism, September 11 has made it easier for India and the West to work together in expanding the Enlightenment project into the subcontinent and Asia.

Notes

1. Testimony of Ambassador Michael A. Sheehan, Coordinator for Counter Terrorism, US State Department before House International Relations Committee, July 12, 2000.
2. For an incisive analysis of the anti-Western sentiment brewing across the Orient see Ian Buruma and Avishai Margalit, 'Occidentalism', *New York Review of Books*, January 17, 2002.
3. For a comprehensive account of the American alliance with militant Islamic groups in Afghanistan see John K. Cooley, *Unholy Wars: Afghanistan, America and International Terrorism* (2nd edn) (New Delhi: Penguin Books, 2001).
4. A term that has come to describe militant Islamic groups. The word *jihad* is often loosely translated as 'holy war', but is more accurately translated as the 'righteous struggle' that all followers of the Islamic faith are mandated to follow in their lives. In Afghanistan in the 1980s, *jihad* became a slogan against Soviet occupation; now it is interpreted by the radical Islamic groups as a war against Western dominance and a campaign to purify the Islamic world itself.
5. Highlights of General Musharraf's TV address to Pakistan, BBC News Online, January 12, 2002, 18.25 GMT.
6. In his New Year musings at the beginning of 2001 and 2002, Prime Minister Atal Behari Vajpayee proclaimed and reiterated in articles published in newspapers his desire to get off the 'beaten track' in finding a solution to the Kashmir dispute with Pakistan and design a 'future architecture for peace and prosperity for the entire South Asian region'. See Atal Behari Vajpayee, 'My Musings from Kumarakom-I: Time to Resolve Problems from the Past', *The Hindu*, January 2, 2001; 'We Shall Triumph Against Terrorism', *The Hindu*, January 1, 2002.
7. President George W. Bush Jnr, State of the Union Address, January 29, 2002.

CHAPTER 19

Political Violence and Global Order

Paul Rogers

A frequently quoted definition of terrorism is 'the threat of violence and the use of fear to coerce, persuade and gain public attention'.[1] Assigning political motives to terrorism may be considered to provide a legitimacy to acts that public authorities would normally want to deny, but the political context is accepted by most analysts and is accurately reflected in Wardlaw's definition of political terrorism as:

> the use, or threat of use, of violence by an individual or a group, whether acting for or in opposition to established authority, when such an act is designed to create extreme anxiety and/or fear-inducing effects in a target group larger than the immediate victims with the purpose of coercing that group into acceding to the political demands of the perpetrators.[2]

An important aspect of such a definition is that it recognizes that terrorism and political violence are not the prerogative of substate groups. 'Agitational' or 'revolutionary' terrorism may be employed by such groups, but 'enforcement' or 'establishment' terrorism is the province of the state.

This elaboration is essential because state authorities concentrate almost exclusively on threats to their own power, whereas most terrorism is actually conducted by states against their own populations. The attacks on September 11 were widely regarded as unique, not least because of the considerable loss of life, but the use of mass-casualty political violence in the second half of the twentieth century was much more commonly an aspect of state control, and continues to be so.

There have been many examples of massacres of political opponents and non-politically active civilians across the world, from Indonesia to

215

Iraq and from Chile to Guatemala, with many individual periods of violence far exceeding the losses of the September 11 atrocities. The use of chemical weapons of mass destruction by Iraq against the Kurdish inhabitants of Halabjah in March 1988, killing some 5000 people, is a particular example. It was not greatly condemned by Western states, as Iraq was then regarded as a bulwark against Iran.

The use of terror continues in many parts of the world, including in countries that maintain support from Western democracies. Methods include summary detention without trial, torture and the use of para-military death squads and counter-insurgency military action against civilian populations. On any scale of measurement, terrorism is primarily a function of the state, even if the greatest attention is currently given to substate terrorism against Western states.

Even so, this chapter concentrates primarily on substate actors, but it will be argued that the changing 'drivers' or parameters of international security mean that it will be the interaction of state power with anti-state or 'anti-elite' action that will be particularly significant. While my focus in this chapter will, in part, be on the attacks of September 11 and their aftermath and consequences, my principal concern is with the wider issues of international security which, it will be argued, are likely to determine the nature and extent of conflict, including political violence, in the next two to three decades.

My intention is therefore to examine the main 'drivers' of conflict and insecurity, to contrast these with the current Western security paradigm, and to question whether that paradigm is sustainable. I analyse the prospect that advanced urban industrial states are sufficiently vulnerable to political violence and asymmetric warfare that it is in their own self-interest to address root causes of insecurity, and ask whether the impact of September 11 will help or hinder that process.

Trends in Conflict and Insecurity

The three dominant drivers of conflict and insecurity over the next few decades are likely to be socioeconomic divisions, environmental constraints and proliferation of military technologies. The latter results largely from the impetus and momentum of the Cold War years and includes the spread of weapons of mass destruction, ballistic and cruise missiles, area-impact munitions and the capability of paramilitary groups to target nodes of economic or political power using relatively crude devices and tactics.

In terms of socioeconomic divisions, the global trend of recent decades has been for an elite of about 1 billion to move rapidly ahead of the remaining 5 billion, with the ratio of inequality between the richest and poorest fifths of the global population nearly doubling. The gap widened markedly during the 1980s and 1990s and demographic and economic trends suggest a further widening. Elite communities are concentrated in the North Atlantic community and some West Pacific states, but with significant elites in many poor countries, and marginalized minorities in some rich countries.

A form of economic apartheid is emerging as the elite surges ahead of the rest and the globalized free market delivers patchy economic growth but fails to ensure any degree of economic justice. This process is happening in the context of significant improvements in primary education, literacy and communications, resulting in many more people becoming aware of their very marginalization. This, in turn, leads to the phenomenon of the 'knowledgeable poor' and a potential revolution of frustrated expectations.

Frequent results include substantial and increasing pressure to migrate, endemic problems of criminality and, in many parts of the world, anti-elite insurgencies and rebellions often stemming from the development of radical social movements. Among many examples are the Zapatista rebellion in Mexico, the Shining Path in Peru and FARC in Colombia, a bitter anti-authority revolt and civil war in Algeria, a Maoist rebellion in Nepal and protracted insurgencies in several parts of the Middle East and southern and Southeast Asia. Such trends should be expected to continue and increase in impact.

Environmental limitations are primarily felt, so far, in terms of resource conflicts. Smaller-scale examples include conflicts in Africa involving cobalt, diamonds, tantalum and rock phosphates, but the most notable example stems from the remarkable concentration of two-thirds of the world's proven oil reserves in the Persian Gulf. With the United States experiencing an increasing dependence on imported oil, now running at over 60 per cent of consumption compared with 10 per cent 30 years ago, a key component of US security policy has been an extensive military basing in the region, including the Fifth Fleet in the Persian Gulf and a major air force presence in Saudi Arabia. In turn, one of the major motivations of the al-Qaeda network, with considerable local support, has been an increasingly violent opposition to this presence.

In the longer term, though, certain global environmental impacts are likely to be even more significant. In the 1980s, the first evidence of global environmental change effected by human activity became apparent with the developing problem of ozone depletion caused by CFC pollutants. That was a relatively simple matter to address and some action has been taken, although not sufficient to prevent some serious environmental problems. Much more important is the phenomenon of climate change caused primarily by release of carbon gases due to excessive combustion of fossil fuels.

Until recently it was assumed that climate change would have its primary impact in temperate latitudes, causing substantial problems; not least in the form of severe weather events. These effects would at least be experienced mainly by wealthy countries that would best be able to cope. What is becoming clear is that climate change is likely to have profound effects on the tropical and subtropical land masses where the great majority of the world's people live.[3] A progressive 'drying out' of the tropics is thought likely, with profound effects on the ecological carrying capacity of some of the world's most fertile croplands. The effects of this would be to cause regional food deficits that would far outstrip even the major famines of the past century, putting an immense strain on sociopolitical systems and greatly exacerbating migratory pressures.

Overall, the combination of socioeconomic divisions and environmental constraints implies enhanced problems of environmental conflict, insecurity stemming from mass migration and, above all, anti-elite insurgencies, some of them transnational in nature and effect. The results of such developments are inherently unpredictable, but what should be expected is that radical and extreme social movements are likely to develop that are frequently anti-elite in nature and draw substantial support from the marginalized majorities.

In different contexts and circumstances, such groups may have their roots in political ideologies, religious beliefs, ethnic, nationalist or cultural identities or, more likely, a complex mixture of several of these. They may focus on individuals or groups, but the most common feature is likely to be an opposition to existing centres of power.

They may be substate groups directed against the elites in their own state or foreign interests, or they may hold power in states in the south, and will then no doubt be labelled as 'rogue' states as they direct their responses to the north. What can be said is that, on present trends, anti-elite action will be a core feature of the next 30 years, driven in part by widening socioeconomic divisions exacerbated by environmental constraints.

Furthermore, such movements may, in some cases, engage in extreme action, including the willingness to cause mass casualties. They may well draw their leadership from well-educated and relatively wealthy sectors of society. If they succeed in effecting anti-elite revolutionary change, they may introduce rigid and authoritarian regimes in which they themselves constitute new elites. For the most part, the movements and resulting centres of political power will be male-dominated.

Such trends are in progress in the context of a demonstrated capability of political violence to affect centres of power, although some notable attempts of the mid-1990s did not achieve their full impact. Even so, there are many examples, from the Sendero bombing of elite neighbourhoods in Lima, through to the bombing of the Colombo central business district by the LTTE. An Algerian group made a failed attempt to crash a hijacked plane in the centre of Paris in 1994, and a Japanese religious sect attempted to killed thousands by releasing nerve gas into the Tokyo subway the following year. In the mid-1990s the Provisional IRA undertook a sustained programme of economic targeting of city-centre and transport network bombings in the UK, having a substantial if largely unacknowledged political impact.[4]

US forces overseas have experienced political violence over two decades, from the Beirut bombing of the embassy and marines barracks in 1983 through to the Khobar Towers and USS *Cole* bombings the following decade and the attacks on embassies in Nairobi and Dar es Salaam. Perhaps most significant was the attempt to destroy the World Trade Center in 1993, an attack which, if it had succeeded, would have killed ten times as many people as the atrocities of September 11, 2001.

There is thus a strong record of anti-elite action by radical groups seeking political change, although this was not widely recognized prior to September 11. What is even less recognized is the connection between such action and the wider issue of the changing security parameters, even though such an analysis is not new. An early example was the work of Edwin Brooks, more than 25 years ago, who was concerned at the risk of

> a crowded, glowering plant of massive inequalities of wealth buttressed by stark force yet endlessly threatened by desperate people in the global ghettos ...[5]

The US Security Paradigm

How does this analysis of international security trends compare with the outlook from the West in general and the United States in particular? Is there any indication that the core 'drivers' of potential insecurity need to be addressed, or is it a matter of maintaining the existing order?

President Clinton's first CIA Director, James Wolsey, characterized the post-Cold War security challenge for the United States by saying that the US has slain the dragon (the Soviet threat) but now lives in a jungle full of poisonous snakes.[6] The jungle includes the two potential rivals of Russia and China, at least in the long term, and two zones of continuing instability, north-east Asia and the Middle East. The latter is particularly significant because of the remarkable concentration of oil reserves. The less clear-cut threats include terrorism and disorder stemming both from 'rogue' states and failed states, especially where they affect US interests. This outlook would be accepted, to an extent, by principal US allies in Europe and elsewhere, but usually in a less clear-cut form and with certain concerns about the lack of a nuanced view, not least in relation to the Middle East.

In the US, the post-Cold War military posture changed radically during the 1990s. The army, navy and air force all lost around 30 per cent of their personnel while transforming themselves in the direction of rapid deployment capabilities, long-range force projection, counter-insurgency and special operations. The Marine Corps, with its amphibious capabilities, retained most of its strength. Military budgets may have been cut, but the resultant forces are considerable, especially in the absence of any kind of threat from the defunct Warsaw Pact, and are, by a very substantial measure, the most powerful in the world today.

Some major NATO allies have followed a similar path, but the United States is pre-eminent, the overall direction being to sustain and enhance a capability to intervene in regional conflicts where national interests are considered to be at risk. Taming the jungle has replaced slaying the dragon. The exact nature and capabilities of those 'snakes' may not be too clear, a problem expressed with remarkable candour by President Bush in one of his early campaign speeches (January 2000):

> it was a dangerous world and we knew exactly who the 'they' were. It was us versus them and we knew exactly who 'them' was. Today we're not so sure who the 'they' are, but we know they're there.

In spite of the many military changes, the view on the Republican right in the latter part of Clinton's second term was that the US was not properly fulfilling its role of ensuring the enhancement of US interests internationally, and a markedly unilateralist stance developed initially in the Republican-controlled Congress. This is part of a wider view that the twenty-first century should be seen as the American Century.[7] Prior to the election of President Bush, this mood had been demonstrated by the refusal of the Senate to ratify the Comprehensive Test Ban Treaty, and by opposition to proposals for an anti-personnel landmine ban and moves towards an international criminal court.

After the election and prior to September 11, the unilateral stance included withdrawal from the Kyoto Protocols on climate change, a disinterest in Middle East peace proposals, a cessation of the diplomatic engagement with North Korea, opposition to UN proposals on the control of terrorism and an increasingly critical stance on the negotia-tions to strengthen the 1972 Biological and Toxin Weapons Convention. Not that the United States was unilateralist in all things, a point made admirably by Charles Krauthammer, writing in June 2001:

> Multipolarity, yes, when there is no alternative. But not when there is. Not when we have the unique imbalance of power that we enjoy today – and that has given the international system a stability and essential tranquility it had not know for at least a century.
>
> The international environment is far more likely to enjoy peace under a single hegemon. Moreover, we are not just any hegemon. We run a uniquely benign imperium.[8]

Thus, where it is in US interests to have agreements, then they are acceptable, as with NATO expansion and NAFTA. But the policy is highly selective and fits a paradigm in which US security interests are paramount and where the only way to ensure peace and prosperity is for the US to have freedom of action, whatever the effects on the world in general and even its allies in particular.

The Implications of September 11

There was remarkable support for the United States in the immediate aftermath of the atrocities of September 11, 2001, together with an expectation that one result would be a recognition in Washington of the need for close multilateral cooperation in any response. In the event, the response, outside of intelligence and security collaboration, was of a substantial military operation that was primarily unilateral. This involved joining opposition forces in the Afghan civil war to defeat the Taliban regime, using a sustained bombing campaign that also resulted in the deaths of several thousand civilians. Most of the Taliban militia withdrew without surrendering and melted back into their communities, with very little of the leadership killed or captured.

This applied also to the al-Qaeda network which had its facilities in Afghanistan hugely disrupted, but lost few of its leaders and dispersed successfully to the extent that a senior FBI official concluded that it had been cut back in its potential for action by perhaps 30 per cent.[9]

In the immediate aftermath of the most intense phase of the war, Afghanistan experienced a degeneration into warlordism and banditry except in a few centres of population, notably Kabul, where an international security assistance force provided some stability. Meanwhile, the United States was able to extend its bases into Afghanistan, Tajikistan, Kyrgyzstan and Uzbekistan, to maintain a military presence in Pakistan and even to obtain basing facilities for tanker aircraft in Bulgaria, the first presence of foreign troops in that country since 1946.

More generally, the September 11 attacks and the resulting war on terror have greatly reinforced the unilateralist outlook. In the wider context, this has included strong opposition to further multilateral negotiations on strengthening the bioweapons convention, the establishment of military tribunals meeting in secret to try presumed terrorists and the withdrawal from the Anti-Ballistic Missile Treaty. This last decision, in early December 2001, coincided with a large 'ripple-fire' test of the Trident strategic nuclear missile system, a potent reminder of the US desire to acquire missile defences while retaining the world's most powerful offensive nuclear forces.

In relation to the 'war on terror' itself, there has been an intensification in both words and action. As well as the establishment of an extended network of bases across Central Asia, increased military assistance has been given to the Philippines in its counter-insurgency operations against Islamic militants. The Fiscal Year 2003 defence budget will see a very substantial increase in military spending in addition to increases already agreed for 2002. The 2003 budget will rise by a figure nearly 150 per cent of that of the entire UK defence budget, with considerable emphasis on those aspects most relevant to low intensity and counter-insurgency operations. Maintaining control has become the dominant theme of the security paradigm.

The rhetoric, too, reflects these budgetary developments. The underlying theme is more than the well-rehearsed 'if you are not with us you are against us', for there is a clear emphasis on Washington deciding who is 'against us'. Most notable was the 2002 State of the Union Address in which President Bush referred to an 'axis of evil' encompassing North Korea, Iraq and Iran; the latter being included greatly to the surprise, and consternation, of European diplomats.

Future Trends in Political Violence – and Alternatives

What is the relevance of the attacks of September 11 and their after-math to the more general analysis of trends in international insecurity? Will it make a re-examination of the Western security paradigm more or less likely? The first point to emphasize is that the al-Qaeda attacks did not come from a desperate underclass of marginalized peoples across the globe, driven to violence by frustration of the possibilities of peaceful change. Even so, the context of the development of the network is relevant in several respects.

First, the September 11 attacks did demonstrate in a horrifying manner the vulnerability of highly developed states to asymmetric paramilitary action. Second, al-Qaeda's support stems, in part, from an opposition to the US military presence in the Gulf, boosted by disaffection from among the 'demographic bulge' of educated young people in the region. Finally, and most significant, the reaction of the United States has not been to address the core issues underlying the strength of this and other networks, but rather to seek to maintain control with great vigour and expanded military force.

The more general analysis suggests that the core drivers of socioeconomic divisions and environmental constraints will lead to increased instability and conflict, much of it represented by an increasing tendency towards anti-elite insurgencies. These will, on occasions, result in considerable violence, including the risk of mass casualty attacks similar to or worse than those of September 11. In turn, there will be vigorous counter-insurgency actions, both by the military and paramilitary forces of local elites, and by substantial action by the US in its war on terror. The longer-term result is likely to be a cycle, or perhaps a spiral, of violence between elites and radical anti-elite movements.

While a short-term alternative might involve far greater cooperation for anti-terrorist actions with a strong emphasis on multilateral approaches, longer-term action requires some fundamental changes in Western policies aimed at reversing socioeconomic divisions and engaging in effective environmental management linked to sustainable economies. This requires radical changes to policies on the debt crisis, the promotion of trade reforms specifically linked to the trading prospects of the South and the encouragement of economic cooperation for gendered and sustainable development. It also requires a radical reappraisal of northern attitudes to economic growth, centred on effective action on climate change and excess resource use.

In the aftermath of September 11, the short-term prognosis for such a change in the paradigm is negative. In the United States, at least, the combination of a notably right-wing administration, especially in security terms, with the traumatic and far-reaching domestic effects of the attacks, has produced a reinforcement of the existing paradigm of maintaining control, keeping the lid on problems of instability and threats from the jungle full of snakes. There is little or no attempt to understand or address the core issues.

Endless War?

While sympathy for the United States over the effects of the New York and Washington attacks remained strong in Europe for some months, there was increasing concern over the unilateralist stance, both before and after September 11. To varying extents, European governments have taken a different view from that of the US on a wide range of issues: from arms control issues such as missile defence, the test ban treaty and the control of bioweapons, anti-personnel landmines and light arms transfers, through to a greater concern over stability in Northeast Asia and the Middle East. There remains a broadly shared view on some global issues such as WTO, IMF and World Bank activities, but European concern is much higher on issues such as debt and climate change. All this is within the context of a real concern over the clear determination of the US to act as a single-minded superpower, with little interest espoused for the views of its putative allies.

More widely, there is in the majority of the world a developing analysis that is wildly different from the world view from Washington. One analysis, published soon after the attacks, condemns them as horrific, despicable and unpardonable, but cautions against an automatic 'iron fist' response that ignores the underlying context. It points to the frequent use of indiscriminate force by the US and to the bitter mood throughout much of the Middle East and Southwest Asia, directed partly at the US but also against autocratic states dependent on continuing US support. The analysis concludes:

> The only response that will really contribute to global security and peace is for Washington to address not the symptoms but the roots of terrorism. It is for the United States to re-examine and substantially change its policies in the Middle East and the Third World, supporting for a change arrangements that will not stand in the way of the achievement of equity, justice and genuine national

sovereignty for currently marginalised peoples. Any other way leads to endless war.[10]

The prognosis, at least for the present, has to be one of endless war, with a substantially increased risk of political violence, both by elites and against elites. An alternative possibility is that the trauma of September 11 might encourage individuals, citizen groups, intellectuals and indeed political leaders to recognize the long-term security signifi- cance of what has happened and to redouble efforts towards a more equitable and stable world.

It is essentially a matter of choice, and the next decade is likely to prove pivotal in determining the degree of international instability and political violence. The early effects of September 11 suggest a hardening of the old paradigm, but there is every chance that it may be possible to further analyse and demonstrate the futility of that approach. The responsibility for those in a position to do so, whether academics, activists, politicians or many others, is considerable.

Notes

1. Quoted in Sean Anderson and Stephen Sloan, *Historical Dictionary of Terrorism* (Metuchen, NJ, and London: The Scarecrow Press, 1995). This includes a helpful discussion of the conceptualization and definition of terrorism.
2. Ibid.
3. David Rind, 'Drying Out the Tropics', *New Scientist,* May 6, 1995.
4. For an analysis of the use of economic targeting by paramilitary groups see Paul Rogers, 'Political Violence and Economic Targeting – Aspects of the Provisional IRA Strategy, 1992–97', *Civil Wars,* vol. 3, no. 4 (2000), pp. 1–30.
5. Edwin Brooks, 'The Implications of Ecological Limits to Growth in Terms of Expectations and Aspirations in Developed and Less Developed Countries', in Anthony Vann and Paul Rogers (eds) *Human Ecology and World Development* (London and New York: Plenum Press, 1976).
6. Statement by James Wolsey at Senate Hearings, February 1993.
7. See the Project on the New American Century, an interest group promoting a vigorous US foreign policy, with supporters including Vice President Cheney and Secretary of Defense Rumsfeld, <www.geocities.com/newamericancentury/>.
8. Charles Krauthammer, 'The Bush Doctrine: ABM, Kyoto and the New American Unilateralism', *Weekly Standard,* June 4, 2001, Washington, DC.
9. The view of the acting assistant director of the FBI's counter-terrorism division. See Walter Pincus, 'Al Qaeda to Survive bin Laden', *Washington Post,* December 19, 2001.
10. Walden Bello, 'Endless War', *Focus on the Global South,* Manila, September 2001. This and other analyses are available at <www.focusweb.org>.

CHAPTER 20

World Politics as Usual after September 11: Realism Vindicated

Colin Gray

Because the now global media lives by what appears to be new in the 'news', any dramatic event is liable to be retailed as the herald of a new era. The dramatic quality of an event, however, is not an entirely reliable guide to its significance. September 11 may score a perfect ten for shock effect, indeed it could have been inspired by a Hollywood storyboard, but really what does it signify for the future of world politics?

In this chapter I advance the quite unremarkable argument that the eternal lore of statecraft still holds. Moreover, I suspect strongly that history textbooks a century hence will vary with reference to September 11 only insofar as some will accord the events of that day a fat footnote, while others will allow it a paragraph in the text. In other words, there is much less to September 11 than met the eye late in 2001. The domain of this chapter covers two distinctive kinds of terrain. First, September 11 and its immediate consequences must be interrogated for what it says about the working of world politics: is realism vindicated? Second, if realism is judged to be alive and well, has September 11 effected any noticeable major changes in political behaviour within the realist paradigm? For example, does it seem probable that any lasting political realignment will emerge as a legacy of the atrocities? On the grandest scale, might a global coalition against terrorism take shape, or, more exclusively, might the G-8 states function as a true 'concert' of powers? As we shall see, smart money will avoid both those bets.

It is, perhaps, more than a little curious to debate the proposition that recent events have seen 'realism vindicated', because it is difficult to identify an alternative paradigm for world politics which is suitably rich in explanatory power. The realist canon assumes a structurally anarchic world wherein necessarily self-helping states – the principal players – seek power and influence in pursuit of their national interests. All of the players, main characters and walk-ons, have followed a realist script. The world has not been, and is not about to be, politically transformed. To the limited degree to which one can find evidence of transformation, of arguably revolutionary change, it lies in the manner in which the United States applied its military power against the hapless holy warriors of the Taliban. Even in that relatively dramatic realm, though, the traditional lore of strategy still holds. Today's 'joint warfare', melding special operations forces, unmanned aerial vehicles, long-range bombers (dropping JDAMs[1]) and space systems, certainly is an innovation in the tactical and operational threads to strategic history. But, in their day, so also were the railway, the electric telegraph, indirect artillery fire and extensive mechanization. What we have witnessed thus far in the military dimension of the war against those presumed to be guilty for September 11, has been technically impressive indeed. What we have not witnessed in the war to date is any convincing evidence that the realist world (dis)order is either undergoing some transformation, or is revealed to be conceptually deficient in satisfactory explanatory power.

Realism is so broad a church that it is not useful, or even practicable, to attempt in a short chapter rigorously to test the validity of its many precepts. Instead, it should be enlightening to outline and discuss an argument that covers the principal facets of international political behaviour from September 11 to the present. Lest I have failed to flag my thesis with the necessary clarity thus far, my case is to the effect that the methods and content of statecraft are, and will remain, very substantially unchanged by the evidence of the new style in mass terrorism. It may be worth my mentioning the fact that if the actual (the First and Second World Wars and the Holocaust) and potential (a superpower nuclear Third World War) horrors of the twentieth century failed to effect radical change in the means and methods of world politics, it is hardly likely that isolated terroristic atrocities, no matter how televisual, would succeed in their turn. So what have we seen since September 11?

1. Reaffirmation of the validity of the motivations behind Athenian statecraft as interpreted by Thucydides – fear, honour and interest.[2]
2. No plausible evidence suggesting the emergence of a new world order, perhaps one governed either by the whole global community through the agency of the United Nations or, more likely, by a new concert of Great(er) Powers (effectively the G-8 polities).

3. The appearance of a new maturity in information-led long-range air power, dependent upon target intelligence gathered on the ground and transmitted via satellite. Whether or not a true transformation is occurring in the US armed forces, there is no doubt that September 11 and the subsequent military campaign have fuelled American debate over the future of defence policy and planning.

Given the many varieties of realism, it is no easy matter to test its/their validity as the authoritative set of terms of engagement in world politics.[3] The best I can do here is to pose some questions of recent behaviour to see if any flags are raised arguably signalling policy motives and objectives, or commitments to a new *modus operandi*, which appear challenging to the realist paradigm. To be specific: are states, particularly the most powerful of states, ceasing to act primarily in self-regarding ways with reference to their own security? Are non-state actors, both international institutions and transnational organizations (especially those of a 'terroristic' bent), changing the game of world politics? Is military power of a 'regular' kind of sharply declining relevance in a new era of 'asymmetric' conflict?

If anything, September 11 and its immediate aftermath have provided compelling evidence to encourage fresh recognition of the authority of the realist canon. The script for statecraft was first written by the Greeks and the Romans, now it is played by Americans, Russians, the Chinese and bands of murderous religious zealots. The CNN factor, and the instant global scrutiny it enables, has the consequence that the means and methods for the suppression and punishment of history's losers generally have altered somewhat since ancient times. Mass crucifixions and impalings are long out of fashion, though we can be confident that there would be satellite channels eager to carry them, should the commercial opportunity beckon. There can be little doubt that today's Americans are more generous victors than were yesterday's Athenians and Romans. Nonetheless, when we allow for cultural differences and for the military options granted by the leading edge of modern technology, the practice of imperium, indeed of the stability deriving from a hegemonic order, is not that distinctive from ancient times to modern.

Great Powers, even hegemonic Great Powers, do not always perform competently as the rules of world politics indicate to be appropriate. But international political and strategic affairs run along realist lines, whether or not statesmen have talent for the game. The only question is, how well, or poorly, do they play? Today, in the very early 2000s, we

are striving to cope with the consequences of eight years of drift in
American high policy, because President Bill Clinton had no real
interest in, or understanding of, foreign affairs. This lack of sustained
presidential attention, taken together with an administration short of
outstanding talent in the domain of foreign and defence policy, translated into a 1990s decade unshaped by the only polity that could have
given it forward-looking prudent definition for the construction of a
postwar order worthy of the name. The Blair government's periodic
public commitment to an ethical foreign policy, at the least to doing
good in the world, has been as embarrassingly pretentious as it has
proved militarily infeasible. When ethics require muscular enforcement, there is no acceptable substitute for military commitment by the
hegemon. For reasons that we shall ponder, today's international order
ultimately is shaped and disciplined – to the degree that it can be – by
the hegemonic power. The Bush administration may have unilateralist
tendencies, but those tendencies do reflect the genuine loneliness and
uniqueness of responsibility that attends solitary superpower status.

Let us consider briefly the fundamental questions posed above. Are
states ceasing to act in primarily self-regarding ways with reference to
their own security? Recall that realist theory, both structural-defensive
and of the John Mearsheimer offensive kind,[4] requires states to look
primarily to their own survival, given the essential anarchy that is
world politics. Following September 11, the United States, whose
'honour' was offended grossly, asserted itself ruthlessly to wreak
military destruction upon such of its foes as it could target. The demonstration of military competence was truly impressive; the intelligence
story, alas, was much less so. Most of the world's 'terrorists' can sleep
easily in their beds, and the leading state sponsors of terrorism need not
quake, because the American hegemon is only talking about a crusade;
there is no prospect of it actually pursuing such. The reason, of course,
is that old-fashioned geopolitics and geostrategy continue to comprise
the serious business of national security policy. Terrorism and similar
asymmetric menaces may be the threat *du jour*, but the prudent realists
who now command the American ship of state are not confused over
the distinction between first- and second-order perils.

The United States is behaving towards al-Qaeda exactly as did
imperial Rome towards the Jewish zealots (and indeed towards any
revolting minority). For the sake of its reputation, its priceless 'honour',
rather than out of fear or even interest, the hegemon must hunt down
its irregular foes to the last man and to the ends of the earth, if need be.
Such a campaign is not performed primarily as a service for world order

directly, though that is likely to be a beneficial by-product, but rather as a reaffirmation of hegemonic dignity and *pour encourager les autres*. In addition to the revenge motive in US policy which has been plain to see, the hopefully merciless pursuit of al-Qaeda is important if the United States is to continue to command the respect that it needs to ease some of the burdens of hegemony. The world will become far more dangerous if regional opportunists are encouraged to pull the eagle's feathers by any apparent evidence of a loss of hegemonic will to power.

What of the other state players in post-September 11 politics? Putin's increasingly illiberal Russia has calculated in best *realpolitik* fashion, that the path of cooperation with an assertive United States has much to recommend it. Putin knows that Russia's most serious geopolitical problem in the twenty-first century is a rising China, not an enlarging NATO or even a hegemonic US. By acting the responsible statesman over al-Qaeda, Putin obtains near absolution for his sins against decency in Chechnya, is wooed as a mover and shaker of world events – which is flattering to a country currently objectively challenged on almost every metric of relative power – and fuels the hopes of those enlightened folk in the West who would like to see the old NATO demolished by *de facto* or *de jure* Russian membership. To repeat the point, looking to the longer term, Putin knows that he will need a US alliance to contain China in Asia.

The Chinese shed crocodile tears for September 11 and have been somewhat chastened by the evidence of the new style in 'joint' warfare practised by the United States. China has some modest conjunction of interests with the United States in chasing terrorists (as indeed do most countries – terrorism is a near universal phenomenon), but those interests do not begin to compete with Beijing's interest in the humbling of the current hegemon and the reduction of its influence in East Asia. The long-term struggle for ordering authority in East Asia is truly a serious business; hunting down handfuls of fanatics is not.

I will not waste the reader's time by arguing the painfully obvious vindication of a brutal realism that, for a leading example, has Indo-Pakistani relations in its grip. If there is some benign transformation under way in the means and methods most characteristic of world security politics, it has yet to reach the subcontinent.

It is perhaps instructive to offer passing comment upon the British performance after September 11. Britain has sought to increase its influence, certainly to 'punch above its weight', by serving as America's faithful lieutenant. The United States has not been prepared to share campaign direction (strategy) or war-fighting duties seriously with

Britain, but it has been content to condone Mr Blair as global traveller
for the forces of good over evil, and to tolerate, if not quite encourage,
a leading British peacekeeping role in post-Taliban Afghanistan. The US
armed forces, keyed for effectiveness to the provision of hi-tech fire-
power, do not really 'do' peacekeeping. The armed forces, realistically
or not, adhere to a warrior ethos and to a doctrine of war that seeks to
achieve decisive military success. Peacekeeping is for somewhat lesser
breeds, like the Canadians, the Nigerians and the British.

My next basic question asked if non-state actors, international institutions and transnational bodies are changing the game of world
politics? Has the decline of the state proceeded so far that the realist
paradigm is approaching an absurdity?[5] Well, the experience of
September 11 to the present suggests not. It is true that al-Qaeda is a
gloriously transnational organization, but it is also true that it can
flourish only with some significant measure of official state acquiescence, if not necessarily actual sponsorship. Perhaps to the surprise of
some, but certainly not to we classical realists, states, their territoriality
and their sovereign prerogatives, continue to rule in world politics. For
all the allegedly burgeoning relations of complex interdependence and
suchlike sophisticated nexi, traditional state-centric behaviour, in
pursuit of eminently realist goals, explains the course of contemporary
events. The UN, NATO, even the G-8 (for those who are speculating
about a return to a concert system of international security), have none
of them played genuinely independently influential roles in the
protracted crisis. In a hegemonic order like that, extant, international
institutions, even alliances for collective defence, can act only so as to
add legitimacy to the policy will of the hegemon. For the time being,
US military prowess is trumps in world politics.

On the distaff side of international order, it seems improbable that
transnational actors such as al-Qaeda will shape the (in)security environment for decades to come. Compared with the unpleasantness in
Indo-Pakistani relations, the ambition of China to be sovereign
throughout maritime East Asia, and the determination of Russia to
regain positions of authority in the imperial marches lost in 1991,
transnational terrorism is pretty small beer. Geopolitics, not various
transnationalisms (including 'civilizations'), shapes the mainstream of
historical events.

Have events since September 11 taught any useful lessons about the
relevance of 'regular' military power? For all the excited chatter about
'asymmetric' threats and warfare,[6] what actually has happened over the
past several months? The answer is that regular US conventional

military power has battered the third- or fourth-rate military capabilities of the Afghan Taliban into a state of collapse. The frequently
imperfect political intelligence behind the aerial targeting cannot
detract seriously from the judgement that US military power, employed
in a novel mix of joint effort, has performed magnificently. It is true
that the enemy proved not to be an overly worthy foe, but nonetheless
the US offensive air campaign was a marvellous demonstration of state-
of-the-art hegemonic military ascendancy.

Periodically, most recently in the early 1970s and then again in the
1990s, it is fashionable to discern a sharply declining utility to the
threat or use of military force in world politics. Would that that speculative perception were accurate. The truth of the matter is that
international order today is ultimately sustained either by the threat of
superior military muscle (in a hegemonic or concert system), or by a
balance of military power. The bulk of the action against the al-Qaedas
of this world will have to be undertaken by intelligence agencies and
their hit squads, and by police forces and financial investigators, but
regular military power has an essential role to play in discouraging
states from playing host to terrorists.

Al-Qaeda is not going to bring down Western civilization, while it is
not by any means certain that September 11 has the potential to
mobilize the disaffected masses of Islam. On balance, for all the tactical
ingenuity displayed on September 11, al-Qaeda's strategy must tenta-
tively be judged an abysmal failure. Although, on the one hand, a
dramatically painful blow was struck at American pride, on the other
hand, the measured yet lethal American response has revealed to all
interested observers just what it means to be a hegemon. If the course
of contemporary history is challenging in notable ways to the realist
paradigm, I must confess to being blind to the evidence. As was
suggested earlier, the major and minor players in the current international political context are all following a script that has powerful
precedents in Greek and Roman history.

I will conclude this chapter by presenting some 'lessons of
September 11 and after', though in truth they are more akin to redis-
covery of what should be blindingly obvious to any student of history.

1. International order needs a sheriff. World opinion, opulent international debating fora and alleged shifts in values away from the
   atavistic attractions of violence, can none of them handle the
   strategic traffic when disorder needs to be stamped on.

2. Today, the American hegemon is the only possible sheriff. Americans do not care very much about the Balkans, they care not at all about Africa, and – until very recently – they had barely heard of land-locked Central Asia. In short, a great deal of murder and mayhem will be tolerated in the world by a hegemonic power that is attentive to a careful definition and rank-ordering of its national interests. However, when the United States wishes to act it is literally unstoppable by any combination of polities and institutions. America's debacle in Somalia in 1993–94 was an exception which proves the rule. As a hegemonic power the contemporary United States believes it has rights that match its burdensome duties. For a recent example, the unilateral US decision to withdraw (legally) from the Anti-Ballistic Missile Treaty regime, though universally unpopular abroad, was taken because Americans are painfully aware of the exceptional risks that they will run as *the* sheriff for order.

3. Great Powers seek to increase their influence. The several principal variants of realist doctrine offer distinctive, albeit generally compatible, explanations of why Great Powers behave as they do. Suffice it to say that events since September 11 underline the continuing authority of this third precept. As we noted above, Russia, China and Britain, to which short list we should add India, Iran and even Germany, have all been seeking opportunistically to make gains in political influence in the current context. Journalistic speculation about fundamental realignments in world politics, keyed to the overhyped 'war on terror', is so much nonsense. States, especially the greater states, have only a minor interest in chasing down *their own* irritating terrorists; their major interest lies in shaping their international relations to the national advantage.

4. Crusades are not profitable or practicable. It is the American way in statecraft to ideologize the basically mundane. Current US policy is not about waging a war on terrorism (a linguistic atrocity, if nothing else); rather is it about restoring national honour after the humiliation of September 11. There can be no war on terrorism because the concept carries so much political baggage that it continues to defy efforts at substantive definition. No one is really all that interested in chasing terrorists, let alone freedom fighters, who menace someone else. Realists of all stripes know this. Higher policy considerations of a geopolitical character soon serve to discourage expansive adventures against terrorists writ large and territorially widely scattered. If anyone believes that the twenty-first century will witness a concerted US-led crusade against the evils of terrorism, he

or she should be encouraged to read the basic texts on realism in world politics.

5. Concert statecraft is not feasible today. We classical realists have no quarrel with concert diplomacy, but we do not believe it to be practicable in the contemporary world. There cannot be an oligopolistic organization – the G-8, of course – functioning roughly in concert, when power, especially military power, is distributed as unevenly as it is today. From time to time the greatest of the contemporary Great Powers will be in need of positive security cooperation from another G-8 member, as was the United States over logistical access to Central Asia. However, the informal rules of a true concert system eschew unilateralism and oblige all the players to pay due deference to the vital interests of the other members of the concert, as they elect to define those interests. By political culture and by current military primacy, the United States cannot function even as only a first among equals in a G-8 concert, let alone as just another Great Power. For good, and occasionally for ill, and not entirely by grand design and purpose, the United States is the keystone in the arch of a hegemonic order in world politics.

Notes

1. JDAMs (Joint Direct Attack Munitions) are 1-ton bombs fitted with satellite guidance kits and fins for precise navigation.
2. Robert B. Strassler (ed.) *The Landmark Thucydides: A Comprehensive Guide to The Peloponnesian War* (New York: Free Press, 1996), especially p. 43.
3. See Jack Donnelly, *Realism and International Relations* (Cambridge: Cambridge University Press, 2000).
4. John J. Mearsheimer, *The Tragedy of Great Power Politics* (New York: W.W. Norton, 2001).
5. See Martin van Creveld, *The Rise and Decline of the State* (Cambridge: Cambridge University Press, 1999).
6. Colin S. Gray, 'Thinking Asymmetrically in Times of Terror', *Parameters*, vol. XXXII, no. 1 (Spring 2002).

CHAPTER 21

A New Global Configuration[1]

Fred Halliday

There are two predictable, and nearly always mistaken, responses to any
great international upheaval: one is to say that everything has changed;
the other is to say that nothing has changed. We have heard much of
both in the aftermath of September 11, 2001, just as, a decade or so
earlier, the same two polar positions were articulated after the earth-
quakes of that time, the collapse of the Berlin Wall, the Gulf War and
the dissolution of Yugoslavia.

September 11 did not 'change everything': the map of the world
with its 200 or so states, the global pattern of economic and military
power, the relative distribution of democratic, semi-authoritarian and
tyrannical states remains much the same. Many of the greatest threats
to the world, and many of the problems which are least susceptible to
traditional forms of state control (the environment, migration, the
drugs trade, AIDS), long pre-dated September 11. The 40 or so societies
that were riven by war before September 11, from Colombia to
Palestine, remain so. In a more specific sense, some of the changes that
have become evident since September 11 were already incipient: the
more unilateral assertion of US power by the Bush administration, a
rhetoric of cultural conflict coming out of both Western and Islamic
societies, intervention by OECD states to offset an anticipated recession, and a pervasive retreat, by states and commentators alike, from a
commitment to universal codes of human rights.

Yet this recognition of continuity downplays the degree to which
the attacks on the US 'homeland' have reshaped, or promise to reshape,
the world in which we live. That some of these changes are evolu-
tionary, reformist, rather than revolutionary, or absolute, does not
diminish their importance. One can indeed suggest that it is reform, at
least as much as revolution, which has in modern times done more to

remodel the world. It is early days yet, and the conflict which
September 11 spotlit, but did not begin, has many a year to run. But, in
summary terms, there are at least five major ways in which the world
after September 11, and the world that we could have anticipated had
September 11 not happened, is now a different place.

First, there has been a marked increase in the focus and assertion of
US power. The US was, prior to September 11, the dominant world
power in every significant index, with the possible exception of
football.[2] Yet it was uncertain as to how to exert this, wavering between
a multilateral approach, favoured by Clinton, and quite tenaciously
pursued by his administration, and the unilateral, which is not the
same as isolationist, policy favoured by Bush. The signs of that unilateralism were evident enough in the first few months: rejection of
Kyoto, stalling on OECD regulation of tax havens, sliding out of
chemical warfare conventions, national missile defence, and sneering
at the UN, to name but a few. September 11 has forced the Bush administration to reverse some of these policies and stall on others. Yet is has
both substantially reinforced the commitment of the US administration to asserting US power and, even more so, altered the mood within
America to one of support for this course of action. The president's
State of the Union Address of January 29, 2002, and his $50 billion rise
in US defence spending, were evidence enough of this.

Equally importantly, however, September 11 has led much of the
rest of the world to seek to work more closely with the US. Washington
has, in this crisis, cashed in its power: when the call for cooperation
comes, it has proven hard to refuse. Here lies the second of the great
changes brought about by September 11: some US allies have moved
further away, notably Saudi Arabia, but the overall diplomatic balance
sheet has been to America's advantage. Russia has, with its own benefits
in mind, tried to consolidate a new strategic and political collaboration
with Washington: Bush has not given Moscow what it wants, and has
alarmed Russia by its long-term plans to station forces in Central Asia,
but a degree of greater understanding now exists. China too, to the
alarm of some in the Middle East, who look to it as the only permanent
member of the Security Council not to have a colonial past, joined the
counter-terrorist campaign.

Against this, however, lies the third of the outcomes of September
11, the consolidation, to a degree latent but not present before that
date, not of an alternative military or economic bloc but of something
else, a global coalition of feeling against the US. The basis of much
orthodox theory of international relations is the concept of 'balance of

power': this means not an equal distribution of power, but a self-correcting mechanism, whereby, if one state becomes too strong, others form a countervailing alliance against it. This happened in response to Napoleon in the 1800s and to Hitler in the 1940s. This version of balance of power did not work in the period since the end of the Cold War: there was no countervailing bloc of military, or economic, powers. Rather everyone seemed to want to 'bandwagon', to join the US bloc and its associated international institutions, like NATO and the WTO.

However, if states bandwagon, popular opinion does not. Just as hegemonic control is more focused on 'soft' power, so too is opposition to it. This is very evident post-September 11. At the level of popular feeling across the world, and not just in the Muslim world, a kind of countervailing balance of affect is taking shape. Hence the opposition of much of Latin America to support for the US campaign, widespread objections in East Asia and in normally anti-Muslim India. Loosely associated with globalization, this too will not easily go away. One of the greatest, and possibly most permanent, consequences of this crisis will lie in its reinforcement of anti-Americanism.

A fourth dimension is that of management of the global economy. September 11, by depressing certain important sectors of the market – airlines, tourism, oil, insurance – and by spreading a wider lack of confidence on the part of investors and consumers, has accentuated a trend towards recession that was already evident. In the energy field, it has pushed down global demand for oil – there is now surplus capacity of around 3 million barrels of oil a day, with world output at around 75 million: this has not only precipitated a fall in oil prices, with no evident floor in sight, but has also led to a price war between OPEC and the main non-OPEC producers (Russia, Norway, Mexico).

On the consumer side, there is renewed concern by the US and other OECD states to reduce dependence on the oil of the Gulf, site of two-thirds of the world's reserves, but now felt to be a region of enduring instability: non-Gulf producers, notably Russia, the Caspian states and Venezuela, are pressing their case. Russia appears to have got some of what it wants, including a commercial and strategic share in any Western plans to build a pipeline from the Caspian Sea to Turkey outside Russian control. The Caspian states, notably Azerbaijan and Kazakhstan, are offering military and oil cooperation to the US: but their own regimes may not be the most long-lasting. As for Venezuela, its ideal strategic location, in the western hemisphere, is for the moment offset by US anger at President Chavez's independent foreign policy, which has included criticism of the action in Afghanistan.

[handwritten marginalia: are, the bad acts to evidence of failing economies working or europe liberal institutions banding together to bolster its power. vs US, china etc? (all dependent on perspective.)]

The most important economic shift, above all, is that September 11 has brought the state, and not least the US state, back into the management of the world economy: neo-liberal faith in the market, already frayed, has now been further eroded as the governments of the developed world promise to subsidize ailing sectors, use fiscal adjustment and lower interest rates to offset the crisis. One open question is how all this will affect the longer-term fate of the euro: the stability pact is already under pressure, and George Bush is not likely to worry much about what happens to this putative rival to the dollar. But the reversal of state policy, across the OECD, through state and international financial institutional intervention, is considerable.

In terms of regional power politics, the fifth dimension of change, the area most affected is that of West Asia. Pakistan seems to have been able to talk itself out of its isolation, and many hundreds of millions of dollars of debt, by switching to the US side. Provided the military regime of General Musharraf holds, and its prospects looked better once the Afghan war had subsided, it will be able to enjoy improved relations with the outside world: a stable Afghanistan would open up the prospect of the oil and gas pipelines of Central Asia coming southwards to Pakistani ports. Iran benefited in the short run: in the weeks after September 11 its relations with the UK and even the US improved, and Foreign Minister Kharrazi met Colin Powell in New York. Iran made it clear it did not want to control Afghanistan or get its fingers burnt there: the victory of the Northern Alliance, Persian-speaking in the main, gave Iran some new influence there and in Central Asia as a whole. This short-term improvement was not to last: by early 2002 Iran's own conservative factions and the US administration were combining to stoke a new confrontation.

The situation for the Arab world is rather different. Any further US campaign against al-Qaeda will involve operations, overt or in the shadows, against its networks in two other countries, and ones where the state is weak or non-existent, Yemen and Somalia. For its part, the Iraqi regime knows that it too may be on the target list for US action: success in Kabul seems to have emboldened the US hawks on this matter. Europeans will try to restrain Washington, but action against Iraq, as, following Bush's 'axis of evil' speech against Iran, must remain a possibility. The Arab states of the Gulf are also in an uncomfortable situation, given the rise of pro-Qaeda sentiment amongst young people in recent years. Saudi Arabia, above all, finds itself with a population that is strongly anti-American. This population is also increasingly critical of the ruling family because of unemployment and the elite's disproportionate take of oil and investment revenues.

The Saudi regime has tried to offset this by reducing cooperation with the US, but in doing so it has deeply antagonized the country on which it relies for its ultimate survival. Time has, in a way, overtaken the cautious, and often indecisive, rulers of these oil-producing states. Washington may belatedly be getting the military facilities and some of the tracer information on terrorist suspects and finances it has asked for from Riyadh, but no president will find it easy to risk American lives to defend the House of Saud. Strategists in Washington are already thinking the unthinkable: if Saudi Arabia enters a serious crisis, it may, as did two other states formed around the same time in the 1920s, Yugoslavia and the USSR, break up. The question then becomes how to preserve the Western, and global economic, interest in the oil and gas regions of the East without remaining embroiled in the domestic politics. It has not come to this yet, but it may.

Finally, the overall context for these changes, and for what was in any case in train, is that of globalization. While September 11 challenges some aspects of globalization, notably a sense of rising global optimism in culture and economics, and freedom of movement for travellers and migrants, it has also given the opportunity for a more sober, and perhaps therefore sustainable, model of globalization to be discussed. The institutions of global financial and macroeconomic management will now be put to the test and given greater political support. Some greater urgency may, as was evident in the November 2001 WTO meeting in Doha, enter discussion of global trade liberalization and an improved distribution of wealth.

These policy issues are, however, taking place within a context defined by another set of controversies and options about values. The most obvious of these concerns the question of culture, and the relation of culture to universal or relative values. September 11 did not settle this question, but it has thrown the relativist, or communitarian, argument on to the defensive: on the one hand, as public argument in West and East has shown, the claim that there is *one* communal or traditional interpretation of text of belief is questionable; on the other, the invocation of difference to legitimate criminal acts, or culturally phrased denial of responsibility and international obligation, is a bit harder to make.

There has also been an important shift, of great relevance in the aftermath of September 11, about who is responsible for the upholding and violation of human rights. For a long time the answer was that this was the responsibility of states. But the 'non-state', be it the family, the tribe, the vicinity or the self-proclaimed representative of the oppressed is also responsible for human rights violations. Debates on, for example, violations of the rules of war or violence against women or racism have highlighted the combined responsibility of states *and* societies for human rights violations.

All of this has been made more difficult, prior to and subsequent to the US attacks, by the ever-widening scope of what are classed as 'human rights' issues: a concern with the political rights of individuals has been matched by a commitment to social and economic rights, and, by extension, with the rights of collective groups, be these nations, women, children, refugees or disabled people. In addition, the scope of human rights concern, and activism, has also come to include what were earlier seen as separate issues, encoded in the Geneva Conventions of 1949, binding states, and the 1977 Additional Protocols, involving opposition groups, about the legitimate use of violence.

This set of interrelated ethical and rights issues has, however, demonstrated that, while no policy can neglect these questions, the certitude that there is one simple answer on human rights grounds or one clear 'ethical' option may be misleading. Those involved in distributing humanitarian assistance may have to buy off warlords and indicted war criminals with percentages of fuel, food and medicine. Those concerned with the rights of individuals, not least women, may have to override the supposedly 'authentic' or 'traditional' values of religions and communities. A more robust and critical stand towards the claims of community and difference may be one desirable consequence of the more edgy human rights debate prompted by September 11.

Much has been made of the challenge posed by September 11 to globalization. It can be argued that it has weakened the liberal optimism that underlay globalization, not least with regard to security of travel. But it may also be a challenge that brings out a stronger, more resilient commitment to globalization. It has reminded those who, in a rush of liberal or cosmopolitan optimism, or in a semi-anarchist radical critique of global institutions, may have forgotten that without global security, and a security sustained by capable and determined powers, there will be no globalization at all. A commitment to military security as one universal good needs to be combined with a broader but unflinching commitment to democratic and secular values. Such a commitment is, as much as security, a prerequisite for any long-run resistance to terrorist attack. This sober but pertinent message may be one of the positive outcomes of the upheavals of the autumn of 2001.

Over time, the consequences of September 11 will be decided by the factor that itself caused this crisis: politics, and of three broad kinds.

The first is the politics of the US itself. The Bush administration in particular, and the US state in general, have in the short run emerged strengthened from this crisis. It remains to be seen what it does with this strength and how far it can sustain its new advantages. The second is the politics of the Middle East and of the Muslim world. It is unclear what this earthquake will bring down, or leave standing, but the tremors are substantial. Finally, there is the broader context, the coalition of states that has supported the US 'war' on terrorism, and the pervasive bloc of resentment that opposes it. These are the sinews of globalization, the foci of cooperation and opposition forged after September 11. Their longer-term shape is by no means preordained.

Notes

1. An earlier version of this article was published in Mark Leonard (ed.) *Re-Ordering the World* (Foreign Policy Centre, 2002).
2. Fred Halliday, *The World at 2000* (Basingstoke: Palgrave, 2000), chapter 6.

Part III
Worlds

CHAPTER 22

Democracy and Terror in the Era of Jihad vs. McWorld

Benjamin R. Barber

A week after the trauma of the first large-scale assault on the American homeland, more successful than even its scheming perpetrators could possibly have hoped for, President George Bush joined the abruptly renewed combat with Jihadic terrorists by deploying the rhetoric of retributive justice: 'We will bring the terrorists to justice,' he said gravely to a joint session of Congress, 'or we will bring justice to the terrorists'. The language of justice was surely the appropriate context for the American response, but it will remain appropriate only if the compass of its meaning is extended from retributive to distributive justice.

The collision between the forces of disintegral tribalism and reactionary fundamentalism I called Jihad (Islam was not the issue) and the forces of integrative modernization and aggressive economic and cultural globalization (the US was not alone responsible) I called McWorld in my *Jihad vs. McWorld*[1] has been brutally exacerbated by the dialectical interdependence of these two seemingly oppositional sets of forces. In that critical examination of the relationship between globalization and fundamentalism, I warned that democracy, caught between a clash of movements each of which for its own reasons seemed indifferent to freedom's fate, might suffer grievously. It is now apparent, as the US successfully concludes the first phase of a military offensive against Jihad (understood not as Islam but as militant fundamentalism), that democracy rather than terrorism may still become another victim of the battle being waged.

Only the globalization of civic and democratic institutions is likely to offer a way out of the global war between modernity and its aggrieved critics. Democracy responds both to Jihad and to McWorld. It responds directly to the resentments and spiritual unease of those for whom the trivialization and homogenization of values is an affront to cultural diversity and spiritual and moral seriousness. However, it also answers the complaints of those mired in poverty and despair as a consequence of unregulated global markets and of a capitalism run wild because it has been uprooted from the humanizing constraints of the democratic nation state. By extending the compass of democracy to the global market sector, it can promise to those wishing to join the modern world and take advantage of its economic blessings, opportunities for accountability, participation and governance; by securing cultural diversity and a place for worship and faith insulated from the shallow orthodoxies of McWorld's cultural monism, it can address the anxieties of those who fear secularist materialism and are fiercely committed to preserving their cultural and religious distinctiveness. The outcome of the cruel battle between Jihad and McWorld, which will be won only if democracy is the victor, will depend upon the capacity of moderns to make the world safe for women and men in search of both justice and faith.

A Democratic Front

If democracy is to be the instrument by which the world avoids the stark choice between the sterile cultural monism of McWorld and the raging cultural fundamentalism of Jihad, neither of which services diversity or civic liberty, then the US, the UK and their allies will have to open a crucial second civic and democratic front aimed not against terrorism *per se* but against the anarchism and social chaos – the economic reductionism and its commercializing homogeneity – that have created the climate of despair and hopelessness which terrorism has so effectively exploited. A second democratic front will be advanced not only in the name of retributive justice and secularist interests, but in the name of distributive justice and religious pluralism.

The democratic front in the war on terrorism is not a battle to dissuade terrorists from their campaigns of annihilation. Their deeds are unspeakable, and their purposes can neither be rationalized nor negotiated. When they hijacked innocents and turned civilian aircraft into lethal weapons, these self-proclaimed 'martyrs' of faith in truth subjected others to a compulsory martyrdom indistinguishable from mass murder. The terrorists offer no terms and can be given none in exchange. When Jihad turns nihilistic, bringing it to justice can only take the form of extirpation – root, trunk and branch. Eliminating terrorists will depend on professional military intelligence and diplomatic resources whose deployment will leave the greater number of citizens in the US and throughout the world sitting on the sidelines, anxious spectators to a battle in which they cannot participate, a battle in which the nausea that accompanies fear will dull the appetite for revenge. The second front, however, engages every citizen with a stake in democracy and social justice, whether within nation states or in the relations between them. It transforms anxious and passive spectators into resolute and engaged participants – the perfect antidote to fear, as activated passengers on commercial flights have recently learned as they participate in subduing would-be terrorists and bombers.

Because an outraged and wounded American nation demands it, and because terrorists bent on annihilation will not yield to blandishments or inducements, the first military front must be prosecuted. Terrorists are looking not for bargains but for oblivion. Yet it will be the successful prosecution of a second civic front in the war rather than the strictly military campaign that will determine the outcome in the long term. It, too, in President Bush's words, will be a war for justice, but a war defined by a new commitment to distributive justice: a readjudication of north–south responsibilities, a redefinition of the obligations of global capital as it faces the claims of global justice and comity, a repositioning of democratic institutions as they follow markets from the domestic to the international sector, a new recognition of the place and requirements of faith in an aggressively secular market society. The war against Jihad will not, in other words, succeed unless McWorld is also addressed.

To democratize globalism and render McWorld less homogenizing and trivializing to religion and its accompanying ethical and spiritual values will, to be sure, do nothing to appease the terrorists, who are scarcely students of globalization's contractual insufficiencies. Jihadic warriors offer no quarter, whether they are the children of Islam, of Christianity or of some found blood tribalism; they should be given none. These Jihadic warriors detest modernity – the secular, scientific, rational and commercial civilization created by the Enlightenment as it is defined by both in its virtues (freedom, democracy, tolerance and diversity) and its vices (inequality, hegemony, cultural imperialism and materialism). What can enemies of the modern do but seek to recover the dead past by annihilating the living present?

Terrorists then cannot themselves be the object of democratic struggle. They swim in a sea of tacit popular support and resentful acquiescence, however, and these waters – roiling with anger and resentment – prove buoyant to ideologies of violence and mayhem.

Americans were themselves first enraged and then deeply puzzled by scenes from Islamic cities where ordinary men, women and children who could hardly be counted as terrorists, nonetheless manifested a kind of perverse jubilation in contemplating the wanton slaughter of American innocents. How could anyone cheer such acts? Yet an environment of despairing rage exists in too many places in the Third World, and also in too many Third World neighbourhoods of First World cities, enabling terrorism by endowing it with a kind of a quasi-legitimacy it does not deserve. It is not terrorism itself but this facilitating environment against which the second-front battle is directed. Its constituents are not terrorists, for they are themselves terrified by modernity and its costs, and as a consequence vulnerable to ameliorative actions if those who embrace democracy can find the will to take such actions. What they seek is justice, not vengeance. Their quarrel is not with modernity but with the aggressive neo-liberal ideology that has been prosecuted in its name in pursuit of a global market society more conducive to profits for some than justice for all. They are not even particularly anti-American: rather, they suspect that what Americans understand as prudent unilateralism is really a form of arrogant imperialism, what Americans take to be a kind of cynical aloofness is really self-absorbed isolationism and what Americans think of as pragmatic alliances with tyrannical rulers in Muslim nations such as Egypt, Saudi Arabia and Pakistan are really a betrayal of the democratic principles in which Americans claim to believe.

A War within Civilization

Hyperbolic commentators such as Samuel Huntington have described the current divide in the world as a global clash of civilizations, and warn of a cultural war between democracy and Islam, perhaps even between 'the West and the rest'. However, this is to ape the messianic rhetoric of Osama bin Laden – who called for precisely such a war. The difference between bin Laden's al-Qaeda terrorists and the poverty-stricken Third World constituents he tries to call to arms, however, is the difference between radical Jihadic fundamentalists and ordinary men and women concerned to feed their children and nurture their religious communities. Fundamentalists can be found among every religious sect and represent a tiny, aggravated minority whose ideology contradicts the very religions in whose names they act. The remarkable comments of the American fundamentalist preacher Jerry Falwell interpreting the attacks on New York and Washington as the wrath of God being vented on abortionists, homosexuals and the American Civil Liberties Union no more defines Protestantism than the Taliban defines Islam. The struggle of Jihad against McWorld is not a clash of civilizations but a dialectical expression of tensions built into a single global civilization as it emerges against a backdrop of traditional ethnic and religious divisions, many of which are actually created by McWorld and its infotainment industries and technological innovations. Bin Laden without modern media would have been an unknown desert rat. Terrorism without its reliance on credit cards, global financial systems, modern technology and the internet would have been reduced to throwing stones at local sheiks. What we face is not a war of civilizations, but a war within civilization, a struggle that expresses the ambivalence within each culture as it faces a global, networked, material future and wonders whether cultural and national autonomy can be retained; the ambivalence within each individual juggling the obvious benefits of modernity with its equally obvious costs.

From Seattle and Prague to Stockholm and Genoa, street demonstrators were protesting the costs of this civilizational globalization long before September 11, 2001. Yet, although President Chirac of France acknowledged after the dissident violence of Genoa months before the attacks in New York and Washington that 100,000 protesters do not take to the streets unless something is amiss, they have mostly been written off as anarchists or know-nothings. More media attention has been paid to their theatrics than to the deep problems those theatrics are intended to highlight. After September 11, some critics even tried to lump the anti-globalization protesters in with the terrorists, casting them as irresponsible destabilizers of world order. But the protesters are the children of McWorld and their objections are not Jihadic but merely democratic. Their grievances concern not world order but world disorder, and if the mostly young demonstrators are a little foolish in their politics, a little naive in their analyses and a little short on viable solutions, they understand with a sophistication their leaders apparently lack that globalization's current architecture breeds anarchy, nihilism and violence. They know too that the greater number of those in the Third World who seem to welcome American suffering are at worst reluctant adversaries whose principal aim is to make clear that they too suffer from violence, even if it is less visible and destroys with greater stealth and over a longer period of time than the murderous schemes of the terrorists. They do not want to belittle American suffering but to use its horrors to draw attention to their own. How many of these 'enemies of McWorld', given the chance, would prefer to enjoy modernity and its blessings if they were not so often the victims of modernity's unevenly distributed costs? How many are really fanatic communists and how many are merely instinctive guardians of fairness who resent not capitalism's productivity but only the claim that in the absence of global regulation and the democratic rule of law, capitalism can possibly serve them. It is finally hypocrisy rather than democracy that is the target of their rage.

For those living in the Second and Third Worlds to the south of the US, Europe and Japan, globalization too often looks like an imperious strategy of a predominantly American economic behemoth; what we understand as the opportunities to secure liberty and prosperity at home too often seem to them but a rationalization for exploitation and oppression in the international sphere; what we call the international order is too often for them an international disorder. Our neo-liberal antagonism to all political regulation in the global sector, to all institutions of legal and political oversight, to all attempts at democratizing globalization and institutionalizing economic justice looks to them like brute indifference to their welfare and their claims for justice. Western beneficiaries of McWorld celebrate market ideology with its commitment to the privatization of all things public and the commercialization of all things private, and consequently insist on total freedom from government interference in the global economic sector (*laissez-faire*). Yet total freedom from interference – the rule of private power over public goods – is another name for anarchy. And terror is merely one of the many contagious diseases that anarchy spawns.

What was evident to those who, before September 11, suffered the economic consequences of an undemocratic international anarchy beyond the reach of democratic sovereignty was that while many in the First World benefited from free markets in capital, labour and goods, these same anarchic markets left ordinary people in the Third World largely unprotected. What has become apparent to the rest of us after September 11 is that that same deregulated disorder from which financial and trade institutions imagine they benefit is the very disorder on which terrorism depends. Markets and globalized financial institutions, whether multinational corporations or individual currency speculators, are deeply averse to oversight of nation states. McWorld seeks to overcome sovereignty and makes its impact global. Jihad, too, makes war on sovereignty, using the interdependence of transportation, communication and other modern technological systems to render borders porous and sovereign oversight irrelevant. Just as jobs defy borders, haemorrhaging from one country to another in a wage race to the bottom; just as safety, health and environmental standards lack an international benchmark against which states and regions might organize their employment; so too anarchistic terrorists with loyalty to no state and accountable to no people range freely across the world, knowing no borders can detain them, no united global opinion can isolate them, no international police or juridical institutions can interdict them. The argument laid out in what follows then proposes that both Jihad and McWorld undermine the sovereignty of nation states, dismantling the democratic institutions that have been their finest achievement without discovering ways to extend democracy either downwards to the subnational religious and ethnic entities that now lay claim to people's loyalty or upwards to the international sector in which McWorld's pop culture and commercial markets operate without sovereign restraints.

Ironically, it is the terrorists and not the leaders of the US who acknowledge and exploit the actual interdependence that characterizes human relations in the twenty-first century. Theirs, however, is a perverse and malevolent interdependence, one in which they have learned to use McWorld's weight jujitsu-style against its massive power. Yet even as it fosters an anarchic absence of sovereignty at the global level, the US has resisted the slightest compromise of its national sovereignty at home. The US has complained bitterly in recent years about the prospect of surrendering a scintilla of its own sovereignty, whether to NATO commanders, to supranational institutions such as the International Criminal Tribunal, or to international treaties such as those banning landmines or regulating fossil fuels (in response to global warming). Even today as the US successfully prosecutes a military campaign against terrorism surrounded by a prudently constructed coalition, it has made clear that it prefers 'coalitions' to 'alliances' because it wants to be free to target objectives, to develop strategy and to wage war exactly as it wishes. It still shies away from 'nation building' and other strategies that might entangle it in the web of interdependence.

Yet terrorism has already made a mockery of sovereignty. What was the hijacking of airliners, the calamitous razing of the Twin Towers of the World Trade Center, the brash attack on the Pentagon, but a profound obliteration of American sovereignty? Terrorism is the negative and depraved form of that interdependence which in its positive and beneficial form we too often refuse to acknowledge. As if still in the nineteenth century, the US has persuaded itself that its options today are to preserve an ancient and blissfully secure independence that puts Americans in charge of American destiny, or to yield to a perverted and compulsory interdependence that puts foreigners and alien international bodies like the United Nations or the World Court in charge of American destiny. In truth, however, Americans have not enjoyed a real independence since sometime before the great wars of the twentieth century; certainly not since the advent of AIDS and the West Nile virus, of global warming and an ever more porous ozone layer, of a job 'mobility' that has decimated America's industrial economy and of restive speculators who have made 'capital flight' a more 'sovereign' reality that any conceivable government oversight. Interdependence is not some foreign adversary against which citizens need to muster resistance, it is a domestic reality that has already compromised the efficacy of citizenship in scores of unacknowledged and uncharted ways.

It was the interdependence of the US with the world and the interdependence of shared economic and technological systems everywhere on which the Jihadic warriors counted when they brought terror to the American homeland. They not only hijacked America's air transportation system, turning its airplanes into deadly missiles; they provoked the nation into closing it down entirely for nearly a week. They not only destroyed the cathedral of American capitalism at the World Trade Center, they forced capitalism to shut down its markets and they shocked the country into deep recession of which the stock market in freefall was only a leading indicator. How can any nation claim independence under these conditions?

In the world before McWorld, there was genuine independence for democratic sovereign nations, and sovereignty represented a just claim by autonomous peoples to autonomous control over their lives. In Andrew Jackson's premodern, rural America where communities existed in isolation, where there was no national system of transportation or communication, systematic terror was simply not an option: there was no system. There was no way to bring America to its knees because in a crucial sense America did not exist, not at least as a collectivity of interdependent regions with a single interest – not until after the Civil War and the Industrial Revolution that followed it. Today there is so much systemic interactivity, so highly integrated a global network, so finely tuned an integral communications technology, that it has become as easy to paralyse as to use the multiple systems and networks. Hence, the decision that would-be sovereign peoples face today it not the felicitous choice between secure independence and an unwanted interdependence, it is only the sobering choice between, on the one hand, a relatively legitimate and democratic and useful interdependence which, however, is still to be constructed and which leaves sovereignty in tatters; and, on the other hand, a radically illegitimate and undemocratic interdependence on the terms of criminals, anarchists and terrorists, an interdependence that is already here and which will triumph in the absence of a democratizing political will.

In short, we can allow either McWorld and Jihad – Hollywood cowboys and international desperadoes – to set the terms of our interdependence; or we can leave those terms to transnational treaties, new global democratic bodies and a new creative common will. We can have our interactivity dictated to us by violence and anarchy or we can construct it on the model of our own democratic aspirations. We can have a democratic and useful interdependence on whatever common ground we can persuade others to stand on, or we can stand on the brink of anarchy and try to prevent criminals and terrorists from pushing us into the abyss.

It will be hard for defenders of modernity – whether of McWorld's markets or democracy's citizenship – to have it both ways. Terrorism turns out to be a depraved version of globalization no less vigorous in its pursuit of its own special interests than are global markets, no less wedded to anarchist disorder than are speculators, no less averse to violence when it serves terrorists' ends than marketers are averse to inequality and injustice when they represent the 'costs of doing business'. It is their instinctive reading of this equation that turns poor people into cheering mobs when Americans experience grievous losses. It is their perception of overwhelming hypocrisy that leads them to exult what we would wish them to grieve.

In his address to Congress, President Bush said 'you are with us or you are with the terrorists'. Americans may appreciate the impulse to divide the world into good and evil (even though it smacks of the Manicheanism for which Americans excoriate their fundamentalist adversaries), but enemies of the US (and more than a few of its friends) are likely to find this discourse misleading if not hubristic – for a US that comprehends the realities of interdependence and wishes to devise a democratic architecture to contain its disorder cannot ask others to join it or 'suffer the consequences'. It is not for the world to join the US: McWorld already operates on this premise and the premise is precisely the problem; certainly anything but a key to the solution. It is rather for the US to join the world on whatever terms it can negotiate on an equal footing with the world. Whether a product of arrogance or prudence, the demand that the world join the US simply will not secure results. It defies the very interdependence to which it is addressed. It assumes a sovereign autonomy the US does not and cannot enjoy.

The US and Anarchic Global Capitalism

In the last ten years the US has intensified its commitment to a political culture of unilateralism and faux autonomy that reinforces rather than attenuates the effects of McWorld. There is hardly a multilateral treaty of significance to which the US has shown itself willing to subscribe in recent times – whether the Kyoto Protocol on global warming, or the ban on landmines or the comprehensive test ban treaty. Indeed, after a month or two of diplomacy with President Putin of Russia, President Bush simply walked away from the Anti-Ballistic Missile Treaty in order to be able to develop and deploy his missile defence shield. There is hardly a single international institution that has not been questioned, undermined or abandoned outright by the US in the name of its 'need' to protect its sovereign interests. Only the competing need to gather a coalition to underwrite its anti-terrorist military strike compelled the American government finally to pay its UN dues and to commit to modest amounts of simple humanitarian aid that should have been a function of normalcy. The US still spends a smaller percentage of its GNP on foreign aid – less than 0.01 per cent – than any other developed nation in the world.   Other nations spend double that, and the goal of the United Nations is that the figure should reach 0.07 per cent.

   The Bretton Woods institutions, such as the International Monetary Fund and the World Trade Organization (heir to the General Agreement on Tariffs and Trade) could be of real succour in the effort to construct a more democratic globalism, were they to be put to the kinds of developmental and democratic purposes for which they were originally designed in postwar Europe. Instead they have been cast by the democratic governments that control them as undemocratic instruments of private interest – seeming tools of banks, corporations and investors (which to an untoward degree also control the policies of the international financial institutions' member governments). Anarchism in the global sector is no accident: it has been assiduously cultivated.

   Yet what is terrorism but a depraved version of this global anarchism – one which, for all its depravity, is as vigorous and self-justifying as global markets? It, too, profits from the arrogant pretence of claims to national sovereignty. It, too, benefits by the absence of international executive police and juridical institutions. It, too, exploits global anarchy to ferment national anarchy and the further weakening of the capacity of nations to control their own destinies, either apart or together. In late nineteenth-century America when the federal government was markedly weaker than it is today, America looked locally rather like social relations look today globally. Lawlessness came easy, both to the robber barons of growing capitalist metropolises and the robber desperadoes of the western prairies. Then, too, the outlaws prospered in the suites as well as in the streets.

The global sector today seems driven by the same anarchy in which burgeoning forces of what our own bankers have called wild capitalism spread both their productivity, which we welcome, and their injustices, which we try to ignore. Wild capitalism is not alone: alongside it rage reactionary forces of wild terrorism. Against capitalism's modern message, Jihadic fundamentalism spreads its anti-modern message, sowing fear and nurturing chaos, hoping to bring democracy no less than capitalism to its knees. The war between Jihad and McWorld takes no prisoners. It cannot serve democracy, however it turns out.

The democratic project is to globalize democracy as we have globalized the economy; to democratize the globalism that has been so efficiently marketized. The issue is no longer utopian longing for global democracy against the siren call of consumerism or the passionate war cries of Jihad; it is the securing of safety. Following September 11, global governance has become a sober mandate of political realism.[2]

However, it will not be easy for America to overcome the reassuring myth of national independence and innocence with which it has lived so comfortably for 200 years. Before it traded in the currency of McWorld that made it the global merchandiser, America had invented a simpler story about itself. In the Puritan myth of the City on the Hill, in the Enlightenment conceit of a *tabula rasa* on which a new people would inscribe a fresh history, Americans embraced Tom Paine's quaint and revolutionary notion that on the new continent humankind could literally go back and start over again as if at the beginning of the world. Europe's cruel torments, the ancient prejudices and religious persecutions would be left behind. Safeguarded by two immense oceans, at home on a bountiful and empty continent (the red man was part of the new world's flora and fauna), Americans would devise a new experimental science of government, establish a new constitution fortified by rights and, with the innocence of newborn peoples, write a new history. Slavery, a great civil war, two world conflagrations, totalitarian regimes abroad could not dissuade America from its precious self-definition. Even as the oceans became mere streams that could be crossed in an instant by invisible adversaries, even as the pressures of an impinging world grew too complex to yield to simplicity, America imagined it might, with its vaunted technology, re-create virtual oceans, deploying a magic missile shield that would ward off foreign evil.

Was America ever really a safe haven island in the tainted streams of world history? Was it ever any more innocent than the children of every nation are innocent? Human nature is everywhere morally ambivalent, the better angels cooing into one ear, their demonic cousins crowing into the other. Americans seem to know no evil, even when they do it. To others the claim to innocence is an assertion of hypocrisy – among the deadliest of sins for Muslims and others who watch the US demonize others and forgive itself.

If ever such an age of innocence existed in the US, terrorism brought it to a close. How could the myth of independence survive September 11? The Declaration of Independence that announced a new coming, a new kind of society, had achieved its task of nation building by the end of America's first century. To build the new world that is now required calls for a new Declaration of Interdependence, a declaration recognizing the interdependence of a human race that can no longer survive in fragments – whether the pieces are called nations or tribes, peoples or markets. There are no oceans wide enough to protect a nation from a tainted atmosphere or a spreading plague, no walls high enough to defend a people against a corrupt ideology or a vengeful prophet, no security strict enough to keep a determined martyr from his sacrificial rounds. Nor is any nation ever again likely to experience untroubled prosperity and plenty unless others are given the same opportunity; suffering, too, has been democratized and those most likely to experience it will find a way to compel those most remote from it to share the pain. If there cannot be an equity of justice there will be an equity of injustice; if all cannot partake in plenty, impoverishment – both material and spiritual – will be the common lot. That is the hard lesson of interdependence.

In a certain sense, to declare interdependence is merely to acknowledge what is already a reality. It is to embrace willingly and constructively a fate terrorists would like to force on sovereign nations. Their message is: 'Your sons want to live, ours are ready to die.' The democratic response must be: 'We will create a world in which the seductions of death hold no allure because the bounties of life are accessible to everyone.'

In the wake of two centuries of either quiescent isolationism or aggressive unilateralism, with only a few wartime pauses for coalition building and consultation, the US is inexperienced in the hard work of creative interdependence and international partnership. When the US discerns problems in international treaties (the Kyoto Protocol on global warming, the landmine ban, the International Criminal Court) and it cannot negotiate its way in; it has made a habit of simply walking out. When international institutions like UNESCO and the United Nations and international conferences like the Durban Racism meeting resonate with hostility, it withdraws in an arrogant pique instead of participating with a view to make its influence felt. The missile shield with its attendant requirement that the US abandon the ABM Treaty is a typically unilateral and hubristic instance of the United States' inclination to go it alone. The shield (actually a tactic to permit continued interventions without fear of retaliation) is technologically infeasible. More importantly, when terrorists cannot be kept off domestic flights and individual 'sleepers' engage in biological and chemical warfare from within, intercepting multiple warheads and their multiplying decoys without a hitch, even if it one day becomes possible, is irrelevant. The missile shield once again isolates the US from a world it ought to participate in changing.

Ronald Reagan imagined a virtual bubble that would keep the nation safe from foreign nightmares, but the nightmares reached American shores in the bright light of morning and there is no shield against terror except a confrontation with its complex global genealogy. It is a peculiarly American conviction that technology can take the place of human ingenuity and action in warding off trouble. Smart bombs are given preference over smart people, missiles that 'think' take the place of policy makers who think; electronic listening posts replace culturally and linguistically adept human agents. Technology is the last redoubt of the vanishing independence of the US, the means by which it aspires to keep alive the fading dream of sovereign autonomy. Yet technology itself, like the science from which it arises, is a product of transnational communities and is a better symbol of interdependence than independence. McWorld itself, with its reliance on global communications technology, teaches that lesson.

The Global Democratic Deficit

When the US finally turns from its mythic independence and acknowledges the real world of interdependence, it will face an irony it helped create: the international institutions available to those who wish to make interdependence a tool of democracy and comity are few and far

between. McWorld is everywhere, CivWorld is nowhere. But Nike and
McDonald's and Coke and MTV can contribute nothing to the search
for democratic alternatives to criminal terrorism. In the melancholy
dialectic between them, they inadvertently contribute to its causes.

The encompassing practices of globalization nurtured by McWorld
have in fact created a radical asymmetry: they have managed to globalize markets in goods, labour, currencies and information without
globalizing the civic and democratic institutions that have historically
comprised the free market's indispensable context. Put simply, capitalism has been removed from the institutional 'box' of laws and
regulations that has (quite literally) domesticated it and given its sometimes harsh practices a human face. To understand why taking
capitalism 'out of the box' has been so calamitous, we need to recall
that the history of capitalism and free markets has been one of synergy
with democratic institutions. Free economies have grown up within
and been fostered and contained and controlled by democratic states.
Democracy has been a precondition for free markets – not, as econo-
mists try to argue today, the other way round. The freedom of the
market that has helped sustain freedom in politics and a spirit of
competition in the political domain has been nurtured in turn by
democratic institutions. Contract law and regulation as well as cooperative civic relations have attenuated capitalism's Darwinism and
contained its irregularities, its contradictions, and its tendencies
towards self-destruction around monopoly and the eradication of
competition. On the global plane today, the historical symmetry that
paired democracy and capitalism has gone missing. We have globalized
the marketplace willy-nilly because markets can bleed through porous
national boundaries and are not constrained by the logic of sovereignty; but we have not even begun to globalize democracy, which –
precisely because it is political and is defined by sovereignty – is
'trapped' inside the nation-state box.

The resulting global asymmetry, in which both states and markets
serve only the interests of markets, damages not only a well-
functioning democratic civic order, but also a well-functioning international economic order. The continuing spread of the new
globalization has only deepened the asymmetry between private vices
and public goods. McWorld in tandem with the global market economy
has globalized many of our vices and almost none of our virtues. It has
globalized crime, the rogue weapons trade, and drugs, pornography
and the trade in women and children made possible by 'porn tourism'.
Indeed, the most egregious globalization has been the globalization of

the exploitation and abuse of children in war, pornography, poverty and sex tourism. This aspect of globalization entails that slow suffering, the deliberately paced violence, that has created so fertile a ground for recruiting terrorists. Indeed, it is terrorism itself along with its propaganda that has been most effectively globalized – sometimes (ironically) using the modern technologies of the world wide web and the worldwide media to promote ideologies hostile both to technology and to anything smacking of the worldwide or the modern. Following September 11 and up until that last glimpse of his gaunt and hunted face at the end of 2001, Osama bin Laden was a regular on the channels of McWorld (including their new Arab language competitors). McWorld's conduits were used for the attack on McWorld.

Globalization has been complete in the private sector then, but lacks anything resembling a civic envelope. Thus it cannot support the values and institutions associated with civic culture, religion and the family; nor can it enjoy their potentially softening, domesticating and civilizing impact on raw market transactions. No wonder Pope John Paul said in his Apostolic Exhortation on the Mission of the Roman Catholic Church in the Americas: 'If globalization is ruled merely by the laws of the market applied to suit the powerful, the consequences cannot but be negative.'[3] One expects the Pope to moralize in this fashion. More startling is a similar message from another more powerful pope of the secular world, who wrote recently:

You hear talk about a new financial order, about an international bankruptcy law, about transparency, and more ... but you don't hear a word about people ... Two billion people live on less than two dollars a day ... We live in a world that gradually is getting worse and worse and worse. It is not hopeless, but we must do something about it now.[4]

The moralist here is the hardheaded James Wolfensohn, president of the World Bank, who has begun to replace the Bank's traditional energy and industrialization projects thought to favour the interests of foreign investors with environmental and health projects aimed at the interests of the populations being directly served.

International institutions already exist, of course, that might serve as building blocks for a global democratic box into which the economy could safely be put. The international financial institutions conceived at Bretton Woods after the Second World War to oversee the reconstruction of the shattered European and Asian economies were intended originally to function as regulatory agencies to assure peaceful, stable and democratic redevelopment under the watchful eye of the victorious allied powers. Although the World Bank and the IMF (and later the GATT and the WTO that grew out of it in 1995) were ostensibly forged as instruments of democratic sovereign nations designed to guide and regulate private sector interests in the name of public sector reconstruction, over a period of time they became instruments of the very private sector interests they were meant to channel and to keep in check. Those who today call for their elimination in the name of transparency, accountability and democracy might be surprised to learn that these norms were once regarded as among the postwar financial order's primary objectives. Given the role that the modern institutions representing this order play as potential pieces in a global regulatory infrastructure, one way to begin the process of global democratization would be to redemocratize them and subordinate them to the will of democratic peoples.

Globalization does not, of course, occur in a vacuum. Its corrosive impact on democratic governance and our inability to put international financial institutions that are nominally already at the service of democracy to real democratic use is augmented by a cognate ideology of privatization that is prevalent both in the international scene and within the countries whose economies are being globalized. McWorld is accompanied by this ideology of privatization – what Europeans often call neo-liberalism, and what George Soros has labelled market fundamentalism (an appropriate implicit comparison to Jihadic fundamentalism) – is an ideology that saps democracy by attacking government and its culture of public power. By arguing that markets can do everything government once did better than government, and with more freedom for citizens, privatization within nation states opens the way for a deregulation of markets that in turn facilitates the globalization of the economy. It softens up citizens to accept the decline of political institutions and tries to persuade them that they will be better off – more 'free' – when their collective democratic voice is stilled, when they think of themselves not as public citizens but private consumers. Consumers are poor substitutes for citizens, however, as corporate CEOs are poor substitutes for statesmen.

On the fateful morning of September 11, 2001, no American or German or free Afghan called Bill Gates or Michael Eisner to ask for assistance in dealing with terrorism. Long-neglected public institutions reacquired overnight their democratic legitimacy and their role as defenders of public goods. Can this renewed legitimacy be employed on behalf of international institutions dedicated to public rather than private goods? If it can, new forms of civic interdependence can be quickly established. The ideology of privatization has always confounded private and public modes of choosing. Consumer choice is always and necessarily private and personal choice. Private choices, autonomous or not, cannot affect public outcomes. Democratic governance is not just about choosing, it is about public choosing, about dealing with the social consequences of private choices and behaviour. In the global sector this is crucial, because only public and democratic decisions can establish social justice and equity. Private markets cannot, not because they are capitalist but because they are private. In Rousseau's language, through participation in the general will, global citizens can regulate the private wills of global consumers and global corporations.

Rousseau understands the vital difference between public and private liberty, a difference that may go to the heart of Pope John Paul's complaint that 'the human race is facing forms of slavery which are new and more subtle than those of the past, and for far too many people, freedom remains a word without meaning'. To think that shopping is what freedom means is to embrace the slavery against which the Pope warns (though of course the Pope is a thoroughly unmodern man, if not yet a Jihadic warrior).

There are many things governments cannot do very well but there are many others things that *only* governments can do, such as regulate, protect and sometimes subsidize and redistribute – not because it does them particularly well or even 'better' than the market, but because they are public things for which only 'we' (the public) can be held accountable. These *res publica* include education, culture, incarceration, transportation, defence, health care and, yes, the human genome. They include the war on terrorism. And they include the construction of a fair and equitable international order that offers every people (and every person) equal access and equal opportunity. Put simply, the struggle against Jihad (which is itself a holy 'struggle' against us) can succeed only if it is also a struggle on behalf of genuine transnational public goods against the private interests manifest in McWorld.

Capitalism is an extraordinarily productive system. There is no better way to organize human labour for productivity than mobilizing a billion private wills motivated by self-interest. It fails miserably at distribution, however, which is necessarily the object of our public institutions, motivated by the search for common ground and a way to overcome the private conflicts and private inequalities that arise out of private production. Domestically, most nation states have struck the balance: that is the meaning of democratic capitalism. Internationally, there is only a raging asymmetry that is the first and last cause of that anarchism in which terror flourishes and terrorists make their perverse arguments about death to young men and women who have lost hope in the possibilities of life.

The war between Jihad and McWorld cannot be won. Only a struggle of democracy against not only Jihad but also against McWorld can achieve a just victory for the planet. A just, diverse, democratic world will put commerce and consumerism back in its place and make space for religion; it will combat the terrors of Jihad not by making war on it but by creating a world in which the practice of religion is as secure as the practice of consumption and in which the defence of cultural values is not in tension with liberty but part of how liberty is defined. Terror feeds off the parasitic dialectics of Jihad and McWorld. In a democratic world order, there will be no need for militant Jihad because belief will have a significant place; and there will be no advantage to McWorld because cultural variety will confront it on every television station and at every mall, the world over. When Jihad and McWorld have vanished as primary categories, terror may not wholly disappear (it is lodged in a small but impregnable crevice in the dark regions of the human soul), but it will become irrelevant to the hopes and aspirations of women and men who will have learned to love life too much to confuse religion with the courtship of death.

Notes

1. Benjamin R. Barber, *Jihad vs. McWorld* (New York: Ballentine Books, 1996).
2. For an account of the new democratic realism see Benjamin R. Barber, 'Terrorism and the New Democratic Realism', *The Nation*, January 4, 2002.
3. Pope John Paul's Apostolic Exhortation, cited in the *New York Times*, January 24, 1999.
4. James D. Wolfensohn, president of the World Bank, cited by Jim Hoagland, 'Richer and Poorer', *Washington Post* National Weekly Edition, May 3, 1999, p. 5.

CHAPTER 23

How to Fight a Just War

Jean Bethke Elshtain

From President George W. Bush to the average man and woman on the street, Americans since September 11 have evoked the language of justice to characterize their collective response to the despicable deeds perpetrated against innocent men, women and children on September 11. When they do this, they tap into a complex tradition called 'just war'. The origins of the just war tradition are usually traced back to St Augustine's fourth-century masterwork, *The City of God*.[1] In that great text, Augustine grapples with the undeniable anti-violence of Christian teaching. He comes to the conclusion that wars of aggression and aggrandizement are never acceptable. But there are occasions when resort to force may be tragically necessary although violence is never a normative good. What, then, makes it justifiable? For Augustine, the most potent justification is to protect the innocent – those in no position to defend themselves – from certain harm. If one has compelling evidence that harm will come to persons unless action involving coercive force is taken, a requirement of neighbourly love may be a resort to arms. Self-defence is trickier. According to Augustine, it is better for the Christian as an individual to suffer harm rather than to commit it. But are we permitted to make that commitment to non-self-defence for others? No, surely not.

The upshot of Augustine's reflections, refined over time, is that a primary rule for those committed to just war is non-combatant immunity or the so-called principle of discrimination, meaning that non-combatants must not be the *intended* targets of violence. A further implication is that a carefully worked out and unprovoked act of terror against non-combatants of one's own country is an injury – an act of war – that demands a response. That response involves just punishment, not in order to inflict grievous harm on the non-combatants of a country whose operatives have harmed your citizens but to interdict in order to prevent further harm and to punish those responsible for the harm that has already occurred. In so doing, one reaffirms a world of moral responsibility and justice.

What Governments Are For

When a wound as grievous as that of September 11 has been inflicted on a body politic, it would be the height of irresponsibility – a dereliction of duty, a flight from the serious vocation of politics – to fail to respond. The Christian tradition tells us that government is instituted by God. This does not mean that every government and every public official is godly but, rather, that he or she is charged with a solemn responsibility for which there is divine warrant. It is extreme bad faith to agree that government is thus ordained but then to disdain those who take up its important tasks. A *political* ethic is an ethic of responsibility. The just war tradition offers a way to exercise that responsibility. This way of thinking rejects both the 'anything goes' ethic of Machiavellian *realpolitik* and an ethic that forswears action if that action takes the form of coercion and commits a country to the use of armed force in a responsible and limited way.

In the immediate aftermath of the events of 9/11, I said to a friend, 'Now we are reminded of what governments are for.' None of the goods human beings cherish – including politics itself – can flourish absent a measure of civic peace and security. Those that lurk and plot in darkness and secret, that operate stealthily, and that refuse to accept responsibility for wrongdoing perpetrate harm beyond the immediate violent event. They force good into hiding as we retreat behind closed doors. What good do I have in mind? The simple but profound good that is mothers and fathers raising their children, men and women going to work, citizens of a great city making their way on streets and subways, ordinary people buying airplane tickets in order to visit their grandchildren in California, business men and women en route to transact business with colleagues in other cities, the faithful attending their churches, synagogues and mosques without fear. This quotidian idea, this basic civic peace, is a great good. It is not the peace of the City of God. That awaits the end-time. In the meantime, we live in a world of tragic conflict and a world of comparative justice in which the good may not be the best but it is far, far better than the worst that human beings have devised and are capable of. As Martin Luther put it, 'If the lion lies down with the lamb, the lamb must be replaced frequently.'

Beating swords into ploughshares and spears into pruning hooks, a world in which 'nation shall not lift up sword against nation, neither shall they learn war any more', is a vision connected with certain conditions, as Kenneth Anderson reminds us in an essay in the *Times Literary Supplement*.[2] For the prophet tells us that the condition of eschatological peace is one in which the Lord's house has been established everywhere and all 'go up to the mountain of the Lord ... For out of Zion shall go forth the law, and the world of the Lord from Jerusalem.' We are not there yet, to put it mildly. It isn't even clear that we *should* get there under the conditions of late modernity with its pluralisms of ways of life.

Nevertheless, the ordinary civic peace that horrific violence disrupts and attempts to destroy offers intimations of eschatological peace and is a good to be cherished and not to be made light of. It is a good that we charge our public officials with maintaining. If we live from day to day in fear of deadly attack, the other goods we rightly cherish become difficult. Human beings are soft-shelled creatures. We cannot reveal the fullness of our being, including our deep sociality, if airplanes are flying into buildings and cities become piles of rubble composed in part of the mangled bodies of victims. We can neither take this civic peace for granted – as we have learned so horribly – nor shake off our responsibility for helping to respect and to promote the norms and rules whose enforcement is constitutive of civic peace. St Augustine taught us that we should not spurn worldly vocations, including the tragic vocation of the judge – tragic because he or she can never know for certain whether punishment is being meted out to the guilty and not the innocent. But we depend on judges and others to uphold a world of responsibility, a world in which people are not permitted to 'devour one another like fishes', in Augustine's pithy phrase.

Restraint in War

Public officials are charged with protecting a people. As those extraordinary firemen in New York City said, simply, 'It's my job.' This is their right authority – another vital dimension of the just war tradition and one aimed at limiting freelance, opportunistic and individualistic violence. So even as just war permits limited resort to arms, it challenges the anything goes approach to violence. Responding justly to injustice is a tall order, for it means that it is better to risk the lives of one's own combatants than to intentionally kill 'enemy' non-combatants. It is often difficult to separate combatants from non-combatants, but try one must. The restraints internal to the just war tradition encode the notion of limits to the use of force. Many of these rules and stipulations have been incorporated into international agreements, including several Geneva Conventions. During and after a conflict we assess the conduct of a war-fighting nation by how its warriors conducted themselves. Did they rape and pillage? Were they under careful rules of engagement or was it a free-for-all? Was every attempt made to limit civilian casualties knowing that, in time of war, civilians are invariably going to fall in harm's way? It is unworthy of the solemn nature of these matters to respond cynically or naively. As theologian Oliver O'Donovan put it in the British journal *The Tablet* at the time of the Persian Gulf War, just ask yourself, would you rather have been a citizen of Berlin in 1944 or a citizen of Baghdad during the Persian Gulf War? The answer is obvious, given both the nature of modern weaponry and US targeting strategy aimed at avoiding civilian targets as well as important cultural centres and houses of worship.

Since the Vietnam War and the restructuring of the US military, pains have been taken to underscore the codes of ethics that derive from the just war tradition in US military academies and in the training of American soldiers. No group in the US pays more attention to ethical restraint on the use of force than does the US military. We do not kill or even threaten to kill nearly 3000 civilians because that number of our own civilians have been murdered by perpetrators who scarcely deserve the name of either soldier or warrior. We put soldiers into combat rather than unleashing terrorists. The soldier, in contrast to the terrorist, seeks to search out and to punish those responsible for planning, aiding and abetting, and perpetrating an evil deed. Just punishment is different from revenge. Revenge repudiates all limits; just punishment observes restraints. The course charted by the Bush administration has been both complex and restrained. The US did not rush to retaliate. Careful planning crafted a multipronged strategy, at once military, diplomatic, economic, cybernetic and rhetorical. Messages were decoded and money flows were cut off. Support through front organizations was dried up. The rabid anti-American and anti-Semitic monotone of much of the press in the Arab world was countered with a message that was more nuanced – Americans being nothing if not self-critical, often to the point of self-flagellation – and that defended the US and its policies at one and the same time. This was a rather extraordinary thing for a wounded and aroused superpower to do. That the president and his advisers have been aware of the need for restraint is evident in the renaming of a mission that was first dubbed 'Operation Infinite Justice' by the military with a more modest name that does not suggest a utopian goal: 'Operation Enduring Freedom'. Another sign is the ongoing insistence that the US response is not aimed at a whole people or nation or religion or way of life but is, instead, directed at those who defame their own religion, who drag their own people into harm's way, and who perpetrate an ideology that has as its end the deaths of babies, people in wheelchairs, mothers and fathers, brothers and sisters, uncles and aunts, grandmothers and grandfathers, friends and lovers, going about their daily routines. And why should they die? Simply because they are infidels – they are Americans. The aim of terrorism is terror. The terrorists did not issue a set of demands. They did not demand negotiation or else. They simply murdered. That is why one does not negotiate. There is nothing to negotiate about. Thus the talking ends and the call to responsible action begins.

This is an extraordinary moment in American history. On September 11, the US sustained a greater loss of life in a single day than ever before in its history, easily topping the previous norm for a day of death – the Battle of Antietam during the bloody American Civil War. Americans tell us that they are prepared for this different kind of war, but the numbers of those who support action against terrorism begin to waver when the question is put as to whether this force would be acceptable if 'innocent men, women and children' are the victims. No war, as I have already indicated, can be fought without putting non-combatants in harm's way, but the American people favour doing everything possible to limit this damage. One reason why the US wearied of the Vietnam War was the realization that fighting a guerrilla war meant that the US simply could not distinguish combatants from non-combatants and that, even without horrors like the My Lai massacre, American soldiers were put in the impossible position of regarding everyone as 'the enemy'. That is not the case here.

A Nation's Honour and Responsibility

So respond the US has and respond it shall. It is a vital concern that the entire world should stop those who use civilians against other civilians by turning a great symbol of human freedom of movement – the commercial airplane – into a deadly bomb. To this end, it is necessary to cut off terrorist finances, to decode their messages, to disrupt their networks and, finally, to interdict and to punish the terrorists themselves – means that are consistent with just war constraints. The US is prepared to put its combatants in harm's way to punish those who put American non-combatants in harm's way and have no compunction about mass murder. That is the burden of the just warrior. And that is his or her – and a nation's – honour.

In the dark days of Nazi terror, a brave young German theologian, Dietrich Bonhoeffer, who had been moving toward pacifism, committed himself to a conspiracy to assassinate Adolph Hitler, to cut off the head of the snake. He asked, who stands fast? Bonhoeffer observed that the great evil that had appeared among the German people had 'played havoc with all our ethical concepts'. He was particularly severe in his criticism of those who

> flee from public altercation into the sanctuary of private *virtuousness*. But anyone who does this must shut his mouth and his eyes to the injustice around him. Only at the cost of self-deception can he keep himself pure from the contamination arising from responsible action.[3]

Obedient and responsible action. One who cares about these, Bonhoeffer taught us, asks the question, how is the coming generation to live?

We know what happens to people who live in pervasive fear. It isn't pretty. It invites lashing out, and severe isolation from a desire to protect oneself. It encourages harsh measures because – and in this Thomas Hobbes was right – we simply cannot live as human beings if we live in constant fear of violent death. Two weeks after the horror of 9/11, my daughter, the mother of two of our grandchildren, and I found ourselves discussing the need for a plan should there be a biological or chemical attack. Who would pick up all the children, the grandchildren? Where would we rendezvous? Should one buy gas masks? Should one discuss any of this with two five-year-olds and a seven-year-old? Already JoAnn, Christopher and Bobby are drawing pictures of planes flying into buildings and asking, 'What happens if Grandma's plane is hijacked?' We reassure them, knowing that the correct answer cannot be spoken aloud to children. Of course, we all must die one day. But we are called to life. There are times when that call to live demands – *demands* – action against those claimed by death. Osama bin Laden has insisted that the Americans will be defeated because they want to live, whereas young members of al-Qaeda want to die. He didn't say that they are unafraid to die but, rather, that they desire death. It has claimed them. Those claimed by life are not afraid to die, but they know that we are called to tend to the quotidian, to the everyday business of living in decency and with dignity. That is why we fight. It has nothing to do with American megalomania, or errant nationalism, or narrow pride. It has to do with a just response to aggression and the responsibility that a great nation with a preponderance of power, but one nonetheless vulnerable for all that, must feel toward her own citizens, first, but toward the possibility of a measure of peace for all humankind as well. To that end, those whom Michael Ignatieff, in an essay in the *New York Review of Books*, tagged 'apocalyptic nihilists' must be defeated.[4] Now is not the time for pessimism but for resolve and determination in the recognition that no one will play a role in helping to build up the infrastructures of societies now riven by political and economic collapse – hence a ripe breeding ground for apocalyptic nihilism – if the United States does not lead the way. That is the burden of empire and it is time that Americans faced up to it. September 11 shocked Americans into this sober recognition and they cannot back down. No responsible leader or country wants them to, even as many complain about American power. Americans can be carefree no longer. That is the grim lesson of September 11.

Notes

1. St Augustine, *The City of God* (Penguin: London, 1985).
2. Kenneth Anderson, 'What Kind of War Is It?', *Times Literary Supplement*. Visited at Crimes of War Project website, <http://www.crimesofwar.org/index.html>.
3. Dietrich Bonhoeffer, *Letters and Papers from Prison* (Macmillan Collier Books: New York, 1998), p. 5.
4. Michael Ignatieff, 'It's War – But it Doesn't Have to be Dirty', *Guardian*, October 1, 2001.

CHAPTER 24

Terrorism or Intercultural Dialogue

Bhikhu Parekh

How should we respond to terrorist attacks of the kind that occurred on
September 11? The question has received several answers, of which two
are most influential. First, some argue that the perpetrators of these evil
acts are callous and inhuman monsters driven by a blind hatred of the
West, especially the United States. Since they are non-state agents, they
are strictly speaking not at war with us, but they are most certainly in
a state of war with us. We have a duty to defend ourselves and to do
everything in our power to put them out of action. We cannot reason
with them because they are not rational beings but nihilists determined
to inflict maximum harm on us. The only language they understand is
that of force. They do, of course, claim in self-justification that they
have grievances against us, which their peaceful appeals have failed to
redress. However this is a specious argument. It turns every act of injustice into a licence for terrorism, and that is a recipe for chaos. What is
more, the long terrorist list of injustices is largely suspect, for these so-
called injustices are the results of their own badly managed societies
and cannot be blamed on us. And even if we bore responsibility for
some of these, tackling or even discussing them now would widely be
taken to legitimize terror.

Second, some argue that while terrorist acts deserve to be punished
or pre-empted, we also need to look at their context and causes. They
do not occur in a historical and moral vacuum. Their agents are human
beings like the rest of us, a mixture of good and evil, and do not enjoy
throwing away their lives and turning their wives into widows and
children into orphans. They risk their lives in terrorist acts because they
feel humiliated, trampled upon, unjustly treated, and see no other way
of redressing their grievances. Rather than concentrate only on their
reprehensible deeds, we must address their deeper causes. We should

not put terrorists outside the pale of rational discourse but engage in a dialogue with them, understand their grievances, see if they are genuine, ask ourselves whether we bear any responsibility for these, mend our ways when we think we do and, when we don't, persuade them why they need to put their own house in order. Although such a dialogue is not easy against the background of spectacular terrorist acts, it is absolutely essential. We have seen dead bodies and desperate struggles for safety, and heard heart-rending last-minute messages, all of which tend to overwhelm and unhinge us. It is therefore of the utmost importance that we should not lose our moral balance and perspective by allowing our sense of justice to remain trapped within the grip of vivid and horrifying images.

Of the two, the first response, though understandable, is deeply flawed. It makes no attempt to understand the agents and the wider context of their actions, and all too conveniently dismisses them as inhuman monsters. Once they are so perceived, it becomes easier to argue that the only way to deal with them is to terrorize them, to treat them with such severity that neither they nor their supporters would ever dare to repeat these deeds. This reduces us to their level and weakens our moral authority to condemn them, for although our ends are infinitely superior our methods are the same. If terrorism is reprehensible, anti-terrorist terrorism is no better.

When people are embittered and brutalized and prepared to throw away their lives, nothing we do to them will terrorize and deter them. Whatever we do to them only confirms their poor opinion of us and hardens their resolve. There is a limit to what we can do to intimidate and terrorize potential terrorists, and once these are exhausted, we are left without resources. By contrast, terrorist methods are limitless. When hijacking planes becomes difficult, planting bombs takes its place. When that is stopped, suicide bombing becomes common, extending to women and before long to children. And if that becomes impossible, biological warfare and hitherto unimagined forms of terror appear on the horizon. Liberal societies are by their very nature vulnerable to attacks at many different points. While their capacity to protect themselves is necessarily limited, there are no such limits on the opportunities available to the terrorist.

It took only 20 determined terrorists to cause massive havoc in New York and Washington. It is inconceivable that millions of sulking and disaffected people from whose ranks they came cannot continue to throw up similar numbers in future. Terrorists require not only finances, training, and so on, but also a supportive or acquiescent body of people, a justifying ideology, and widely perceived grievances around which to mobilize support. Dismantling their networks is never enough; we also need to tackle their cultural and political roots and win the battle for the minds and hearts of ordinary people. This is why Western leaders have repeatedly insisted, sometimes disingenuously, that Islam is a religion of peace, that it does not justify suicide and killing the innocent, that their struggle is not against Muslims or Islam, and so on. Terrorism is both a military and a political problem, and cannot be tackled by military means alone.

The initial response of the United States government to the events of September 11 was mature and belonged to the second type. While condemning the attacks and vowing to bring their perpetrators to justice, its spokesmen appreciated the need to address their deeper causes. Increasingly the United States government began to veer towards the first response and is now firmly committed to it. Several factors seem to have played a part in this change, such as the relative ease with which the Taliban government was removed, the Israeli government's intransigence, domestic electoral considerations, the temptation to settle old scores with Iran, Iraq, North Korea and other states, the excitement of flexing the military muscle, and the heightened sense of existence offered by the incredible upsurge in American patriotism and sense of national solidarity. Whatever the explanation, hunting down and eliminating potential terrorists and deterring others is now more or less the sole objective. Prisoners taken in Afghanistan are not only harshly treated but humiliated, partly out of a sense of revenge and partly to strike terror in the hearts of their sympathizers. Over 1000 foreign nationals have been arrested with little explanation, and many are still being held though none has been charged. Ordinary legal processes are suspended in favour of military tribunals with the power to execute suspects on the basis of evidence neither disclosed to them nor subject to their challenge. Every country that is suspected of supporting potential terrorists is declared a legitimate military and economic target and threatened with dire consequences. The whole world is divided up into friends and foes. The latter, the 'axis of evil', are under intense pressure; and the former are told that even if they strongly disagree, America will go its own way. The United States is the sole judge of who is or is not a potential terrorist, and the sole executioner of its verdict. Welcoming this exclusive reliance on the big stick, Charles Krauthammar wrote in the *Washington Post* that the United States must create the 'psychology of fear' in order to command 'deep respect for the American power'.

As one would expect in these circumstances, the US government's rhetoric and behaviour are sadly beginning to display a remarkable resemblance to those of the terrorists. The latter call the United States an evil civilization; the United States says the same about them. They say they are fighting for 'eternal moral verities', the United States says it is fighting for values that are 'right and unchanging for all people everywhere'. They say that every state working in league with the United States is a legitimate target; the United States says the same. Terrorists aim to create global fear by demonstrating that even the centres of American financial and military power are not beyond their reach; the United States aims to do the same. Both claim divine blessings for their respective projects; both talk of a clash of civilizations, a long and bitter war, and a fight to the finish; both want to stand and act alone, are driven by rage and hatred, and claim absolute superiority for their respective ways of life.

All this goes to show how mistaken it is to adopt the first, punitive approach and to see terrorism as an exclusively military problem. The United States ends up becoming the mirror image of its enemy and profoundly corrupting the integrity of its way of life. It is led to cut legal and moral corners, to violate the rule of law, to authorize intelligence agencies to do things that transgress international norms, to interfere in the national lives of vulnerable states, to militarize the psyche of its own people, and to encourage dangerous passions. As I observed earlier, such methods rarely succeed in achieving their objectives and only end up escalating the spiral of violence. Given its fairly extensive list of terror-sponsoring states, the United States also risks getting dragged into wars on many different fronts, making enemies, provoking widespread hostility, and so on – precisely what it needs to avoid and what the terrorists desperately desire. The Muslim population in the world is likely to form about a quarter of the world population by 2024, and the United States cannot afford to alienate vast masses of them, especially as it badly needs access to their vast and vitally necessary reserves of gas and oil.

The Case for Dialogue

I suggest that the only effective way to counter terrorism is to adopt the second approach outlined above. Potential terrorists and their sponsors or supporters must obviously be deterred by all legitimate means, including carefully gathered intelligence, financial squeeze, domestic vigilance and, when necessary, a judicious use of force. At the same time we must also address the deeper roots of terrorism that drive otherwise decent men and women to build up enormous rage and hatred, and so blunt their moral sensibilities that they cannot see anything wrong in taking innocent lives. We need to reassure them that injustices worry us as much as they worry them, that they can count on us to tackle these, that they do not need to take the law into their own hands, and that we are partners in a common cause. International terrorism is not caused by poverty and global inequality. The poor and the oppressed know that their enemies are located within their countries. And although Western prosperity attracts them, they do not resent or hate it and seek instead to become part of it by legal or illegal immigration. They obviously wish, as does any morally sensitive person, that the West would use its resources and influence to eliminate poverty and minimize global inequalities in its own long-term interest as well as for humanitarian reasons, but they do not go and bomb Western cities. The West arouses their anger and hatred only when, in their view, it bears at least some responsibility for their predicament, either by propping up the domestic system of injustice or by inflicting additional injustices and humiliations on them. If we are to tackle the roots of terrorism, we need to enter their world of thought, understand their grievances and explore why they think we bear responsibility for these.

This calls for a dialogue between Western and non-Western societies, especially Muslim societies whose sense of injustice is the most acute and from which almost all the recent terrorists have sprung. The point of the dialogue is to deepen mutual understanding, to expand sympathy and imagination, to exchange not only arguments but also sensibilities, to take a critical look at oneself, to build up mutual trust, and to arrive at a more just and balanced view of both the contentious issues and the world in general. The dialogue cannot achieve these objectives if it is reduced to a public relations exercise, or is too frightened to offend, or too obsessed with political correctness to be honest. It must be robust, frank and critical, telling the truth as each party sees it, but always in the knowledge that the dialogue cannot be allowed to fail, for the only alternative to it is violence and bloodshed. In order that the dialogue can permeate and shape the consciousness of decision makers, commentators and ordinary citizens, it should occur at all levels ranging from serious academic discussions to international conferences, the United Nations and the popular media in Western and Muslim societies.

The dialogue is necessarily multistranded and at various levels. It is obviously about substantive economic, political and other issues, the immediate causes of conflict and violence. Since all such issues have historical roots and are embedded in historical memories, the dialogue also has an inescapable historical dimension, and involves arriving at a broadly agreed view of the past. And since human beings define their interests and identities and their relations with others from within their culture, the dialogue has a strong cultural component as well. We cannot hope to understand why Muslim societies feel strongly about certain issues or define them in certain ways unless we understand their wider systems of meaning and values or cultures. And similarly Muslim societies cannot understand the West without understanding the internal structure, dynamics and tensions of Western civilization. The dialogue between Western and Muslim societies thus moves freely between substantive issues and their historical interpretations and cultural contexts, and is necessarily complex and messy.

Contrary to the current rhetoric, there can be no clash between cultures or civilizations. Cultures do not speak or fight; rather, people speak and fight from within and about their cultures. Cultures, further, are not homogeneous wholes and contain different strands and currents of thought. Cultures or civilizations therefore do not clash, only their particular strands and interpretations do. There is no inherent clash between Islam and the West. Some strands within Islam fit nicely with some strands within the West, and on some readings of them, Islamic and Western civilizations share much in common. It all depends on what one takes to be their central values and how one interprets these. Islam is not a homogeneous entity with an unchanging essence. There are in fact many Islams just as there are many Wests. The Indian Islam is different from the Saudi, and both are different from their Indonesian, Afghan, Iranian, Tunisian and Bosnian counterparts. And each of these is internally contested. Ayatollah Khomeini's politicized and militant understanding of Islam was fiercely attacked by several traditionalist Ayatollahs, who thought it a profound distortion of Islam and insisted on a clear separation between religion and the state, a view for which some of them were placed under house arrest. As for the West, it is made up of a complex and sometimes contradictory set of views and values derived from very different sources. And since different Western societies interpret and combine them differently, no two Western societies or their cultures or forms of Christianity are exactly alike.

Since all societies are internally diverse, we should not homogenize them, generalize about them, or allow anyone the sole authority to speak for them. Furthermore, they all have admirable and abominable qualities, this being as true of the Western as of Muslim societies, and none should be demonized or declared 'evil'. For that very reason, each needs to be critical of itself and avoid the deadly vices of self-righteousness and moral arrogance. A society unable to engage in a critical dialogue with itself and tolerate disagreement is unable to engage in a meaningful dialogue with others. It is only when participants recognize and respect these basic conditions of a dialogue that the latter can be meaningful.

Muslim and Western Voices

I have argued above for a dialogue between Western societies, especially the United States, and Muslim societies.[1] How would such a dialogue proceed? Each would obviously speak with different voices and emphasize different things about itself and the other. In order to get to the heart of their deepest disagreements, I shall simplify and polarize the dialogue and sketch, on the basis of the utterances of their intellectuals and political leaders, what each thinks and would want to say to the other. I shall begin with the kind of opening statement Muslim leaders might make.

You, the United States of America, are driven by an overweening ambition to dominate the world. Since you enjoy military superiority over the whole of the rest of the world put together, a dominance without parallel in human history, you want to use it to turn other societies into pliant instruments of your will. You have used vulnerable states to serve your interests and left them in a mess when they outlived their value. Despite all your talk of human rights and democracy, whenever progressive forces emerged in many parts of the world, you subverted them, as when you toppled Mussadiq in Iran, Lumumba in the Congo and Allende in Chile; when you trained and helped terrorists in Guatemala, Nicaragua, Angola and Argentina; when you endorsed the mass murders of Samuel Doe, Suharto and Pinochet, and when you invaded Grenada. You were so determined to avenge your defeat in Vietnam and destabilize the Soviet Union that you stoked powerful religious passions in Afghanistan and armed and trained Mujahideen and Islamic terrorists without any thought for the long-term danger this posed to Afghanistan and Pakistan. To contain Iran, you encouraged a most brutal war between it and Iraq. And when the latter thought it could count on your support and punish Kuwait for helping itself with Iraqi oil during its war with Iran, you sent it mixed messages. And when it foolishly invaded Kuwait, you hit it hard, imposed on it impossible conditions, and continue with a regime of punitive sanctions. You have been grossly biased in your response to the Israel–Palestine conflict, demanding impossible concessions from the Palestinians and endorsing the belligerence of Ariel Sharon, a man with a shabby past who is disowned by the progressive forces in his own country. You are Israel's staunch ally but not its true friend. You well know that Israel is a small country, that the Arabs will one day become strong and prosperous, and that they would then seek to avenge the humiliations and injustices the current Israeli government continues to heap on them. Israel has no choice but to continue to depend on your contingent goodwill, to militarize its way of life, and to distort its great inspiring ideals. If you were its true friend, you would in its own long-term interest tell it a few home truths. You would not, partly because of the obvious pressure of the misguided Israeli lobby and partly because you want to tie that talented country to your apron string, make it do your dirty job in that region, and use its quarrels with its neighbours to sell them arms and increase your power over them.

You are firmly convinced that your way of life is the best, that you represent 'the city on the hill', and that you have a God-given right to shape the rest of the world in your image. You are determined to turn the world into a consumerist paradise, inhabited by self-absorbed and self-satisfied people who like their Coca-Cola and hamburgers, their Hollywood movies, their freedom to do as their fancy dictates, and who are guided by no deeper moral and spiritual goals. You do not appreciate that the good life can be lived in several different ways; some better than others, but none absolutely the best. Your way of life has its obvious merits such as extensive liberties, personal autonomy, vibrant civil society, material comforts, enormous self-confidence and the spirit of equality, but it also has its limitations. It breeds aggression, self-centredness, corporate stranglehold over the political process, media manipulation of public opinion, absence of mutual concern, blindness to the limitations of the human will, callousness to those who cannot compete, and so on. While other societies have much to learn from you, you too can learn much from them. Rather than cherish and foster the rich diversity of the multicultural world, you aggressively universalize your way of life, dismissing those who resist you as 'medieval' and even evil. With that end in mind, you push for globalization, deregulation, the opening up of domestic markets, the dismantling of the public sector, and structural adjustment programmes, so that your poorly regulated multinationals can have a free run of the whole world. When your direct pressure does not work, you use the IMF and the World Bank to achieve this goal as if these international agencies were nothing more than branches of your Treasury.

While exhorting the rest of the world to respect international law and treaties, you flout them at will. You refused to ratify the Kyoto Treaty on climate change, the International Criminal Court, and the ban on anti-personnel landmines and biological weapons, and you refused to pay your dues to the United Nations. You unilaterally decided to break the Anti-Ballistic Missile Treaty with Russia, and you walked out of the Durban Conference on racism when its agreed protocol did not go your way. You are becoming a moral free-rider, benefiting from others' willingness to discharge their share of the collective burden but refusing to discharge yours when it damages your short-term interest. If you are not careful you risk being branded an arrogant bully who would only relate to the world on its own terms. Your enormous power has rightly made you a world leader and you have the potential to be a great force for good. Sadly, you insist on behaving like a self-absorbed nation state pursuing its narrow interest behind the rhetoric of world leadership.

You display a powerful Manichean thrust. The world for you is made up of 'goodies' and 'baddies'. You and those who go along with you repres-ent the former; the rest are evil and must be defeated. You define your identity in terms of a real or imaginary hostile other, are constantly looking for enemies, and are at peace with yourself only when at war with others. For 40 years, you fought the Cold War and caused much havoc. When that ended, you found a new enemy in the shape of Islamic funda-mentalism. You have now found another in Islamic terrorism, and your war with it will, in your own words, keep you busy for a long time. This will boost your arms industry, will help the Republicans win the forth-coming congressional and even the presidential election, will promote right-wing social and economic agendas, and will give you the opportunity to settle old scores with some countries. A cynic might think that you needed Osama bin Laden's blood-curdling rhetoric to give your collective life moral meaning and purpose. It is about time you asked yourself why your civilization has become so war-dependent and militarist, and why you scare the rest of the world, including your friends.

Muslims have remained backward, divided and confused, and that has spawned fundamentalism and even terrorism. The blame for that lies at the doors of the colonial powers, and more recently at yours. You support despotic and feudal regimes in Muslim societies, and actively help them or at least acquiesce when they crush democratic movements. Can you think of one occasion when you sincerely and actively supported the latter? Divided, ill-governed and oppressed Muslim masses turn to their radically redefined religion to generate a sense of community, to mobilize their moral resources, to fight corruption, to forge unity with other Muslim societies, to regain a sense of pride, and to live out their vision of the good society. You feel frightened because religion does not fit into your secular world view, rejects some of your rules of the game, and mobilizes Muslim masses around causes that threaten your interests. You therefore increase your support for oppressive forces, and further alienate and embitter the masses. They are not by nature or habit anti-Western or anti-American, but are made so by your actions. They are drawn to fundamentalists because the latter play up anti-American sentiments and promise to stand up to you. Terrorism is one way to do this.[2] It is the only form of power available to the weak, the only means of asserting their pride and drawing attention to their anger and injustice. You are wrong to think that they are 'jealous' of your way of life or 'resent' your prosperity and power. Since they have no wish to follow your way of life, they cannot be jealous of it. And they do not want your power and wealth either because their goals and ideals are different. All they want is to get you off their backs so they can freely build their way of life. Millions of Muslims strongly disapprove of the terrorist attacks on you, for these go against the basic principles of Islam, give it a bad name, endanger the lives of Muslims in the West, and invite reprisals. However, they understand the anger and frustration that inspired these evil deeds, appreciate the sacrifices and altruism of their perpetrators, and cannot honestly condemn them without qualification. They are keen to help you to put an end to such acts if only you would agree to mend your ways and join them in exploring how best to redress their long-festering grievances.

I have briefly sketched the kind of honest opening statement Muslim spokesmen might make in their dialogue with the West. For its part, the latter would want to make an equally robust statement, which might take the following form.

You, Muslims, misleadingly claim that yours is a religion of peace. Islam is an absolutist religion claiming superiority over all others and driven by the hegemonic ambition to convert the world to its way of life. It insists that the Qur'an is the sole authentic and exhaustive revelation of God, and that Mohammed is the last of the prophets. It pours scorn on the so-called idolatrous religions including Hinduism which it has despised for centuries, and on such others as Confucianism which in its view are not religions at all. It does, of course, show respect for Judaism and Christianity but only as primitive first drafts of Islam, and takes a somewhat patronizing view of Moses and Jesus. This is why Islam extends its proselytizing activities to their followers, never granted the latter full equality, and harasses them in countries where it is in power. It is true that

Islam is currently engaged in a dialogue with these religions. However, one should not read too much into this. The initiative for the dialogue has come not from Islam but from them. The dialogue is confined to a few intellectuals, is limited to areas of mutual cooperation, and is not allowed to challenge Islam's belief in its absolute superiority. And Islam has welcomed it in order to neutralize these two powerful religions and enjoy the freedom to carry on its proselytizing activities elsewhere.

You are not content to assert the absolute superiority of your religion. You are also driven by a hegemonic political ambition. You constantly hark back to your 'glorious' period of military and political expansion, your rule over large parts of Europe, Asia and elsewhere, the Ottoman Empire, and so on. You resent Europe for defeating and marginalizing you, and now want to replace the West as a global power. This is why you want to unite the umma, to exploit your natural resources of gas and oil, to use these to challenge the West and build up your economic power, and to acquire sophisticated nuclear and other destructive technology. You have imperialist designs, and your attack on Western or American imperialism is not born out of a sincere desire to get rid of all imperialism but is part of a larger strategy to impose your own.

You talk of your great civilization and its superiority to ours. Nothing can be further from the truth. No Muslim society today has much to be proud of. All are corrupt, autocratic, degenerate, materialist, violent, and oppressive of their minorities, women and dissident sects. You claim that this is because they are not truly Islamic and have bartered away the true principles of Islam for the consumerist idolatry of the secular West. This is nonsense. No two Muslims are agreed on what a truly Islamic society is like. For some only the umma can be the legitimate unit of governance; others justify the existing nation states. For some, Islam requires communal ownership of property; others disagree. For some, it requires rule by the mullah; for others, it calls for a moderately secular state. Indeed, since the general and vague statements of the Qur'an can be interpreted in different ways, the very idea of a truly Islamic state is deeply problematic. Furthermore, whenever a self-styled 'truly' Islamic state has come into existence, it has turned out to be worse than others. The Taliban regime was endorsed by many a fundamentalist Muslim including bin Laden. The regime was most oppressive and brutal, raping women whose chastity it claimed to safeguard by imposing the veil, persecuting Shi'as, grossly abusing political power, plundering public property, harassing followers of other religions, destroying rare Buddhist statues, and so on.

You blame the West for your current predicament. You could not be more mistaken. Many non-Muslim societies have had no difficulty devel-

oping themselves. There is no reason why you should have lagged so far behind. Many of you sit on vast natural resources, and could have used these to modernize yourselves as well as the less well-resourced members of the umma. The West did support some of your despotic rulers. However, all states, including the Muslim states, pursue their interests, and it is wrong to expect the West to be altruistic. What is more, it was and is open to your leaders to organize your masses around a democratic agenda. You either did not do so or did it in a manner that failed to resonate with popular aspirations. It is most irresponsible of you to blame the West for not fighting your battles for you and not giving you a democratic system on a platter. It is about time you began to think and behave as adults taking charge of your destiny rather than as children passively praying for a Western Santa Claus to bring you the gifts of new ideas and institutions.

You argue that you disapprove of fundamentalism and terrorism, and that those involved are mad people who have hijacked your great religion. This is an intellectual and political cop-out. It does not explain why your religion was hijacked, why there was no resistance, why this happened in some but not other Muslim countries, and why a powerful alternative view of Islam was not developed and canvassed by your leaders. The responsibility for the corruption and misuse of your religion lies fairly and squarely on the shoulders of your political, religious and intellectual leaders. They need to take a most critical look at it and ask what tendencies within it are susceptible to fundamentalist and terrorist interpretations and need to be fought or reinterpreted. They must also explore how Islam can come to terms with modernity, including modern science, liberal and democratic values, the spirit of critical inquiry, and independent thought. These and other ideas are an inescapable part of our collective life today, and also have much to be said for them. Islam needs to engage in a critical dialogue with them, adopting what is valuable and rejecting what is shallow and misguided. Contrary to what your conservative leaders say, millions of Muslims when given a choice have opted for many a Western value and practice, such as the freedom to challenge orthodoxy, to choose a career, to run their lives themselves, to protest against oppression and injustices, to enjoy the normal pleasures of life, to read Western literature, and to watch Western movies. It is about time you acknowledged the reality of these and other choices, and provided viable alternatives to the naively anti-modernist readings of your traditions and religion.

I have sketched above the broadest outlines of the discursive framework within which a badly needed dialogue can take place between Western and Muslim societies. The views I have attributed to each side are based on the public and private remarks of their spokesmen, and are inevitably partisan, extreme, polemical, hurtful and sometimes deeply offensive. Since they are widely held and form the often unarticulated background against which each perceives and relates to the other, they need to be stated, confronted and carefully examined. Some of the points made by each against the other are likely to be fiercely resisted by the latter; others are based on ignorance or wilful or honest misunderstanding; yet others are accepted by at least the more reflective among them. Neither the Western nor even most Muslim societies are monolithic. Each has its internal critics, and can count on them to treat these criticisms with respect and use them to take a fresh and careful look at their society.

The dialogue is at various levels, and the consensus secured at one level facilitates it at others. The dialogue is about specific political issues and conflicts, such as the Israel–Palestine conflict, sanctions on Iraq, American support for the Saudi regime, the reconstruction of Afghanistan, and global inequality and poverty. Our aim here should be to ensure that each side better understands the concerns and constraints of the other and strives to reach a mutually acceptable compromise. The dialogue is also about the interpretation and legacy of history such as the past Western interferences with Iran, Iraq, Egypt, Lebanon, Afghanistan and Pakistan, and our hope here is that each side will, through better mutual understanding, lift the burden of history and learn to face the future with a fresh and charitable perspective. The dialogue at the cultural level is the most challenging, but it cannot be avoided. While some contentious issues can be tackled by themselves, others cannot, and even the former will not have a lasting solution unless they are embedded in better intercultural understanding. Our hope here is that Western and Muslim societies (as well as all others) will avoid the interrelated vices of narcissism and demonization of the other, will appreciate each other's strengths and inadequacies, and will develop over time a shared global perspective in which deep differences are admitted but not allowed to get out of control.[3]

Notes

1. For a further discussion, see my *Rethinking Multiculturalism* (Basingstoke: Palgrave, and Harvard University Press, 2000).
2. 'When the world is so thoroughly monopolised, when power is so frighteningly consolidated by the technocratic machine and the dogma of globalisation, what means are there for turning the tables but terrorism? In

dealing all strong cards to itself, the system forced the Other to change the rules of the game.' Jean Baudrillard in *Le Monde*, November 2, 2001.

3. '... in closing the door on the era of sovereign independence and American security, anarchic terrorism has opened a window for those who believe that social injustice, unregulated wild capitalism and an aggressive secularism that leaves no space for religion and civil society not only create conditions on which terrorism feeds but invite violence in the name of rectification. As a consequence, we are at a seminal moment in our history – one in which trauma opens up the possibility of new forms of action.' Benjamin Barber, *The Nation*, January, 21, 2002. This wise and courageous remark deserves sympathetic attention.

CHAPTER 25

Rethinking Common Values[1]

Sissela Bok

I

In 1840, John Stuart Mill pointed to the contrast between those who waxed lyrical about 'our enlightened age' and those who stressed only the inequities, the loss of independence and the suffering accompanying such progress.[2] In that debate as in most controversies in social philosophy, Mill maintained, both sides were 'in the right in what they affirmed, though wrong in what they denied'. Failure to perceive opposing perspectives forced each side into needless rigidity. It mattered, therefore, to recognize the importance 'of antagonist modes of thoughts; which, it will one day be felt, are as necessary to one another in speculation, as mutually checking powers are in a constitution'.

Reactions to the news of the terrorist attacks on the World Trade Center and the Pentagon on September 11, 2001 – not only of horror, anger and grief, but also of jubilation and *Schadenfreude* – brought to public attention modes of thought that were more antagonist than those that Mill discussed. At issue were violations of fundamental moral prohibitions on the taking of innocent human life: violations common to all major religions, yet proclaimed by the perpetrators of the attacks and their leaders to have been divinely ordained. The scale and impact of the attacks were unprecedented, but the violations were anything but novel in human history; and even as the planes hit their targets, campaigns of terrorist killing were under way in conflicts in Africa, the Middle East and Asia in the name of a variety of religions and belief systems.

Is it still possible to speak of common values in the aftermath of September 11, as societies attempt to meet shared threats? What kinds of agreement on basic moral values would facilitate collective responses to challenges – and challengers – that themselves stop at no national, linguistic or other boundaries? How might a closer study of 'antagonist modes of thought' provide the necessary constraints on speculation that Mill compared to the mutually checking powers in a constitution? And what countervailing forces can support such efforts in practice?

Before the millennial celebrations in the year 2000, the media had resonated with contrasting proclamations regarding human prospects and the role of shared values: glowing claims about the spread of democracy and the promises of technology for health and well-being competed with grim prognostications about the spreading ravages of the HIV/AIDS pandemic and other diseases, the exhaustion of water, fuels and other resources, the extinction of ever more numerous species, the spread of terrorism and civil wars, and the proliferation of weapons of mass destruction.

Authors of such clashing forecasts are less likely to disagree about facts regarding, say, past scientific attainments or existing levels of poverty than in their conclusions. Most agree, for instance, that levels of income, literacy and life expectancy are now far higher for a much larger proportion of people than at the turn of the previous century. In 1900, infant mortality still ravaged rich and poor families alike in all societies, and average life expectancy at birth was almost half what it is today. Likewise, the proportion of people living on less than $1 a day has declined from 28 per cent in 1987 to 23 per cent in 1999. Meanwhile, however, the actual number of people having to subsist on the equivalent of a dollar a day has nearly doubled since 1970. At the beginning of the twentieth century, there were barely as many people alive on earth at all as the 1.2 billion who now have to subsist on the equivalent of one dollar a day and who lack sufficient food or water.

To the extent that those making forecasts for the century dwell primarily on the growing numbers either of those whose lives have improved or who are living in misery, their projections will be skewed, as Mill pointed out, by what they deny, gloss over, ignore or set aside as insignificant. The same is true in many other controversies. The skewing may be more pronounced still if those on opposing sides leave out of the account the role of values, either taking that role for granted or seeing it as of little significance in the general scheme of expected improvement or deterioration in human prospects. It may just be, however, that the central role of fundamental values seen in reactions to the September 11 attacks has contributed to a sobering rethinking of the most sweeping claims regarding the future.

II

In September 2000, world leaders assembled at the United Nations in New York for a Millennium Summit. The presidents, prime ministers and other representatives of over 150 states who had come together concluded by signing a sonorous United Nations Millennium Declaration, setting forth an expansive set of common values. Among these were freedom, equality, solidarity, tolerance, respect for nature and shared responsibility – in other words, ideals that have conspicuously *never* been held in common by all or even most societies at any time in history.

Among the signatories were leaders of some of the most oppressive and aggressive regimes on earth; yet they, too, agreed to uphold the Declaration's panoply of values and to combat violence, terror and crime. Likewise, representatives of the states discriminating most severely against women were at one with the rest in claiming to resolve to ensure that (by 2015) children everywhere, boys and girls alike, will be able to complete a full course of primary schooling, and that boys and girls will have equal access to education.[3]

The Millennium Declaration never rang more hollow than after the September 11 attacks the following year, offering harrowing evidence that the values so ringingly proclaimed, including the rejection of terror, are not nearly universal. The conclusion seems inevitable: any view that clusters of values such as those enumerated in the Declaration are universal is simply erroneous; it represents a mistaking of what many long to see as universal for what is all too obviously the case.

Scepticism in the face of such rhetoric about common values is surely needed. But indiscriminate scepticism has dangers all its own. It can lead those disenchanted by inflated claims about common values to swing over to imagining that societies in fact share no values whatsoever, and in turn to fatalistic acceptance of dismal projections. In this regard, too, the aftermath of the September 11 attacks proved instructive. True, they received no unanimous condemnation and evoked, instead, rejoicing by some and measured approval by others; but the vast outpouring of sympathy for the victims from so many countries was striking, as was the horror widely expressed at the transgression of the most fundamental moral requirements of respect for innocent life.

What might these moral requirements be? And might the ways in which they have been thought to be common to human societies have to be rethought in the aftermath of the attacks? In my book *Common Values*, I pointed to accumulating historical and anthropological research showing that the claim that societies share no values whatsoever is erroneous. No community can survive long without some limited set of internal constraints on violence, deceit and fraud, and some positive duties of mutual care and reciprocity, along with rudimentary procedures and standards for what is fair and just. These basic values are indispensable to human coexistence, though far from sufficient, at every level of personal and working life and of family, community, national and international relations.

As Charles Darwin pointed out in *The Descent of Man*, humans share with many animal species a disposition to provide mutual care and support; and 'No tribe would hold together if murders, robbery, treachery, &c., were common; consequently, such crimes within the limits of the same tribe are "branded with everlasting infamy".'[4] Darwin added, however, that such crimes 'excite no such sentiment beyond these limits'. Even the most fundamental constraints, such as those he mentioned, are shared in the sense that they have been indispensable everywhere within communities; but they are precisely not shared in another sense – that of being recognized by all as applying to outsiders, strangers, enemies. Indeed, they are not even shared by all within any single community.

These values have surely also been violated within all societies, even as they have often been held not to apply to outsiders and enemies at all. But any community – no matter how small or disorganized, no matter how hostile toward outsiders, no matter how cramped its perception of what constitutes childcare, say, or torture – requires at least rudimentary forms of nurturing and of internal curbs on violence, deceit and betrayal in order to survive.

The danger of ignoring the existence of shared but limited values takes many forms. It becomes easier to dismiss all talk about values as mere rhetoric, without making distinctions between vacuous invocations of vast lists of ideals and efforts to protect basic human rights. Such an attitude can facilitate, in turn, passivity in the face of atrocities, on the grounds that there can be no meaningful discourse about shared values or even understandings across cultural and linguistic boundaries. And many who dismiss the existence of shared values fall prey to unquestioning acceptance of erroneous prognostications and in turn to insufficiently carefully calibrated responses to stark violations of the most basic among these values.

Once we can conceive of these values as being so widely shared, we have a basis for dialogue and debate about how to extend them beyond the narrowest confines. These values can also offer criteria and a broadly comprehensible language for critique of existing practices. Within societies they can buttress arguments against leaving out certain groups when it comes to fundamental forms of respect. Across societal boundaries, taking these values seriously can support arguments that they should hold everywhere; and that cross-cultural critique is fully justified when it comes to political or religious practices such as torture, slavery, terrorism or human sacrifice, as well as to doctrines that endorse such practices.

III

In *The Age of Extremes*, Eric Hobsbawm held that the twentieth century 'was without doubt the most murderous century of which we have record, both by the scale, frequency, and length of the warfare which filled it, barely ceasing for a moment in the 1920s, but also by the unparalleled scale of the human catastrophes it produced, from the greatest famines in history to systematic genocide'. By contrast (much like those thinkers to whom Mill pointed as waxing lyrical about 'our enlightened age'), Hobsbawn called the nineteenth century a century 'of almost unbroken material, intellectual, and moral progress, that is to say of improvements in the conditions of civilized life'.[5] Yet such a characterization of their century would surely come as a surprise to Frederick Douglass, Abraham Lincoln, Susan B. Anthony, Joseph Conrad, and all who bore witness to evils such as slavery, war and genocide in their time.

Just as looking back at the nineteenth century in a purely benign light requires considerable air-brushing, so accounts of evils held to be unique in the twentieth century can blur the awareness of remarkable innovative countervailing forces for survival and for human flourishing. Even as hatred and violence flourished in the twentieth century, movements have arisen in response to these threats. Just as technological advances in weaponry and industry have magnified the threats, so technology has come to the aid of non-violent and restorative means of combating them. Non-governmental groups are using the internet to mobilize efforts such as that to ban landmines or to combat the resurgence of child kidnapping and slavery, and research has accelerated on ways to resolve conflicts, to foster restorative institutional change and to protect human rights.

Even in the past decade, new resources have come into being that could contribute greatly to a collective effort to deal with the forms of violence that now ravage communities the world over. We can now draw on the experience of the International Criminal Tribunals in Rwanda and the former Yugoslavia, of the Truth Commissions beginning in 1974, and especially on the South African Truth and Reconciliation Commission under the leadership of Archbishop Desmond Tutu. We are learning to recognize the ways in which basic values can be thwarted and eroded, and how violence can take over the human mind. New information comes to light each year from fields as diverse as neurology, genetics, primate studies, public health, psychiatry and politics about the indoctrination into growing tolerance for violence, pitilessness toward victims, and sometimes sheer pleasure in killing.

These countervailing forces, bringing to bear new institutions, movements and resources of leadership, research and diplomacy, are too often neglected by those writing to sum up the history of the twentieth century. Jonathan Glover's *Humanity: A Moral History of the Twentieth Century*, for example, dwelt primarily on that century's horrors – its wars, its genocides, its totalitarianisms.[6] Such books are important, and we ignore them at our peril. Even their one-sidedness is understandable, signalling their authors' recoil from cheap, unseeing optimism and reminding readers of unspeakable crimes and desperate human suffering from which it is so easy to turn aside. But they must be read alongside others, in full recognition of the antagonist modes of thought of which Mill spoke, in any effort to strive for the balance of perspectives that he saw as necessary.

In *The Twentieth Century*, J.M. Roberts addressed the difficulty of achieving a balanced perspective on a century of which one has been a part, and of making predictions for the future. He left out of the account neither the evils of that century nor the countervailing forces marshalled against them. All things considered, he regarded 'the bloodshed which is a central fact of the twentieth century' to be outweighed by what he saw as an extraordinary shift in human consciousness over the course of the century: the fact that increasing numbers the world over no longer believed suffering and unhappiness to be the preordained lot of human beings. He referred to factors such as the unprecedented and revolutionary growth in the world's wealth, the much greater choice open to individuals and the huge outflowing of information making possible a new degree of shared experience; and also to the vast differences these factors brought about for women, half the human race, 'even if much of it still remains only potential'.[7]

IV

Almost 2000 years ago, the Roman philosopher and statesman Seneca wrote to console a mother so distraught after the death of her son that she asked how she could go on living after such a loss.[8] He compared her choice – of whether to engage once more in life or give up – to that of whether or not to travel to a city such as Syracuse, on the island of Sicily. Just as that city had the balmiest of winters, a great harbour, many beauties and much that would fill a visitor with wonder, so its inhabitants endure oppressive and unwholesome summers, and suffer under the tyrant Dionysus, 'that destroyer of freedom, justice, and law, greedy of power even after knowing Plato'.

> You will see man in his audacity leaving nothing untried, and you will yourself be both a spectator and a participant in mighty enterprises ... But there, too, will be found a thousand plagues, banes of the body as well as of the mind, wars, robberies, poisons, shipwrecks, distempers of climate and of the body, untimely grief for those most dear and death – whether an easy one or only after pain and torture no one can tell. Now take counsel of yourself and weigh carefully the choice you would make; if you would reach these wonders, you must pass through these perils.

We still have the opportunity, as Seneca told Marcia she would have if she chose to engage in this world, of being both spectators and participants in 'mighty enterprises'. We still live in that world of contrast – a world of extraordinary beauties and wonders, but also of great evils and perils. True, a number of the plagues that ravaged communities in Seneca's time have been vanquished; but others such as that of HIV/AIDS have arisen, capable of reaching across the world with a speed far greater than that of any previous epidemic. Likewise, many tyrants have been defeated and self-rule is possible for more persons than ever in history; at the same time, regimes that deny peoples the most basic freedom and justice have more powerful means at their disposal than ever and can threaten liberty, even survival, far beyond their frontiers.

As in Seneca's time, so in ours, the difficulty can be one of seeing not merely the evils of our time, so often noted, but also the remarkable, innovative countervailing forces for survival and for human flourishing. Nothing assures that these countervailing forces will win out, but to neglect them is to invite needless and debilitating fatalism with respect to what the future holds in store, and a standing aside, a choice to be merely a spectator, not a participant, in times of crisis.

Initial reports indicate that the September 11 attacks brought about a shift in priorities in personal as well as collective life – a rethinking of what values matter most directly for purposes of survival and thriving. Such reactions went far beyond the instinctive first response of self-protection and of reaching out to immediate victims. Many reassessed not only their travel plans but also their commitment to work, family and community life. Psychologist Howard Gardner has pointed out that far more people on American college campuses are now considering careers in public service and teaching.[9] In the international debate, many argue that the new sense of urgency must govern not only immediate responses of self-protection against aggression but also efforts to deal with life-threatening conditions of poverty, disease and humanitarian emergencies worldwide. The question for the future will be one of how lasting and how far-reaching such reactions will be. As Joseph Stiglitz has stated,

> September 11 has resulted in a global alliance against terrorism. What we now need is not just an alliance *against* evil, but an alliance *for* something positive – a global alliance for reducing poverty and for creating a better environment, an alliance for creating a global society with more social justice.[10]

Notes

1. This chapter draws in part on three of my books: *A Strategy for Peace: Human Values and the Threat of War* (London: Vintage Books, 1989), *Mayhem: Violence as Public Entertainment* (Boulder, CO: Perseus Books, 1998) and *Common Values* (Columbia, MO: University of Missouri Press, 2002).
2. John Stuart Mill, 'Coleridge' (1840) in Marshall Cohen (ed.) *The Philosophy of John Stuart Mill* (New York: The Modern Library, 1961), p. 62.
3. Barbara Crossette, 'UN Meeting Ends with Declaration of Common Values', *New York Times*, September 9, 2000, pp. A1, A4.
4. Charles Darwin, *The Descent of Man* (1859) (Princeton, NJ: Princeton University Press, 1981), p. 101.
5. Eric Hobsbawm, *The Age of Extremes: A History of the World, 1914–1991* (New York: Pantheon Books, 1994), p. 13.
6. Jonathan Glover, *Humanity: A Moral History of the Twentieth Century* (London: Jonathan Cape, 1999).
7. J.M. Roberts, *The Twentieth Century: The History of the World, 1901–2000* (New York: Viking Press, 1999), pp. 839–40.
8. Seneca, 'To Marcia on Consolation', *Moral Essays II*, trans. John W. Basore (Cambridge, MA: Loeb Classical Library, 1932), pp. 59–63.

9. Howard Gardner, 'In the World of Work's Realignment, "good" careers move to the forefront', *Boston Globe*, February 24, 2002, p. E1.
10. Joseph E. Stiglitz, 'Globalism's Discontents', *The American Prospect*, Winter 2002, Special Supplement, p. A21.

CHAPTER 26

Narratives of Religion, Civilization and Modernity

Chris Brown

The purpose of this chapter is to examine some narratives of religion, civilization and modernity in the context of the conflict of which the events of September 11, 2001, were a manifestation. To begin with, it may be helpful to get a sense of how things look to the participants on the front line of this conflict.[1] How do they characterize what they are doing? What kind of stories do they tell in order to make sense of their own actions and that of their enemies?

Wars of Religion?

Osama bin Laden and al-Qaeda clearly place themselves and their enemies in a theological context. They understand themselves to be fighting on behalf of Islam against the enemies of God, in a struggle that has been under way since the time of the Prophet. Bin Laden's various videos are shot through with references to this struggle; the US is the 'Hubal of this age' (a reference to a stone idol that stood in the Kaaba in Mecca prior to the triumph of Islam) and, literally, 'Satanic'; that is, actually in league with the devil.[2] The US is only the most recent centre of idolatry, but by entering into an alliance with Satan has aligned itself with past enemies of God – Crusaders, Zionists, the imperialists who relieved the siege of Vienna in 1683 (on September 11/12, as it happens) and destroyed the Caliphate after the First World War (which the enemies of God promoted for this purpose). This perspective, of course, does not rule out a certain degree of political opportunism on the part of bin Laden; his recent emphasis on Palestine – as opposed to what appears to be his real focus, Saudi Arabia and the Gulf – is obviously intended to draw attention to that aspect of US foreign policy most opposed by the overwhelming majority of

Muslims, its support for Israel. Still, the sense that al-Qaeda members have that they are acting in the name of God and against God's enemies is real, and provides a partial explanation of their ruthlessness and cruelty – there is nothing like a sense of divine mission for overriding normal human inhibitions in this area. 'Kill them all and let God sort out the innocent', an orthodox Bishop was reported to have remarked during the Albigensian crusades.

Bin Laden's theology is, of course, somewhat unorthodox. His particular take on Islam is a minority position, condemned by the majority of 'responsible', 'respectable' Islamic religious leaders. At the same time, it clearly has quite substantial appeal to ordinary Muslims, even those who do not have a stake in the conflicts in Palestine and the Gulf. Even those Muslim leaders who condemned the terrorism of 9/11 – the majority – have been reluctant to see US power being used against 'the Muslims' in Afghanistan, and it is interesting that it is in these terms that the US is often condemned. Just as the Muslims of northern Nigeria identify themselves in religious rather than ethnic or cultural terms by naming their sons Osama, so the (Muslim) critics of US action in Afghanistan express their criticisms in religious terms – even though the US has been acting with the support of the indisputably Muslim Northern Alliance in that country. Muslims killing each other is one thing, Americans joining some Muslims in killing other Muslims is quite another.

Predictably, Western leaders have worked hard to avoid characterizing the current conflict in religious terms. Rarely have Muslim leaders been in such demand; President Bush and Prime Minister Blair have taken every opportunity to involve cooperative Muslims in the various state occasions at which the victims of 9/11 were mourned (rightly, since there were many Muslims killed in the Twin Towers) and have tried hard to get their approval for the coalition's actions in Afghanistan and elsewhere. Those Western leaders who have gone off message have been greeted with stern disapproval. Italy's Silvio Berlusconi was metaphorically carpeted for making the kind of observations about Western superiority to Islam that were only the mirror image of the positions held by many, perhaps most, Muslims. George W. Bush was briefly in disgrace for referring to the Coalition's actions as a 'crusade'; admittedly this was naive, even though it seems doubtful that he was using the term as anything other than a generic description of morally driven action, but had he defended himself by making the point that the original Crusades were launched partly in response to Islamic aggression in the Levant, that many Muslim leaders at the time allied with the Crusaders, and that the latter were no more (nor less) violent than their enemies, he would have compounded the offence.

As these remarks suggest, the West's handling of the religious dimension of the current conflict has been based on a rather irritating, if perhaps politically understandable, double standard. Christians such as Tony Blair and George W. Bush – undeniably sincere in their beliefs, but living in a world where religious conviction is tinged with irony – cannot express their own deeply held convictions in explicitly Christian terms for fear of alienating the decidedly un-ironic beliefs of their coalition partners in Pakistan and the Arab world. The sensibilities of the latter – however irrational – have to be respected; and, indeed, respect in this case seems to mean actually pandering to the irrational. The implicit assumption seems to be that it would be both unfair and unsafe to subject Muslim beliefs, attitudes and behaviour to the kind of robust criticism common in Western societies. The most perfect expression of this kind of reverse racism was given by the British journalist Robert Fisk, who, when beaten up by some Afghan refugees simply for being a Westerner, explained afterwards that he understood their position, given the indignities and violence to which they had been subjected.[3] It is doubtful whether he would have been equally tolerant of the actions of the – astonishingly few – New Yorkers who turned on Muslims in the immediate aftermath of September 11. The obvious explanation is that Muslims as individuals cannot be held morally responsible for their acts in the way that New Yorkers can – as Fisk puts it, denying their capacity to be moral agents with perhaps unintentional clarity, their brutality 'was entirely the product of others, of us'. More on this later. In the meantime, if not defined in terms of religion, how have Western leaders understood the current crisis?

No Clash of Civilizations

President Bush succinctly answered this rhetorical question in his post-9/11 address to the joint houses of Congress: 'This is the world's fight. This is civilization's fight.' The war on terrorism is constructed on this basis: on the one side is the civilized world; on the other, those who employ terror, whomsoever they may be and in whatever cause. Thus the particular content of the ideology of the terrorist is rendered irrelevant, and the specifically religious content of al-Qaeda's position is not to be answered, save by the generalized assertion that all of the world's religions are part of the civilization that al-Qaeda has attacked – the readings from the Qur'an that Tony Blair has frequently called in aid have been designed to support this position; as he put it on October 2 to the Labour Party Conference, 'Jews, Muslims and Christians are all children of Abraham.' Presumably some other patriarch, Noah perhaps, will be needed to pull Hindus and Buddhists into this particular big tent.

It should be noted that for *neither* side in this conflict is a 'clash of civilizations', in Samuel Huntington's terms, taking place, even if the *Sunday Times*, in reprinting his original article with this title, described it as 'uncannily prescient' (October 14, 2001).[4] Neither the Coalition against Terror nor the al-Qaeda network regard each other as civilized. From the Coalition's point of view the various civilizations identified by Huntington are all on the same side against the forces of barbarism, the terrorists. From al-Qaeda's perspective the conflict is between the true followers of God and God's enemies, who include those so-called Muslims who align themselves with the United States and, worse, have allowed the US and the UK to pollute the sacred soil of Arabia. The pluralism of Huntington's original conception of a clash of civilizations is absent from the narratives of *all* the participants in this particular conflict. For this reason, his solution to the 'clash' – a pluralistic recognition of difference within an international order that de-emphasizes universal notions such as human rights – appeals to none of the combatants currently engaged in Afghanistan and elsewhere; this particular version of international society depends upon a mutual recognition of legitimacy that is absent in this case. Neither terrorists nor Satanists can expect to be recognized as legitimate participants in a dialogue of civilizations. Huntington's more recent identification of this as the 'age of Muslim wars' may be more to the point – so long as it is understood, as it is by Huntington, that most Muslim wars involve Muslims on both sides, and many involve only Muslims.[5] Narratives of religion and civilization are employed by the participants in the current conflict, but not in ways that make it possible to understand the perspectives of both parties under the same heading. Religion and civilization are understood by both sides in ways that ensure that they do not apply to the other. There is, however, one narrative to which, rather surprisingly, both sides can relate, and that is a narrative of modernity. Clearly underpinning the speeches of Western leaders such as Blair and Bush is the conviction that they represent the modern world while al-Qaeda are, in some sense, a throwback to an earlier time, with a medieval theology and atavistic notions of society – Tony Blair's aforementioned speech to the Labour Party is a model in this respect, tying in the war against terrorism with a critique of the Taliban's rule in Afghanistan, extended meditations on the nature of globalization and a homily on the importance to the modern world of the international community acting with one voice in this matter. In this respect, at least, these leaders are representative of Western society more generally – even critics of US action in Afghanistan generally condemn also the so-called primitivism of the Taliban.

The contrast between the modern and the primitive works well also for the responsible and respectable Muslim leaders who wish to distance themselves from bin Laden without, of course, distancing themselves from the faith which he claims to profess. They can describe him and his followers as misguidedly working to an understanding of Islam that is inappropriate for the modern world where, for example, the notion of *jihad* is best understood in terms of spiritual rather than physical struggle. Moreover, they can build from this base to make the further, political, point that these primitive ideas would have no appeal to the majority of Arabs or Muslims were it not for Western support for Israel and for corrupt Muslim leaders, although this latter point, unlike the former, tends not to be made openly in the Arab world. It is the insensitivity of the West, particularly the US, to the legitimate grievances of the Muslim world that allows al-Qaeda to flourish. This story, of course, links up with the one Robert Fisk tells about his role as the victim of Afghan violence. The people who beat him up were behaving badly but they were goaded into this bad behaviour by the Americans – indeed if he had been in their position, the victim of American bombing, he would have done the same thing – but to respond to the events of September 11 in the same way would be intolerable, because modern people are to be held morally responsible for their actions and ought not to allow themselves to be provoked, while primitives do not know any better. The policy advice implicit in this narrative is clear: while primitives are unpredictable and violent now, the hope is that if we behave better to them they will become more like us – in which case they will no longer have a free pass allowing them to beat up Robert Fisk and carry out other atrocities.

Perhaps surprisingly, to complete the circle, a narrative based on a contrast between modernity and primitivism can also be espoused, albeit not in these terms, by al-Qaeda, the Taliban and other so-called 'fundamentalist' Islamic groups such as Hamas in Palestine. In this case, of course, primitivism is read as a term of approval. Part of the religious message these groups are putting forward is that they represent a kind of purified, uncompromising Islam which can quite readily be characterized as primitive and atavistic insofar as it is intended to re-establish contact with the faith of the Prophet and the original community of

Believers. The idea of primitive nomadic peoples burning out the corruption associated with city life has been a regular trope of the sociology of Islamic societies since at least the time of the philosopher, historian and sociologist Ibn Khaldun (1332–1406 CE), and bin Laden's presentation of himself in the mountains of Afghanistan wearing traditional dress, carrying a rifle and often on horseback plays to this image; probably consciously.

Narratives of Modernity

At this point doubts begin to arise; it is generally good policy to worry about any account that seems to serve quite so many interests, and bin Laden's home video collection seems a good place to begin to question a narrative of modernity and primitivism in which he features as a primitive. In these videos he portrays himself as the fearless leader of an incorrupt and incorruptible movement bearing down on the corruption of the Saud family and their satanic American supporters – but Osama bin Laden is himself the product of the wealthiest strata of Saudi society, and many of his most active supporters are drawn from the professional classes. Nothing unusual about that, it might be thought – think of Lenin and the Leninists in 1917, very few actual workers there – but what is commonplace for revolutionaries sits rather less well with the supposed representatives of a purified religion. The very extensive use of video technology and the internet, and the sophisticated management of relations with the Arabic-language TV station al-Jazeera, suggests a decidedly unprimitive sense of public relations. It is interesting that Mullah Omar, the Taliban leader and a rather more plausible primitive, has eschewed such modern inventions and, in keeping with the traditional Islamic ban on images that represent the human figure, has refused to allow himself to be photographed. If bin Laden were prepared to cite a Shi'ite precedent he could point to the iconography of the Ayatollah Khomeini in support of the appearance of his own face on so many banners and T-shirts, but even so there is something suspiciously modern about his sense of PR.

Once this suspicion is let off the leash, the narrative of the modern and the primitive collapses – if al-Qaeda were genuinely primitive we would not have heard of them, or certainly not in the way in which they have made themselves known to the world at large. Rather, Osama bin Laden is as modern a figure as Tony Blair, but represents a different *kind* of modernity. This is the key point – contrary to a great deal of thinking in this area, there are potentially a number of ways of being modern, and not just the one way espoused by the liberal, largely post-Christian, humanist West. The world view of the latter has, indeed, dominated the last half-century to such an extent that it has ceased to be understood as the particular perspective it is. The application of scientific knowledge and rationality to production within the context of a capitalist economy; the subjection of all accounts of the ultimate ends of life to the same rationality, which has induced a self-consciously ironic dimension to even deeply held religious and social beliefs; the notion that representative forms of democracy are the only legitimate basis for political power; and the spread of a human rights culture in which the privileges once extended only to rich and powerful white males are understood as legitimate only if universally available – this actually rather disparate set of ideas and propositions has come to be seen not as disparate, and thereby separable, but as a package that, taken as such, gives meaning to the notion of modernity within Western society and, with the onset of globalization, within a nascent global society.

However, even a sketchy knowledge of the history of ideas, and indeed of the political history, of the last two centuries reveals that the various elements of the package can, in fact, be taken apart and either allowed to stand alone or be recombined in different ways to create alternative but equally 'modern' accounts of society. The authoritarian modernizers of the second half of the nineteenth century, and the fascist movements of the first half of the twentieth, wanted, in different ways, to create industrial societies devoid of irony, without representative institutions, and without extended human rights, and in this they are followed by contemporary 'fundamentalist' movements. Such fundamentalists want a world with modern technology, but with scientific rationality confined to the technical; a world with IT, mass media and 'infotainment', but with its content strictly regulated; a world where the community of Believers exercises political power, but non-believers are disenfranchised; and – a consistent theme of fundamentalism of all varieties – a world where women remain subjected to men, and transgressive sexual identities are delegitimized. In short, they want a world devoid of irony, a world in which individuals do not distance themselves from their own beliefs, and they see no reason why such a world cannot encompass the creature comforts of modernity, which is why it is not uncommon for fundamentalists to do rather well for themselves – we are familiar with this from the lifestyles of Christian TV evangelists in the US, but it seems from news reports that Mullah Omar's compound in Kandahar was also, as an estate agent might say, well-appointed.

So, are al-Qaeda and their ilk 'Islamo-fascists' as writers as diverse as Francis Fukuyama and Christopher Hitchens have suggested?[6] This designation correctly links such groups to alternative, authoritarian notions of modernity and is reasonable enough, so long as it is understood that there are also 'Christo-fascist', 'Judaeo-fascist' and 'Hindu-fascist' movements at loose in the world; it should also be noted that the specific beliefs of these modern groups make it more difficult for them to form cross-cultural alliances than was the case with their predecessors. Islamo-fascists are the most prominent of these groups and, perhaps, the most ruthless and unpleasant – not because of any features specific to Islam as a religion, but because of the particular conditions to be found within the so-called world of Islam; in particular the failure of any state or society with a majority Islamic population to offer a convincing, non-fundamentalist model of modernity. What keeps Christian and Jewish fundamentalism at bay is the fact that Western society provides satisfactory outlets for its youth either in the mainstream or in anti-establishment but non-fundamentalist counter-cultures.[7] The Mohammed Attas of the post-Christian West generally end up in merchant banks or working for Greenpeace. Hindu fundamentalists have become the government of India, and have found themselves obliged to compromise and temporize in order to stay in power in a state where the commitment to the rule of law and constitutionalism runs deep. Islamic movements have never found themselves in such a position.

So, in conclusion, are the forces of radical Islam doomed to be defeated, and, if not, what can be done to bring about such a defeat? If they actually were primitives, then it would be possible to believe that the tide of history will, eventually, leave them stranded – and much Western thinking seems to make this assumption. But if they represent an alternative modernity then no such guarantee is available. Fascism and National Socialism did not collapse of their own contradictions, but rather succumbed to superior force after a struggle that, had it been in a better cause, one would have to describe as heroic. The willingness of the al-Qaeda to continue fighting when all is lost can be seen in this light. Therefore, the opponents of Islamo-fascism have to be prepared to fight for what they believe in, and the intelligent use of military force will, inevitably, be one component of the struggle.

It is, however, of the utmost importance that such an application of force does not betray the values of the conception of modernity that it is designed to promote. In part, this is a matter of following, as far as possible, the rules of war and not endorsing gratuitous violence, but it also involves preserving a sense of irony, which is ultimately what distinguishes 'our' modernity from 'theirs'. To have an ironic commitment to the values associated with freedom of thought and human rights means to hold these values wholeheartedly, while acknowledging that they cannot rest upon some ultimate sense of what is true or false. To believe passionately in something while holding on to the thought that one might, just possibly, be wrong; to be able to insert a degree of distance between oneself and one's beliefs, is terribly difficult but also liberating, and the capacity to function in the world in this way is precisely what fundamentalists lack.

For this reason it is important that we recognize all the different kinds of heroes in the current struggle: the NYFD, the NYPD and Rudy Giuliani (the heroes of 'Ground Zero') for sure; Tony Blair, perhaps; but also those who have preserved a sense of distance, some of the critics of action in Afghanistan – not the Fisks who apologize for tyranny, or the usual America-haters, but the more thoughtful critics who have no illusions about the dangers of al-Qaeda but have legitimate doubts about the ability of military power to combat the network. More controversially, the humorists and satirists who have punctured the tendency to self-righteousness in our thinking about 9/11, a tendency closely aligned to fundamentalism, should also be recognized. Here the splendid headlines and stories of *The Onion* ('America's Finest News Source' online at <www.theonion.com>) define the right attitude: its first post-9/11 issue of September 26, 2001, contained such expressions of determination as 'America Vows to Defeat Whoever It Is We're at War With', the stern 'Hijackers Surprised to Find Selves in Hell: "We Expected Eternal Paradise for This" Say Suicide Bombers', as well as the helpful 'God Angrily Clarifies "Don't Kill" Rule'. Such irreverence is, literally, what we should be fighting for – the sense of humour it reveals offers a stark contrast to, say, bin Laden's grim amusement, captured on video, at the fact that many of the hijackers of 9/11 did not realize they were on a suicide mission. It exemplifies the capacity to step back and recognize one's own occasional absurdity without allowing this distancing to undermine one's basic values, and it is precisely this which distinguishes a narrative of modernity that endorses and sustains human freedom from its fundamentalist alternatives.

Notes

1. I am grateful to Toni Erskine, Fred Halliday, Andrew Mason and Michael Yahuda for their helpful comments – but, of course, responsibility remains entirely mine.

2. Michael Scott Duran's 'Somebody Else's Civil War' in James F. Hoge Jnr and Gideon Rose (eds) *How Did This Happen?: Terrorism and the New War* (New York: Public Affairs, 2001) is an excellent guide to al-Qaeda's understanding of Islam.
3. Robert Fisk, 'My Beating by Refugees is a Symbol of the Hatred and Fury of this Filthy War' *Independent*, December 10, 2001.
4. Samuel Huntington, 'The Clash of Civilizations', *Foreign Affairs*, vol. 72 (1993), pp. 22–49; *The Clash of Civilizations and the Remaking of World Order* (New York: Simon and Schuster, 1996).
5. Samuel Huntington, 'The Age of Muslim Wars' *Newsweek*, Special Davos Edition, December 2001–February 2002, pp. 6–13.
6. Francis Fukuyama, 'The Real Enemy' *Newsweek,* Special Davos Edition, December 2001–February 2002, pp. 58–63; Christopher Hitchens, 'The Fascist Sympathies of the Soft Left', *Spectator*, September 29, 2001, pp. 10–11.
7. Jewish fundamentalists *in Israel*, however, have proved as violent as their Muslim counterparts.

CHAPTER 27

Unnecessary Suffering

Andrew Linklater

The violent acts of September 11 and the war against al-Qaeda and the Taliban are unique in raising profound questions about how modern societies should deal with many diverse forms of human suffering. Modern societies face the challenge of ensuring that efforts to protect innocent civilians from terrorist attacks do not damage the moral ideal of freeing all human beings from unnecessary suffering. They face the challenge of ensuring that the 'civilizing process' of eradicating indefensible violence does not have the paradoxical effect of creating 'decivilizing processes' that cause many human beings avoidable distress and injury.[1]

These moral concerns have dominated public discussion from the time a broad coalition formed to wage war against al-Qaeda and the Taliban. Relief organizations warned of the dangers of added misery to the Afghan people, and powerful voices emphasized the moral duty to spare civilians unnecessary suffering in war. Fears were raised that the military conflict and accompanying statements about a war between the civilized world and the evil of terrorism would encourage pernicious representations of Muslims. The arrest, treatment and future trial of terrorist suspects has produced concerns about threats to civil liberties and the rule of law. The coalition with governments which are guilty of human rights violations has raised serious questions about the West's claim to be the leading custodian of humane values. Many observers have argued the war against terrorism will lack legitimacy unless the powerful nations undertake to reduce global inequalities and end extreme poverty. And, not least, many have insisted that the global war against terrorism cannot succeed without bold initiatives to secure justice for the Palestinian people.

The events of September 11 have raised large questions for a world which made important progress in the twentieth century in making avoidable suffering a moral problem for humanity as a whole. The development of the international law of war and international criminal law, the global human rights regime, and (more controversially) an emerging norm of humanitarian intervention are evidence of progress in regarding unnecessary suffering as a central problem which all states should endeavour to solve. A crucial – perhaps the central – question raised by September 11 is whether the vision of a world in which fewer human beings are burdened with preventable suffering has been dealt a blow from which it will not easily recover.

Four discourses which emerged in the days after September 11 cast some light on how this question might be answered: the narrative of the war of civilization against evil, the discourse of the international duties of liberal states, the language of multiculturalism and religious tolerance, and the narrative of Great Power responsibilities for promoting global reform. The interaction between these discourses casts important light on the current relationship between 'civilizing' and 'decivilizing' processes in the current world order.

The War of Civilization against Evil

The UN Secretary-General, Kofi Annan, described the atrocities as 'an attack on the whole of humanity, and all humanity has a stake in defeating the forces behind it'.[2] Others called the terrorist attacks a 'crime against humanity' and stressed the crucial legal idea that the whole human race has a common interest in the apprehension and punishment of those that commit terrible acts of violence. However, very different policy conclusions can be drawn from these comments. The essence of the first discourse was captured in a striking claim made by Edward Luttwak in a television interview in the immediate aftermath of the September 11 attacks. The United States, he argued, had looked on bemused as the Taliban violated the rights of women and destroyed sacred monuments. But September 11 changed everything. By failing to hand over those responsible for the atrocities, the Taliban acquired 'the right to be destroyed'.

Appeals to this language are hardly surprising, and it is scarcely credible that any US president could have withstood public pressure to attack the Taliban. But the first discourse legitimated what Dick Cheney called a 'dirty war' with unclear objectives and an indefinite timescale. For the more hawkish members of the US administration these objectives included an appetite for concluding the unfinished war against Saddam Hussein.

Fears that the United States would unleash terrible violence leading to tens of thousands of civilian casualties and the total disregard for human rights were expressed in the week of the terrorist attacks.[3] As it was, wiser counsel prevailed in the first stage of the war, and in that period three dissenting discourses emerged in opposition to unsettling 'decivilizing processes'.

Liberal States and their Humanitarian Obligations

The first of these discourses made the simple point that the terrorist attacks could have been depicted as criminal acts rather than as acts of war. Defending this theme, Geoffrey Robertson called for a revised 'Lockerbie solution' in which terrorist suspects would be tried in courts of law which could enjoy legitimacy in the eyes of the non-Western world by including Muslim judges.[4] The point was that the discourse of war against evil ran against powerful trends since the end of the bipolar era to strengthen international criminal law. Anti-Western sentiment, not least in the Muslim world, was thought likely to increase given further evidence of the United States' uneven regard for international law.

Concerned about decivilizing processes, this legalist language reminded liberal states of their obligations to non-liberal societies in times of war. Legal and moral obligations to prevent unnecessary suffering to civilians and duties of care to prisoners of war were emphasized, as were long-term duties not to abandon Afghanistan to the warlords once again.

Reports that international lawyers were involved in decisions about the selection of military targets seemed to suggest that modern war must be fought (or be believed to be fought) with greater respect for moral constraints than in the past. The just war tradition has long argued that civilian deaths are morally defensible as long as the level stands in proportion to the goals for which the war is fought, although deciding the level of acceptable civilian casualties has never been an exact science. There is now reason to think that informed Western publics are less willing than ever to believe official pronouncements on proportionality and less inclined to tolerate what they think is the unnecessary suffering of civilians.

The cynic might protest that targeting errors and the reliance on cluster bombs hardly dented public support for the war in the US and the UK. Western publics, it might be thought, are less concerned about the plight of 'distant strangers' than about keeping their own military personnel out of harm's way. There is much truth in this, but the cynic protests too much. With the 'Kosovo wobble' fresh in their minds, the war was conducted with a mixture of caution and anxiety, recognizing that public support is notoriously fickle and likely to weaken when casualties 'on either side' reach unacceptable levels, however defined.

It is vital to remember that the war against al-Qaeda and the Taliban brought humanitarian aid to a sudden end, and many humanitarian organizations called for the suspension of the war so that the vulnerable could receive essential supplies following prolonged drought. The refugee problem served to compound the crisis. The United States and its coalition partners responded that humanitarian relief would not reach the endangered while the Taliban remained in power. But the decision to place significant numbers of Afghans in harm's way prompted questions about the coalition's long-term obligations to post-Taliban Afghanistan.

The decision to cooperate with the Northern Alliance to defeat the Taliban led to deep concerns about its fitness to govern given its past human rights record and involvement in the global drugs trade. An immediate issue following the collapse of Mazar-e-Sharif was whether the victorious would slaughter Taliban prisoners, and the question of whether the victors have failed in their legal and moral duty of care to prisoners of war – unlawful combatants, as the US administration has called them – awaits a satisfactory answer.[5] Suspicions that the liberal world does not wish to be encumbered by humanitarian law of war in wars with illiberal societies have not been allayed. However, discussions about the need for a broad-based coalition government found support during the war against the Taliban, as did duties to support the political and economic reconstruction of post-Taliban Afghanistan most simply by despatching this complex task to the United Nations. But the liberal world's willingness to make a long-term commitment to the reconstruction of Afghanistan has yet to be severely tested.

Religious Tolerance and Multiculturalism

A second dissenting discourse emerged because official claims about the war against evil appeared to inflame or legitimate xenophobic and racist sentiments. A related factor was the evidence that a version of Huntington's thesis about the possible clash of civilizations seemed to enjoy considerable support in the Muslim world. In response to the decivilizing effects of the so-called 'clash of civilizations' and evidence of increasing violence against Muslims, this second dissenting discourse defended the ideals of religious tolerance and multi-culturalism.

In his speech to the Labour Party Conference three weeks after the terrorist attacks, Tony Blair stressed the need to distinguish terrorism from Islam, and this theme was subsequently highlighted in a series of articles in Middle Eastern newspapers written in the hope of winning the so-called 'propaganda war'. Blair spoke of the need for 'greater understanding between nations and between faiths, adding that '[it] is time the West confronted its ignorance of Islam. Jews, Muslims and Christians are all children of Abraham.' His claim that the 'true followers of Islam are our brothers and sisters in this struggle', and that 'bin Laden is no more obedient to the proper teaching of the Koran than those crusaders of the twelfth century who pillaged and murdered, represented the teaching of the gospel', appealed for a global interreligious alliance against international terrorism.[6] In newspaper articles and public statements, Blair referred to the peaceful nature of Islam, adding that its prohibitions of violence against innocent civil-ians formed part of the common moral ground with the Christian tradition.

Without question, the task of maintaining a diverse and precarious military coalition was one reason for such pronouncements, but it would be a mistake to suppose their function was just strategic. However, interesting claims emerged in the aftermath of Blair's appeal for an intercivilizational alliance against terrorism. Salman Rushdie's twist on this theme was that the attacks of September 11 were inextri-cably linked with 'paranoid Islam' which is 'the fastest-growing version of Islam in the world' and the lamentable consequence of the failure to 'be reconciled with modernity'. Rushdie referred to arguments for 'a reformation in the Muslim world' and added that modernist Muslims had a duty to resist fanatics who had 'hijacked' their religion.[7]

The plea for religious tolerance has been played out in interesting ways, not least in the UK as the debate over the future of faith schools, loyalty tests for immigrants, the law of blasphemy and legislation against the incitement of religious hatred all reveal.[8] Here we see in national microcosm the outlines of what seems certain to be a prolonged global debate about the long-term relationship between some versions of Islam and secular modernity.

Remaking World Order

The final dissenting discourse has its origins in media reports of Palestinians celebrating the violence of September 11, in the obvious levels of support for bin Laden in the Muslim world and in the unwillingness of many in the West to applaud the idea that the terrorist attacks could be explained away as the work of 'fanatics' dedicated to 'violence and savagery'.[9] This last notion implied that the attacks of September 11 were as unintelligible (not least because they were suicide attacks) as they were reprehensible. The language of evil carries the obvious implication that there is nothing in the behaviour of the victims or the wider society which could be said to explain – or to have contributed to – the acts of violence.

In fact, the reasons for bin Laden's hatred of the United States were well-known and the motives of his supporters were not hard to understand.[10] The deeply controversial question, especially in the United States, was whether the United States could reasonably conclude – as the language of evil would have it – that there is no need to re-examine its own role in world politics. In a bold challenge to this view, Chalmers Johnson argued that it would be a mistake to 'think that we in the United States are entirely blameless for what happened' on September 11. Johnson went on to argue that the 'suicidal assassins ... did not "attack America", as our political leaders and the news media like to maintain; they attacked US foreign policy'. For Johnson, September 11 was a form of 'blowback' as the United States reaped the rewards of its imperial policy towards radical Third World societies including, crucially, support for state terrorism.[11]

The call for national soul-searching was unlikely to command widespread support in a society clamouring for revenge and disposed to regard such comments as deeply unpatriotic. Be that as it may, its chief merit was to raise the challenging question of whether the language of evil and fanaticism soothed the US public and distracted attention away from the urgent question of how a post-imperial foreign policy could tackle at least some of the root causes of terrorism. The notion that the Great Powers should be 'Great Responsibles' striving to create a world order which would seem legitimate in the eyes of the global poor did not go unsupported. In his speech to the Labour Party Conference, Blair said 'the starving, the wretched, the dispossessed, the ignorant, those living in want and squalor from the deserts of Northern Africa to the slums of Gaza, to the mountain ranges of Afghanistan: they too are our cause'.[12] Blair spoke of the need to combine military action with global reform. For his part, President Bush maintained that a Palestinian state which was compatible with Israel's security was part of the long-term vision of US foreign policy, only to be accused of appeasement by Sharon, as violence between Israel and Palestine intensified.

It would be foolish to discount the possibility of a renewed effort to broker a new deal between Israel and the Palestinians but not to discount major global reform. Unsurprisingly, Blair's references to the importance of the Kyoto Protocol in his Conference speech did not seize the imagination of the US administration, and a break with neo-liberal economic fundamentalism is not about to occur. Nor is the US commitment to multilateralism guaranteed, given that the Bush administration has repeatedly said it will 'go it alone' if necessary. In his Party Conference speech, Blair said the current time 'is an extraordinary moment for progressive politics' despite the misery of September 11, but there are few reasons for optimism. Compassion seems set to lose out in the struggle to deal with threats to security.

The Significance of the Revolt of the West

We have to ask how far legitimate efforts to combat terrorism have jeopardized other values of importance. These include the duty to protect individuals from violence and unnecessary suffering in war, from human rights violations caused by their own governments, from demeaning representations whether they originate inside or outside their societies, and from the harmful consequences of general indifference to poverty and disadvantage. We need to ask how far the discourse of war as against criminality has damaged the ideal of a world legal order that upholds the ideal of justice between cultures, how far the willingness to put large numbers of civilians in harm's way and to risk humanitarian relief has increased anti-Western sentiment, how far an alliance with unsavoury regimes has damaged Western claims to be custodians of human rights, how far claims that the coalition is not engaged in demeaning Islam and the suggestion that the majority of Muslims have more in common with Western liberals than with the exponents of 'paranoid Islam' suggest will prevail, how far anything will be done to reduce global inequalities and to deal with environmental harm, and, finally, how far the affluent West can escape the charge of indifference to the poor and to the plight of the Palestinians. These are the larger values at stake in the war against al-Qaeda and the Taliban.

The exponent of *realpolitik* might argue that it is absurd to expect Western states to carry such a moral burden. Their first priority is to provide for the security of their citizens under conditions of terrible uncertainty. On this score, states have discharged their primary obligations by creating a broad coalition of states against global terrorism, by promoting new forms of intelligence cooperation and by freezing the assets of suspected terrorist organizations as part of the invisible war against terrorism. Here is evidence of real progress in making unnecessary suffering which results from indiscriminate violence a matter for the whole world. From this standpoint, those that focus centrally on civil liberties, human rights and the international law of war miss the central point which is that liberal democracies are at war with a new threat which requires unusual remedies involving unwelcome but unavoidable compromises.

We have seen how different discourses since September 11 have resisted efforts to confine the moral agenda and the public debate to traditional security concerns. We have seen how these discourses have been used to widen the discussion to include the ideals of promoting human security and conforming with liberal principles of human decency in times of war. This is what the clash between the different discourses is ultimately about.

The claims for human decency are crucially important if we regard the violence of September 11 (as well as support for the Taliban and al-Qaeda amongst Muslim groups) as the most recent, violent manifestation of the unfinished 'revolt against the West'. It is worth remembering that the whole species is now enclosed within a sovereign states system. Since the era of decolonization, new states have been among the most vocal champions of state sovereignty, and some of the keenest advocates of non-intervention are to be found in the Third World. But a sense of exclusion from the benefits of Western modernity has long been widespread amongst the peoples of the new states, and deep resentment of the West's cultural dominance and antipathy to its social and political values have been no less important. This hostility to Western values seems to have grown in recent years, and most notably in the Muslim world – hence the continuing revolt against the West exemplified by the unexpected atrocities of September 11.

To ask if progress in defeating global terrorism may jeopardize other worthwhile objectives is to ask if the means of combating terrorism seem likely to deepen non-Western grievances about global inequalities of power and wealth and the relentless incursion of Western secular values. It is to ask whether decivilizing processes will deepen

Governance Hotspots: Challenges We Must Confront in the Post-September 11 World[1]

Saskia Sassen

Travelling around the world since September 11, I have found one theme becoming louder and louder in many places outside the US, both in the global north and global south, by critics of the attacks who share our horror and do not want to see such violence ever again anywhere in the world. The theme is, in a nutshell, that the attacks on the US and the war against organized terrorism should not keep us from seeing and remembering all the other struggles going on and the larger landscape of rage and hopelessness engulfing more and more people. This theme is either not welcome in the US, starting with the government, or is seen as being a chance to re-run old slogans. And yet, what one hears and reads outside the US should be attended to and positioned as a 'decentred' view; not necessarily an opposite view, but one that does not have the US suffering and interests at its centre. As social scientists we should be able to do this, even at a time when this is not politically correct. In my research about globalization, I have come to see that decentring the production of knowledge about globalization is crucial for a better analysis.

Moving on after September 11 will require more than just eliminating organized terrorist networks and providing humanitarian aid, crucial as these two interventions are. There is a much larger set of issues that needs to be addressed – by world and country leaders, by the supranational system, by NGOs, by global civil society, by corporate economic actors. Many of these issues are specific to each country and are inevitably centred in the internal dynamics and struggles of each; others concern the further development of global governance institutions. Most of these issues precede September 11: they involve often long-term trends and conditions. September 11 has repositioned them in a more urgent landscape: the inexplicability of these terrorist attacks on US soil has had the effect of an incipient recoding of the miseries of the global south as potential causes. But this still leaves us very far from an acknowledgement of any responsibility by the US government and corporations for these miseries.

Here I address what have emerged as two difficult governance hotspots in this larger context of challenge. Examining them is a way of dissecting the nature of the challenge and identifying specific governance deficits. The two issues are, first, the debt trap in which a growing number of governments are caught and which leads to, among other things, a sharp growth in illegal trafficking of people; and, second, immigration, a process caught in a whole series of new contradictions. Both of these will require innovations in our conceptions of governance. Both show that as the world is more interconnected, we will need more multilateralism and internationalism, but that these will have to consist of multiple and often highly specialized cross-border governance regimes, and that simply relying on overarching institutions will not do. While I confine myself here to the role of governments, it is clear that new forms of collaboration with civil society and supranational institutions are part of this effort.

I examine these two governance hotspots from the perspective of the countries of the global north and their self-interest rather than broader issues of social justice and humanitarian concern. The latter are crucial, yet utilitarian arguments might be more persuasive to many. The notion that addressing debt and immigration is in the self-interest of the global north, rather than simply a matter of social justice *vis-à-vis* the global south, is the more difficult argument to make. Indeed, such an argument has not quite been developed and I do not claim to succeed at it here.[2] What follows are some elements towards such an argument.[3] It is important to emphasize that one's positionality does make a difference. If I were to produce an account from the perspective of a country in the global south, the issues would not be exactly the same. At the same time, examining these particular issues as part of a larger discussion about September 11 and its meaning is one way of decentring the discussion in that it is not exclusively centred in the suffering and losses experienced by the US. The policy position this leads to is one that emphasizes the mutual interests of the global south and north and hence the desirability of multilateralism and internationalism.

Interdependence

Among the many issues that September 11 brought to the fore is the fact that globalization has not only facilitated the global flows of capital, goods, information and business people, as was the intent of its 'framers': it has also facilitated a variety of other entanglements. The list is long, and what follows are just some of the more dramatic instances, in no particular order. Global trade, tourism and migration have enabled diseases and pests present in many parts of the global south which we in the rich countries could forget about, to come north: tuberculosis is back in the US and typhoid fever is in the UK, the encephalitis-producing Nile mosquito has made its first appearance in the global north and so have a growing number of others. As governments become poorer they depend more and more on the remittances of immigrants in the global north and hence have little interest in the management of emigration and illegal trafficking of people. The pressures to be competitive make governments in poor countries cut their health, education and social budgets, thereby further delaying development and stimulating emigration and trafficking. Powerful states cannot fully escape bricolage terrorism nor global organized terrorism. In brief, the interdependencies are many, they are multiplying and they bring the socioeconomic devastation of the global south closer to the global north.

Terrorism is a distinct and extreme act which requires a specific ingredient, and is hence fed by much more than socioeconomic devastation. The globally organized and coordinated terrorism of September 11 is an even more extreme act than much of the more localized and more available forms of terrorism we see around the world today. The added ingredient for terrorism can take shape in many different ways. Further, terrorism may not always be as purposeful as in the case of its main forms today, whether September 11, the earlier IRA actions in Northern Ireland, or the ongoing acts by Hamas and Jihad in Israel.

Against this context, socioeconomic devastation cannot be seen as a cause for terrorism, but it can be seen as a breeding ground for extreme responses, including illegal trafficking in people and the successful recruitment of young people for terrorist activity, both random and organized. An example of extreme response was what we now know was the case with the militarized gangs in the aftermath of the Bosnian conflict: there were no jobs and there was no hope for these young men, so the most exciting option was continuing warfare. This is also the case with some of the gangs in devastated inner cities in the US (though not all gangs, since now we also know that many inner-city gangs are actually contributing to social order and making life more manageable in devastated neighbourhoods). In the global south, the growth of poverty and inequality and the overwhelming indebtedness of governments which then have fewer and fewer resources available for development, are all part of the broader landscape within which rage and hopelessness thrive. If history is an indication, it is only minis-cule numbers who will resort to terrorism, even as rage and hopelessness may engulf billions. But the growth of debt and unem-ployment, and the decline of traditional economic sectors, is feeding multiple forms of extreme reactions, such as, for example, an exploding illegal trade in people, largely directed to the rich countries.

The Need for New, Specialized Multilateralisms

After a decade of believing that markets could take care of more and more social domains, we must now accept that markets cannot take care of everything. For instance, use by organized terrorist networks of the financial system comes on top of previous recognition that money laundering, the black net and tax evasion, for example, have all bene-fited from the liberalization and globalization of financial markets. These abuses of the system signal the limits of liberalization and private governance and call for a reinsertion of governments in the global financial system and in other cross-border domains.

However, this reinsertion of governments is of a very different sort from the earlier state-centred and largely domestic types. Today it calls for multilateral and internationalist measures. A good case in point is the recent announcement by the US, the UK and the EU of legislative and regulatory measures aimed at the financial transactions of terror-ists. They will use the Financial Action Task Force (FATF), the world's main anti-money laundering body, to seek agreement from its 31 member countries to join the effort to make a new set of rules binding on members and the rest of the world.[4] Governments are asked to take on legal powers to freeze terrorist assets, and to include in this effort not only mainstream banking but also money-service businesses such as the *hawala* system, Islam's version of the correspondent banking of medieval Europe's Lombards.

Part of the challenge is to recognize the interconnectedness of forms of violence that we do not always recognize as being connected (or, for that matter, as being forms of violence). For instance, the debt trap in the global south is far more significant than many in the global north recognize. The focus tends to be on the size of these debts, and these are indeed a small fraction of the overall global capital market estimated in 2000 at about $68 trillion (the value of internationally traded derivatives, the leading financial instrument in the global capital market). There are at least two utilitarian reasons why rich countries should worry. First, since these debts do not simply concern a firm, but a country's government, they destabilize global order in multiple, often micro ways: more poverty and disease in the global south, with all their consequences, from illegal trafficking to further deterioration of our increasingly fragile ecosystem. Second, the debt trap is entangling more and more countries and has now reached middle-income countries, those with the best hopes for genuine development. The Argentine government's default – the largest such default ever in history – is, perhaps, the most dramatic instance, with its enormous instability and suffering. Together these various negative trends keep on reducing the portion of the globe in which it is 'safe' for the global north to pursue its interests, whether it be those of its large firms, its investors or its tourists.

Generally, it is becoming evident that even as we experienced a 'decade of unprecedented peace and prosperity' in the 1990s, in the language of our leaders, a growing number of countries in the global south experienced accelerated indebtedness and unemployment, the decay of health and social services, and of infrastructure. There are two distinct issues that matter for the argument here. One is that even if the spread of misery will largely not touch the global north directly and hence, from a narrow utilitarian logic, can be seen as of little concern to the global north, it does destabilize global order and reduce the possibilities for future operations. The other is that the spread of misery can lead to extreme acts by a minority of people and organizations in these countries that may have direct or indirect impacts on the global north, partly enabled by the infrastructure for globalization largely developed by the global north.

Perhaps one of the clearest indications of a direct effect in the last few years is the exploding illegal trade in people, largely directed to the rich countries. Using the latest available data, the United Nations estimates that 4 million people were trafficked in 1998, producing a profit of $7 billion for criminal groups.[5] As the global north has put increasing pressure on governments in the global south to open up their economies to foreign firms, these countries have become poorer even as certain sectors within them have become very rich. Governments and large sectors of the population in many of these countries have come to depend more and more on the remittances of immigrants in the global north, which overall are estimated at an annual $70 billion dollars over each of the last few years. This has also meant that these governments have little interest in the management of emigration and illegal trafficking. Further, the pressures to be competitive make governments in poor countries cut their health, education and social budgets, thereby hampering development and stimulating emigration and trafficking.

The Debt Trap: Breeding Despair

The International Monetary Fund (IMF) formally recognizes 41 countries as being hyper-indebted and unable to redress the situation. This figure is rising. It is no longer a matter of loan repayment but a fundamental new structural condition which will require innovation in order to get these countries going. One consequence is that the debt cycle for poor countries has changed and that debt relief is not enough to address the situation. One of the few ways out – perhaps the only one – is for the governments of the rich countries to take a far more active and innovative role.

It is always difficult to accept that an effort that mobilized enormous institutional and financial resources does not work, but we now know that what has been done thus far about government debt in the global south will not solve the problem. Even full cancellation of the debt will not necessarily put these countries on to a sustainable development path. Had the Jubilee 2000 campaign to cancel all existing debt of poor countries succeeded, it would not necessarily solve the basic structural trap. There is enough evidence now to suggest that a new structural condition has evolved from the combined effect of massive transformations in the global capital market and the so-called economic 'liberalization' related to globalization. Middle-income countries are also susceptible, as the financial crises of 1997 and 1998 indicated.

If key features of the global capital market can have severe impacts on what are some of the richest economies in the world, such as South Korea, Brazil or Mexico, one can imagine the impact on poor countries. While all countries, including the US and the UK, have in fact implemented versions of structural adjustment programmes to lower expenditures by states on the social agenda, the impact on poor countries has been devastating. The bundle of new policies imposed on states to accommodate new conditions associated with globalization includes: structural adjustment programmes (SAPs), the opening up of economies to foreign firms, the elimination of multiple state subsidies and, it would seem almost inevitably, financial crises and the prevailing types of programmatic solutions put forth by the IMF. It is now clear that in most of the countries involved, whether Mexico and South Korea or the US and the UK, these conditions have created enormous costs for certain sectors of the economy and of the population. In the poor countries these costs have been overwhelming and have not fundamentally reduced government debt but rather have entrapped these countries in a syndrome of growing debt.

In the 1990s we have seen a whole new set of countries become deeply indebted. In addition, most countries which became deeply indebted in the 1980s have not been able to overcome that debt. Over these two decades many innovations were launched, most importantly by the IMF and the World Bank through their structural adjustment programmes and structural adjustment loans, respectively. SAPs became a new norm for the World Bank and the IMF on the grounds that they were a promising way of securing long-term growth and sound government policy. The purpose of much of this effort was and is to make states more 'competitive', which sounds fine – but it typically means sharp cuts in various social programmes in countries where these programmes are already inadequate in their coverage.

The actual structure of these debts, their servicing and how they fit into debtor countries' economies, suggest that most of these countries will not be able to pay this debt in full under current conditions. According to some estimates, from 1982 to 1998 indebted countries paid four times their original debts, and at the same time their debt stocks increased fourfold.[6] Debt service ratios to GNP in many of the heavily indebted poor countries (HIPCs) exceed sustainable limits. Many of these countries pay over 50 per cent of their government revenues toward debt service or 20–25 per cent of their export earnings. Africa's debt service payments reached $5 billion in 1998, which means that for every $1 in aid, African countries paid $1.4 in debt service in 1998. What is often overlooked or little known is that many of these ratios are far more extreme than what were considered unmanageable levels in the Latin American debt crisis of the 1980s. Debt to GNP ratios are especially high in Africa, where they stood at 123 per cent, compared with 42 per cent in Latin America and 28 per cent in Asia. The IMF asks HIPCs to pay 20–25 per cent of their export earnings toward debt service. In contrast, in 1953 the Allies cancelled 80 per cent of Germany's war debt and only insisted on 3–5 per cent of export earnings debt service. These are also the terms asked from Central Europe after the collapse of communism.

There is considerable research showing the detrimental effects of such debt on government programmes for women and children, notably education and health care – clearly investments necessary to ensure a better future. Furthermore, the increased unemployment typically associated with the austerity and adjustment programmes implemented by international agencies to address government debt have also been found to have adverse effects on women. Unemployment, both of women themselves but also more generally of the men in their households, has added to the pressure on women to find ways to ensure household survival. Subsistence food production, informal work, emigration and prostitution have all grown as survival options for women.

What can be done to pull these countries out of the debt trap? Poor countries need to import goods for basic needs and for development. Most are heavily dependent on imports of oil, food and manufactured goods. Few poor countries can avoid trade deficits – of 93 low- and moderate-income countries, only 11 had trade surpluses in 2000. These countries would like to export more, as is evidenced by the setting up recently of a new African Trade Insurance Agency supporting exports to, from and within Africa. Such specialized and focused efforts hold promise.

These countries need loans for these imports. Most exporters, especially from the global north, will only accept payment in dollars or other high-value currencies. This further renders native currencies valueless. Once they have debts, interest payments and other debt-servicing costs escalate rapidly and their currencies are likely to devaluate further. For these countries, borrowing in the leading foreign currencies is a debt trap. Their position is radically different from that of the rich countries, for example the US has a $300 billion trade deficit and no problem getting loans at good rates, but foreign lenders are unlikely to want to hold loans denominated in the currencies of less developed countries. Furthermore, lenders will ask for much higher interest rates from poor countries. This produces a debt trap that continues to reproduce itself.

We do not need a lender of last resort to bail out rich investors. We need a lender of first resort to help the global south to pay for needed, development-linked imports, in their own currencies if at all possible and through reasonable loans. The logic is that this would make poor governments less dependent on private lenders who demand leading currencies, and who even then charge these governments a premium and would never accept their weak currencies. The government debts of poor countries, and perhaps increasingly of middle-income countries as well, need to be taken out of the global capital markets and placed in the domain of the interstate system. Keynes already proposed this in the 1940s when the IMF was created, and the IMF has recently gone in this direction with its plan to provide early financing before a crisis, rather than bailing out rich countries' investors.

Immigration: Unsustainable Contradictions

Immigration is at the intersection of a number of key dynamics that have gained strength over the last decade and in some cases after September 11. Among the most prominent are the conditions described above which are likely to function as inducements for emigration and trafficking in people, much of it directed to the global north. A second set of conditions is the demographic deficit forecast for much of the global north. A third is the increasingly restrictive regulation of immigration in the global North, to which we must now add new restrictions after September 11 in a context of both growing interdependence and the strengthening of civil liberties in the global north.

What I want to extricate from this bundle of issues is the existence of several serious tensions among these different conditions. Let me focus, first, on the increasingly restrictive immigration policies in much of the global north along with the sharpening demographic deficit in these same countries which experts see as requiring rising immigration; and, second, on the growing military, economic and political interdependencies worldwide which will tend to facilitate as well as produce new migrations and refugee flows.

Even as the rich countries try harder and harder to keep would-be immigrants and refugees out, they face a growing demographic deficit and rapidly ageing populations. According to a major study (Austrian Institute of Demography, 2001), at the end of the twenty-first century, the population size in Western Europe will have shrunk by 75 million (under current fertility and immigration patterns) and almost 50 per cent will be over 60 years old – a first in its history. Where will they get the new young workers they need to support the growing elderly population and to do the unattractive jobs whose numbers are growing, some of which will involve home and institutional care for old people? The export of older people and of economic activities is one option being considered now, but there is a limit to how many old people and low-wage jobs can be exported. It looks as though immigration will be part of the solution.

However, the way in which the countries in the global north are proceeding is not preparing them to handle this. They are building walls to keep would-be immigrants out, thereby feeding illegal trafficking. At a time of growing refugee flows, the UN High Commissioner for Refugees faces an even greater shortage of funds than usual. This will also feed illegal trafficking of people. And anything that involves the development of infrastructures for illegal trafficking will easily bring about an expansion and diversification of illegal trafficking of all sorts – not just people, but also arms and drugs. The aftermath of September 11 has further sharpened the will to control immigration and resident immigrants, especially in the US but also in several European countries. The reduction in civil liberties will not facilitate the need to learn how to accommodate more immigration to respond to the future demographic turn.

Economic and politico-military globalization bring with them an additional set of factors for immigration policy. They intensify, multiply and diversify these interaction effects. If we accept that immigration flows are partly embedded in these larger dynamics, then we may eventually confront the necessity of a radical rethinking of what it means to govern and regulate immigration flows. Such a radical policy rethinking has been worked out with trade through the Uruguay Round of the General Agreement on Tariffs and Trade (GATT) and the creation of the World Trade Organization. Such a policy rethinking is also becoming evident in military operations, with the growing weight of international cooperation, United Nations' consent and multilateral interventions; and it is being done for telecommunications policy and other areas that require compatible standards across the world. However, there has been little innovation in immigration policy, a fact often explained by invoking the complexity and intractability of the issues.

In this context it is important to emphasize that many of the policy areas that have seen enormous innovation are also extremely complex, that the policy reformulation could not have been foreseen even a decade ago, and, perhaps most importantly, that the actual changes on the ground (for example, globalization) in each of these domains forced the policy changes. From where I look at the immigration reality the changes brought about by the growing interdependencies in the world will sooner or later force a radical rethinking of how we handle immigration. Taking seriously the evidence about immigration produced by vast numbers of scholars and researchers all over the world could actually help because it tends to show us that these flows are bounded in size, time and space, and are conditioned on other processes; they are not mass invasions or indiscriminate flows from poverty to wealth.[7]

We will need regionally focused multilateral approaches involving the governments of both emigration and immigration countries, as well as a range of non-governmental actors, to develop the capacity to manage migration flows. This means recognizing that migration flows are part of how an interconnected world functions. The challenge that lies ahead will demand that all countries involved move beyond current conceptions of immigration policy in the receiving countries and that the governments of sending countries, notorious for their lack of involvement and indifference, join in this effort.

Beyond the crucial objective of effective socioeconomic development that makes it possible for people to stay in their countries, there are specific migration-linked issues. For instance, a very particular and utilitarian beginning that might motivate rich countries concerns precisely the emerging demographic and labour force asymmetries. We have recognized the emergence of a global labour market for high-tech, financial and legal experts, and to that end we have set up multilateral systems and institutional protections and guarantees for these workers (for example, in the North American Free Trade Agreement (NAFTA) and in the GATT); now it is time to recognize that there is an emerging global labour market for low-wage workers as well (maids, nannies, nurses, and so on) and that they deserve the institutional protections and guarantees given to professional workers.

Conclusion

The events of September 11 have produced a new set of constraints and opportunities. Governments have had to re-enter domains from which they had withdrawn. Forms of openness that had come to be considered crucial for a global economy – such as enabling international business travel – are now subject to new restrictions. We are seeing a re-nationalizing of governments' efforts to control their territory after a decade of liberalization. But we are also seeing new types of cross-border government coalitions, especially the US-led war on terrorism and the legal, police and surveillance actions this has entailed.

In an era of privatization and market rule we are facing the fact that governments will have to govern a bit more. But it cannot be a return to old forms – countries surrounding themselves with protective walls. It will take genuine multilateralism and internationalism and some radical innovations. The two cases I briefly examined here bring to the fore the need for specialized multilateral collaboration among specific sets of countries.

The world today faces new governance challenges. Growing interconnectedness has given new meaning to old asymmetries as well as creating new ones. Rising debt, poverty and disease in the global south are beginning to reach deep into the rich countries. Many of these conditions need to be addressed through fairly specialized and focused multilateral efforts. National governments will have to become involved, along with non-governmental actors and supranational organizations.

Notes

1. An earlier version of this chapter was originally prepared for the Social Science Research Council (US), September 11 website, <http://www.ssrc.org/sept11/>.
2. There are two important qualifications with which I agree but do not address here. First, there are moral arguments which could be read as demonstrating the utility of the more moral policy decision (see for example the work by Joseph H. Carens, 'Membership and Morality: Admission to Citizenship in Liberal Democratic States, in Roger W. Brubaker (ed.) *Immigration and the Politics of Citizenship* (New York: University Press of America, 1989), pp. 31–49) and even some elements in the Jubilee 2000 campaign for debt cancellation. I see this as a different type of logic from what I try to present in this chapter. Second, there is a large literature that shows the advantages of immigration for highly developed economies (for example, Alejandro Portes and Rubén G. Rumbaut, *Immigrant America: A Portrait* (Berkeley, CA: University of California Press, 2000)). I distinguish this from the broader argument I present here about the utility of developing specialized multilateral and internationalist forms of governing cross-border migration flows and of handling the growing indebtedness of the global south.
3. I have developed some of this at greater length in my *Guests and Aliens* (New York: New Press, 1999).
4. The UN passed a convention in 1999 aimed at suppressing and criminalizing the financing of terrorism and at the sharing of pertinent information. After September 11 this convention has gained new importance.
5. These funds include remittances from prostitutes' earnings and payments to organizers and facilitators in these countries.
6. According to Susan George, the south has paid back the equivalent of six Marshall Plans to the north. See Asoka Bandarage, *Women, Population and Crisis* (London: Zed Books, 1997). See also Eric Toussaint, 'Poor Countries Pay More Under Debt Reduction Scheme?', <www.twnside.org.sg/souths/twn/title/1921-cn.htm>.
7. See John Isbister, *The Immigration Debate: Remaking America* (West Harford, CN: Kumarian Books, 1996); Stephen Castles and Mark J. Miller, *The Age of Migration: International Population Movements in the Modern World* (2nd edn) (New York: Macmillan, 1998); Max Castro, *Free Markets, Open Societies, Closed Borders?* (Berkeley, CA: University of California Press, 2000).

CHAPTER 29

Testing Patriotism and Citizenship in the Global Terror War

Richard Falk

The imperatives of patriotism and citizenship are increasingly subjective and contested in a world of overlapping identities, accelerating mobility, daily engagements with cyberspace and societal confusions about the role of the state, nationalism and sovereignty in the hierarchy of political virtues. These features of patriotism and citizenship are intensified in the American context because of the combination of insulation and global involvement that defines its current place in the world. In writing about the country, the former American poet laureate Robert Pinsky has suggested that '[a] country is the things it wants to see', and it certainly seems to be the case that the horizon of national vision narrows still further when a society feels deeply wounded and profoundly threatened.[1]

From the morning of the attacks on the World Trade Center and the Pentagon, the American people and their leaders seemed unified in their resolve to respond as effectively as possible. President George W. Bush expressed this resolve in his September 20 speech to a Joint Session of Congress:

Tonight we are a country awakened to danger and called to defend freedom. Our grief has turned to anger, and anger to resolution. Whether we bring our enemies to justice, or bring justice to our enemies, justice will be done.

This call was immediately reinforced by the language and urgency of war – an undertaking that seemed plausible, even unavoidable, given the magnitude of the harm inflicted and the newly exposed American vulnerability to mega-terrorism. It was the manifest intent of the perpetrators to wage a merciless war directed at all Americans, Jews,

'Crusaders' and the general lack of confidence in the capabilities of the United Nations. Under these circumstances of the September 11 attack, the al-Qaeda commitment to a grandiose war that had demonstrated real capabilities to inflict major damage and an unabashed genocidal intent, the United States had little choice but to respond in a war mode, but hopefully taking full account of the special character of the adversary as a non-state, multistate network and as something entirely new and different in the annals of warfare.

It was further to be expected that the American military response should be immediately focused on Afghanistan, where the al-Qaeda network had its headquarters and enjoyed what appeared to be a close collaborative relationship with the extremist Taliban regime. It was against this background that there occurred in the United States an unprecedented display of flag-waving patriotism, a celebration of America linked in the political and moral imagination with the evil 'other', the demonization of Osama bin Laden and all those who perpetrated or supported in any way such a massive crime against humanity.

This patriotic fervour needs also to be understood as a response to the realization that bin Laden's attack on the US was greeted with mixed emotions in many parts of the Islamic world, and particularly the Arab world. In the same speech delivered to assembled members of Congress and other notables, President Bush posed the question that bothered ordinary Americans, 'Why do they hate us?', and gave this answer: 'They hate what they see right here in this chamber – a democratically elected government. Their leaders are self-appointed. They hate our freedoms … .' Such a self-serving explanation further encouraged the American understanding of the challenge of September 11 as in essence a geopolitical soap opera pitting good against evil. The mainstream media in the US reinforced this moralistic imagery by cheerleading the moves toward war and excluding any expression of dissenting or sceptical voices. This unconditional celebration of American life, values and institutions, without a scintilla of willingness to listen to anti-American grievances so prevalent in the Arab world and zero receptivity to self-criticism, has produced a patriotic fever with dangerous implications for Americans as well as others.

Again, these implications can be most vividly apprehended by the manner in which President Bush has rallied the country in his two major speeches setting forth the American response to September 11. I would highlight here three disturbing expressions of this mode of perception. In the initial address on war aims to the Joint Session, Bush laid down a challenge to the rest of the world in highly charged hegemonic language: 'Every nation, in every region, now has a decision to make. Either you are with us, or you are with the terrorists.' Such an approach, while understandable from the narrow perspective of counter-terrorism, seems oblivious to the existence of moral and legal limits on the use of force, and exhibits no respect for either the sovereignty and security interests of others or for their views on global security. There was no language in official American discourse on the response recognizing the importance or relevance of such limits, or even of taking account of the views of others.

This unilateralist tenor, while slightly disguised by the efforts to construct an inclusive counter-terrorist coalition of states, was given a more disturbing twist in Bush's State of the Union Address (January 29, 2002) in which he directed belligerent warnings toward North Korea, Iran and Iraq, calling them to account as an 'axis of evil', a rhetoric recalling both the Second World War fascist coalition of axis powers and Ronald Reagan's designation of the Soviet Union as 'the evil empire'. Such threats were being directed at governments that were not generally seen as posing a threat to the United States, and were in no meaningful or manifest way connected with the al-Qaeda network. And finally, the patriotic moment has been variously invoked to stifle criticisms of state security measures that interfere with the normal civil liberties of Americans, and especially of resident immigrants from the Islamic world. Attorney-General John Ashcroft reacted in venomous vein – 'My message is this: your tactics only aid terrorists' and 'give ammunition to America's enemies'. A similar vindictiveness has been consistently expressed by US officials in their unrelenting moves to prosecute John Walker Lindh, a 20-year-old teenage American convert to radical Islam, for his participation on the side of the Taliban in their struggle against the Northern Alliance, which after September 11 became the military ally of the United States. The essential message being sent by US officialdom, and dutifully transmitted by the media (especially television), is that there is no legitimate room for American doubts or opposition to the militarist course being charted by the White House.

Patriotism, Citizenship and Nationalism

The basic energy of patriotism is of course emotive, understood as love of country, an affirmation of a bonded political community of fellow citizens sharing memories and identities, as well as a willingness to make sacrifices for the sake of the collective well-being, and especially the security and survival, of the country. In the modern era, the sovereign state has become the main focus for these sentiments, especially for large and well-governed states. States have also tried to resolve issues of multicultural identity by conferring nationality as a matter of law, and issuing passports, claiming to be nation states. In fact, the psychological foundations of group identity may not correspond with state boundaries, thus creating a variety of tensions, including in their most intense forms separatist struggles for national self-determination and claims for the protection of minority rights.

Citizenship implies full and non-discriminatory membership in a political community; the most important by far being sovereign states. The idea of citizenship is increasingly applied to other political communities, supporting the notion of a European citizen and even a world citizen. One impact of globalization and the rise of regional political communities is to establish multiple identities and a non-exclusive sense of citizenship. War is a throwback to simpler times of exclusivity, a tribal sense of passionate solidarity that is incapable of objectivity. War creates a special regime of intensified patriotism and nationalism, and maximizes the duties of the citizen, especially the obligation of young males to serve in the armed forces. This most serious claim of wartime over the life and destiny of such young citizens makes it necessary to believe ardently that the cause is worth the dying and killing. It has also established a powerful, often jingoistic, symbiosis between nationalism as ideology and patriotism as creed. It is notable to observe that when this symbiosis is absent, as it was in relation to the humanitarian peacekeeping missions of the 1990s – most notably in Somalia under UN auspices, where even 18 American combat deaths were quickly regarded as politically unacceptable. The patriotic idea is only mobilizing when it can draw on nationalist security goals, and these remain mired in an anachronistic statist vision of world order that has not yet adapted to the fundamental changes wrought by globalization.

The United States is a prototypical successful sovereign state. It is rich and powerful and enjoys the undivided support of the overwhelming majority of its citizens, despite an exceptional degree of ethnic, religious and cultural diversity within its boundaries. Its foundation myths and historical experience generate pride and love of country for most of its citizenry on most issues. The American Civil War and the defeat in Vietnam, as well as the Great Depression of the 1930s, have tested national unity, but the outcome in each instance has borne witness to the resilience of the country as a coherent entity. Its republican form of government associates patriotism with the affirmation of the freedom and rights of citizens, including the right to dissent from national policy. Part of the self-glorifying American epic narrative is its supposed reluctance as a country to engage in warfare. However, once engaged, there is a tendency to view the conflict as one between America's forces of good and the enemy's forces of evil, and thus an unwillingness to agree upon compromises which appear in such settings as pacts with the devil. The First and Second World Wars were both so conceived, as was the Cold War and the Gulf War, and so is the current war on global terror. Victory is thus seen in totalistic terms; unconditional surrender is demanded and normal constraints governing conduct in war are largely ignored so as to reach a victorious outcome sooner and at a lesser cost. Negotiation, diplomacy and deference to international law and the UN are consistently subordinated to military effectiveness, and the almost religious degree of assurance that whatever is done is in furtherance of America's just cause and of benefit to the world as a whole. No dose of history has been able to weaken this self-redeeming sense of American moral exceptionalism, and talented 'communicators' such as Ronald Reagan, and now George W. Bush, knew very well how to tap into this seemingly infinite reservoir of American innocence and call forth a patriotic response of unquestioning approval for policies, however dubious, from the perspective of law and morality.

Such a background does not tell the whole story. The United States has emerged over the last several decades as the unquestioned leader of the world, a position based on military power, technological innovation, economic prosperity, diplomatic role and cultural vitality. At the same time, the complex developments understood beneath the rubric of 'globalization' have deterritorialized all states, including the United States. Such deterritorializing has given great historical weight to networked forms of organization, changing the nature of conflict and creating this new phenomenon bureaucratically described in the United States as 'asymmetrical warfare', better conceived as warfare by the weak directed at the vulnerabilities of the strong. September 11 epitomizes such warfare waged by an extremist network willing to embark upon suicidal missions to inflict harm on its stronger enemy. Of course, the response inverts the dynamics of the asymmetry, with the technologically more powerful, established state wreaking havoc and devastation anywhere on the planet at virtually no human cost to itself. The type of tribal patriotism that has emerged in the United States since September 11 has exhibited almost no capacity to interpret the world scene in light of these new realities, but has shaped a nationalist mood that is rooted in the mainly obsolescent attitudes and perceptions of a territorially constituted world order.

There is also a normative dimension that needs to be considered in clarifying concerns about the impact of the type of American patriotism that is defining this special moment of global crisis for the American people. To begin with, there has been a long struggle during the past century to limit the recourse and conduct of war as much as possible. The carnage of two world wars encouraged an idea of world order that sought to minimize the role of war in regulating the relations among states. Limiting war to conditions of self-defence and in situations authorized by the UN Security Council expressed these aims in a form that was geopolitically ineffectual. The UN role was hampered at its inception by the veto given to permanent members and by not being entrusted with independent capabilities to challenge the ethos of sovereignty. To the extent that major wars were avoided, it was not a result of constraining legal rules, but rather of the prudence of political leaders, especially associated with deterrent approaches to security induced by the presence of nuclear weaponry. The existence of this weaponry on both sides of the Cold War cleavage meant that compromises and stalemates were often more attractive than going all out for victory, as in the Korean and Vietnam Wars. These outcomes were inconsistent with the standard American approach to its wars – fight only just wars, but then go all out to win. In these instances, the wars were never successfully 'sold' as just and necessary, the human costs to America never seemed entirely worthwhile, and the inconclusive endings made many disillusioned, convinced that young Americans had died in vain.

With the collapse of the Soviet Union, earlier American attitudes toward war have re-emerged by stages, and have been extended with dogmatic clarity to the struggle against global terrorism. In the 1990s the revived moralism of US foreign policy was explained to the public either as a defensive and strategic response to aggression, as in the Gulf War, or in the ethical language of humanitarian diplomacy, as in Somalia, Bosnia, and especially the Kosovo War. The attacks of September 11 on the symbolic and substantive core of American primacy in the world, together with the genocidal ethos of the perpetrators, has generated an American response that is committed to total victory. Such a commitment takes on added credibility because the visionary outlook of Osama bin Laden and al-Qaeda cannot be deterred (as was the Soviet Union, and even Iraq in the 1990s) and may have at its disposal a large cadre of suicidal warriors prepared to attack the US and Americans in the future. Beyond this, more than in past wars, there are no battlefields or delimited enemy territories, and so it more difficult to achieve a consensus as to what the war is about. The war in Afghanistan did resemble earlier wars to the extent that there were 'battlefields' associated with Northern Alliance operations against Taliban forces and in relation to the effort to destroy the al-Qaeda base areas at the Tora Bora cave complex and elsewhere. Still, there is an indeterminacy about the outcome, with al-Qaeda obviously suffering a setback in Afghanistan, but most of its leaders and many of its fighters appearing to elude capture or death, and possibly escaping to fight another day. Furthermore, in the background are unresolved controversies about the character of terrorism, such as whether it should be associated with anti-state violence in the setting of nationalist struggles for self-determination, particularly in instances where the targeted state has itself relied on violence directed at civilian society. Part of the objection to the expansion of the war by the Bush administration is this matter of the scope and nature of terrorism, but it is also the issue of whether, as in the 'axis of evil' speech, there is a sufficient link between some governments, terrorist groups and weaponry of mass destruction to validate recourse to preventive war and military intervention.

In fact, the al-Qaeda global terrorist network can be anywhere, but is nowhere. Its operational units can lodge themselves as sleeper cells in the midst of the United States itself. Under these conditions it is to be expected that Americans will pull together at home and pursue all-out victory in the war. Patriotic zeal lends enthusiasm to the undertaking, recognizing and validating the sacrifices made by those who fight and pushing the citizenry to mobilize the resources needed to win the war.

Why, then, should there be concerns about the role of patriotism in this setting of responding to 9/11? In essence, these concerns arise because waving the American flag so vigorously has made it more difficult to set limits on the response, and these limits are necessary for both pragmatic and normative reasons. It has seemed that the American leadership has itself been genuinely engulfed in this tidal wave of patriotic feelings, which is leading it to undertake a far wider war than is necessary given the scope of the threat. There has been a refusal by American leaders to define national goals and defensive responses with precision. This has led to the adoption of foreign and domestic policies of a dubious and dangerous character that engage issues that are not really raised by the September 11 attacks.

Patriotism Reformulated

In times of crisis when a society is threatened by an external enemy, there is a strong tendency to express patriotic feelings through tribal and ultra-nationalist displays of unconditional support. September 11 accentuated this tendency due to its abrupt exposure of American vulnerability and anxieties that more of the same would likely follow. The anthrax scare coming weeks later solidified these sentiments of solidarity, which were further strengthened by periodic messages from the US government to the citizens to stay alert in view of indications that additional attacks were in the offing. In this respect, the patriotic mood was a result of both the extreme character of the circumstances arising from the attacks and a quite contrived campaign to mobilize popular enthusiasm for the war policies that was brilliantly coordinated by the White House and the mainstream media.

If the United States was truly a beleaguered country fighting for its survival against far stronger adversaries, such a fusion of nationalism and patriotism would not only be natural but would probably be of great functional value. One thinks of the Vietnamese or Palestinian struggles for self-determination against overwhelming odds as important historical examples. But the post-September 11 realities facing the United States, and indirectly the rest of the world, were decidedly different. For one thing, part of the menace associated with al-Qaeda extremism is that it arises out of grievances associated with American behaviour that have a wide resonance throughout the Arab world, especially in relation to the American responsibility for Palestinian suffering; and less pronouncedly, yet still significantly, especially given the awareness provided by al-Jazeerah TV coverage, and the persistent bombing and punishing sanctions imposed on the people of Iraq for more than a decade. Osama bin Laden pointed to such grievances especially in his more recent interviews, although his own turn against the United States seemed to derive mainly from hostility toward the House of Saud's rule in Saudi Arabia; particularly its acceptance during the Gulf Crisis in 1990 of large contingents of American military forces in close proximity to the most holy Islamic sites.

Because the United States government mobilizes for war in a tribalist manner that absolutizes group solidarity and identity, it is disabled from reflecting upon its own conduct, and is unwilling to take steps that might address those grievances of others that are just and in accord with international law and morality. Worse than this, it is seduced by its own hyperbolic rhetoric about terrorism into throwing its weight behind oppressive policies of great severity. Instead of confining its defensive claims to the threats posed by the al-Qaeda network, the Bush administration has generalized its struggle so as to take on 'terror' in general, although selectively defined. At this point, a justifiable defensive posture by the US morphs into an interventionary one directed at the unfinished struggles of peoples seeking self-determination. To add Hamas, Hezbollah, Islamic Jihad, and Jaish-I-Mohammed to the 'terrorist underworld', as Bush did in his State of the Union Address, is to associate terrorism exclusively with non-state actors, when in fact violence against the civilian population is engaged in by both sides and with greater ferocity by the states in question, whether Israel or India. The proper role for the United States in these conflicts is to work toward a just solution that brings peace and accommodation, and not to confuse its response to September 11 with policies of support for a variety of state terrorisms.

This expanded sense of what is 'terrorism' also operates regressively as a green light for other governments seeking to deal with micro nationalisms within their borders. In the aftermath of the attacks on the US, the Soviet Union has stepped up its repressive policies toward Chechnya, as has China in its administration of the restive Uighers in Xinjiang Province in this period. Worst of all, Ariel Sharon intensified his extremely violent occupation of Palestinian territories, and has been supported all the way by Washington. The point about patriotism here is that a global leader is not just defending itself but is always setting rules of the game for others, and has a particular responsibility to ensure that such rules do not perpetuate ongoing wars, thereby adding to injustice and suffering.

National patriotism can also morph a legitimate defensive response into a frightening form of expansionism and hegemonic pretension, as when President Bush designates North Korea, Iran and Iraq as 'an axis of evil', implying that such countries might become targets for military attack and coercive diplomacy if they make moves unwelcome in Washington, especially the acquisition of weaponry of mass destruction. These governments have not even been accused of involvement in September 11 and pose no threat to the United States, but rather are threatened by the United States, including by its arsenal of nuclear weaponry. To assert such preventive war prerogatives without even seeking the backing of coalition partners, much less a willingness to proceed by way of the UN, is to take on a domineering role that threatens to a degree the sovereign rights of every state on the planet and poses serious war dangers to all peoples in the world. Such policies also have to be understood in the context of the foreign policy of the Bush administration prior to September 11, which was notable for its self-conscious unilateralism (the Kyoto Protocol, the Anti-Ballistic Missile Treaty, the Protocol to the Biological Weapons Convention, for example) and its determination to proceed with missile defence and the weaponization of space despite the objections of almost every one of its closest allies. The disregard of even NATO in its definition of war aims is bound to challenge the Euro-American relationship in ways that are at present unpredictable.

I am not suggesting that this entire litany of concerns can be attributed to the surge of national patriotism, but it has paved the way, at least in the United States, and to some extent in Europe. Bipartisanship has reached such extremes that Democratic Party leadership is mainly eager to present itself as beating the drums of war as loudly as its Republican counterparts. Citizens have been half scared and half convinced that the call for unity means a suspension of criticism and conscience. Even the lamentable treatment of Taliban/al-Qaeda prisoners at Guantanamo and the refusal to accept the application of the Geneva Convention raises only the mildest of criticisms, and mainly at the margins. In this instance, a self-defeating arrogance is evident in relation to the treatment of prisoners, as it is Americans, with their far-flung commitments and individualist ethos, who would benefit most over time from a show of respect for Geneva standards. If the United States can decide when captured individuals are 'unlawful combatants', why can't others do the same, or worse? National patriotism is a powerful and risky vaccine that immunizes the body politic against self-criticism.

In a globalizing world there is another way of being patriotic that reconciles love of country with responsibility to humanity: cosmopolitan patriotism.[2] Such attitudes have started to form in the midst of the deterritorializing of economic, social and cultural life, and seem to have affected segments of public opinion in Europe.[3] Cosmopolitan patriotism accepts the right of a people and a country to defend its fundamental rights, whether struggling for self-determination or dealing with an aggressor. At the same time, such a patriotic outlook sees the self from without as well as from within and is receptive to criticism, and seeks to live by the rule of law rather than to dominate by the rule of force. The citizenry of the United States is being tested in this period to shape a response to September 11 that restores its security but also contributes to the peace and justice in the world, and especially in the Arab and Islamic world. Such contributions relate to doing more to ensure that the poor benefit from economic growth and the patterns of globalization, to using its diplomatic muscle to end tragic encounters of the sort that have cast such dark shadows over Palestinian and Israeli lives for decades, to working for more capable and trusted international institutions, especially the United Nations, and to supporting the deepening of respect for human rights and the international rule of law.

Cosmopolitan patriotism combines love of humanity with love of country, and does not imply a renunciation of national identities or affinities. It is more alive to the degree to which globalization alters our sense of time and space than is its nationalist counterpart. National patriotism is premised on a world order that is decisively defined by autonomous sovereign states, each dependent for survival and prosperity on the successful exercise of its unconditional dependence on self-help. This dependence overrides any considerations of morality and law that may stand in the way of expedient action taken for the sake of survival and security. It inclines toward viewing an adversary as 'evil' and regarding its own reality as 'good', especially under conditions of hostility and trauma. National patriotism does not perceive any dangers flowing from its own excesses of power, whereas cosmopolitan patriotism seeks to substitute the security of community for the security associated with military capabilities. The United States and most of its citizenry, as powerful (and rich) beyond the reality of other states, seems more resistant to cosmopolitan considerations at present, treating them as superfluous and diversionary from the basic self-help challenge to restore a national sense of security in the aftermath of September 11.

A United States guided by the spirit of cosmopolitan patriotism could turn the tragedy of September 11 into an inspirational moment in the early history of the twenty-first century. At the moment such a prospect is as remote as landing a man on the moon must have seemed in the 1930s. As the old world order of states and wars is being transformed by networks and digital potency, we must reconceive politics as *the art of the impossible*.

Notes

1. Robert Pinsky, *An Explanation of America* (Princeton, NJ: Princeton University Press, 1979), p. 8.
2. Martha Nussbaum et al., *For Love of the Country: Debating the Limits of Patriotism* (Boston, MA: Beacon Press, 1996); Bart von Steenbergen, *The Conditions of Citizenship* (London: Sage, 1994).
3. Elizabeth Pond, *The Rebirth of Europe* (Washington, DC: Brookings Institution, 1999); Dusan Sidjanski, *The Federal Future of Europe: From the European Community to the European Union* (Ann Arbor, MI: University of Michigan Press, 2000).

CHAPTER 30

Peace, Poetry and Pentagonese

Patricia J. Williams

Things fall apart, as Chinua Achebe put it, in times of great despair. The American nightmare that began with the attacks on the World Trade Center and the Pentagon, has, like an earthquake, been followed by jolt after jolt of disruption and fear. In the intervening six months (as of this writing), yet another airplane crashed, this time into a residential section of New York City. Anthrax contamination succeeded in closing, for varying lengths of time, all three branches of government. From the tabloids to the *New York Times*, major media outlets have had their centres of operation evacuated repeatedly. The United States Postal Service has been tied in knots. Hundreds of anthrax hoaxes have stretched law enforcement beyond all capacity. Soldiers guard all our public buildings.

Almost 4000 Americans died in planes, collapsing buildings or of anthrax toxin in the first weeks after that morning in September; tens of thousands more lost their jobs. Some 5000 Arab residents between the ages of 18 and 33 were summoned for interrogation by the FBI. And 20 million resident aliens live suddenly subject to the exceedingly broad terms of a new martial law. Enron, one of the world's largest energy brokers, collapsed from the weight of its own corruption, bringing down with it a significant chunk of the world economy. President Bush produced a new budget with such enormous increases in military spending that legislators across the country scurried to slash education, welfare, child care and health programmes. Even while we try to follow the president's advice to pick ourselves up and go shopping, punchdrunk and giddily committed to soldiering on as before, we know that the economic and emotional devastation of these events has only begun to register.

We have never been a nation able to grieve easily or properly – to turn off the yammering on CNN and the yelling on Fox, to disconnect the telephone, surround ourselves with friends and come to terms with the magnitude of this tragedy. But we must do something like that in order to move on unencumbered and outspoken, rather than trying to stop time by mutely uncritical allegiance to that day – that unified, yes, but horrifically frozen moment in our lives.

As the enormity of the destruction settles in and becomes less dreamlike, more waking catastrophe, American society begins to face those long-term tests that inevitably come after the shock of so much loss and change. We face the test of keeping the unity that visited us in that first moment of sheer chaos. We face the test of maintaining our dignity and civility in a time of fear and disorder. Above all, we face the test of preserving the rights and freedoms in our Constitution and its Bill of Rights.

Few in the United States question the necessity for unusual civil measures in keeping with a state of emergency. But a number of the Bush administration's subsequent laws, orders and policies are deservedly controversial: the disregard for international treaties and conventions; strict controls on media reports about the war and its casualties; secret surveillance and searches of citizens' computers; widespread ethnic profiling; indefinite detention of non-citizens; offers of expedited American citizenship to those who provide evidence about terrorists; and military tribunals with the power to try enemies in secret, without application of the usual laws of evidence, without right of appeal, yet with the ability to impose the death penalty. Although there have been leaked reports that the administration is thinking about conforming the tribunals to at least the minimal standards of due process, at the time of writing no such qualification has formally occurred.

Opportunity for legislative or other public discussion of these measures has been largely eclipsed by the rapidity with which most of them have been pushed into effect. This speed, one must accede, is in large part an exigency of war, and in some lesser but still significant part, the product of an administration making the most of unusually high popularity ratings. In any event, the president has successfully enlarged the power of the executive to an unprecedented extent, while limiting both Congressional input and the check of the judiciary.

The War on War

Overall, we face one of the more dramatic constitutional crises in United States history. First, while national security mandates some fair degree of restraint, blanket control of information is in tension with

the Constitution's expectation that freedom of a diverse and opinion-
ated press will moderate the tyrannical tendencies of power. We need
to have some inkling of what is happening on the battlefield in our
name. On the domestic front, moreover, the First Amendment's protection of free speech is eroded if even peaceful dissent becomes casually
categorized as dangerous or unpatriotic, as it has sometimes been in
recent weeks. This concern is heightened by the fact that the war has
been framed as one against 'terror' – against unruly if deadly emotion-
alism – rather than as a war against specific bodies, specific land,
specific resources. Again, a war against terrorism is a war of the mind,
so broadly defined that the enemy becomes anybody who makes us
afraid. Indeed, what is conspicuous about American public discourse
right now is how hard it is to talk about facts rather than fear.

I worry too about the degree to which we keep referring to these
enemies as 'The Evil Ones' or 'The Bad Guys' – such odd terms, as
though our leaders were speaking to very young children. By this, al-
Quaeda is placed in an almost biblical narrative, ready to be smote
down, cast out. In this model, giving The Evil Ones so mundane a
forum as a trial is like literally 'courting' the devil. While this sort of
embedded language has certainly galvanized the American public in a
time of great crisis, it is not a useful long-term model for a democratic
secular government trying to fight real political foes, particularly state-
less enemies who are religious zealots in their own right.

Indeed, the very name of the agency recently established to calm our
fear – the Office of Homeland Security – has a chilly ambiguity about
it. The word 'homeland' has burrowed its way into ordinary conversa-
tion and multiplied with astonishing rapidity. It is not just the curious
name of an office merging police and intelligence functions. It is a
lower-case reference to purple mountains' majesty and all those fruited
plains. Suddenly, 'America the Beautiful' has become some sort of bad
translation from the German. Like 'Fatherland' or 'empire', labels
channel unspoken allegiances. I wonder about the line drawing such an
odd term was calculated to evoke – it sounds at once intimate and
abstract – like the good-guy quadrant in some strategic computer game?
Like the Bush team's attempt to sound mythic? Like some effort to
denationalize and fuse enemy status with that of domestic criminality
– as in home wreckers, home invaders, domestic abusers? Some weird
echo of Disneyland, Legoland, or Never-Never Land?

There has got to be an angle. 'Homeland Security' is the new office of
what they keep calling 'psy-op' after all. Psy-op, or psychological operations, is apparently a kind of cross between Madison Avenue and the star

chamber. A calculated brew of advertising tricks – including puffery, packaging, mass hypnosis and disinformation – it includes the sort of strategies that were used to reduce Manuel Noriega to a quivering mass of submission: the US military purportedly blared relentless, sleep-defying hard rock at the building where he was holed up and I guess eventually he came out with his hands up. It's a strategy of insinuation and disguise, used by all sides in any given new age conflict, even al-Qaeda. In a National Public Radio broadcast, Dr Gerald Post, an adviser to the CIA and professor of something called 'political psychology', described an al-Qaeda handbook found on one of the defendants in the first World Trade Center bombing, in 1993. He discussed passages in which operatives are advised to 'blend in', to stay clean-shaven, not to talk too much over coffee, and to pay their parking tickets in a timely fashion. Perhaps it was not Dr Post's intended result, but I found myself extremely alarmed. The bottom line of his advice seemed to be that you can trust no one, so just call the FBI about every move your suspiciously average neighbours make. I felt the seduction of that suspicion (six or seven overly clean-cut colleagues who have offended me over the years immediately leapt to mind) and yet also (as a terse coffee-drinker who always pays her parking tickets on time) a deep fear of the same.

Better Safe ...

In a struggle that is coloured by a degree of social panic, we must be very careful not to allow human rights to be cast as an indulgence. There is always a certain hypnosis to the language of war – the poetry of the Pentagon, a friend calls it – in which war means peace, and peacemongering invites war. In this somewhat inverted system of reference, the Christian iconography of the bleeding heart does not beat within the corpus of law but rather in the bosom of those whose craven sympathies amount to naive and treacherous self-delusion. Everywhere one hears what, if taken literally, amounts to a death knell for the American dream: rights must be tossed out the window because 'the Constitution is not a suicide pact'.

However, accepting rational reasons to be afraid, the unalloyed ideology of efficiency has not only chilled free expression, but has left us poised at the gateway of an even more fearsome world in which the 'comfort' and convenience of high-tech totalitarianism gleam temptingly; a world in which our Americanness endures only with hands up! so that our fingerprints can be scanned, and our nationalized identity can be scrutinized for signs of suspicious behaviour.

This brings me to the second aspect of our constitutional crisis; that is, the seeming endorsement by a majority of Americans of encroachments upon freedom from unreasonable searches and seizures. The establishment of the new Office of Homeland Security and the passage of the so-called USA Patriot Act has brought into being an unprecedented merger between the functions of intelligence agencies and law enforcement. What this means might be clearer if we used the more straightforward term for intelligence: spying. Law enforcement agents can now spy on us, 'destabilizing' citizens and not just non-citizens. They can gather information with few checks or balances from the judiciary.

Morton Halperin, a defence expert who worked with the National Security Council under Henry Kissinger, worried, in the *New Yorker* magazine, that if a government intelligence agency

> thinks you're under the control of a foreign government, they can wiretap you and never tell you, search your house and never tell you, break into your home, copy your hard drive, and never tell you that they've done it.

Moreover, says Halperin, upon whose own phone Kissinger placed a tap,

> Historically, the government has often believed that anyone who is protesting government policy is doing it at the behest of a foreign government and opened counterintelligence investigations of them.[1]

This expansion of domestic spying highlights the distinction between punishing what has already occurred and preventing what might happen in the future. In a very rough sense, agencies like the FBI have been concerned with catching criminals who have already done their dirty work, while agencies like the CIA have been involved in predicting or manipulating future outcomes – activities of prior restraint, in other words, from which the Constitution generally protects citizens.

The third and most distressing area of constitutional concern has been Mr Bush's issuance of an Executive Order setting up military tribunals that would deprive even long-time resident aliens of the right to due process of law. The elements of the new order are as straightforward as trains running on time. The president would have the military try non-citizens suspected of terrorism in closed tribunals rather than courts: no requirement of public charges, adequacy of counsel, usual rules of evidence, nor proof beyond a reasonable doubt. The cases would be presented before unspecified judges, with rulings based on the accusations of unidentified witnesses. The tribunals would have the power to execute anyone so convicted, with no right of appeal. According to polls conducted by National Public Radio, the *Washington Post* and ABC News, approximately 65 per cent of Americans wholeheartedly endorse such measures.

'Foreign terrorists who commit war crimes against the United States, in my judgment, are not entitled to and do not deserve the protections of the American Constitution', says Attorney-General John Ashcroft in defence of tribunals.[2] There are a number of aspects of that statement that are worrisome. The reasoning is alarmingly circular in Ashcroft's characterization of suspects who have not yet been convicted as 'terrorists'. It presumes guilt before adjudication. Our system of innocent until proven guilty is hardly foolproof, but does provide an essential, baseline bulwark against the furious thirst for quick vengeance, the carelessly deadly mistake – albeit in the name of self-protection.

It is worrisome, too, when the highest prosecutor in the land, Attorney-General John Ashcroft, declares that war criminals do not 'deserve' basic constitutional protections. We confer due process not because putative criminals are 'deserving' recipients of rights-as-reward. Rights are not 'earned' in this way. What makes rights rights is that they ritualize the importance of solid, impartial and public consensus before we take life or liberty from anyone, particularly those whom we fear. We ritualize this process to make sure we don't allow the grief of great tragedies to blind us with mob fury, inflamed judgements and uninformed reasoning. In any event, Bush's new order bypasses not only the American Constitution but the laws of most other democratic nations. It exceeds the accepted conventions of most military courts. (I say all this provisionally, given that the Bush administration is urging the enactment of similar anti-terrorism measures in Britain, Russia, and that troublesome holdout, the European Union.)

As time has passed since the order was published, a number of popular defences of tribunals have emerged: we should trust our president, we should have faith in our government, we are in a new world facing new kinds of enemies who have access to new weapons of mass destruction. Assuming all this, we must wonder if this administration also questions whether citizens who are thought to have committed heinous crimes 'deserve' the protections of American citizenship. The terrorist who mailed 'aerosolized' anthrax spores to various Senate

offices is, according to the FBI, probably a lone American microbiolo-
gist. Although we have not yet rounded up thousands of
microbiologists for questioning by the FBI, I wonder if the government
will be hauling them before tribunals – for if this is a war without
national borders, the panicked logic of secret trials will surely expand
domestically rather than contract. A friend observes wryly that if the
reasoning behind the order is that the perpetrators of mass death must
be summarily executed, then there are some CEOs in the tobacco
industry who ought to be trembling in their boots. Another friend who
works with questions of reproductive choice notes more grimly that
that is exactly the reasoning used by those who assault and murder
abortion doctors.

'There are situations when you do need to presume guilt over innocence', one citizen from Chattanooga told the *New York Times*.[3]
Conservative talk-show host Mike Reagan (and son of former President
Ronald Reagan) leads the pack in such boundlessly presumed guilt by
warning that you might think the guy living next door is the most
wonderful person in the world, you see him playing with his children,
but in fact 'he might be part of a sleeper cell that wants to blow ... you
... AWAY'.[4] We forget, perhaps, that J. Edgar Hoover justified sabotaging
Martin Luther King and the 'dangerous suspects' of that era with
similar sentiment.

In addition to the paranoia generated, the importance of the right to
adequate counsel has been degraded. Attorney-General Ashcroft's
stated policies include allowing federal officials to listen in on conversations between suspected terrorists and their lawyers. And President
Bush's military tribunals would not recognize the right of defendants to
choose their own lawyers. The tribunals also challenge the right to a
speedy, public and impartial trial. More than 1000 immigrants have
been arrested and held, approximately 800 with no disclosure of identities or location or charges against them. This is 'frighteningly close to
the practice of "disappearing" people in Latin America', according to
Kate Martin, the director of the Center for National Security Studies.[5]

Finally, there has been an ominous amount of public vilification of
the constitutional right against self-incrimination. Such a right is, in
essence, a proscription against the literal arm-twisting and leg-pulling
that might otherwise be necessary to physically compel someone to
testify when they do not want to. It is perhaps a rather too-subtly-
worded limitation of the use of torture.

While not yet the direct subject of official sanction, torture itself has
suddenly gained remarkable legitimacy. Callers to radio programmes say

that we don't always have the 'luxury of following all the rules'; that, given recent events, people are 'more understanding' of the necessity for a little behind-the-scenes roughing up. The unanimity of international conventions against torture notwithstanding, one hears authoritative voices – for example, Robert Litt, a former Justice Department official – arguing that while torture is not 'authorized', perhaps it could be used in 'emergencies', as long as the person who tortures then presents him- or herself to 'take the consequences'. Harvard Law School Professor Alan Dershowitz has suggested the use of 'torture warrants' limited, he insists, to cases where time is of the essence.

Most alarming of all, a recent CNN poll revealed that 45 per cent of Americans would not object to torturing someone if it would provide information about terrorism. The figures also show that many of those same Americans seem to feel that such measures will affect only a few non-citizens, and that the real subject of such measures will be Osama bin Laden. 'They had to do it this way because you can't make a law against just one person', opines a friend.

Yet there are about 20 million non-citizen residents in America. By the terms of President Bush's order, all those people are now effectively living under martial law. I think that's a tad overbroad; although for the sake of argument, I will concede that my opinion is presently a minority voice in America. Rather, I wish to pursue my concern that the practical divide between 'aliens' and 'citizens' is a very thin one, one that is melting away quickly beneath the sun of this go-for-the-throat, to-hell-with-human-rights rage.

Virtual Reality

If Osama bin Laden is the icon by which non-citizens are deprived of constitutional protections, my sense is that O.J. Simpson has re-emerged as the justification for doing the same to certain citizens. 'We wouldn't want Johnnie Cochran defending Osama', I keep hearing. 'He'd end up in Florida, playing golf with O.J.'

The Simpson case, a wholly anomalous piece of bread and circus, has come to symbolize a widely shared and unfortunately politicized understanding of the criminal justice system. The 'O.J.' case represents the misuse of public resources, the helplessness of prosecutors, the predatory nature of defence lawyers in particular and of trial lawyers generally, the cravenness of judges and the bias of black jurors. The case remains an object lesson in the sensational potential of reality TV. And in the fallout, the English language gained an ugly new phrase –

'playing the race card' – that has been used to pulverize any constructive discussion of race or civil rights since.

The problem is that this rendering of the Simpson case is deeply misleading, and its reappearance in the context of whether Osama bin Laden should be tried or just 'offed' is dangerous.

To back up a bit, when Simpson was acquitted of murdering Ron Goldman and Nicole Brown Simpson, the big question was why a very racially mixed jury (it intrigues me that people always think of that jury as 'all black') acquitted him when the whole of the rest of the world wanted to hang him. Most people blamed the supposed stupidity of the jurors. But I think Simpson was acquitted not so much because defence lawyers befuddled the wits of the jury – however much the media bemoaned Alan Dershowitz's and Johnnie Cochran's theatre – but more because the prosecution's chief witness, officer Mark Furhman, lied on the stand, was caught at it, and was ultimately convicted of perjury for it. There really are very few cases where you can ever get a conviction if the credibility of a major prosecution witness is as shaky as that.

Moreover, people who live in Los Angeles – the jury pool, in other words – were perhaps more aware than the rest of the nation of the Los Angeles Police Department's history of flagrant frame-ups, particularly racialized ones. The now notorious revelations of corruption in the LAPD's Rampart Division grew out of this precise concern: hundreds of criminal cases had to be dismissed in Los Angeles in the last few years because of officers so eager to convict that they suppressed relevant evidence, or relied too heavily on snitches intent upon plea bargaining their way to lighter sentences, or lied, or framed or even attacked mostly minority defendants.

To this day, few people recognize the relation between the attitudes of the jury pool in the Simpson case and the Rampart scandal. I don't wish to settle whether this kind of so-called 'jury nullification' also amounts to reasonable doubt or not. My only point is that the practised corruption – of lowered evidentiary standards, of self-interested witnesses, of other such shortcuts to conviction – poisons not just individual cases but the public trust and perception of fairness upon which all else rests.

To bring this back to military tribunals, such trust-eroding 'street justice' is precisely the 'cure' now being proposed in the name of 'avoiding' more O.J.-like trials: indefinite detention in undisclosed locations, less than unanimous decisions to convict, execution without right of appeal, unidentified informants paid with promises of expedited American citizenship, undue weight to ethnic profiling, and so on. And therein lies the unsettling meeting point between the fates of those who dwell in the 'mean street' and those in the 'Arab street'. People who have been marked as 'suspect', or 'other', regardless of whether they are citizens or non-citizens, understandably want – yes, even deserve – the Johnnie Cochrans of the world out there making sure the prosecution lives up to its burden of proof rather than just sending out a posse because a CNN poll says you did it.

I sometimes wonder if the role of defence attorneys has become too hard to see in our culture – it's such an ancient function. It's about becoming an extension of the defendant. A 'mouthpiece' in the literal sense. It is democratizing to have an advocate who knows the law and, theoretically, at least, can present one's side as nominally well as the prosecution. Alas, it is also true that none of this makes us feel better about the fact that celebrity status, extreme wealth and not one but teams of lawyers can sometimes whip up a script – like those hard-working Hollywood propagandists we are told the government has hired – that no one could resist.

What's that about the exception proving the rule? It is as wrong-headed to think that O.J. Simpson represents the mass of citizens who are viewed as suspect profiles (and who are overwhelmingly poor, who are already convicted with far too much dispatch, and who can rarely afford even one never mind a dream team of lawyers) as it is to think that Osama bin Laden represents the 20 million resident aliens in the US, who, if summoned before a military tribunal – just to begin with – would not have even the right to choose their own lawyers.

While fully acknowledging the stakes of this new war, I worry that this attitude of lawless righteousness is one that has been practised in oppressed communities for years. It is a habit that has produced cynicism, riots and bloodshed. The always urgently felt convenience of torture has left us with civic calamities ranging from Abner Louima – a Haitian immigrant whom two New York City police officers beat and sodomized with a broom handle because they mistook him for someone involved in a bar-room brawl – to Jacobo Timerman in Argentina to Aleksandr Solzhenitsyn in the Soviet Union: all victims of physical force and mental manipulation, all people who refused to speak or didn't speak the words their inquisitors wanted to hear, but who were 'known' to know something. In such times and places, the devastation has been profound. People know nothing so they suspect everything. Deaths are never just accidental. Every human catastrophe is also a mystery and mysteries create ghosts, hauntings, 'blowback' and ultimately new forms of terror.

The problem with this kind of 'preventive' measure is that we are not mindreaders. Even with sodium pentathol, whose use some have suggested recently, we don't and can't know every last thought of those who refuse to speak. Torture and 'extracted' confessions are investments in the right to be all-knowing, in the certitude of what appears 'obvious'. That certitude is the essence of totalitarianism. Those who justify it with confident proclamations of 'I have nothing to hide, why should they?', overlap substantially with the class of those who have never been the persistent object of suspect profiling; who have never been harassed, stigmatized, generalized or feared just for the way they look.

The human mind is endlessly inventive. People create enemies as much as fear real ones. We are familiar with stories of the intimate and wrong-headed projections heaped upon the maid who is accused of taking something that the lady of the house simply misplaced. Stoked by trauma, tragedy and dread, the creativity of our paranoia is in overdrive right now. We must take a deep collective breath and be wary of perse- cuting those who conform to our fears instead of prosecuting enemies who were and will be smart enough to play against such prejudices.

Collateral Damage

I worry about this tendency to create new enemies beyond the ones we have reason to fear. I worry that, on the one hand, great grief allows us to feel that we have merged with the world, all boundaries erased in deference to the commonality of pain and the bedrock of human exis- tence. But traumatic loss can also mean – sometimes – that you want to hurt anyone in your path. Anyone who is lighthearted, you want to crush. Anyone who laughs is discordant. Anyone who has a healthy spouse or child is your enemy, is undeserving, is frivolous and in need of muting. And as for anyone who disagrees ...

When I served as a prosecutor years ago, I was very aware of this propensity among victims, the absolute need to rage at God or whomever is near – for that is what great sorrow feels like when the senses are overwhelmed. You lose words and thus want to reinscribe the hell of which you cannot speak. It is unfair that the rest of the world should not suffer as you have.

This is precisely why we have always had rules in trials about burdens of proof, standards of evidence, the ability to confront and cross-examine witnesses. The fiercely evocative howls of the widow, the orphan, the innocently wronged – these are the forces by which many a lynch mob has been rallied, how many a posse has been motivated to bypass due process, how many a holy crusade has been launched. It . easy to suspend the hard work of moral thought in the name of Ultimate Justice, or even Enduring Freedom, when one is blindly grief-stricken. 'If you didn't do it then your brother did', is the underlying force of blood feuds since time began. 'If you're not with us, you're against us', is the dangerous modern corollary to this rage.

'Give the government the power to assassinate terrorists', comes the call on chat shows. 'Spare us the circus of long public trials', say the letters to the editor.

I used to think that the most important human rights work facing Americans would be a national reconsideration of the death penalty. I could not have imagined that we would so willingly discard even the right of habeas corpus. I desperately hope we are a wiser people than to unloose the power to kill based on undisclosed 'information' with no accountability.

It is good to remember that Dr Martin Luther King's message was far more complex than the naive rosiness to which he's often reduced. He insisted upon equal protection even for those we do not like. He insisted on due process of law even for those whom we have reason to fear. And he demanded that we respect the humanity of even those whom we despise. We have faced horrendous war crimes in the world before. The Second World War presented lessons we should not forget, and Nuremberg should be our model. The United States must reconsider its objections to the jurisdiction of the International Criminal Court. Our greatest work is always keeping our heads when our hearts are broken. Our best resistance to terror is the summoning of those principles so suited to keep us from descending into infinite bouts of vengeance and revenge with those who wonder, like Milton's Stygian Counsel:

Will he, so wise, let loose at once his ire,
Belike through impotence, or unaware,
To give his Enemies their wish, and end
Them in his anger, whom his anger saves
To punish endless ...

Notes

1. Jeffrey Toobin, 'Crackdown', *The New Yorker*, November 5, 2001, p. 60.
2. *New York Times*, November 15, 2001, p. A1.
3. *New York Times*, November 18, 2001.
4. The Mike Reagan Show, WBRO (Providence, RI), November 14, 2001.
5. *New York Times*, October 30, 2001, p. B1.

CHAPTER 31

The Continuity of International Politics

Kenneth N. Waltz

On the morning of September 11, 2001, terrorists toppled the Twin Towers of the World Trade Center, symbols of world capitalism. They then struck a section of the Pentagon, symbol of America's military might. Apparently organized by Osama bin Laden and executed by members of al-Qaeda, the terrorists' acts were roundly condemned worldwide. Yet one wonders how deep and lasting the impact on American policy and on international politics will be.

The biggest early effects were felt in the policies and politics of the United States. The new Bush administration instantly turned from strident unilateralism to urgent multilateralism. The new multilateral approach, however, was adopted only to meet immediate and pressing requirements. The United States needed the police and intelligence capabilities of other states in order to track and apprehend terrorists. However, the American military response flatly refuted the subtitle of a newly published book: *The Paradox of American Power: Why the World's Superpower Can't Go it Alone*, by Joseph S. Nye. America organized and conducted the Afghanistan campaign on its own, rudely rebuffing Prime Minister Blair's offer of British troops to share in the fighting. Other indications that the Bush administration's multilateral impulses are strictly limited abound. By proclaiming a 'war against terrorism', Bush raised terrorists to the dignity of soldiers, and almost casually assigned to American forces the impossible task of militarily defeating an 'ism'. President Bush nevertheless claimed that prisoners held at Guantanamo were criminals, not soldiers, and thus unprotected by the Geneva Convention. America's attempt to make its own international rules (in disregard of the well-being of Americans fighting abroad who may be captured by countries that refuse to call them soldiers) is an extreme example of unilateralism. New challenges have not changed old habits. I offer just two more examples. NATO foreign ministers promised to bring Russia directly into NATO consultations. Lord Robertson, NATO's secretary-general, proposed giving Russia equal status with other members, including the right of veto, on problems of terror and regional stability.[1] But America's Afghanistan campaign went beautifully, and nothing more has been heard about NATO's becoming 19 + 1. When world leaders, dressed in their Tang dynasty jackets, were bonding at the APEC conference in Shanghai last October, President Bush gave the impression that he and President Putin would find agreement on interpretations of, and modifications to, the Anti-Ballistic Missile (ABM) Treaty. Instead Bush renounced the treaty and gave notice of America's withdrawal from it.

Early in the Bush administration consultation with other countries meant that we would tell them what we intended to do and then do it whether they liked it or not. Except on limited and specific matters, the practice has not changed. Some changes, however, are more pronounced. September 11 lifted Secretary of State Colin Powell from near invisibility to prominence, though one wonders how well diplomatic prominence will translate into influence on policy. Having campaigned against nation building, President Bush now embraces it as American policy in Afghanistan, though one wonders whether he will show the same zeal for nation building that he has shown for war fighting. The war against terrorists changed Pakistan from sanctioned pariah to favoured partner, but throughout the Cold War Pakistan has risen in, or fallen from, American favour depending on the thrust of threats from the Soviet Union. One must wonder, as Pakistanis do, whether the pattern will persist. In the name of fighting terrorists, liberties of both American citizens and resident aliens have been curtailed. This, one fears, may last.

Fighting terrorists provided a cover that has enabled the Bush administration to do what it wanted to do anyway. The administration got from Congress all of the money it sought for national missile defence. Terrorist acts torpedoed the earlier cross-party agreement on reductions. The administration abrogated the ABM Treaty without strident complaints at home or abroad. The administration obtained whopping increases in the budgets for the armed services in order to fight and defend against the weak forces the terrorists can muster. Although terrorists can be terribly bothersome, they hardly pose threats to the fabric of a society or the security of the state.

Terrorists have caused America to change its policy and behaviour in the near term, but the changes run in the direction that earlier policies had set. Are changes in the structure of international politics and the behaviour of nations more notable? One reads in the *New York Times* that 'the world has changed, developments in technology have given small groups of people the kind of destructive power once only available to national governments'.[2] Supposedly the weak have become strong – but have they? By cleverly picking their targets, terrorists have often been able to use slender resources to do disproportionate damage. The diplomatic historian John Lewis Gaddis claims that national security has now become truly 'national' with the homeland at risk, and calls this 'a revolution in strategic thinking'.[3] Have the terrorist attacks produced a strategic revolution, or do they leave the underlying conditions of international politics largely intact? For most countries throughout history, including the United States during the war of 1812, the homeland has at times been at risk.

Since the Soviet Union's disappearance, international politics has been marked by three basic facts. The first is the gross imbalance of power in the world. Never since Rome has one country so nearly dominated its world. In 1997 America's expenditure on its armed forces exceeded that of the next five big spenders; by 2000, the next eight. The defence budgets of most countries are stable or declining, while America's rises at an accelerating pace. Economically, technologically and militarily, the United States is far and away the leading country. No other country or combination of countries can hope to challenge it within a generation. After the defeat of the Soviet Union, the United States became the vengeful victor. It maintained its grip on the foreign and military policies of Western Europe and added three countries of the old Soviet empire to NATO's roster while announcing that more would follow. Old members of NATO showed no enthusiasm for, or willingness to bear the cost of, NATO's enlargement, but nevertheless supinely acquiesced in America's aggrandizement. The war on terrorists now enables the United States to establish bases on Russia's southern border and to further its encirclement of China as well as Russia. Secretary of Defense Donald Rumsfeld has announced that, if necessary to prosecute the war against terrorists, the United States will move militarily into 15 more states. In his January 29, 2002, State of the Union Address, President Bush targeted the next three countries (Iraq, Iran and North Korea) who may feel our wrath and threatened to move into any country 'timid in the face of terror'. Driving the threat home, he added: 'And make no mistake about it: if they do not act, America will.'[4] Today Afghanistan and the Philippines; tomorrow, who knows?

Terrorism does not change the first basic fact of international politics – the gross imbalance of world power. Instead, the effect of September

11 has been to enhance American power and extend its military presence in the world.

The second basic fact of international politics is the existence of nuclear weapons, most of them in the hands of the United States, and their gradual spread to additional countries. Again, terror furthers trends already in being. Having agreed with Russia to reduce its nuclear arsenal, the United States announced in January 2002 that instead of dismantling warheads it would place them in storage. And even though September 11 showed that national missile defences are irrelevant to the most likely modes of attack, the Bush administration used terror as a cover for renouncing the ABM Treaty.

The best one can say about missile defences is that they won't work. (If they did, an offence–defence race would result, with all too familiar consequences.) Missile defences are easily thwarted. In the nuclear business, offensive weapons are much cheaper than defensive ones. Other states can multiply their warheads; they can confound defences by deploying decoys and spreading chaff; they can outflank defences by delivering warheads in any of many different ways – by plane, by ships, by cruise missiles, by missiles fired on depressed trajectories. Missile defences would be the most complicated system ever mounted, and the system would have to work with near perfection in meeting its first realistic test – the test of enemy fire. Some warheads may get through, and both the attacked and the attacker will know that. No president will rely on such a system but will instead avoid actions that might provoke an attack. With or without defences, the restraints on American policy are the same.

The worst thing about nuclear defences is that, even though they will leak like a sieve, they will have damaging effects on others and on the United States as well. American intelligence reports state that American nuclear defences may prompt China to multiply its nuclear arsenal by ten and to place multiple warheads on its missiles.[5] Where China leads, India and Pakistan will follow. The result, President Putin fears, may be 'a hectic and uncontrolled arms race on the borders of our country'.[6] Japan, already made uneasy by China's increasing economic and military capabilities, will become uneasier still as China acts to counter America's prospective defences. Since the new Bush administration is rending the fabric of agreements that brought nuclear weapons under a modicum of control, and since nothing has been offered to replace it, other countries try harder to take care of themselves. North Korea, Iraq, Iran and others know that the United States can be held at bay only by deterrence. Weapons of mass destruction are the only means by which they can hope to deter the United States. They cannot hope to do so by relying on conventional weapons. During the Cold War the United States used nuclear weapons to offset the Soviet Union's conventional strength. Other countries may now use nuclear weapons to offset ours. On matters of nuclear weapons, as on others, American unilateralism prevails. The Bush administration refuses to ratify treaties that the United States sponsored (the Comprehensive Test Ban Treaty) and to honour treaties that it has ratified (the ABM Treaty).

Terrorists do not change the second brute fact of international politics: nuclear weapons govern the military relations of nations that have them. Moreover, American policies stimulate the vertical proliferation of nuclear weapons and promote their spreading from one country to another.

The third basic fact of international politics is the prevalence of crises that plague the world and in most of which the United States is directly or indirectly involved. Argentina is an economic and political mess; Chechnya is a running sore on the Russian body politic; North Korea and South Korea, both heavily armed, are as usual at daggers drawn; the Taiwan problem affects every state in the region; the disintegration of Indonesia, should it occur, threatens to destabilize Southeast Asia; the longstanding Indian–Pakistani conflict over Kashmir is exacerbated by the war against terrorists, as is the unending conflict between Palestine and Israel. If the United States decides to move into other countries militarily or to strike at them, more crises will be added to the already long list.

Terrorists do not change the third basic fact of international politics: the persistence and accumulation of crises. Indeed, by pursuing terrorists and threatening to attack states that harbor them the United States will add crises to an already long list.

Rather than interrupting the continuity of international politics, increased terrorist activity is a response to changes that have taken place in the last two decades. Before the decline and disappearance of the Soviet Union, weak states and disaffected people could hope to play off one superpower against the other. Now the weak and disaffected are on their own. Unsurprisingly, they lash out at the United States as the agent or symbol of their suffering. The terrorist acts of September 11 have prompted the United States to enlarge its already bloated military forces and to extend its influence into parts of the world that its tentacles had not already reached.

Fortunately or not, terrorists contribute to the continuity of international politics. They further trends already in motion. Why, one may wonder, does the prospect of terror not change the basic facts of international politics? All states – whether authoritarian or democratic, traditional or modern, religious or secular – fear being their targets. Governments prize stability, and most of all they prize the continuation of their regimes. Terror is a threat to the stability of states and to the peace of mind of their rulers. That is why President Bush could so easily assemble a coalition a mile wide.

Yet, because terror is a weapon wielded by the weak, terrorists do not seriously threaten the security of states. States are therefore not compelled to band together to shift the balance of world power. Terrorist attacks do not change the two main bases of international politics or alter the condition of recurring crises. That is why, although a mile wide, the anti-terrorist coalition is only an inch deep.

Notes

1. Patrick E. Tyler, 'Gingerly, NATO Plans Broader Role for Moscow', *New York Times*, December 7, 2001, p. A11; Michael Wines, 'NATO Plan Offers Russia Equal Voice on Some Policies', *New York Times*, November 23, 2001, p. A1.
2. Alexander Stille, 'What is America's Place in the World Now?', *New York Times*, January 12, 2002, p. B7.
3. Ibid.
4. 'President Bush's State of the Union Address to Congress and the Nation', *New York Times*, January 30, 2002, p. A22.
5. Steven Lee Myers, 'Study Said to Find US Missile Defense Might Incite China', *New York Times*, August 10, 2000, p. A1.
6. Patrick E. Tyler, 'Putin Says Russia Would Add Arms to Counter Shield', *New York Times*, June 19, 2001, p. A1.

Notes on the Contributors

Amitav Acharya is a Professor at Nanyang Technological University, Singapore, and Deputy Director of the Institute of Defence and Strategic Studies. His latest book is *Constructing a Security Community in Southeast Asia: ASEAN and the Problem of Regional Order* (2001).

Abdullahi Ahmed An-Na'im is Charles Howard Candler Professor of Law, Emory University, Atlanta, USA. He taught law at the University of Khartoum, Sudan, and has held visiting appointments at several North American and European universities. He served as Executive Director of Human Rights Watch (Africa), based in Washington DC in 1993–95.

Desmond Ball is Special Professor in the Strategic and Defence Studies Centre at the Australian National University, Canberra. He is the author of books and articles on nuclear strategy, security developments in Asia, and intelligence matters.

Benjamin R. Barber is Gershon and Carol Kekst Professor of Civil Society and Wilson H. Elkins Professor, School of Public Affairs, University of Maryland. He is the author of *Jihad Versus McWorld* (1995), *Strong Democracy* (1984) and, most recently, *The Truth of Power: Intellectual Affairs in the Clinton White House* (2001).

Thomas J. Biersteker is Director of the Watson Institute for International Studies and Henry R. Luce Professor of Transnational Organizations at Brown University. His next book is *The Emergence of Private Authority in Global Governance*, co-edited with Rodney B. Hall. He chairs the US Social Science Research Council's Global Security and

355

Cooperation Committee and co-directs the Watson Institute's Project on Targeted Financial Sanctions.

Sissela Bok is Senior Visiting Fellow at the Harvard Center for Population and Development Studies. Her books include *Lying: Moral Choice in Private and Public Life* (1999), *Secrets: On the Ethics of Concealment and Revelation* (1989), *A Strategy for Peace: Human Values and the Threat of War* (1990), *Mayhem: Violence as Public Entertainment* (1998) and *Common Values* (1995, 2002).

Ken Booth is E.H. Carr Professor and Head of the Department of International Politics, University of Wales Aberystwyth. His next book is *Security, Community and Emancipation*.

Chris Brown is Professor of International Relations at the London School of Economics. His books include *International Relations Theory: New Normative Approaches* (1992) and *Understanding International Relations*. His *Sovereignty, Rights and Justice*, is forthcoming.

Barry Buzan is Research Professor of International Studies at the University of Westminster and a Project Director at the Copenhagen Peace Research Institute (COPRI). His books include *People, States and Fear* (1983, 1991) and *International Systems in World History: Remaking the Study of International Relations* (with Richard Little, 2000).

Michael Byers teaches international law at Duke University, North Carolina and is currently Visiting Fellow at Keble College and the Centre for Socio-Legal Studies, Oxford University. He is the author of *Custom, Power and the Power of Rules* (1999) and a regular contributor to the *London Review of Books*.

Noam Chomsky is Institute Professor at Massachusetts Institute of Technology, where he has been on the faculty since 1955. His most recent books include *New Military Humanism* (1999), *A New Generation Draws the Line* (2000), *Rogue States*, (2000), *9-11* (2001) and *Understanding Power* (2002).

Michael Cox is Professor of International Politics, University of Wales Aberystwyth. He has recently edited *E.H. Carr: A Critical Appraisal* (2000) and *Empires, Systems and States* (with Tim Dunne and Ken Booth,

2001). He has written the introduction to the new edition of E.H. Carr, *The Twenty Years' Crisis* (2001).

James Der Derian is Professor of Political Science at the University of Massachusetts at Amherst and Research Professor of International Relations at the Watson Institute for International Studies at Brown University, where he directs the Information Technology, War and Peace Project. His most recent book is *Virtuous War: Mapping the Military-Industrial-Media-Entertainment Network* (2001).

Tim Dunne is Senior Lecturer in the Department of International Politics, University of Wales Aberystwyth. He is the author of *Inventing International Society* (1998) and editor of *Human Rights in Global Politics* (with Nicholas J. Wheeler, 1999), and *How Might We Live?: Global Ethics in a New Century* (with Ken Booth and Michael Cox, 2001).

Jean Bethke Elshtain is the Laura Spelman Rockefeller Professor of Social and Political Ethics at the University of Chicago. She is the author of *Democracy on Trial* (1995) and has written extensively on the just war tradition.

Richard Falk retired in 2001 from Princeton University after 40 years as a faculty member. He is currently Visiting Professor at the University of California at Santa Barbara. His most recent books are *Religion and Human Global Governance* (2001), *Human Rights Horizons* (2000) and *Predatory Globalization* (1999).

Lawrence Freedman is Professor of War Studies and Head of the School of Social Science and Public Policy, King's College, London. His books include *Cold War: A Military History* (2001), *Kennedy's Wars: Berlin, Cuba, Laos and Vietnam* (2000), and *The Evolution of Nuclear Strategy* (2nd edn, 1989).

Francis Fukuyama is Bernard Schwartz Professor of International Political Economy at the Paul H. Nitze School of Advanced International Studies at Johns Hopkins University. He is author of *The End of History and the Last Man* (1992), *Trust: The Social Virtues and the Creation of Prosperity* (1995) and *The Great Disruption: Human Nature and the Reconstitution of Social Order* (1999).

Colin S. Gray is Professor of International Politics and Strategic Studies at the University of Reading. He is an adviser to the US and British governments. His book *Strategy for Chaos: RMA Theory and the Evidence of History* is forthcoming.

Fred Halliday is Professor of International Relations at the London School of Economics. He is the author of *The World at 2000* (2000) and *Two Hours that Shook the World: September 11 2001, Causes and Consequences* (2001).

Robert O. Keohane is James B. Duke Professor of Political Science, Duke University, North Carolina. His books include *After Hegemony: Cooperation and Discord in the World Political Economy* (1984), *International Institutions and State Power: Essays in International Relations Theory* (1989) and *Power and Interdependence: World Politics in Transition* (with Joseph S. Nye Jnr, 1997; 3rd edn, 2001).

Andrew Linklater is Woodrow Wilson Professor of International Politics at the University of Wales Aberystwyth. His books include *Men and Citizens in the Theory of International Relations* (1982), *Beyond Realism and Marxism* (1990) and *The Transformation of Political Community* (1998).

William Maley is Associate Professor of Politics, University College, University of New South Wales, Australia. He is author of *The Afghanistan Wars* (2002) and editor of *Fundamentalism Reborn? Afghanistan and the Taliban* (1998).

C. Raja Mohan is the Strategic Affairs Editor of *The Hindu*, a leading English-language daily published in New Delhi, India. He has been Senior Fellow at the Institute for Defence Studies and Analyses in New Delhi, and has published widely on the security politics of the subcontinent.

Bhikhu Parekh is Centennial Professor at the London School of Economics after many years as Professor of Political Theory at the University of Hull. His books include *Rethinking Multiculturalism* (2000) and *Gandhi* (2001). He is a Labour Peer in the House of Lords.

Paul Rogers is Professor of Peace Studies at Bradford University. A second edition of his most recent book is *Losing Control: Global Security in the 21st Century* (2000).

Saskia Sassen is the Ralph Lewis Professor of Sociology at the University of Chicago, and Centennial Visiting Professor at the London School of Economics. Her most recent books are *Guests and Aliens* (1999) and *Global Networks/Linked Cities* (edited, 2002). She is Chair of the newly formed Information Technology, International Cooperation and Global Security Committee of the Social Science Research Council.

Avi Shlaim is a Professor of International Relations and Fellow of St Antony's College, Oxford. His books include *Collusion across the Jordan* (1988), *The Politics of Partition* (1990, 1998), *War and Peace in the Middle East: A Concise History* (1995) and *The Iron Wall: Israel and the Arab World* (2000).

Steve Smith is Pro Vice Chancellor (Academic Affairs) and Professor of International Politics at the University of Wales Aberystwyth. He was the founding editor of the Cambridge University Press 'Studies in International Relations' series and has recently been elected President of the International Studies Association (2003–04). His books include (with Martin Hollis) *Explaining and Understanding International Relations* (1990).

Immanuel Wallerstein is Director of the Fernand Braudel Center for the Study of Economies, Historical Systems, and Civilizations, Binghamton University, and Senior Research Scholar at Yale University. He is the author of *The Modern World-System* (3 volumes, 1974, 1980, 1989) and most recently of *The End of the World As We Know It* (1999).

Kenneth N. Waltz is Ford Professor Emeritus of the University of California at Berkeley. He is presently Adjunct Professor and Senior Research Associate at the Institute of War and Peace Studies, Columbia University. His books include *Theory of International Politics* (1979) and *The Spread of Nuclear Weapons: A Debate* (with Scott Douglas Sagan, 1998).

Patricia J. Williams is Professor of Law at Columbia University in New York City. Her column 'Diary of a Mad Law Professor' appears in *The Nation*. She is the author of *Seeing a Colour-Blind Future: The Paradox of Race* (1997).

INDEX

368 *Worlds in Collision*

Laqueur, Walter 9
Latin America 30
    reaction to 9/11 attack 133, 237
law, due process of 347
Lebanon 39, 51, 83, 130–1, 134
Lee Kuan Yew 30
liberal states, humanitarian
    obligations 305–6, 310
Liberation Tigers of Tamil Eelam
    (LTTE) 219
Liberia 77
Libya 89, 122
Liechtenstein 83
Likud Party 173–4, 175
Lima 219
Lindh, John Walker 327
linkage 173, 178, 180–1
    deferred 173, 174
Lippmann, Walter 154
Litt, Robert 343
Locke, John 30
Lockerbie bombing 169
Louima, Abner 345
Lumumba, Patrice 276
Luther, Martin 264
Luttwak, Edward 304

Machiavelli, Niccolo 15, 21, 99, 264
McVeigh, Timothy 7, 142
Madrassas 211
Mahar, Bill 108
Mahathir, Mohammed 196
Malaysia 49, 195–6, 197, 199, 200,
    201
Malley, Robert 176
Mao Tse-tung 86
Martin, Kate 68
Mauritius 83
Mazar-e-Sharif 43, 306
Mearsheimer, John 229
Mecca, Great Mosque 33
media
    and dramatic events 226, 228
    forecasts 285
    information 115
    and intercultural dialogue 274
Megawati Sukarnoputri 198
Mexico 33, 217
Meyers, General 109

migration 217
military action
    and accuracy 12, 14, 86, 106, 266
    justification for 12–13
military tribunals 157, 272, 340–1,
    342, 344–5
Mill, J.S. 284, 285, 289
Mills, C. Wright 115
Milosevic, Slobodan 7, 11, 41, 77, 85,
    91
MIME-NET (military-industrial-
    media-entertainment network)
    112, 113, 115
mimetic war 109–10
missile defence 118, 120, 256, 334,
    349
    and Anti-Ballistic Missile Treaty
    222, 254, 257, 351
modernity 28, 248, 250, 297–301
    and globalization 253, 296–7, 299
    Islam and 31–2, 34–5, 213, 247,
    296–7, 307
    and primitivism 297–8
    and values 301
modernization 30–1, 32
Le Monde 97
money laundering 70, 75, 78, 82,
    316
Moussaouri, Zacarias 53, 56, 65, 200
Mubarak, Hosni 86, 198
Mujahideen 45, 95, 207, 276
multiculturalism 20, 277, 304, 306–7
multilateralism 314, 316–18, 323–4
    United States and 119, 221, 236,
    309, 348–9
Musharraf, Pervez 3, 146, 195, 210,
    211–12, 238
Muslim Brotherhood 147
Muslims
    backwardness of 278, 280
    imperialist designs 280
    reactions to 9/11 attack 7, 154,
    195, 279, 308, 326
    size of population 273
    stereotyping 4
    and terrorism 9–10
    Western view of 279–81
    see also Islam
Mussadiq, Mohammad 276

religious fundamentalism 18,
248–9
response to 9/11 attack 155,
272–3, 325–6, 330–1, 332–3
responsibilities 33
security 120, 156–7, 202–3,
220–2, 338–9, 350
and self-defence 12, 18, 119, 121,
121–4, 330
sponsorship of terrorism 163,
273
support for despotic regimes 119,
278–9
tactics 95–7
and UN 129–30, 144, 278
unilateralism 118–21, 144,
159–60, 220–1, 327, 348–9
and American superiority 57–8,
236
European concern over 224
and international agreements
222, 224, 256–7, 278, 333–4
and superpower status 229
see also Anti-Ballistic Missile
Treaty; coalition against
terrorism; Kyoto
and universal values 28, 29, 44,
67
and warfare 278, 328–30
and world domination 57–8, 125,
155, 276–7, 329, 350
unmanned aerial vehicles (UAVs) 44,
67
Uruzgan 63
US Marine Corps 220
US Space Command 69
USA Patriotic Act 157, 340
USS *Cole* 62, 219
Uthman ibn 'Affan 165
Uzbekistan 119, 121, 201, 222

Vajpayee, Atal Behari 212
values
and culture 239
universality of 28, 29–30, 275,
284–91
Western 28, 29, 30, 86–7, 205,
277, 310
see also common values

Vedrine, Hubert 97
Venezuela 237
Viet Minh 99
Vietnam 88, 90
Vietnam Syndrome 106, 157
Vietnam War 43, 86, 266, 267, 330
violence, understanding 289
Virilio, Paul 113
'virtuous war' 105–6, 115

Wahhabis 31, 32–3, 35
war on terrorism 37, 44–5, 198, 348
broader agenda 31–2, 172, 303,
332–3
casualties 12, 105–6, 119
civilization against evil 304–5
critics of 301
democratic front 246–8
effect on South Asian subcontinent 205–14
and extension of American power
155–6, 159, 350
and humanitarian aid 306, 309
and information 337–8
and intelligence 65–8
as intercultural struggle 28
and international law 135, 311
justification for 164–5
legitimate targets 92–3, 122–3,
128, 132, 263–4, 266–7, 305–6
lessons from 46
and media 109–10, 111
mimetic war 109–10
negative consequences of 97–8,
167
objectives 18, 39–40, 95–6, 304–5
popular opposition to 237
popular support for 197–8
and pre-emptive action 158–9
propaganda 111–12
religious dimension 294–6, 307
restoring honour 233–4
and unnecessary suffering 303–4,
305, 309, 310
US strategy 40–2, 43–5
and victory 19, 20, 39, 44,
99–100, 300, 330–1
and world economy 99
Wardlaw, G. 215